CAREER
OPPORTUNITIES
IN POLITICS, GOVERNMENT,
AND ACTIVISM

CAREER OPPORTUNITIES IN POLITICS, GOVERNMENT, AND ACTIVISM

Joan Axelrod-Contrada

Foreword by
U.S. Senator

John Kerry

Ferguson
An imprint of ☑® Facts On File

Career Opportunities in Politics, Government, and Activism

Ferguson
An imprint of Facts On File, Inc.
132 West 31st Street
New York NY 10001

Library of Congress Cataloging-in-Publication Data

Axelrod-Contrada, Joan.
  Career opportunities in politics, government, and activism/Joan Axelrod-Contrada;
  foreword by U.S. Senator John Kerry.
      p.   cm.
  Includes index.
  ISBN 0-8160-4317-5
  1. Civil service—United States. 2. Public administration—United States. 3. United States—Officials and employees.
I. Title.
  JK692 .A94 2003
  320.973′023—dc21   2002010476

Ferguson books are available at special discounts when purchased in bulk quantities for businesses, associations, institutions, or sales promotions. Please call our Special Sales Department in New York at (212) 967-8800 or (800) 322-8755.

You can find Ferguson on the World Wide Web at http://www.fergpubco.com

Cover design by Nora Wertz

Printed in the United States of America

VB Hermitage 10 9 8 7 6 5 4 3 2 1

This book is printed on acid-free paper.

CONTENTS

FOREWORD

Almost four decades ago, my generation was inspired by President John F. Kennedy's call to public service. He challenged Americans everywhere with words that have been repeated countless times in our nation: "Ask not what your country can do for you; ask what you can do for your country." Many of us answered that call by joining the military, fighting for civil rights, or volunteering in the Peace Corps and Volunteers in Service to America (VISTA). Some answered that call by joining the government in a different way—as staff members committed to making government work better for our fellow citizens.

Much has changed since the era that some called Camelot. But one condition remains the same—or in many ways has taken on a new importance in an era when too many are cynical—the need for talented and committed individuals to pursue careers in public service: teaching, volunteering for campaigns and running for office, and organizing in the community.

This book outlines the countless opportunities out there to get involved in public service. Joan Axelrod-Contrada recognizes the necessity for a talented and dedicated workforce to participate in careers of public service. By making the information on how to research and obtain these jobs more accessible, Ms. Axelrod-Contrada is providing an invaluable service for those about to enter the job market for the first time or for those seeking a more fulfilling line of work.

Your challenge is to pick the job that reflects your interests and abilities, to become part of something bigger than you, and to be part of an effort to make a real contribution to our society. Unfortunately, there is a gap between the increasing number of young people who engage in community service and those who dedicate their careers to public service. The staggering statistics show that although more college-aged students volunteer in a variety of community outreach programs, fewer are seeking careers in the government and fewer are showing any desire to run for public office. We need to turn those numbers around, and in my judgment, this book offers a wonderful jumping off point.

In this time of complex challenges, we are seeing a boom of public and private sector partnerships that are increasing both the options and compensation for a career in service. This exciting climate fosters constant change. Rarely do people in these fields stay at the same desk for long. As you gain more experience, new opportunities continue to present themselves. In fact, you don't have to work in the government to make an impact on our political system. This book offers information not only on opportunities within government, but on positions that run the gamut of activism and service. To help you navigate this confusing road this book maps out typical, though evolving qualifications for specific jobs and opportunities.

Most importantly, though, you will find in these pages both a blueprint and a road map to finding a position that helps you keep faith with your most passionately held convictions about government, about our society, and about how you can, in your own way, build on the tradition of public service as an "honorable profession." Indeed, in this time of enormous social, economic, and political challenge for our nation, it must be.

— Senator John Kerry

INDUSTRY OUTLOOK

Why look for a career in politics, government, or activism?

Just about everyone offers the same answer: to make a difference. Something draws people like radar to the pressing issues of our day. Whether they want to improve their own communities, analyze policy initiatives, or advocate for social justice, they understand the importance of public involvement. They know from the election of 2000 that every vote counts and from the terrorist attacks of 2001 that tragedy can awaken a new spirit of public consciousness. People in politics, government, and activism have the satisfaction of knowing at the end of the day that something they said or wrote could improve the lives of thousands of people.

Although people today have much the same desire "to serve" as their predecessors, the public realm itself has changed dramatically over the years. On the political front, the waning role of the old-time party bosses has contributed to the burgeoning growth of the relatively new political consulting industry. Meanwhile, years of downsizing and outsourcing have changed the old government-centered system to a new one in which nonprofit and private organizations play a prominent role. Jobs once held by government employees are now contracted out to think tanks, consulting firms, and nonprofit social-service organizations.

The National Association of Schools of Public Affairs and Administration, which tracks the employment of its graduates, has seen a marked shift in placement by sector over the years. In 1989, 21 percent of graduates found positions in the national government, whereas by 2000 the number had dropped to 12 percent. Employment in the nonprofit sector rose during the same period from 11 to 16 percent.

In *The New Public Service,* Paul Light, of the Brookings Institution, describes how the "lifer" of old has given way to the "switcher" of today. Instead of being lost for good, many jobs have simply been reassigned to other sectors. Someone who worked as an analyst for a government agency might, years later, do the same type of work for a think tank with a government contract. It is not uncommon for individuals to move back and forth between sectors.

All this is good news for you, the job seeker. As employment has become more diversified, different sectors need to compete more for talent. In the federal government, industry sources say that the upcoming retirement of thousands of baby boomers will create a need for new talent. Some government agencies are offering incentives such as the repayment of student loans to appeal to a new generation of public-spirited candidates also courted by businesses and nonprofits.

Yet, as has any industry, public service has its drawbacks. Government employees face the pressure of trying to get things done while navigating bureaucracies and weighing public input. Nonprofit employees cope with the stress of funding pressures and shoestring budgets. Private consultants contend with the challenges of balancing the public good with the bottom line. And all face lingering misconceptions of politics, government, and activism among the very public they are trying to serve.

Nevertheless, despite lingering stereotypes of corrupt public officials, unimaginative bureaucrats, and wild-eyed activists, observers believe that a more appreciative view of the public sector may be taking hold. In the wake of the terrorist attacks of September 11, 2001, people who had long viewed government as an intrusion have come to see it more as a necessary protector. Public officials showed leadership. Government rose to new challenges. And nonprofit organizations mobilized their volunteers.

In the fictional world of television, too, depictions of public officials and civil servants appear to be growing more positive. A 2001 study by the Council for Excellence in Government examined television portrayals of elected officials and civil servants between 1992 and 1998 and 1999 and 2001. Whereas seven out of 10 shows in 1992–98 showed politics as corrupt, cynical, or unrepresentative, three out of four shows in the 1999–2001 period presented political institutions as effectively serving the public interest. NBC's *West Wing,* in particular, has won acclaim for portraying the public sector in a sophisticated and textured way.

In the real-life world of politics, the path to elected office is particularly difficult and precarious. Few opportunities exist for long-term paid careers. Many elected officials view their positions as a "calling" rather than as a career. Someone passionate about community issues, for instance, might prefer to remain at the local level rather than mount a risky and expensive bid for higher office. Unlike appointed officials such as city managers who can climb the career ladder by moving to progressively larger communities, elected officials generally only run for office in the jurisdiction where they have established residency. Hence the opportunities for a lifetime career as an elected official are extremely rare.

Career prospects appear brighter for the behind-the-scenes professionals who devise strategy for political campaigns. The relatively new profession of political consulting has grown by leaps and bounds, as political candidates as well as businesses, interest groups, labor unions, and other organized bodies turn to professionals to produce state-of-the-art campaigns. The American Association of Political Consultants estimates that more than a billion dollars is spent yearly on campaign communication.

Political consultants travel in the same circles as lobbyists, political action committee (PAC) administrators, and other up-and-coming political professionals who tend to generate controversy wherever they go. Depending on one's point of view, these political professionals are either dedicated activists or unscrupulous opportunists. Is negative advertising a useful device or a dirty trick? Is grassroots lobbying an expression or a corruption of democratic ideals? Are PAC professionals mobilizing citizens or hindering campaign reform? Political professionals wrestle with these kinds of questions every day.

The adrenaline-charged world of political campaigns might, at times, seem a world apart from the hard work of governing that follows. "Bureaucrats," as government employees have been called, have changed the face of the world. As the National Association of Schools of Public Affairs and Administration observes, bureaucrats have helped develop the Internet and put a man on the Moon.

Although much has been written about government cutbacks, the federal government remains the nation's largest employer, according to the U.S. Department of Labor's *Occupational Outlook Handbook*. Federal agencies oversee the environment, education, emergency management, public health, and countless other issues. They set guidelines for everything from the safety of meat to the amount of money Americans pay each year in income taxes.

Many positions—program manager and management analyst, for example—can be found at all levels of government, but staffers at the local and state levels are closer to the results of their labor than their counterparts in the federal government. They see potholes being fixed and new schools being built on their way home from work. State government, which serves as a link between the local and the federal, has assumed new regulatory powers as a result of the "devolution" of power from the federal government.

Charitable nonprofits are the fastest growing sector—ahead of government and private industry—in the nation, according to the Independent Sector, a nonprofit, nonpartisan coalition of more than 700 national organizations, foundations, and corporate philanthropy programs. The number

of nonprofit organizations soared from 739,000 in 1977 to 1.19 million in 1997.

Typically, nonprofit organizations offer lower salaries than government or the private sector but provide the benefits of a casual workplace where individuals can quickly assume high levels of responsibility, industry sources say. Often, it is easier to find positions in the nonprofit arena than in government or business.

In many nonprofit organizations dedicated to social change, staffers serve as jack-of-all trades activists. A general rule of thumb is that the smaller the organization—and many are small—the more likely individuals are to take on a variety of responsibilities. A single person might research issues, manage programs, fund-raise, organize grassroots support, and educate the public.

Most important, people must believe in the mission of their organizations. Ideas once considered radical—environmental protection and women's rights, for example—have become widely accepted. Advocacy groups press for social change while nonprofit administrators manage programs to combat problems such as hunger and homelessness. A relatively small but highly influential network of research institutes (think tanks), meanwhile, prepare reports on issues such as education and the economy.

In today's world, the abilities to understand complex organizations and draw competing interest groups to the table are in high demand. The National Association of Schools of Public Affairs and Administration recently embarked on a Public Service Career Initiative to attract students to public service by showing young people involved in such dynamic activities as negotiating environmental policy, helping the homeless, providing emergency management services, and directing a community-based nonprofit agency. Debunking the stereotype of the unimaginative bureaucrat, each of the new public servants appears to be saying, "Look, Ma! I'm a bureaucrat!"

You, too, can be part of this world. Whether you want to work in Washington, D.C., or a small town in rural America, the opportunities are there. You could design political polls, help victims of disaster, research legislation, or direct programs for a nonprofit advocacy organization. The list goes on and on. As long as you have a zest for hard work, you'll be able to find just the right niche for your talents and interests. This book is just the beginning. The possibilities are endless, so go out there and make a difference!

ACKNOWLEDGMENTS

Special Thanks

Before I acknowledge the many professionals who contributed to the research of this book, I would like to thank the special people who made this project possible. First, to my husband, Freddy, and children, Amanda and Rio, thanks for your incredible love and support. Next, to my editor, James Chambers, thanks for your patience and willingness to understand the depth and complexity of this project. And, finally, to Senator John Kerry, thank you for caring enough about this book to write its Foreword. My gratitude to the many people who assisted me with their time and knowledge:

Lisa Abrams, J.D. (author, *The Official Guide to Legal Specialties*); American Planning Association; American Political Science Association; Helen Anderson (Director of Internships, The Fletcher School, Tufts University); Warren H. Anderson (former Speechwriter for the United States Army and the Joint Chiefs of Staff); Van Anderson (National Recreation and Park Association); Randy Arndt (National League of Cities); Association for Public Policy Analysis and Management; Patti Jo Baber (American League of Lobbyists); Denise Baker (Massachusetts Municipal Association); Noreen Banks (Access Center: Networking in the Public Interest); Julio Barreto (National Association of Housing and Redevelopment Officials); Dave Beattie (Hamilton Beattie & Staff); Tobe Berkovitz (Professor, Boston University); Maurice Bisheff, Sheryll Schroeder, and Mary Haynes (International Institute of Municipal Clerks); Dr. James Brademus (University of Illinois); Laura Brem (former Paralegal, Federal Trade Commission); Michael Brintnall (Executive Director, National Association of Schools of Public Affairs and Administration); Judith Brown (International Personnel Management Association); Dr. Anne L. Bryant (National School Boards Association); Dr. Martha Burk (National Council of Women's Organizations); Katie Burnham (Society for Nonprofit Organizations); Carol Carson (Massachusetts Ethics Commission); Jacqueline Clark and Christine Curtis (U.S. State Department); Craig Coletta (National Association for Community Mediation); Relmond Van Daniker (National Association of State Auditors, Comptrollers, and Treasurers); Joan Day and Paul Hatch (New Hampshire Employment Security); Sandy Deaton (Kentucky Legislative Research Commission); Lloyd Dennis (former Speechwriter for Secretary of the Treasury, Dennis and Associates); Erik Devereux (Association for Public Policy Analysis and Management); Lawrence S. DiCara, Esq. (former Boston City Councilor);

Kevin Doyle (Environmental Careers Organization); Douglas Duckett, Daryll Griffin, Scott Milinski (National Public Employer Labor Relations Association); Frank Duehay (former Mayor of Cambridge, Massachusetts); Dr. George C. Edwards III (Texas A & M University; *Presidential Quarterly*); Susan Ellis (Energize, Inc.); John Esson (Environmental Careers Center); Mary Flanders Aicardi (Personnel Director, Town of Watertown, Mass.); Mary Ford (former Mayor of Northampton, Mass.); Netfa Freeman (Social Action and Leadership School for Activists); Dr. Shari Garmise (Council for Urban Economic Development); Maureen Gillmer (Anne Arundle County, Md., District Attorney's Office); Dorca Gomez (Massachusetts Commission against Discrimination); Maureen Grieco (Executive Director, Connecticut Democrats); Anya Guilsher (Central Intelligence Agency); Jean Halloran (Consumer Policy Institute, Consumers Union); Charles Hardin (Council for Government Reform); Deirdre Healey (AmeriCorps Recruiter); Audrey Heffron (Florida State University); Suellen Honeychuck (National Capital Area Paralegal Association); Jonathan Hite (Northampton, Mass., Housing Authority); Stan Hutton (Clarence E. Heller Charitable Foundation); Meredith Janik (Georgetown University Career Center); Bob Johnson (Anoka County, Minn.); Helen Jones (Florida Commission on Ethics); Rich Jones (National Conference of State Legislatures); Peter Kennerdell (PAC Consultant); Michael Klare (Professor, Hampshire College); Carl Koechlin (Fenway Community Development Corporation, Boston); Paul Lawler (American Economic Development Council); Karen Lederer (University of Massachusetts-Amherst, Women's Studies); Donna Lucas (American Association of Political Consultants); John McCamman (House Administrative Assistants Association); Joe McDaniel (American Society of Association Executives); David McDonald (Human Resources, State of Massachusetts); Tom McClimon (U.S. Conference of Mayors); Michael Meit (National Association of City and County Health Organizations); Ray Meserve (Massachusetts Municipal Association); Joshua Miller (Professor, Smith College School of Social Work); Rene Moller (Internship Coordinator, United Nations); Sonja Nash Murray (Fund for Public Interest Research); Michael Nilsen (National Association of Fund Raising Executives); Carolyn Van Noy (Council on Government Ethics Laws, Seattle Ethics and Election Commission); Costas Panagopoulos (Executive Director, Political Campaign Management Program, New York

University); Linda Patton and Barbara Palassis (South Carolina Department of Health and Environmental Quality Control); Peace Corps (Peace Corps Regional Office, Boston, Mass.); Michael Pearse (Congressional Research Service); Christopher Porter *(YourCongress.com);* Lynn Preuth (Greater Cincinnati chapter, American Society for Public Administration); Roy Priest (National Congress for Community Economic Development); Beryl A. Radin (Professor of Public Administration and Policy, Rockefeller College at the State University of New York at Albany); Patricia Read (Colorado Association of Nonprofit Organizations); Dr. Barbara Reinhold (Director, Smith College Career Development Office); Don Reuter (North Carolina Association of Government Information Officers); Kristin Riggin (National District Attorneys Association); Sherri Rowland (National Association of State Auditors, Comptrollers, and Treasurers); Kristi Rudelius-Palmer (Human Rights Resource Center, University of Minnesota); Greg Sam (Municipal Management Assistants of Northern California); Chris Santarsiero (Executive Director, Connecticut Republicans); Joanne Scanlan (Council on Foundations); Connie Schmidt (The Election Center); Lynn Schultz-Writsel (Equal Justice Works); Baillee Servin (The Management Center); Patricia Shaughnessy (Northampton, Mass., Regis-trar of Voters); Beth Sheehy (former Congressional Page); Betsy D. Sherman (International City/County Management Association); Michael Sheward (National Association of Government Communicators); Bill Shingleton (Center for Responsive Politics); J. C. Squires (National Association of Local Government Auditors); Kimberly Stanton, Ph.D. (Robert F. Kennedy Center for Human Rights); J. K. "Hoopy" Stinger, Jr. (Executive Director, State Personnel Board); John Thomas (Independent Sector); Dr. James Thurber (Director, American University Center for Congressional and Presidential Studies); Carolyn Torma (American Planning Association); Amy Tucci (American Public Human Services Association); Cheryl Guidry Tyiska (National Organization for Victim Assistance); Sean Walsh (Office of the Governor, North Carolina); Brian Weberg (National Conference of State Legislatures); Kathryn Weeden (Senate Page School); Peter Wendel *(Campaigns & Elections* magazine); Vanessa White (Association of Schools of Public Health); Lane Windham (American Federation of Labor-Council of Industrial Organizations [AFL-CIO] Media Outreach); Meg Yetishefsky (Connecticut Department of Administrative Services, American Association for Affirmative Action); Billy Zwerschke (President, International Association of Emergency Managers).

INTRODUCTION
How to Use This Book

Welcome to a world of possibilities. Whether you dream of running for political office, planning cities, monitoring legislation, fighting for a cause, or joining the Peace Corps, this book should help you get started. The possibilities are endless. You could start out as a congressional page and work your way up to president of the United States.

This book was written for the practical idealist, someone who wants to know what it takes to make a difference. Beyond that, however, the jobs in this book are widely varied, appealing to a variety of types of people: political junkies, public servants, program specialists, policy wonks, grassroots activists, social entrepreneurs, and adventurers, to name a few.

Sources of Information
This book required extensive research in a variety of sources to capture the depth and complexity of these jobs. Sources include

- Industry professionals, including representatives of national associations and working professionals
- Association and employment websites
- Books, magazines, and newspaper articles
- College career centers

When people say that there is an association for everything, they are right. And that is good news for job seekers. The websites of professional associations are veritable gold mines of information. Many post job listings, helpful career advice, and news about upcoming conferences and other networking opportunities.

The Internet also has given rise to broader-based employment websites that serve as virtual career counselors. Nonprofit employment sites such as Idealist and the Access Non-Profit Jobs Clearinghouse allow viewers to punch in keywords like *activism/organizing* and a field like *environmental* and see job openings around the country.

Yet, for all the wonders of modern technology, there is no substitute for curling up on the couch with a good book. The research for this book involved countless trips to libraries and school career centers.

How This Book Is Organized
Career Opportunities in Politics, Government, and Activism is organized into three main categories, even though real life defies such simple groupings. In reality, the three sectors often overlap. For instance, Lobbyist, which is in the Activism section of the book because of its links to nonprofit organizations and interest groups, could easily have been included in the Politics section alongside Political Consultant.

As a result, this book is a lot like a buffet, with jobs, like dishes, laid out on a table—the table of Contents, that is. Be sure to browse all of the Contents so you don't miss anything. If a job title strikes you, chances are that you are on the right track, no matter where in the book the position is described.

The Job Profiles
Career Profile and Career Ladder
Each job profile begins with a chart for easy browsing. The Career Profile on the left summarizes the main duties, alternate titles, salary ranges, employment prospects, and prerequisites of education, experience, and special skills.

The Career Ladder diagram on the right shows a typical career path, including the positions above and below each job. If a job is entry level, the positions of Student, Intern, or Volunteer often precede it.

Position Description
Every effort has been made to provide well-rounded descriptions that neither glamorize nor denigrate jobs that are sometimes controversial, bureaucratic-sounding, and perplexing to outsiders. The Position Description uses plain and simple language to answer questions such as What's a typical day like? What kinds of questions need to be answered? What types of projects are handled? Each job in this book involves a mix of responsibilities, which are often bulleted for easy reading.

Salaries
Salary ranges are based on either surveys by national associations or the U.S. Department of Labor's Bureau of Labor Statistics or estimates by knowledgeable sources. Sometimes, though, salaries might rise or fall a bit in response to economic or political changes. Also, you might find jobs that fall below or above the general range, as salaries vary from one employer and geographic location to the next.

Employment Prospects

Employment prospects for job seekers are ranked on a scale from poor to fair, good, or excellent. When employees retire or new jobs are created, employment prospects generally improve for newcomers. Also, expect same changes due to economic or political trends. However, do not despair if a job you are interested in has a rating of "poor." Personal determination can help you get the job, even if the going is not easy.

Advancement Prospects

Advancement prospects deal with your chances of moving up once you get the job. Often, job holders can move in a variety of directions—private, public, and nonprofit—good news for anyone with a fair amount of ambition or wanderlust.

Education, Experience, Personality Traits

For some positions, graduate degrees are important, whereas for others experience is key. Because civil service exams are not required by most federal jobs and vary so much from one municipality and state to the next, they are rarely mentioned in this section. Instead, this topic is addressed in the Appendixes section Frequently Asked Questions about the Civil Service.

On a more personal level, dedication, commitment, and hard work count for a great deal in this field. If you are looking for an easy, uncomplicated job, you are in the wrong place. The jobs in this book are mentally and emotionally challenging. Employers want people dedicated enough to weather the inevitable setbacks that characterize working for the public good.

Unions and Associations

Professional associations (and some unions) provide valuable information and services to job seekers, including job postings, conferences, and other networking possibilities. In addition, associations such as the National Association of Schools of Public Affairs and Administration link colleges and universities in particular fields of study.

Tips for Entry

This section provides valuable advice on ways to get your foot in the door, find jobs, and locate sources for additional information. Sources repeatedly mention the importance of volunteer experience, whether it is community service, an internship, participation in a political party, help on a politi-cal campaign, grassroots organizing, or something else. The opportunities abound, so get involved in whatever way most suits your interests.

Appendixes

The Appendixes are geared to helping you locate the information you might want but don't know how to find. How to Run for Political Office—the Basics is a step-by-step guide to what is required to get your name on the ballot and your campaign headed for victory. The section Frequently Asked Questions about the Civil Service demystifies the process of applying for government jobs.

Other Appendixes provide information about the federal government's pay scale, employment offices, and organizational structure. The Graduate School Programs Appendix lists names, addresses, phone numbers, and websites of higher-education programs, including those in public affairs, public administration, and public policy. Other Appendixes outline

- Professional associations
- Employment websites
- Advocacy organizations, including political parties
- Trade publications

The Internet

The Internet has revolutionized the world of job-hunting. You can go on-line from your computer at home—or in a school or public library—and find professional associations, surf library catalogs, and browse job ads. All the websites mentioned in this book were accessible when it was being written. However, sometimes web addresses change, so if you find one that does not work, try scanning the home page for a new location. Another option is to enter keywords into a search engine such as Google.com.

This Book Is Yours

By picking up this book, you already have taken the first step toward finding a rewarding career. Curl up on the couch and have fun reading it. You'll be surfing the Net and pounding the pavement before long, I promise.

The jobs in this book will allow you to use your mind and satisfy your soul. So keep on reading. And get involved in something to make the world a better place. The job of your dreams will follow.

Good luck!

PART I
POLITICS

POLITICAL CAMPAIGNS

POLLSTER

CAREER PROFILE

Duties: Researching political campaigns; designing poll questions; supervising interviewers; analyzing data; writing reports

Alternate Title(s): Polling Analyst, Project Director

Salary Range: $30,000 to $500,000+

Employment Prospects: Good to excellent

Advancement Prospects: Good

Best Geographical Location(s): Washington, D.C., state capitals, major cities

Prerequisites:

Education or Training—Master's degree preferred
Experience—Campaign experience
Special Skills and Personality Traits—Passion for politics; understanding of statistical methods; ability to advise client on the most persuasive message(s) and targeting for campaign

CAREER LADDER

```
┌─────────────────────────────────────┐
│          Senior Associate            │
└─────────────────────────────────────┘

┌─────────────────────────────────────┐
│              Pollster                │
└─────────────────────────────────────┘

┌─────────────────────────────────────┐
│   Graduate Student or Campaign Worker │
└─────────────────────────────────────┘
```

Position Description

Pollsters measure and analyze public opinion, acting as doctors of sorts for political campaigns. They take the pulse of the electorate to diagnose the client's strengths and weaknesses and prescribe winning strategies.

As other political consultants do, Pollsters, who are also called polling analysts, typically work for a variety of clients, including interest groups, referendum committees, government agencies, and private corporations, as well as political candidates. Campaign polling has grown by leaps and bounds, as all levels of campaigns are turning to professional Pollsters to determine which issues to play up, where to focus their energies, and whether or not their strategies are working.

Pollsters are increasingly expanding their repertoire beyond traditional polls to include new tools such as focus groups and to survey specific groups of individuals. In the electronic focus group, or dialmeter, participants use a hand-held device to signal degrees of agreement or disagreement with what is said on a television screen.

Pollsters may conduct a variety of polls in the course of any given campaign. The benchmark survey, the first major poll of the campaign, is often followed by trend surveys and tracking polls. Each poll involves a number of steps. Pollsters

- Determine the purpose of the poll
- Select the sample
- Design questions
- Supervise interviewers
- Analyze data
- Write reports

Before drawing up the questions, Pollsters research the campaign, often consulting at length with strategists and in-house analysts. They determine the purpose of each poll before writing the questions. For example, a poll to gain an understanding of the candidate's strengths and weaknesses has a different purpose than one that looks into the general concerns of the electorate.

Pollsters use census tracts and other tools to select random samples for surveys, which are generally conducted by phone. The larger the sample, the lower the margin of error, but also the more expensive the poll.

Many questions have become standard, the exact wording devised and tested over time for its objectivity. On many public issues, people have no opinion at all, so questions should be worded in such a way as not to manufacture one. Most polls follow a standard sequence, beginning with an authoritative introduction and moving into screening questions to determine the respondent's likeliness to vote. Screening questions are tricky because some respondents, wanting to seem to be good citizens, say they will vote in the election but ultimately don't. The poll then moves into substantive questions about the campaign and concludes with demographic questions providing information about the respondent's television-viewing, radio-listening, and newspaper-reading habits as well as personal characteristics such as age, ethnic group, race, and income.

Pollsters can either contract out interviewing (e.g., to telemarketing phone banks or campaign volunteers) or head up their own interviewing operations, often with the help of an in-house field director. Interviewers are trained to stick to the script and avoid biased phrasing. Supervisors use plug-in monitors and call back respondents to check for accuracy.

New techniques in analysis have revolutionized polling. Whereas in the old days Pollsters could only correlate two factors simultaneously and needed weeks to complete polls, now they can analyze multiple responses at once and use rolling average techniques for continuous tracking.

As key strategists, Pollsters prepare reports based on the data for the client. For example, a Pollster might recommend that a candidate air TV ads around sports shows watched by a large share of undecided voters to shore up "soft" support. Yet, for all the new techniques, polling is not an exact science. Polling is controversial, faulted for driving up campaign costs, prompting candidates to pander to public opinion, and inculcating a "horse race" mentality of politics. Supporters, though, say polling gives candidates important feedback about the concerns of the public.

Salaries
Salaries tend to be higher for Pollsters than for other Political Consultants because of the more specialized nature of the work. Most beginning Pollsters have salaries in the $40,000 to $50,000 range, according to industry sources. In response to increased competition, some Pollsters are offering lower fees and less extensive polls to boost business.

Employment Prospects
Employment prospects are good to excellent for individuals with the right training. Polling firms are looking for individuals with experience in political campaigns and a background in quantitative analysis to hold professional-track positions in this rapidly growing industry. A polling firm may handle nonpolitical as well as political clients.

Advancement Prospects
Advancement prospects are good because new analysts, who are generally paired with more experienced members of the team, can acquire more responsibility with time. Individuals on a career track as Pollsters generally start out as Polling Analysts. A junior analyst who has the right education and training can move up to a more senior position. From there, individuals can build up their own client bases and start their own businesses or become senior partners in their polling firm.

Education and Training
Because Pollsters perform specialized quantitative analysis, graduate-school training tends to be more important for them than for other types of political consultants. Insiders recommend a master's degree for individuals looking to become associates in polling firms. Levels of education vary among Pollsters, as some hold Ph.D.s and others learn through fieldwork.

Master's programs in political science or related fields provide training in quantitative-research techniques, with new programs in political management dealing specifically with polling. Internship opportunities provide important hands-on experience.

Experience, Skills, and Personality Traits
Insiders emphasize the need for hands-on experience in political campaigns as well as familiarity with statistical methods. Pollsters must be able to perform two roles: objective analyst and campaign strategist. Those who see the two roles as complementary say they use objective analysis to help the candidates they like win. Maintaining high methodological standards in the heat of campaign battle, however, can be challenging, particularly if the firm has taken on too many clients. Many firms pair senior Pollsters with junior associates to give clients adequate access. Pollsters generally choose to represent either Democratic or Republican clients.

Pollsters must earn the trust of clients to be treated as full members of the strategy team even if the numbers are disappointing. Because campaigns involve teamwork, a good relationship between the Pollster and other members of the team can keep a lid on bickering and time-consuming arguments.

Polling analysts who work primarily on campaigns, as opposed to market research, should have a passion for politics. They tap into their own competitive instincts to help their candidates win. High pressure and frequent travel are integral parts of this job.

Unions and Associations
Many Pollsters belong to the American Association of Political Consultants (AAPC) and/or the American Association for Public Opinion Research (AAPOR).

Tips for Entry
1. Work on a political campaign. Because Pollsters are key members of the strategic team, they should have an understanding of how campaigns work.

2. Look into educational programs in political management, political science, statistics, and/or related fields, as familiarity with quantitative analysis is important in this field. Many programs offer valuable internship opportunities.

3. Read about polling. Newspapers commonly run articles detailing the results of various polls, and books on political consulting provide information about polling.

4. Browse the webpages of the American Association of Political Consultants *(www.theaapc.org)* and the American Association for Public Opinion Research *(www.aapor.org)* for information about conferences and career development.

5. Determine your party affiliation carefully because polling firms tend to be partisan. Become active in the political party of your choice to take advantage of important networking opportunities.

POLITICAL CONSULTANT

CAREER PROFILE

Duties: Providing advice on overall campaign strategy and/or specialized services such as polling, advertising, or direct mail for political candidates and other clients

Salary Range: $30,000 to $250,000

Employment Prospects: Good

Advancement Prospects: Good

Best Geographical Location(s): Washington, D.C.; state capitals; major cities

Prerequisites:

Education or Training—Bachelor's degree or higher

Experience—Several years of campaign experience

Special Skills and Personality Traits—Competitive; quick-thinking; analytical; comfortable in rough-and-tumble world of politics; willing to work long hours and travel

CAREER LADDER

```
┌─────────────────────────────────────┐
│ Senior Associate or Related Profession│
│ (e.g., public relations, lobbying)   │
└─────────────────────────────────────┘

┌─────────────────────────────────────┐
│        Political Consultant          │
└─────────────────────────────────────┘

┌─────────────────────────────────────┐
│      Campaign Worker or Intern       │
└─────────────────────────────────────┘
```

Position Description

Political Consultants are the "hired guns" of candidate and issue campaigns. In the past few decades, industry sources say, the number of Political Consultants has grown enormously, as campaigns that once relied on political parties and volunteers for support have increasingly turned to high-powered professionals for their technological expertise. With a click of a computer mouse, Political Consultants can predict votes, touch up photos, and "dig up the dirt" on the candidate's opponent.

Increasingly, Political Consultants represent not only political candidates but also referendum committees, interest groups, nonprofits, corporations, and international concerns. A labor union, for example, might hire a Political Consultant to advise someone running for a leadership position or identify and mobilize support for a grassroots campaign.

Unlike a Campaign Manager, who works on one campaign at a time, Political Consultants juggle a number of different clients, helping them win whatever campaign they are waging. Some Political Consultants double as lobbyists.

Political Consultants can either provide overall advice or specialize in a particular service such as polling, media advertising, or direct-mail/fund-raising. Many firms keep their size small by subcontracting out to specialists. A Political Consultant specializing in media strategy, for example,

might hire a crew to shoot an ad. Other firms, known as A–Z shops, have full in-house production staffs.

In addition to polling, advertising, and fund-raising, Political Consultants participate in a growing number of specialties, including

- Signature gathering for initiatives and referendums
- Media buying and placement
- Press relations and events
- Opposition and candidate research
- Website consulting

By the time someone becomes a Political Consultant, he or she has usually worked in numerous campaigns. Many start as volunteer or low-paid "worker bees," then move up to management positions with campaigns and/or political parties. They have seen certain patterns repeating themselves. Voters, they discover, can be divided into three basic groups: the candidate's supporters, the opponent's supporters, and the undecided. Political Consultants direct the campaign's message, money, time, and efforts toward building a coalition of supporters and "persuadable" voters large enough to assure victory.

In a typical campaign, the Political Consultant is hired well before the client makes a formal announcement of candidacy. Early in the campaign the Political Consultant develops strategy and looks for support. Can the candidate count on key figures in the political party for financial support? How much money a month must the campaign raise in order to survive? Which events are most important for the candidate to attend?

Political Consultants also conduct research, often with the help of subcontractors, on the record of the candidate and the opponent, the mood of the electorate, and voters' assessments of the candidates. If the campaign progresses to the next level, the Political Consultant is likely to make elaborate preparations for announcement day, planning press packets and endorsements for each stop.

As the campaign progresses, the Political Consultant might work on matters like how to get free publicity to increase the candidate's name recognition and whether or not to respond directly to attacks from the opponent. The final two weeks of the campaign is a time of feverish activity. Campaign ads fill the airwaves, and the candidate attends a nonstop array of events. Phone banks swing into high gear to get out the vote.

On election day, Political Consultants wait anxiously for preliminary, then final, results. Political Consultants celebrate with the winners and commiserate with the losers. Before folding up shop, the Political Consultant might arrange fund-raisers to help a losing candidate recoup some of the campaign debt.

Salaries

Salaries vary, depending on the firm and one's position in it. In the hierarchy of political consulting, junior associates can expect starting salaries of $35,000 to 45,000, compared to about $105,000, the mean salary for principal partners, according to industry sources.

Political Consultants charge clients fees for their services. To protect against sharp drops in salaries during nonelection years, most firms take a variety of clients. Political Consultants also might screen clients to make sure they will be able to pay for their services. In addition to client fees, many Political Consultants receive sizable commissions from advertising.

Employment Prospects

Employment prospects are good because political consulting is a new and rapidly growing industry. Insiders say one needs only a home office equipped with phone lines, computers, faxes, and Internet access to set up shop as a Political Consultant. Most of the estimated 3,000 firms that specialize in campaigns and elections have 10 or fewer staffers, according to *No Place for Amateurs: How Political Consultants Are Reshaping American Democracy* by Dennis Johanson. Many Political Consultants keep their operations small by subcontracting out to specialists when needed.

Although launching a business might be relatively simple, keeping it going is considerably more difficult. Compe-

tition for clients is fierce. Disagreements among partners can lead to acrimonious breakups.

Advancement Prospects

Advancement prospects are good because junior associates can work their way up to senior partner or launch their own business. Political Consultants also can move into positions in related fields such as public relations or lobbying. Because of the competitive nature of the business, some Political Consultants leave the field after experiencing financial setbacks. Others, though, become big-name Political Consultants, basking in the spotlight. They serve as consultants for TV shows such as *The West Wing* or provide political commentary on news shows.

Education and Training

Insiders say the most valuable education and training are gained through "trial-by-fire" on the campaign trail. Academic courses can also be useful in honing the writing, analytical, and critical-thinking skills needed for the job. Some 40 percent of Political Consultants hold graduate degrees, according to a survey by the Pew Center for the People and the Press. Within the past few decades, the new academic field of political management has sprung up specifically in response to the growing complexity of political campaigns.

Programs in political management fall into two basic types: degree-granting and short-term intensive training. Georgetown University and the University of Florida, for example, offer master's degree programs. Some shorter programs are affiliated with universities, such as American University and Yale, and others are offered through members of the industry such as *Campaigns & Elections Magazine* and the American Association of Political Consultants. The national committees of the Democratic and Republican Parties also offer training programs.

Before becoming a Political Consultant, an individual might have worked as a campaign manager, political party operative, or press secretary.

Experience, Skills, and Personality Traits

Most individuals in this field are political junkies drawn to the thrill of competition. This factor—the thrill of competition—ranked as the primary motivator of Political Consultants (outweighing political beliefs, money, and political power) in a survey by the Pew Research Center for the People and the Press. As *Campaigns & Elections Magazine* observed, many Political Consultants see themselves as "the last of the gunslingers."

Political consulting attracts people who thrive in the fast-paced, competitive, rough-and-tumble world of politics. "People who go into social work would not be comfortable in political wars," *Campaigns & Elections Magazine* observed. In the competitive world of political consulting, individuals struggle to maintain high victory-loss ratios.

Whether or not winning takes precedence over high ethical standards, however, is a matter of much debate. The American Association of Political Consultants, which requires members to sign an ethics pledge, allows for negative campaigning as long as the attacks on the opponent are not false or misleading. Insiders say that Political Consultants use negative campaigning because it works. Some Political Consultants blame the media for giving inordinate attention to negative campaigning and delving into the private lives of candidates, thus driving away some talented individuals. Will the public's concerns about negative campaigning and rising campaign costs change the face of the industry? Such questions await a new generation of Political Consultants.

Unions and Associations

Two professional associations—the American Association of Political Consultants and the International Association of Political Consultants—represent members of this relatively new profession. Political Consultants also might be members of other groups such as the American Political Science Association.

Tips for Entry

1. Volunteer to work on a political campaign.
2. Get involved in the political party of your choice.
3. Develop a network of people involved in political matters. Because jobs in this field are rarely advertised, networking helps individuals break in and move up.
4. Check out *Campaigns & Elections Magazine (www.campaignline.com)*. The annual March issue, known as the Political Pages, lists Political Consultants by category.

CAMPAIGN MANAGER

CAREER PROFILE

Duties: Responsible for overall campaign management, including drafting the campaign plan, prioritizing staff activities, and overseeing campaign operations

Alternate Title(s): Campaign Coordinator, Campaign Director

Salary Range: $0 to $8,000/month for approximately six months

Employment Prospects: Fair

Advancement Prospects: Good

Best Geographical Location(s): Campaigns for state or national office

Prerequisites:
Education or Training—Bachelor's degree or higher preferred
Experience—Two to 10 years
Special Skills and Personality Traits—Able to work well with the candidate; politically savvy; well organized; energetic; optimistic; goal-oriented

CAREER LADDER

```
┌─────────────────────────────────────────┐
│  Position in Candidate's Administration  │
└─────────────────────────────────────────┘

┌─────────────────────────────────────────┐
│            Campaign Manager              │
└─────────────────────────────────────────┘

┌─────────────────────────────────────────┐
│            Campaign Staffer              │
└─────────────────────────────────────────┘
```

Position Description

Campaign Managers provide the overall coordination and direction needed to take their candidates to victory on Election Day. Although candidates may have veto power over some key decisions, Campaign Managers usually have authority over everything else. Campaign Managers head up the various elements of the campaign—fund-raising, field operations, and advertising, among them—allowing staff and key volunteers to make their own decisions about details of operation. Campaign Managers work to ensure that all these different elements mesh smoothly and on time.

Sometimes, Political Consultants double as Campaign Managers. In general, though, Campaign Managers work intensively on one campaign at a time whereas Political Consultants juggle a variety of campaigns at once. Sometimes, too, Campaign Managers hire Political Consultants for specialized tasks such as fund-raising or advertising. Another possibility is for the two to work side by side on the same campaign, as Political Consultants provide seasoned advice to Campaign Managers chosen for their ties to the district and the candidate.

Because the position of Campaign Manager requires considerable experience, most individuals have worked their way up to it, starting out as volunteers or low-level staffers. From there, they assume more responsible positions, including Field Coordinator, Finance Director, and Assistant Campaign Manager.

The typical campaign season runs from April to November, with the Campaign Manager on call 24 hours a day. On assuming the position, the Campaign Manager usually helps the candidate draft a campaign plan, a blueprint for the next several months. Over the course of the campaign, the Campaign Manager's role shifts from thinker to doer, as he or she moves from drafting to implementing the plan.

Days are usually packed with activity, as the Campaign Manager travels with the candidate to ensure that everything runs smoothly. If, for instance, the candidate needs "talking points" on economic policy, the Campaign Manager should be able instantly to produce the necessary piece of paper. A typical day might start at 6 A.M. with a trip to the coffee shop or a morning talk show. After an event, the Campaign Manager might coach the candidate, offering advice like

"You're speaking too loudly" or "Slow down and take a deep breath."

Because days are so full, the nighttime hours provide the opportunity for strategizing and catching up on odds and ends. In the middle of the night, the candidate might call with a new plan for mobilizing voters or a quick reminder that a local family of supporters is expecting a lawn sign.

Back in the office, the Campaign Manager recruits supporters and campaign staff and executes the campaign plan. The plan, for instance, might call for a set of newspaper ads in August. By then, the Campaign Manager should already know how much the ads will cost and what they are going to say. In addition, Campaign Managers orchestrate quick responses to changing conditions, ensure that all campaign work is done properly and on time, and monitor finances to stay within the campaign's budget.

Salaries

Industry specialists say that salaries vary by the level of office sought by the candidate—the higher the office, the higher the salary of the Campaign Manager. Most campaigns run from April to November, although presidential campaigns are generally considerably longer—about 18 months.

Whereas many Campaign Managers at the local level are unpaid, those working for state legislative candidates generally earn between $500 and $2,000 a month, although candidates in larger states might pay more. Campaign Managers for U.S. House races generally earn about $5,000 a month or $30,000 for a six-month cycle; those for Senate and gubernatorial campaigns generally earn about $6,000 or $7,000 a month, according to Costas Panagopoulos, executive director of the Political Campaign Management Program at New York University.

Employment Prospects

Employment prospects are fair because Campaign Managers must compete for a limited number of positions, some of which might go to their more seasoned peers in the political consulting industry. Typically, Campaign Managers head up three to five campaigns before choosing a more steady line of work, insiders say. Some Campaign Managers land high-level positions in government such as chief of staff or press secretary. Others become Political Party Operatives or Political Consultants. Still others return to their original line of work, whether it is law, education, or something else. Rarely does a Campaign Manager spend 20 to 30 years in the field.

Advancement Prospects

Advancement prospects are good because a solid record of winning elections opens up doors. A successful Campaign Manager can advance to larger, more influential races or land a position in Washington, D.C., or the state house. Sometimes Campaign Managers who have handled several races and/or had additional training become Political Consultants. Sometimes, too, Campaign Managers decide to run for office. They also might land a key position in the winning candidate's administration or meet influential people on the campaign trail who can help them advance their careers.

Education and Training

Although hands-on experience is vital, insiders agree that a background in certain academic areas can be helpful. Costas Panagopoulos, executive director of the Political Campaign Management Program at New York University, recommends that undergraduates take courses in political science, communications, and marketing.

As political campaigns have become increasingly complex, new degree-granting programs and shorter intensives have sprouted up in the field of political management. Programs are offered through universities, industry organizations such as *Campaigns & Elections Magazine* and the American Association of Political Consultants, and the national and state political parties.

Experience, Skills, and Personality Traits

Campaign experience is crucial, as Campaign Managers perform the role of generals heading up an army of Campaign Workers and Volunteers. Although the Campaign Manager need not be an expert in all aspects of the campaign, he or she should be familiar enough with each of the various elements to make informed decisions.

Most Campaign Managers have worked in a position of responsibility in at least one or two campaigns, although they need not have held the top position. For instance, someone might go from being Finance Director of a U.S. Senator's campaign to becoming Campaign Manager for a candidate for U.S. Representative.

On a personal level, the Campaign Manager must be able to work well with the candidate. Insiders say that candidates generally spend more time with their Campaign Manager than with their spouse. The Campaign Manager should have the candidate's total trust.

Campaign Managers also should be politically savvy, well organized, energetic, and goal-oriented. Their number one goal: winning the election. They should be able to delegate responsibilities and motivate staff even when prospects for the candidate look grim.

"The number one flaw of Campaign Managers is that they try to do too much," said Costas Panagopoulos, executive director of the Political Campaign Management Program at New York University. "They need to be able to delegate to competent team players."

Unions and Associations

There are no unions or associations specifically for Campaign Managers, although state political parties provide important training and networking opportunities. Some Campaign Managers also belong to the American Association of Political Consultants.

Tips for Entry

1. Volunteer for a candidate's campaign.
2. Become active in local organizations and/or your political party.
3. Network: in this, as in many political positions, jobs are rarely advertised.
4. Read more about jobs in campaign management by browsing the Political Resources On-Line jobs board *(www.politicalresources.com),* checking out *Campaigns & Elections Magazine,* and/or reading *The Campaign Manager* by Catherine Golden or other books cataloged under the keyword *campaign.*

POLITICAL PARTY STAFFER

CAREER PROFILE

Duties: Recruiting and training candidates; preparing for conventions; planning events and fund-raisers; supporting candidates and elected officials

Alternate Title(s): Field Director, Communications Director, Finance Director, Political Director, Executive Director

Salary Range: $30,000 to $150,000

Employment Prospects: Fair

Employment Prospects: Good

Best Geographical Location(s): State capitals, Washington, D.C.

Prerequisites:

Education or Training—Bachelor's degree

Experience—One to three years

Special Skills and Personality Traits—Energetic; skillful in communication; well organized; passionate about the party and its issues

CAREER LADDER

> **Political Consultant**

> **Political Party Staffer**

> **Intern or Campaign Worker**

Position Description

Political Party Staffers work to advance their party's candidates and agendas. The party system gives voters a label—a sort of "political brand name"—to help them decide which candidates are most in line with their own interests. Because the two-party system dominates the political landscape, the vast majority of jobs for Political Party Staffers are with the Democratic or Republican Parties.

Both the Democratic and Republican Parties maintain full-time staffs at the national and state levels. Political Party Staffers craft broad messages and supplement the services candidates get from Political Consultants and Campaign Managers. They work under the direction of an elected Chairman or Chairwoman.

On the national front, the Republican National Committee and Democratic National Committee hire individuals for a variety of functions, including communications, fund-raising, and political operations. Each party also has a Senatorial and Congressional Campaign Committee involved in recruiting, training, and financing candidates for the U.S. House and Senate.

At the state level, political parties have established permanent headquarters and beefed up their staffs in recent decades. Much as their counterparts have at the national level, state parties, too, have separate legislative and central committees. Common positions in state parties include Staff Assistant, Communication Director, Finance Director, Political Director, and Executive Director. An entry-level Staff Assistant might be involved in updating the party's databases while more senior Staffers direct the party's operations. The state party, for instance, might kick off a new drive to recruit women.

Much of the work of Political Party Staffers follows the election cycle, which typically begins with recruiting candidates for office. Frequently this involves contacting local party leaders for referrals and talking to prospective candidates. Political Party Staffers then provide training for these new recruits in the nuts and bolts of running for office, including techniques to raise funds and make effective speeches.

Before the state party conventions, Political Party Staffers send information to delegates and coordinate logistics. Endorsed candidates can buy the party's "coordinated campaign" services, which typically include voter files, phone banks, radio ads, and field staffers. Political Party Staffers hire the temporary field help, contract with phone vendors and media consultants, and coordinate events for all statewide candidates.

After the elections, Political Party Staffers provide support to elected officials. If, for instance, there is an argument between party members, a Political Party Staffer might be called in to mediate. Or, perhaps, the mayor of a city wants help in getting more media exposure, so the Political Party Staffer arranges for the mayor to speak at an upcoming event. As the deadlines for the next election approach, Political Party Staffers start recruiting and training the next crop of candidates.

Salaries

Salaries vary according to the level of the position and the size of the political party organization. The executive director of a large state political party might earn more than his or her counterpart at the national level, according to Dr. James A. Thurber, director of the Center for Congressional and Presidential Studies at American University. In general Political Party Staffers can expect to earn between $30,000 and $150,000 a year, depending on their experience, their level of responsibility, and the resources of their party.

Employment Prospects

Employment prospects are fair because much of the work of political parties is done by grassroots volunteers. Most minor parties rely exclusively on volunteers, although a few occasionally hire organizers or other staffers. Industry sources report that the Republican Party generally raises more money than the Democratic Party and so can hire more Political Party Staffers. Most jobs in political parties are filled through word of mouth rather than job ads.

Advancement Prospects

Advancement prospects are good because Political Party Staffers frequently have contact with people who can help advance their careers. In the world of politics, personal contacts often open the doors to new career possibilities. Political Party Staffers commonly refer candidates to Political Consultants and often become Political Consultants themselves. They might also land staff positions for elected officials or become lobbyists.

Education and Training

Insiders observe that the most important education and training result from being out in the field. As one state party executive director put it, "Someone can graduate with a 4.0 in political science and be terrible without the experience."

Nevertheless, a college education can help develop important writing, communication, and analytical skills. New academic programs and training seminars in the field of political management have sprung up in response to the growing complexity of political campaigns.

Experience, Skills, and Personality Traits

Most Political Party Staffers have campaign and/or legislative staff experience. Someone, for instance, might have worked on a few political campaigns and interned for a legislator.

Political Party Staffers should believe in the party's message and be able to communicate it effectively. As do many political workers, Political Party Staffers tend to "eat and breathe" politics. They lead the fast-paced, adrenaline-charged lives of "political junkies." This is not a nine to five job, insiders say: Political Party Staffers frequently work nights and weekends.

Unions and Associations

Both major parties have state and national organizations of young people: Young Democrats, Young Republicans, College Democrats, and College Republicans. Each national and state political party organization handles its own hiring. The Democratic and Republican National Committees have their own personnel offices. Minor parties sometimes work together in organizations devoted to improving ballot access or furthering conservative or progressive agendas.

Tips for Entry

1. Work on a political campaign.
2. Seek an internship with your state or national political party.
3. Look into internships and paid positions with elected officials.
4. Consider working part-time or on a temporary basis to break in. During presidential election years, both major parties enlarge their staffs considerably with temporary and part-time employees. Political parties also hire part-time fund-raisers and temporary field organizers.
5. Search political employment websites for a variety of political positions rather than for jobs specifically with political parties. Helpful sites include GOPjob.com (www.gopjob.com), DEMjob.com (www.demjob.com), the Politix Group (www.politixgroup.com), and Political Resources (www.politicalresources.com).
6. Use the keywords *third party* to find listings of minor political parties.

POLITICAL OFFICE

SCHOOL BOARD MEMBER

CAREER PROFILE

Duties: Represent constituents and exercise public control of schools by setting policy, approving budgets, hiring and evaluating the superintendent, and responding to concerns of constituents; assuming other leadership responsibilities

Alternate Title(s): School Committee Member, Trustee

Salary Range: $0 to $35,000

Employment Prospects: Good

Advancement Prospects: Good

Best Geographical Location(s): Small communities are generally less competitive.

Prerequisites:

Education or Training—No formal requirements; training offered by professional associations for new School Board Members

Experience—Volunteer experience dealing with school and/or community issues

Special Skills and Personality Traits—Articulate; well prepared and organized; committed to providing excellent education for all children; able to work well with others

CAREER LADDER

```
┌─────────────────────────────┐
│   School Board President,   │
│      City Councilor,        │
│  or Other Volunteer Position│
└─────────────────────────────┘

┌─────────────────────────────┐
│    School Board Member      │
└─────────────────────────────┘

┌─────────────────────────────┐
│  Community/School Volunteer │
└─────────────────────────────┘
```

Position Description

School Board Members strive to improve the quality of public education in their communities, sometimes with an eye toward running for higher political office.

Although many members of Congress began their political careers on the school board, the majority of School Board Members lack such lofty political ambitions. They simply want to serve their communities. School Board Members provide critical linking of schools, parents, and the community, confronting such challenges of the 21st century as youth violence, educational testing, and changing demographics.

Most School Board Members see their service as a calling rather than a career. Approximately 90 percent of School Board Members receive little, if any, compensation, according to the National School Boards Association. Most earn their primary income in other occupations. The National Association of School Boards reports that 43 percent of School Board Members hold professional or managerial posts, 12 percent own businesses, and 12 percent are retired.

School Board Members do more than attend meetings: They must also prepare for them, often by making phone calls and poring over mounds of paperwork. First, School Board Members set educational policy for the community. Most boards create a "vision statement" for the district. In addition, School Board Members set policies on a variety of matters such as Internet usage for students, safety in the schools, and school uniforms. School Board Members commonly compile a policy manual, which provides guidance for administrators and others in the district.

Second, School Board Members are responsible for the hiring and evaluation of the Chief Executive Officer, usually called the Superintendent. The relationship between the board and the Superintendent can be a prickly one, particularly if the two do not understand and respect each other's responsibilities: the lay board for *setting* policy and the superintendent, as professional administrator, for *implementing* it.

Third, School Board Members assume responsibility for educational planning, goal setting, and appraisal, with the primary focus of all board decisions on student achievement. For instance, a school district might set the goal of every child's attaining a specified reading level by the end of the third grade. What kind of professional development would enable teachers to achieve this goal? Do some reading systems work better for some students than others? If so, how can the schools best help students with special needs?

Fourth, School Board Members are responsible for setting the overall budget, which is developed by the Superintendent. About 95 percent of the average school district budget is earmarked for wages, benefits, transportation, and other items, according to the National School Boards Association. Because the budgeting process involves several steps, savvy school boards set deadlines when

- A tentative budget will be completed and presented to the board
- The administration will present staff requests to the board
- The Superintendent will make the first formal budget request to the board
- Public hearings will be held
- The budget will be presented to municipal or state officials
- The board will have its final discussion of the budget and adopt it

Fifth, School Board Members communicate with various constituencies. They respond to questions from the media; maintain ongoing, two-way communication with school staff, students, and members of the community; and build collaborative relations with political and business leaders to develop a consensus for student success.

Sixth, School Board Members hear appeals from school staff members or students on issues that involve policy implementation. For instance, if parents are unable to resolve a dispute over discipline with their child's principal, they may take the matter to the school board.

Finally, School Board Members are involved in a variety of other activities, including electing board officers, approving the annual school calendar, and establishing attendance zones for the school district. They also must read lengthy reports, serve on committees, and respond to the concerns of constituents.

Salaries

The vast majority of School Board Members receive little or no compensation for their service. In some communities, School Board Members are compensated on a per-diem or per-meeting basis. On the high end of the range, some large districts offer compensation in the $25,000 to $35,000 range.

Employment Prospects

Employment prospects are generally good, although School Board Members face stiff competition for election in some communities, particularly large urban districts. In other communities, candidates run uncontested. In contested races, candidates who lose on the first try sometimes run again and win, benefiting from increased name recognition.

Running an effective campaign for school board is generally less expensive in small communities than in large urban districts. Overall, candidates in 75.6 percent of all districts spend less than $1,000 to run for school board, according to the National School Boards Association. Most candidates use a combination of their own money and support from friends or family. Less than a third receive contributions from outside sources. Some candidates in large districts, however, spend $10,000 to $25,000 or more to run for school board.

School boards average five or seven people, although board size varies from as few as three to as many as 15. Almost all school boards are elected (fewer than 3 percent are appointed). As with other elected positions, school board candidates must be able to connect with voters to win elections. Candidates who can run on a solid record of accomplishment, often as volunteers in the school or community, have an edge. Insiders say it also helps for candidates to know people in the business and school community.

Advancement Prospects

Advancement prospects depend on one's goals. Within the board itself, members can rise to leadership positions such as School Board President. Some School Board Members pursue other community endeavors such as becoming head of the United Way, finding that their school board service opens up doors. Others run for higher political office such as city council, with prospects that depend on the size of the community and whether or not the race is contested.

Education and Training

Most School Board Members are college-educated, although a bachelor's degree is not required. Eligibility laws differ from state to state, but most states require candidates for school board to be at least 21 years old and registered to vote in the district they want to represent, according to the National School Boards Association. Nearly half of School Board Members are between the ages of 41 and 50. However, younger people are often credited with introducing fresh insights (having recently been students themselves) to school boards.

Training for new School Board Members is offered at the district, state, and national levels. On an informal basis, experienced School Board Members often provide information, encouragement, and guidance to their new colleagues. The district also may have a formal orientation and development program for School Board Members.

National and state school board associations, too, play an active role in educating School Board Members. State school board associations provide workshops for new School Board Members and/or people interested in running for a seat. Both the National School Boards Association and state associations sponsor workshops and conferences on specific issues such as technology and parliamentary procedure.

Experience, Skills, and Personality Traits

School Board Members typically have experience as volunteers in the school or community. Someone involved in the Parent-Teacher Association (PTA), for instance, might decide to run for the school board. A former teacher, too, might decide to run for the board. Although many School Board Members are parents of school-aged children, some candidates in their 20s also win seats on the board.

Many School Board Members find the work more difficult and time-consuming than they expected. To prevent the problems of divided boards, School Board Members should be able to work well with others. Good team players deal with facts rather than personalities, are willing to compromise, and do their homework.

Unions and Associations

The National School Boards Association is a national organization dedicated to fostering excellence in public education through local school board leadership.

Tips for Entry

1. Volunteer to work for an organization involved in school and/or community issues.
2. Attend a school board meeting. Most are open to the public.
3. Ask yourself whether you have what it takes to succeed. Are you willing to work long hours for little or no pay? How well can you handle being in the public eye? Will you be able to compromise with other Board Members?
4. Look into candidacy requirements. Find out whether your school board is elected in November or in April (or some other month) and whether Board Members are elected at large and/or from certain geographical areas. State law often requires all candidates for public office to file financial disclosure statements and to present a nominating petition signed by a certain percentage of registered voters.
5. Participate in workshops and conferences sponsored by state school boards associations and the National School Boards Association. Some local districts also conduct sessions of their own.
6. Remember to factor in the possible costs of running for office. Although many school board campaigns are relatively low budget (limited to such old-fashioned costs as brochures, print advertisements, and bumper stickers), some races are becoming more costly and sophisticated.

CITY COUNCILOR

CAREER PROFILE

Duties: Creating laws, adopting policies, and providing inspiration and motivation to improve the community

Alternate Title(s): Selectboard Member, Alderman/Alderwoman, County Commissioner

Salary Range: $0 to $90,000

Employment Prospects: Fair to poor

Advancement Prospects: Poor

Best Geographical Location(s): Municipalities

Prerequisites:
   Education or Training—No formal requirements
   Experience—No formal requirements
   Special Skills and Personality Traits—Commitment to the community; public speaking experience; endurance; consensus-building skills

CAREER LADDER

```
┌─────────────────────────────────────┐
│               Mayor                 │
└─────────────────────────────────────┘

┌─────────────────────────────────────┐
│            City Councilor            │
└─────────────────────────────────────┘

┌─────────────────────────────────────┐
│      School Committee Member        │
│        or Citizen Activist          │
└─────────────────────────────────────┘
```

Position Description

City Councilors are legislators, much like members of Congress. Both groups draft bills, deal with constituents, and vote on budgets. But, compared to their counterparts on Capitol Hill, City Councilors work on a much smaller scale. A City Councilor might consider a plan for a multithousand- or multimillion-dollar project to build a turn lane at a busy intersection. A U.S. Senator, on the other hand, would be concerned with a multibillion-dollar interstate highway system.

City Councilors work at the street level, dealing with the nitty-gritty details of community life such as potholes, crime, and property taxes. One of the advantages of working at the local level is that results are easy to see. A City Councilor who advocated construction of an additional school, for instance, might pass the new facility every day on the way to work. However, victories like this occur after months, if not years, of hard work. City Councilors are always lining up votes, vying for a majority, or working to build a consensus. In a world where factionalism and infighting are legendary, this is no easy task.

The vast majority of City Councilors are part-time. They balance their political responsibilities with another occupation, such as law or business. Many City Councilors emerge from the ranks of the school committee, a natural progression, considering that schools form a large part of the city council's budget. City Councilors fall into two basic groups:

• District—representing a particular part of the city
• At-large—elected citywide

These two groups differ somewhat in focus. A City Councilor for a district acts as an advocate for a particular neighborhood, asking questions like, What are the needs of different ethnic groups? and How can a certain program benefit the neighborhood? The at-large Councilor needs to juggle the concerns of a broader group of constituents.

Whether elected at large or districtwide, City Councilors need to be generalists to deal with everything from economic development to public safety, social services, and whatever happens to be "hot" at the moment.

If, for instance, constituents are pushing for more affordable housing, a City Councilor might create a plan for increased funding. The Mayor, though, might reject the plan. Should the City Councilor champion an initiative to get permission from the state to float a bond? Or should the City Councilor work on a new housing proposal that could win the Mayor's support? Such tactical decisions can determine whether or not City Councilors are successful in carrying out their agendas. The intensity of work for a City

Councilor depends largely on the nature of the community. Whereas an individual in a small community might take home a few hours of work and attend two or three night meetings a week, the City Councilor of a large city might work considerably longer hours to deal with the more complex problems at hand.

A City Councilor's schedule varies from day to day, but time is generally spent at meetings, such as City Council or committee meetings; in the office, working on correspondence, research, budgets, or planning; or out in the community, meeting with different groups and participating in community events.

In towns and counties, selectboard members and county commissioners perform many of the same duties as City Councilors. Although a county might oversee the courts, corrections, tax assessments, and/or other areas of service, it might lack a charter from the state and so have less authority than a city. A City Councilor might have a higher profile than a county commissioner.

As a local celebrity of sorts, the City Councilor may receive numerous invitations to ground-breakings, parades, wakes, christenings, and weddings. In the case of a blizzard, a City Councilor might be awakened at 3:30 A.M. and work nonstop until 10:00 P.M. Yet, compared to the Mayor, a City Councilor works relatively short hours. A City Councilor is one of several members of a board—a group player rather than a solo performer. A City Councilor might work 15 hours compared to a Mayor's 60 hours a week.

Salaries
Because City Councilor is generally a part-time position, salaries tend to be low. Some communities pay nothing at all. Only a few large cities pay City Councilors in the $50,000 to $90,000 range. More common are salaries in the $10,000 to $30,000 or $0 to $10,000 range.

Employment Prospects
Employment prospects are fair to poor because there are a limited number of slots for City Councilors. Generally speaking, competition is higher in big cities than in smaller communities. Thus a bid for City Council in a smaller community might be more successful.

Advancement Prospects
Advancement prospects are poor because the position of Mayor, the next logical step on the political hierarchy, is generally difficult to reach. Since most City Councilors are part-time, individuals typically return to their primary line

of work. Some City Councilors are retired adults or secondary breadwinners. Others work primarily in another occupation such as business or law.

Education and Training
City Councilors come from all walks of life. There are no formal requirements for this position. Candidates need to "sell" their ideas to voters, who, in turn, decide who is most qualified for the position.

Experience, Skills, and Personality Traits
Many City Councilors have prior experience on a community board such as a civic association, Parent-Teacher Association (PTA), or school committee. As board members, they develop their consensus-building and problem-solving skills.

City Councilors must look at both sides of an issue in order to be fair. Still, they should have the courage of their own convictions.

Dedication counts for a great deal in this field. Few City Councilors are attracted to the job by the salary. Candidates choose to run for office because they want to improve their communities.

Unions and Associations
Although no union or association deals exclusively with City Councilors, individuals might belong to the National League of Cities, state municipal associations, or other groups dealing with municipal issues.

Tips for Entry
1. Look into internships and special opportunities such as city youth councils.
2. Follow the news; keep up with issues of key concern.
3. Attend city council and other community meetings.
4. Carve out a primary occupation with some flexibility. Because most city council positions are part-time, individuals generally need another source of income.
5. Seek a position on another community board such as a civic association, PTA, or school committee. Memberships on these boards often serve as springboards to City Councilor.
6. Become involved in the political party of your choice to take advantage of important networking opportunities.
7. Ask yourself whether you have a large enough network of friends and supporters to launch a successful campaign. Usually, it's easier to win a race when not running against a popular incumbent.

MAYOR

CAREER PROFILE

Duties: Providing overall leadership for the community; setting policy; recommending budgets; appointing members of the local government; balancing out different interests; understanding the needs of citizens; speaking for the municipality

Salary Range: $0 to $130,000

Employment Prospects: Poor

Advancement Prospects: Fair

Best Geographical Location(s): Cities, towns

Prerequisites:

Education or Training—No formal requirements
Experience—No formal requirements
Special Skills and Personality Traits—Strong leadership and communication skills; dedication to the community; honesty; willingness to work long hours

CAREER LADDER

```
┌─────────────────────────────────┐
│  State or Federal Elected Office │
│    or Various Other Positions    │
└─────────────────────────────────┘

┌─────────────────────────────────┐
│              Mayor              │
└─────────────────────────────────┘

┌─────────────────────────────────┐
│          City Councilor         │
└─────────────────────────────────┘
```

Position Description

Mayors steer the course of their communities. Some—such as Fiorello LaGuardia and Rudolph Giuliani—have become legendary figures nationwide. Over the years, Mayors have carved out reputations as fiery eccentrics, cool-headed managers, populists, progressives, power brokers, and visionaries.

As chief executive, the Mayor serves as the local equivalent of President of the United States. Mayors have the most powerful single voice in their communities. They set policy, make appointments, recommend budgets, and speak for their cities. Mayors are credited for the good times and blamed for the bad times. Such power carries an element of glamour. Nevertheless, many Mayors toil for little or no money. They consider the position a "calling" rather than a "career." The hours are so long and the pay so low that only one motive justifies wanting to be Mayor: the desire to serve one's community.

Some Mayors have considerably more power than others. Generally speaking, those elected by the public have more clout than those chosen by a city council. Also, big-city Mayors tend to be more well-known than their counterparts in small cities, many of whom work part-time. A town, too, can have a Mayor, if the charter calls for one. The posi-

tion of Mayor defies easy categorization, as veto powers, term limits, and personalities vary from community to community. A strong leader can emerge from a city chartered for a weak Mayor by virtue of his or her powers of persuasion.

Citizens look to the Mayor for a sense of vision. Over the years, as federal grants have become more scarce, the Mayor has assumed a more entrepreneurial role. In small communities, education typically accounts for more than 50 percent of the budget. Mayors often play an important role in the schools as well as in myriad other community concerns.

Each day is a juggling act: how to balance the needs of different groups, different types of projects, and different time constraints. Mayors attend neighborhood and community meetings, confer with other government officials, serve on state and national committees, initiate and answer correspondence, and set policy priorities and initiatives.

A Mayor might appoint a task force to look into a certain issue of concern. A welfare task force, for instance, might interview citizens to see how welfare reform is working in the community, then report their recommendations. The Mayor would then become an advocate for a plan of action.

As do other elected officials, Mayors need to deal with their colleagues' personalities and egos. Neighborhood representatives, for instance, might demand certain "spoils" in exchange for support on a particular development project. If the Mayor rejects those demands, the project might be held up indefinitely. If, on the other hand, the Mayor agrees to them, he or she might be accused of favoritism. Mayors constantly need to balance advocacy for issues close to their hearts with a sense of fairness to all.

Mayors are under constant scrutiny. Newspaper articles analyze the Mayor's leadership style. Is the Mayor an old-fashioned boss or a modern-day consensus maker? How has the Mayor done on basic services like snow plowing, street cleaning, and trash collection? Has the Mayor initiated any programs to enhance the livability of the city? Does the Mayor have a clear vision for the future?

Success for a Mayor often depends on getting reelected. In a speech to new officeholders reported by the association publication *U.S. Mayor,* one long time Mayor advised the newcomers to focus on five major issues:

- Safe streets
- Jobs
- Housing
- Arts and entertainment
- Schools

Having a set of priorities is important because Mayors can find their efforts scattered in different directions. This job is literally endless. Although all Mayors believe they are qualified by virtue of being elected, some are better prepared and more hardworking than others.

The pace of the work depends on the complexity of the community. In most diverse, large cities, the workload is intense. Mayors are expected not only to perform ceremonial duties, such as welcoming visitors and leading celebrations, but also to be on call 24 hours a day. Despite the extreme pressures, many Mayors find great satisfaction in being the "top dog" in their communities.

Salaries

Salaries range from $0 to about $130,000, according to the National League of Cities. Salaries vary so much that a city with a population of 500,000 might pay a Mayor either $28,000 or $113,000. It all depends on the city.

A position might be officially designated as part-time even though the Mayor essentially works full-time. Some large cities—Dallas, Texas, for instance—have a Mayor designated as part-time. An individual who is retired may be able to devote all his or her time to the position whereas someone else would have to juggle the responsibilities of Mayor with another job. A small city with a part-time Mayor might rely on someone like the municipal clerk to run the government. Some part-time positions are unpaid.

Employment Prospects

Employment prospects are poor because each community has only one Mayor. Many Mayors rose from the ranks of City Councilors. Rising to Mayor, however, can be a difficult—and expensive—task. Even in small cities, campaigning for Mayor can cost $25,000 or more. In the rough-and-tumble world of politics, negative campaigns are common.

Success for a candidate depends on being able to communicate one's ideas effectively to voters. Although the path to Mayor can be a difficult one, the position is open to anyone who is willing to seek it.

Advancement Prospects

Advancement prospects are fair. Although serving as Mayor can open up certain doors, individuals typically move "on" rather than "up." Many Mayors return to their former line of work, for example, business or law, because it is likely to be more lucrative than public office. After serving as the community's "top dog," a Mayor might find the prospect of becoming one of many state or federal legislators unappealing. According to the U.S. Conference of Mayors, fewer than 25 percent of Mayors seek higher office. Those who do have about a 50–50 chance of winning.

Education and Training

There are no formal educational requirements for Mayor. A candidate who is largely self-taught might easily trounce someone with a Ph.D. Voters decide who is more qualified. Specific requirements for eligibility may vary among cities and towns.

Experience, Skills, and Personality Traits

Many Mayors have served first on the city council, where they've had a chance to develop their communications skills. The Mayor needs to be a good communicator to get across his or her message to the people. Communication styles, though, can vary widely. Some Mayors are fiery orators. Others have more of a low-key, conversational style.

Messages often need to be repeated over and over again to lay the proper groundwork for a new agenda. Seasoned Mayors know how to restate a message so the speech doesn't sound "canned." They become adept at using the "bully pulpit" to motivate others. Mayors need to have good interpersonal skills, strong leadership abilities, an abiding interest in their communities, and the ability to withstand pressure.

Unions and Associations

The United States Conference of Mayors represents Mayors of cities with populations of more than 30,000.

Tips for Entry

1. Follow the news and talk to people in local government to familiarize yourself with the position of Mayor.
2. Get a foot in the door by volunteering on a political campaign or for someone already in office. Internships, too, can be good opportunities.
3. Serve the community by volunteering on boards or commissions. Attend community meetings open to the public.
4. Seek a stable job that has some flexibility. Most elected jobs at the local level are part-time, thus requiring officeholders to establish themselves first in another line of work.
5. Take stock of your own priorities for the community and ask yourself whether these are broad enough to attract a multitude of supporters. Can you sell yourself as an effective candidate? Do you have a network of friends and like-minded members of the community?
6. Bear in mind that it's easier to run for Mayor if the race lacks a popular incumbent. In politics, timing is crucial.

DISTRICT ATTORNEY

CAREER PROFILE

Duties: Advocating for the public in criminal-justice matters; overseeing and/or trying cases, administering office policies and procedures

Alternate Title(s): Prosecuting Attorney, County Attorney, State's Attorney, Commonwealth Attorney

Salary Range: $36,000 to $115,000

Employment Prospects: Fair

Advancement Prospects: Good to excellent

Best Geographical Location: Districts with open seats

Prerequisites:

Education or Training—Law degree

Experience—Prosecution experience preferred; extensive trial experience

Special Skills and Personality Traits—Command of the courtroom; sense of fairness; ability to grasp complex issues; willingness to work long hours in a fast-paced environment

CAREER LADDER

```
┌─────────────────────────────┐
│   Judge or Higher Office     │
│     or Private Practice      │
└─────────────────────────────┘

┌─────────────────────────────┐
│      District Attorney       │
└─────────────────────────────┘

┌─────────────────────────────┐
│  Assistant District Attorney │
└─────────────────────────────┘
```

Position Description

District Attorneys combine knowledge of the law with concern about public safety. As the Chief Prosecutor, they oversee and sometimes try high-profile cases, including homicides. They serve as the top law-enforcement official for the district, working closely with the police to protect the safety of citizens. District Attorneys also set office policy, oversee legal matters, and speak out on criminal-justice issues.

The vast majority—95 percent—of District Attorneys are chosen in popular elections; the rest are appointed, according to the United States Department of Justice, Bureau of Justice Statistics. Typically, a District Attorney first works as an Assistant District Attorney, an appointed position. Unlike candidates for the legislature or other political office, District Attorneys must be lawyers, a qualification limiting the pool of candidates. Often, an Assistant District Attorney runs for an office being vacated by his or her boss.

Candidates may have different notions of what it means to be "tough on crime." For one, it may mean providing more community services. For another, it may mean stiffer sentencing.

Many individuals become prosecutors because they are drawn to the drama of the courtroom. Law school graduates typically set out for positions in the prosecutor's office to gain valuable trial experience. They would rather spend their time in the courtroom than behind a desk, researching torts for a senior partner. Assistant District Attorneys fresh out of law school typically start with low-profile cases, such as traffic violations, vandalism, or forged checks. After a while, they move up from misdemeanors to felonies. District Attorneys provide guidance gleaned from their years of experience.

As the chief prosecutor, the District Attorney decides who is charged with which crimes. Insiders say that most defendants are not "evil people" who pose an unquestionable danger to society but, rather, individuals with some weakness of character. One suspect might have committed a robbery when drunk. Another might have had a conflict with a girlfriend and smashed her car. Yet another might have a drug addiction. In the course of a given day, prosecutors make numerous judgment calls. Should the suspect be charged? If so, with what crime? Should the case be plea-bargained or brought to trial? Should the defendant be tried as a juvenile or as an adult?

Most prosecutor's offices are divided into divisions: criminal, sex offender, juvenile, and so on. Assistant District Attorneys make up about a third of the staff; paralegals, investigators, victim advocates, and support staff constitute the rest. Because they head up the office, District Attorneys can launch new programs if they see a need. For example, they might get a grant to start a mediation program or a child abuse unit.

Caseloads in prosecutor's offices tend to be heavy. No sooner is one case solved through trial or plea bargain than a new set of cases piles up on the docket. District Attorneys commonly describe their work as some variation of "shoveling sand against the tides," writes Mark Baker in *D.A.: Prosecutors in Their Own Words.*

Election years often generate renewed attention to criminal-justice issues. If, for example, a referendum on the ballot calls for a change in drug policy, District Attorneys might express their point of view to the media. Prosecutors often can be seen on the TV news, responding to verdicts and expressing opinions about law-enforcement policies.

Although the position varies from state to state, common responsibilities of District Attorneys include

- Overseeing the local police
- Monitoring abuses of the constitutional rights of citizens
- Preparing budgets
- Dealing with personnel issues (e.g., recruiting minority Assistant District Attorneys)
- Assigning cases
- Participating on community task forces dealing with issues such as juvenile crime and sentencing
- Incorporating new technology such as deoxyribonucleic acid (DNA) testing

Salaries

Salaries vary according to the size of the office and whether the position is full time or part time. In small areas, many District Attorneys are part-time employees, earning about $36,000 a year, according to the National District Attorneys Association. Full-time District Attorneys earn approximately $97,000 a year in medium-sized offices and $115,000 in large jurisdictions.

Employment Prospects

Employment prospects are fair because, although the number of positions is relatively small, so, too, is the number of qualified candidates who seek them. Elections for District Attorney differ greatly from other contests in that candidates must be lawyers, preferably with a background in prosecution. When a District Attorney decides not to seek reelection, an Assistant District Attorney typically runs for the position. The median length of service for District Attorneys is six years, according to the Bureau of Justice Statistics.

Advancement Prospects

Advancement prospects are good to excellent because District Attorneys can move in a variety of directions. Many seek judgeships, although these positions can be hard to come by and highly political. Others may seek higher office such as that of attorney general or lieutenant governor. Still others move into higher-paying positions in government or private practice.

Education and Training

Law school and a law degree are required for District Attorneys in order to qualify for office. Assistant District Attorneys are also lawyers. A bachelor's degree, though, may be sufficient for other positions within the office, including investigator, paralegal, and victim advocate.

Law-school students have a variety of undergraduate majors—including political science, criminal justice, and English. Once in law school, individuals interested in becoming prosecutors should take courses in criminal law.

Experience, Skills, and Personality Traits

Most District Attorneys have extensive trial experience. As the chief prosecutor, the District Attorney must have excellent judgment in deciding who is charged with which crimes.

Pressures to keep conviction rates climbing from one political season to the next can be intense. District Attorneys must balance political expediency with political justice, toughness with compassion. "People want you to be tough on crime unless it's their nephew," observed one District Attorney. "Then they want you to be reasonable."

Some defendants, though, are decidedly dangerous. Almost half of all prosecutor's offices in 1996 indicated that a staff member experienced a work-related threat or assault, according to the Department of Justice, Bureau of Justice Statistics. District Attorneys can call upon the support of the police and others.

Seeing human nature at its worst can have a profound impact on prosecutors. Cynicism and paranoia may set in. Insiders say that the best District Attorneys manage to retain their faith in humanity, albeit one tarnished by their gritty exposure to crime. District Attorneys assume an enormous responsibility for dealing with the wrongs committed in society. They should believe in "doing the right thing." As public officials, they must be able to communicate effectively with the public.

Unions and Associations

The National District Attorneys Association represents individuals in the field, as do state associations of District Attorneys.

Tips for Entry

1. Seek an internship in a prosecutor's office.
2. Plan on attending law school if you want to be a District Attorney or Assistant District Attorney. While in law school, seek a clerkship in a prosecutor's office and participate in moot court, in which students prepare and argue a brief in front of a panel of judges.
3. Browse the Internet, using the keywords *prosecutor* and/or *district attorney.*
4. Follow the news to get a sense of the kind of work done by District Attorneys.

STATE LEGISLATOR

CAREER PROFILE

Duties: Sponsoring bills; deciding on legislation; representing constituents; serving on committees; making policy

Alternate Title(s): Senator, Representative, Assembly Member, Lawmaker

Salary Range: $15,000 to $60,000+

Employment Prospects: Fair to poor

Advancement Prospects: Fair

Best Geographical Location(s): Varies

Prerequisites:

Education or Training—No formal requirements

Experience—No formal requirements

Special Skills and Personality Traits—Keen interest in issues and the political process; consensus-making skills; leadership; dedication and stamina

CAREER LADDER

```
┌─────────────────────────────────┐
│  U.S. Congress or Statewide Office │
│       or Other Career             │
└─────────────────────────────────┘

┌─────────────────────────────────┐
│        State Legislator           │
└─────────────────────────────────┘

┌─────────────────────────────────┐
│  Local Political Office or Other Career │
└─────────────────────────────────┘
```

Position Description

State Legislators view their role as midlevel lawmakers in a variety of ways. Some are content to stay where they are, at least for the time being. Others want to move up within the state legislature, perhaps from the House of Representatives to the more prestigious Senate. Still others see their position as a springboard to higher office, as a member of Congress, governor, or a state auditor or treasurer or as secretary of state.

Fifty percent of the Members of Congress and 64 percent of the nation's Governors served previously as State Legislators, according to the National Conference of State Legislatures. State Legislators can also move up to statewide offices such as state treasurer or auditor. Like members of Congress, State Legislators become well-versed in the two-house, two-party system of governing. They sponsor bills, make floor speeches, vote on legislation, represent constituents, determine budgets, and sit on committees.

Over the years state legislatures have become increasingly full-time and professional. The old "slow-witted, cigar-smoking politician" has given way to a younger, more educated breed of legislator, according to *Legislative Life* author Alan Rosenthal. No longer are these bodies inhabited solely by white men. Women and minorities have joined their ranks.

States, meanwhile, have assumed greater importance in the policy-making arena, with larger professional staffs helping busy legislators do their jobs. Such developments notwithstanding, many citizens continue to hold State Legislators (and politicians in general) in low esteem. Ironically, many individuals still want to run for public office, including that as State Legislator. They want the power, the attention, the stimulation, and the chance to make a difference. For many, politics offers the excitement of a "sport" for grown-ups.

The decision to run for office rarely is sudden. Instead, it usually is developed over time. Many State Legislators grew up in politically involved families, participated in school government, and served at the local level. New opportunities have opened up as a result of the breakdown of the political "machine."

Often, State Legislators work full time on government business when the legislature is in session and part-time the rest of the year. Many juggle their legislative duties with another line of work. About 16 percent of State Legislators are lawyers, according to the National Conference of State Legislatures. Fifteen percent identify themselves as full-time Legislators, a number that has grown over the years. Other common occupations include those of entrepreneur and educator.

Legislative schedules vary from state to state. In some states the legislature meets for only a couple of months a year, whereas in others it is full-time. When legislatures are in session, State Legislators commonly work from early in the morning until late at night.

A typical day for a State Legislator is jam-packed with listening, negotiating, debating, and voting. Business is discussed over breakfast, lunch, and dinner. Common responsibilities include

- Conferring with staff
- Meeting with lobbyists
- Talking to reporters
- Attending committee and subcommittee meetings
- Returning phone calls
- Exploring policy issues
- Introducing bills and/or persuading colleagues to cosponsor or support them
- Debating with colleagues
- Voting on legislation

State Legislators voice their own political vision largely through the legislation they sponsor. Senators and Representatives have their own "pet" issues, related to the arts, the environment, health care, or public safety. Sometimes, too, State Legislators sponsor bills to please their constituents. without expecting the legislation to get passed.

After bills are drafted and introduced, they are referred to committees. Some bills simply die in committee. Others are referred to subcommittees or scheduled for hearings. Once a bill is reviewed, the committee schedules it for debate on the floor. Bills may then be approved, amended, referred back to committee, postponed, defeated, or reconsidered.

If approved, the bill is considered by the second house. The second house either concurs, allowing for the bill to pass, or requests changes. The two houses then try to reach an agreement, or the bill is defeated. Bills approved by both houses then go to the governor for a signature or a veto, which the legislature might then override.

State Legislators vote on hundreds of bills a year. Deciding on complex issues with a simple "yea" or "nay" can be especially difficult, insiders say. Party alliances and recommendations from interest groups often help with the decision making.

As the legislative session winds to a close, pressure intensifies. Bills pile up, waiting for decisions. Then, after the final votes have been cast, State Legislators take stock of the session. How productive was it? What were the ups and downs? How many of their own bills were passed?

During the interim, State Legislators spend more time in the district, attending events and talking to people. Insiders say that constituents want a "good man" or "good woman" who cares enough about *them* to seek them out and talk to them personally.

Unlike members of Congress, most State Legislators live in their districts, affording them the opportunity to stay in close touch with their constituents. Working on the state level can be rewarding, as the scale is small enough to allow them to see results. But, for some State Legislators, the chance to move up to the national level is impossible to resist. Instead of running again for State Legislator, these individuals scope out possible seats in Congress.

Salaries

Salaries vary greatly from state to state, according to the National Conference of State Legislatures. State Legislators in New Hampshire make $200 for a two-year term; those in California earn $99,000 a year. Some state legislatures, such as Alabama, pay by the day and/or offer allowances for daily expenses.

Employment Prospects

Employment prospects are fair to poor, depending on the state. Competition is stiffest in large, full-time legislatures without term limits. Seats open up much more quickly in small states *with* term limits. If an incumbent decides not to seek reelection, a newcomer might have a better chance of winning the seat.

Advancement Prospects

Advancement prospects are fair. An individual might fail to win reelection, thus limiting his or her possibilities for advancement, temporarily anyway. Among those reelected, levels of ambition vary from one State Legislator to the next.

Some individuals want to return to their previous careers, which are often more lucrative than serving in the legislatures. Others want to move up within the state legislature, either to leadership positions or from the House of Representatives to the Senate (sometimes called the upper house). Still others seek appointed positions or higher office such as governor or member of the U.S. Congress.

Ascending the political ladder can be extremely difficult. The number of positions decreases as one rises to the next level. Compared to a total of 7,400 State Legislators, there are only 435 U.S. Representatives, 100 Senators, and 50 Governors, according to the National Conference of State Legislatures.

Education and Training

Although anyone, regardless of background, can run for the state legislature, many Senators and Representatives have advanced degrees. States determine their own eligibility requirements for office, requiring candidates to live in the district and be a certain age. In many states, the minimum age is 21 for the House and 25 for the Senate.

Experience, Skills, and Personality Traits

State Legislators have a variety of backgrounds (e.g., law, education, and business) but share an interest in and often a passion for the political process. All need to campaign for office. Fund-raising, public speaking, and problem-solving skills help on the campaign trail. Both on the campaign trail and in office, they must be able to inspire and motivate their constituents and staff.

Being a successful State Legislator depends in large part on having strong consensus-making skills. Some legislatures are known for their intense factionalism. State Legislators must know how to compromise with their colleagues and satisfy the conflicting demands of their constituents. As do many positions in politics, the job of State Legislator requires massive amounts of energy and stamina.

Unions/Associations

The National Conference of State Legislatures provides professional assistance to State Legislators and their staffs.

Tips for Entry

1. Develop an interest in politics and an awareness of the issues of your own community.

2. Get involved in a political campaign for a candidate or an issue.

3. Participate in political party activities. Colleges often have groups affiliated with various political parties.

4. Visit the legislature.

5. Intern or work as a legislative staffer. Some legislators began their careers as legislative assistants or other staffers.

6. Ask yourself whether you would have the stamina and flexibility for this kind of work.

7. Realize that some seats are more competitive than others. A small seat vacated by an incumbent is usually easier to win than a big one held by a popular legislator. The House of Representatives has more seats than the Senate, thus making it the less competitive of the two bodies.

GOVERNOR

CAREER PROFILE

Duties: Serving as top government leader for the state; recommending budgets and programs to the legislature; assuming special judicial powers such as the granting of pardons

Salary Range: $65,000 to $179,000

Employment Prospects: Poor

Advancement Prospects: Good

Best Geographical Location(s): None

Prerequisites:

Education or Training—No formal requirements

Experience—Residency and age requirements varying by state

Special Skills and Personality Traits—Persuasiveness; sharp political instincts; stamina; willingness to listen; commitment; ability to command respect

CAREER LADDER

```
┌─────────────────────────────────────┐
│    Federal Office or Other Career    │
└─────────────────────────────────────┘

┌─────────────────────────────────────┐
│              Governor                │
└─────────────────────────────────────┘

┌─────────────────────────────────────┐
│    Other Political Office or Career  │
└─────────────────────────────────────┘
```

Position Description

Governors are the states' equivalent of the President of the United States. Like the President, the Governor is the chief executive, setting policy, developing budgets, appointing key personnel, and exercising veto power. Four out of five of the latest presidents have served as Governor: Jimmy Carter, Ronald Reagan, Bill Clinton, and George W. Bush.

Governors deal with many of the same issues as Presidents because states have assumed responsibilities once held by the federal government. Distrust of Washington insiders has elevated the nation's Governors to new status over the other two main paths to the presidency: the vice presidency and the U.S. Senate. Whereas Governors used to become U.S. Senators, but not vice versa, now some U.S. Senators are leaving the comfort of their posts to run for Governor. As they see it, being Governor offers an opportunity to get more done because they need not vie for power with 99 other legislators and wait years for key appointments. Governors can use executive power to push through their own initiatives.

Much has changed over the years for U.S. Governors. Whereas Governors in colonial times assumed nearly total control in the name of the Crown, those in the new republic had limited power as a result of short terms and the primacy of the legislature. But, over the years, the rules have changed.

In *Goodbye to Good-Time Charlie: The American Governorship Transformed,* the political scientist Larry Sabato describes how the role of Governor shifted during the second half of the 20th century from society darling to power broker. As states assumed more responsibility for social issues, the once largely ceremonial post of Governor metamorphosed into a powerful vehicle for addressing major concerns such as education and welfare reform. States bestowed new powers on Governors, including longer tenure, control of the budgetary process, appointments of key personnel, and staggered elections to prevent gubernatorial contests from being eclipsed by presidential races. Minorities and women began making inroads into the governorship.

The job of Governor can be broken down into three main areas: policy setting, public relations, and government management. Governors set forth their own policy objectives, whether lowering taxes, revamping education, or generating jobs, but, in the process, must deal with the conflicting demands of taxpayers, interest groups, and legislators. Tensions tend to escalate over the budget, particularly if the opposing party controls the legislature. To assure success in the legislature, some Governors use "arm twisting" techniques such as the threat of a veto or the promise of a future appointment to the bench in exchange for a favorable vote.

Often Governors take their policy objectives directly to the people. A Governor's schedule consists of a dizzying array of public appearances, meetings, phone calls, press conferences, and excursions throughout the state. The Governor might visit an elementary school, attend a housing conference, preside over awards for firefighters, and attend the opening of a state fair. Every year the Governor lays out his or her agenda in a State of the State Address.

In their roles as government managers, Governors meet with department heads, board or commission members, and staff members. Governors act as chief executive officers for the state, presiding over organizations similar in scope to Fortune 500 companies. If a crisis such as a hurricane strikes, the Governor harnesses the power of the state to address it.

Yet, for all its new luster, the role of Governor still depends largely on the quality of the individual. Just as powerful Governors like Woodrow Wilson rose above the institutional constraints of the office, so, too, have contemporary executives squandered or abused their power. Some Governors have left office in disgrace for "selling" pardons or accepting kickbacks. Others have failed to act decisively or acted decisively in ways, such as raising taxes, anathema to the people.

Whatever the situation, the Governor is bound to be in the spotlight. The pollster Louis Harris reported that American citizens are more likely to identify the Governor of their state correctly than one of the two U.S. Senators. Such name recognition was second only to that of the President of the United States.

Salaries

According to the 2002–3 U.S. Department of Labor's *Occupational Outlook Handbook,* annual salaries for Governors range from a low of $65,000 in Nebraska to a high of $179,000 in New York. In addition to their salaries, most Governors receive benefits such as transportation and an official residence.

Salaries for Governors have risen in the past few decades, a trend analysts see as significant. If salaries are too low, they argue, Governors might be tempted to earn money through illegal means. On the other hand, if salaries are too high, the position might attract candidates less serious about public service than about financial gain.

Employment Prospects

Employment prospects are poor because of the scarcity of positions: only 50 within the United States, unless one also includes the commonwealths and territories. Although technically almost anyone can run for Governor, the high cost of campaigning can be a major obstacle. Insiders say that gubernatorial campaigns commonly cost hundreds of thousands of dollars.

Many Governors over the years have been members of well-known political families, like the Rockefellers and Bushes, giving them built-in name recognition. Some widows of Governors have taken over their husbands' seats. In 1975, Ella Grasso of Connecticut became the first female Governor elected in her own right. Since then, 15 women have been elected Governor, according to the National Governors' Association.

Elections are sometimes contested, then decided by the legislature. In 1899, the Governor-elect of Kentucky was assassinated, prompting his opponent to leave the state to avoid implication in the crime.

Advancement Prospects

Advancement prospects are good because the governorship opens up a variety of doors. In addition to going on to the presidency, Governors have become ambassadors, cabinet members, and U.S. senators as well as university presidents, judges, and political party officers.

Seventeen Governors have become President: Thomas Jefferson, James Monroe, Martin Van Buren, John Tyler, James Polk, Andrew Johnson, Rutherford B. Hayes, Grover Cleveland, William McKinley, Theodore Roosevelt, Woodrow Wilson, Calvin Coolidge, Franklin D. Roosevelt, Jimmy Carter, Ronald Reagan, Bill Clinton, and George W. Bush.

The list grows to 19 if one includes Governors of territories not yet incorporated as states at the time of the governorship: William Henry Harrison (Indiana) and Andrew Jackson (Florida). Like Presidents, Governors can be impeached and removed from office by the legislature.

Education and Training

States set their own minimum age and residency requirements but specify no formal criteria for education and training. Approximately half of Governors have law degrees, an asset since government is built upon law. Also helpful is a background in the state legislature or statewide office. Some Governors, though, have backgrounds unrelated to political office.

Experience, Skills, and Personality Traits

Most—but not all—Governors have held prior political office. Many are former State Legislators or have held statewide positions such as attorney general, secretary of state, or state treasurer. Some have carved out names for themselves in other fields. California's Ronald Reagan starred in Hollywood movies; Louisiana's country singer Jimmie Davis popularized the song "You Are My Sunshine"; and Minnesota's Jesse Ventura was a professional wrestler for 11 years. Over the years, several medical doctors have become Governor, as have a florist and a trucker.

Such seemingly unrelated positions might help prepare a Governor for the acting, fighting, arranging, and hard-driving endurance needed for the position. As the most powerful official in a state, the Governor serves as the embodiment of that state. Governors speak for all the people and so need to be able both to listen and to mobilize support. The Governor needs to be part visionary, part manager. Governors must set forth an agenda and persuade people to follow it.

Unions and Associations

Two key associations represent Governors: the National Governors' Association and the Council of State Governments.

Tips for Entry

1. Read books about Governors, including biographies of well-known leaders.
2. Become politically active through student government and/or membership in the political party of your choice.
3. Volunteer or intern at the Governor's office.
4. Identify your own top policy objectives. Most new Governors present a few key issues to the legislature.

U.S. REPRESENTATIVE

CAREER PROFILE

Duties: Campaign for office; attend events and meetings in the district; study staff reports and hear testimony on issues of concern; introduce, examine, and vote on bills; represent constituents

Alternate Title(s): Member, Congressman, Congresswoman

Salary Range: $145,100 to $161,200

Employment Prospects: Poor

Advancement Prospects: Poor

Best Geographical Location(s): Districts without incumbents

Prerequisites:

Education or Training—No formal requirements

Experience—Must be 25 years of age and a legal resident of the state in which elected

Special Skills and Personality Traits—Effective political campaigning skills; strong decision-making abilities; ability to motivate constituents and staff; massive amounts of energy and stamina

CAREER LADDER

```
┌─────────────────────────────────┐
│         U.S. Senator            │
└─────────────────────────────────┘

┌─────────────────────────────────┐
│      U.S. Representative         │
└─────────────────────────────────┘

┌─────────────────────────────────┐
│      Other Elected Office        │
│      or Political Position       │
└─────────────────────────────────┘
```

Position Description

Members of the U.S. House of Representatives live in two different worlds: their home districts and the District of Columbia.

As a result, they are always balancing their role as district representatives with their function as lawmakers, according to Karen O'Connor and Larry J. Sabato, authors of *The Essentials of American Government: Continuity and Change.* U.S. Representatives spend full days in their home districts, holding town meetings and other forums to keep in touch with constituents, then return to Washington, D.C., where they meet with party leaders, colleagues, and lobbyists.

U.S. Representatives differ from their counterparts in the U.S. Senate in several ways. First, unlike U.S. Senators, who serve six-year terms, U.S. Representatives are elected every two years. Next, the House of Representatives is a much larger body, with four times more members than the Senate—435 Representatives compared to 100 Senators. Each state elects two Senators, whereas the number of U.S. Representatives is based on population. Every 10 years districts are redrawn to reflect population shifts indicated by U.S. Census figures.

The U.S. Constitution gives lawmaking powers to both houses. All revenue bills originate in the House of Representatives. The House of Representatives also has the power to initiate impeachment, although the Senate is responsible for trying impeached officials.

Because of its larger size, the House of Representatives is more tightly organized, elaborately structured, and strictly governed than the U.S. Senate. The Speaker of the House wields enormous power. Much of the work of Congress is done in committees. U.S. Representatives serve on at least one committee and several subcommittees. Many seek committee assignments that offer a chance to "bring home the bacon" or build their power and influence within the chamber.

U.S. Representatives use their staffs to research issues and keep in touch with constituents. In large districts, the Representatives' caseworkers may ride "the circuit," taking the helping hand of the congressional office to various stops along the way. When U.S. Representatives visit the district, they often attend fund-raisers and civic events. Insiders say that, because of their two-year terms, U.S. Representatives are constantly running for office.

In Washington, D.C., U.S. Representatives cast their votes on proposed legislation. Often, if a bill is of great interest to constituents, the Representative votes accordingly. In other cases, U.S. Representatives turn to their colleagues, political parties, interest groups, and staff/support agencies for advice.

A typical day for a U.S. Representative begins with a morning committee meeting at 8 A.M. and runs well into the evening. Yet, for all the long hours and hard work, thousands of Americans each year seek a seat in Congress.

Salaries

U.S. Representatives recently earned $145,100 a year—the same salary as U.S. Senators', according to the U.S. Department of Labor's *Occupational Outlook Handbook*. The Senate and House Majority and Minority Leaders earned $161,200.

Employment Prospects

Employment prospects are poor because of the limited number of positions—435 nationwide. Incumbents have certain advantages over their challengers, including name recognition, access to media, and fund-raising clout. In 1998, 97 percent of the incumbents in the U.S. Congress who sought reelection won their primary and general election races, according to the political scientists Karen O'Connor and Larry J. Sabato. Voluntary retirements, regular district changes, and occasional defeats, however, allow newcomers to win election to the U.S. House of Representatives. Compared to that in the U.S. Senate, turnover in the House is relatively high.

Advancement Prospects

Advancement prospects for U.S. Representatives are poor because there are few higher offices to go around, according to Paul S. Herrnson, author of *Congressional Elections: Campaigning at Home and in Washington*. Terms are longer (six years) and turnover is lower in the U.S. Senate than in the House of Representatives, thus making it difficult for Members of the lower house to move up to the upper house of Congress. U.S. Representatives, however, can find opportunities for growth within the House itself. Many U.S. Representatives become subcommittee or committee chairs, and a few rise to top leadership positions, which include Speaker of the House, Majority Leader, Minority Leader, Majority Whip, and Minority Whip.

Education and Training

Although no formal education and training are required for public office, many U.S. Representatives have considerable backgrounds in politics or related fields. In *Congressional Elections: Campaigning at Home and in Washington*, Paul Herrnson observes that individuals who claim law, politics, or public service (many of whom have legal training) as their professions constitute 49 percent of all House members. Business professionals, educators (particularly college professors), entertainers, and white-collar professionals also are fairly well represented in Congress.

Experience, Skills, and Personality Traits

Members of the U.S. House of Representative must be at least 25 years of age; have resided in the United States for at least seven years; and be legal residents of the states where they are elected. Although those are the only formal requirements for office, most U.S. Representatives have considerable experience in politics.

Almost 90 percent of recently elected House Members had previously held another public office, served as a party official, worked as a political aide or consultant, or run for Congress at least once before getting elected, according to Paul Herrnson, author of *Congressional Elections: Campaigning at Home and in Washington*.

Running for office requires massive energy and stamina. Because U.S. Representatives serve two-year terms, those who plan to seek reelection are constantly campaigning for office. They must have the fund-raising, budgeting, public speaking, and problem-solving skills needed to run an effective campaign.

Once in office, U.S. Representatives must be able to lead by motivating and inspiring others. They need to make decisions quickly, sometimes on the basis of limited or contradictory information. They should also know how to reach compromises and satisfy different constituencies. In addition, U.S. Representatives must be able to tackle hard issues and withstand the glare of intense media scrutiny.

Unions and Associations

Political parties, such as the Democratic and Republican Parties, provide support to U.S. Representatives.

Tips for Entry

1. Seek an internship in the U.S. House of Representatives.
2. Work on a candidate's campaign.
3. Become familiar with the issues of your district.
4. Get experience in a lower elected office or other political position.

PRESIDENT OF THE UNITED STATES

CAREER PROFILE

Duties: Serving as chief executive, commander in chief, foreign policy director, and all-around leader of the American people

Alternate Title(s): Head of State, Chief Executive, Commander in Chief

Salary Range: $400,000 a year plus expenses

Employment Prospects: Poor

Advancement Prospects: Poor

Best Geographical Location(s): Helpful to reside in a large state

Prerequisites:

Education or Training—No formal requirements

Experience—Must be natural-born U.S. citizen; at least 35 years old; resident of United States for at least 14 years

Special Skills and Personality Traits—Persuasive; ambitious; politically savvy leader with stamina and grit

CAREER LADDER

```
┌─────────────────────────────────┐
│           Retirement            │
│   (e.g., lecturing, writing,    │
│         charitable work)        │
└─────────────────────────────────┘

┌─────────────────────────────────┐
│           Presidency            │
└─────────────────────────────────┘

┌─────────────────────────────────┐
│       High Political Office      │
│   (e.g., Governor, Senator,     │
│       or Vice President)        │
└─────────────────────────────────┘
```

Position Description

Many people dream of being President of the United States, but few ever approach the dizzying heights of power that mark this position. Hailed as the most powerful leader in the world, the President can trigger war, inspire peace, and alter the course of history. The President is a symbolic leader, drawing together the hopes, fears, aspirations, and disappointments of the American people. In terms of sheer name recognition, the President is the best known person in America.

George C. Edwards III, editor of the *Presidential Quarterly,* describes the presidency as the "most odd and unique" job in America. The position entails unrelenting responsibility and unimaginable authority, the heights of glory and the depths of despair. Despite some notable failures and scandals, the presidency has endured, shaping itself to the demands of changing times.

George Washington, after all, presided over only 13 states, not 50, and had but one aide, his nephew, whom he paid out of his own pocket—a far cry from the executive bureaucracy of the 21st century. Today every personal appearance, utterance, and movement of the President is held up to public scrutiny. Reporters interview Presidents about the most intimate details of their private lives. Comedians lampoon the Oval Office on late-night TV.

Such developments notwithstanding, the Founding Fathers established the loose outlines of the office when they drafted the Constitution. According to Clinton Rossiter, author of *The American Presidency,* the Constitution assigns to the President the following roles:

- Chief of State—acting as figurehead
- Chief Executive—running the government
- Commander-in-Chief—commanding the armed forces
- Chief Diplomat—making foreign policy
- Chief Legislator—initiating and vetoing legislation

As the nation's top leader, the President of the United States helps people make sense of the political process. Instead of wading through congressional committees and executive agencies, citizens can turn to one person—the President—to take charge. Over the years, Presidents have interpreted the Constitution in ways that have expanded rather than limited the position.

Abraham Lincoln, widely regarded as the greatest American President, used unprecedented power to hold the nation together during its darkest hour—the Civil War. Franklin Delano Roosevelt pioneered what has become known as the modern presidency by expanding the federal government into formerly uncharted areas of social welfare during the Great Depression.

Presidents earn much of their authority through the power of persuasion, often known as the "the bully pulpit." Franklin Roosevelt communicated via radio, using his "fireside chats." President Ronald Reagan, a former actor, won the nickname of the Great Communicator.

Whereas some Presidents of the United States—Franklin Roosevelt included—have been able to push legislation through Congress, others have encountered gridlock, particularly when the opposition party has had the reigns of Congress. Some observers say that Americans expect the President, who is a mere mortal, to act like Superman.

The demands on the President of the United States make for a hectic, nonstop schedule, juggling the needs of various constituencies. A typical day in the life of the President involves a whirl of meetings with advisers, working on policy matters, making speeches, and carrying out public functions. The President might go from a symbolic duty like laying the wreath on the Tomb of the Unknown Soldier to signing a congressional bill to meeting with economic advisers to discuss ways to reduce unemployment.

No one can know in advance the dilemmas to be raised or the questions to be asked of the President. President Lyndon Baines Johnson put it aptly when he said, "The recognition of unrelenting responsibility reminds me of the truth of a statement I heard my father repeat many times: 'Son you will never understand what it is to be a father until you *are* a father.'"

Salaries

The President of the United States earns a salary of $400,000, according to the Department of Labor's 2002–3 *Occupational Outlook Handbook*. The salary is only a fraction of what a professional athlete earns. The President and members of the First Family live in the White House. In addition, the President receives an expense account, funds for travel and entertainment, and retirement benefits. A personal staff is ready to satisfy the President's tastes for everything from food and drink to limousines and helicopters.

Employment Prospects

Because the presidency is a hotly contested position held by only one person, employment prospects are extremely poor. Nevertheless, anyone who is at least 35 years old, has lived in the United States at least 14 years, and is a natural-born citizen can serve as President.

In reality, though, few individuals have the experience, support, and endurance needed to win the presidency. No

President since George Washington has made it to office without a fight. Presidential campaigns are notoriously grueling. As Emmet John Hughes points out in *The Living Presidency,* the campaign trail can toughen and ready the President-elect for office. Someone unable to hold up on the campaign trail would be unlikely to cope well with the extraordinary pressures of the Oval Office.

Americans vote for the President of the United States every four years on the Tuesday after the first Monday in November. Delegates to the Electoral College ultimately decide which candidate wins the election.

Despite their differences in style and ideology, American Presidents have been a fairly homogeneous lot: white, male, and overwhelmingly Protestant. One Roman Catholic, John F. Kennedy, was elected President, but so far no woman or member of a racial or ethnic minority has held office.

Advancement Prospects

Advancement prospects are poor because the presidency is the top political position in the United States, making it a hard act to follow. The President is limited to two terms in office. On leaving office, most Presidents retire to lecturing, writing, visiting their presidential libraries, and/or performing charitable work.

A few Presidents of the United States have left office in disgrace. Impeachment, a proceeding with which charges are raised by a legislative branch of a government against civil officials, dates back to ancient Greece. In the United States, only three Presidents—Andrew Johnson, Richard Nixon, and Bill Clinton—were in real danger of being removed from office through impeachment. Richard Nixon resigned from office rather than face a vote for his removal. Votes to convict Andrew Johnson and Bill Clinton fell short of the required margins.

Education and Training

The Constitution specifies no formal requirements for the education and training, but voters look closely at the backgrounds of presidential candidates.

Experience, Skills, and Personality Traits

Most Presidents of the United States have served in high political office as governors, senators, or vice presidents, but what they did beforehand varies widely. Some Presidents (e.g., Richard Nixon) followed a fairly conventional political path, rising from local to national office, while others carved out careers in totally different fields. Jimmy Carter was a peanut farmer; Ronald Reagan, a Hollywood actor; and George W. Bush, an oilman. Whereas Bill Clinton knew from an early age he wanted to be President, many others, including Harry Truman, Ronald Reagan, and George W. Bush, showed no such inclinations.

Scholars offer a variety of theories on what makes for a successful President but agree on a few basic points. Successful Presidents tend to be persuasive, ambitious, extroverted, politically shrewd, resilient, and energetic. Emmet John Hughes in *The Living Presidency,* asserts that successful Presidents share six traits:

- Sense of confidence
- Sense of proportion
- Sense of drama
- Sense of timing
- Sense of constancy
- Sense of humanity

Examples of these traits pepper history. John F. Kennedy's sense of confidence, for example, helped citizens believe in their own capacities and the possibilities of the nation. A sense of proportion can prevent minor incidents from snowballing. Presidents like Theodore Roosevelt with a sense of drama can turn potential disasters into photo opportunities. Those with a sense of timing know when to wait and when to strike. Abraham Lincoln, for instance, chose the opportune moment to end slavery in the states at war with the Union. Successful Presidents also share a sense of stability and compassion.

The traits that make for a successful President of the United States are not always the same as those of a "good person." Franklin Roosevelt's appeal to political melodrama, for example, might be considered a distasteful personal trait, even though it undoubtedly contributed to his success as President. Dwight Eisenhower's dislike of political theatrics, on the other hand, contributed to his ineffectiveness in office ("Good man; wrong profession," one observer said).

Unions/Associations

There is no organization of American Presidents, although scholars meet through institutions such as the Center for the Study of the Presidency in Washington, D.C.

Tips for Entry

1. Recognize that this is a position with no conventional career path. Although almost all Presidents have held high political office, they worked in a variety of different positions beforehand, including farming and acting.
2. Do something very well in the public eye. Ronald Reagan, for example, excelled at giving speeches. All Presidents have shared a sense of ambition, leading them to excel in public.
3. Develop political savvy. Almost all Presidents have held high political office; the position of governor has often opened the door to the presidency.
4. Learn about the successes and failures of past Presidents. Colleges and universities commonly offer undergraduate courses in the presidency through their political science departments, and the Center for the Study of the Presidency, in Washington, D.C., provides lectures, conferences, and fellowships. Books on the American presidency abound.

PART II
GOVERNMENT

LOCAL/STATE—
GENERAL POSITIONS

ADMINISTRATIVE ASSISTANT

CAREER PROFILE

Duties: Providing general administrative support; scheduling and attending meetings; taking notes and messages; conducting research

Alternate Title(s): Management Assistant, Executive Assistant, Executive Secretary, Department Assistant, Program Assistant

Salary Range: $18,000 to $50,000

Employment Prospects: Good

Advancement Prospects: Good

Best Geographical Location(s): Metropolitan areas, state capitals

Prerequisites:

Education or Training—Varies, depending on whether the position is on a professional or nonprofessional track

Experience—Many positions entry-level; some work experience sometimes required in larger jurisdictions

Special Skills and Personality Traits—Flexible; adaptable; skillful in communication

CAREER LADDER

```
┌─────────────────────────────┐
│          Manager            │
└─────────────────────────────┘

┌─────────────────────────────┐
│   Administrative Assistant   │
└─────────────────────────────┘

┌─────────────────────────────┐
│      Intern or Student       │
└─────────────────────────────┘
```

Position Description

Administrative Assistants straddle the line between clerical and management, depending on their educational background and the needs of the employer. Over the years, the term *Administrative Assistant* has become increasingly identified with secretarial work. As government has grown more complex, jobs once known as Administrative Assistant have been retitled to include Town Administrator, Assistant to the Town Manager, and Administrative Analyst.

Nevertheless, some municipalities have retained the title of Administrative Assistant for staffers with high levels of responsibility. In these cases, the Administrative Assistant reports directly to the Select Board or the Town Manager. The Administrative Assistant might develop short- and long-term plans, conduct studies, prepare research, and handle sensitive citizen complaints and confidential employee matters.

Sometimes the *administrative* part of the title is dropped, as in Research Assistant, Grants Assistant, or Assistant to a Top Policy Official. Or the title might be hyphenated, as in Administrative Assistant-Grants Administrator or Administrative-Financial Assistant. A Program Assistant might be

someone with a college degree and a year of relevant experience who does professional-level work developing and implementing programs.

Some professional associations use Management Assistant to encompass a wide range of positions, including not only Administrative Assistants but also higher-level positions such as Administrative Analysts (e.g., budget analysts, management analysts). Generally, Management Assistants perform more complex tasks than Administrative Assistants. A Management Assistant might develop and implement performance measurement systems and coordinate the budget process. This position might require a master's degree in public administration and a few years of professional experience. In Northern California, some Administrative Assistant positions have been upgraded to Management Analyst.

Another title, Executive Assistant, applies to positions assisting top decision makers. The Executive Assistant might track legislative bills and serve as administrative coordinator for the agency, resolving problems and responding to complaints in a confidential manner. Executive Assistants with master's degrees in public administration usually are on their way up the career ladder.

Individuals who prove themselves on the job often are asked to take on more responsibility. An Executive Assistant who gets everyone coffee in the morning might be chairing a meeting in the afternoon. A manager might turn to a trusted Executive Assistant for advice, saying something along the lines of "This language sounds too harsh. How might we change it?" The Executive Assistant might be asked to represent the Manager at meetings and conferences.

Positions tend to be ranked, as in Administrative Assistant I, II, and so forth. At the state level, an Administrative Assistant II might conduct research for the budget director and report on the results.

Generally speaking, Administrative Assistants perform a mix of clerical tasks and special projects. Whereas a low-level clerical worker might simply type a letter, an Administrative Assistant would probably draft it as well. Common responsibilities also include

- Responding to information requests from the public as well as other government personnel
- Serving as liaison to other departments and agencies
- Maintaining databases
- Screening phone calls
- Reserving space, preparing agendas, and taking notes for meetings
- Handling correspondence, including photocopying and faxing
- Assisting in collecting and analyzing data
- Preparing reports

Salaries

Salaries for Administrative Assistants vary widely. Large local and state governments generally pay more than smaller ones. A highly responsible Administrative Assistant for a small town may earn less than a support staffer for a large city or state department.

Employment Prospects

Employment prospects are good because busy managers and administrators need assistants to help ease the workload. A steady turnover rate means new openings are often available.

Advancement Prospects

Many positions offer opportunities for advancement. An Administrative Assistant in the state budget bureau, for instance, might be able to advance to a more responsible position in fiscal policy. Administrative Assistants who make themselves indispensible can, within a few years, rise to key positions.

Education and Training

Generally speaking, the more responsible the job, the more education is required. A bachelor's degree is generally the minimum for positions involving responsible administrative duties. Useful fields of study include public administration, business administration, and political science. An associate's degree in business generally qualifies candidates for positions that are more clerical in nature. Upper management positions, on the other hand, may call for a master's degree.

Experience, Skills, and Personality Traits

Administrative Assistants need to be well-organized, efficient, and articulate. Excellent oral and written communication skills are a must. Many positions also require strong computer skills, particularly in word processing, spreadsheet, database, and related software.

Administrative Assistants are always performing a variety of assignments and so need to be able to prioritize tasks. An Administrative Assistant might work nights and weekends during peak work cycles but be compensated with overtime pay. Individuals must be flexible and adaptable since Administrative Assistants often act as "gophers."

Unions and Associations

The American Federation of State, County, and Municipal Employees (AFSCME) and the National Association of Government Employees (NAGE) are unions that represent government workers. The American Society for Public Administration is a broad-based organization of professionals in local, state, and federal government. State municipal associations provide professional guidance, as do associations that have sprung up specifically for municipal Management Assistants in Arizona, California, Colorado, Illinois, Ohio, and Texas.

Tips for Entry

1. Look for job openings in a variety of places. Check the listings of local and state personnel offices, university career centers, municipal associations, and newspaper classified ads. Many positions are also listed on the Internet.
2. Keep in mind that Administrative Assistant positions may be largely clerical in nature.
3. Seek out internship possibilities. Many government offices use Administrative Interns.
4. Take stock of your short-term and long-term career goals. If you are interested in a particular issue, look for an Administrative Assistant position that deals with it. Develop techniques for upward mobility such as résumé writing, networking, and interviewing skills. If you want to advance to top management positions, consider getting a master's degree in public administration or a related field.

MANAGEMENT ANALYST

CAREER PROFILE

Duties: Gathering and analyzing data; researching trends; preparing reports

Alternate Title(s): Administrative Analyst, Budget Analyst, Program Analyst

Salary Range: $20,000 to $60,000

Employment Prospects: Good to excellent

Advancement Prospects: Good to excellent

Best Geographical Location(s): Large cities, state capitals

Prerequisites:

Education or Training—Bachelor's or master's degree

Experience—Entry-level or some relevant work experience

Special Skills and Personality Traits—Analytical; computer-literate; task-oriented; good with numbers

CAREER LADDER

```
┌─────────────────────────────┐
│          Manager            │
└─────────────────────────────┘

┌─────────────────────────────┐
│     Management Analyst      │
└─────────────────────────────┘

┌─────────────────────────────┐
│      Intern or Student      │
└─────────────────────────────┘
```

Position Description

Management Analysts gather and evaluate information to help managers answer a variety of questions: Is paid sick leave up or down? Are tax revenues increasing or decreasing? How many buildings are being inspected each year? These types of questions are being asked with increasing frequency as government tries to improve its reputation by boosting efficiency.

Much as consultants in the private sector do, Management Analysts in government evaluate an organization's structure and suggest ways to improve efficiency. The trend in government is toward viewing taxpayers as customers. Managers are turning to "performance measurement" to improve customer service. Are taxpayers getting the most for their money? If not, what can be changed? Often Management Analysts use computer spreadsheets to organize their data.

Some Management Analysts work under contract. For instance, a state agency might hire a Management Analyst to improve internal organization and operating procedures. The individual might go to different departments to observe staffers in action, perhaps interviewing them about their particular jobs.

Although Management Analysts in government do much the same work as those in the private sector, they labor under different constraints. Rules and regulations abound. An ordinance from the 1800s might well affect the way a local department is organized today. Often, Management Analysts are ranked by level. Some positions once known as Administrative Assistant have been retitled Management Analyst.

Generally, Management Analysts perform three basic functions: budget analysis, evaluating whether or not the department is operating within budget; management analysis, analyzing general management issues; program analysis, looking into whether or not the program is meeting its goals.

As budget analysts, they advise and assist in establishing budgets to distribute funds efficiently among programs. Their work begins when the heads of various programs or departments submit their budget proposals. Management Analysts compare these to the budgets of previous years. Are the proposed increases workable? Are various departments getting their fair share? Often Management Analysts work closely with managers to fine-tune the budget, which ultimately has to be approved by the head of the agency. Once the budget has been approved, the Management Analyst monitors it, looking at monthly statements to make sure that funds are being used appropriately. Some Management Analysts compare their work with budgets to managing a checking account. They need to make sure that withdrawals do not exceed deposits.

Other analysts deal more with programs. Usually, the *Analyst* in their titles precedes a particular area of expertise, such as Redevelopment Analyst, Traffic Analyst, or Criminal Analyst. An Environmental Analyst, for instance, might have a degree in biology, chemistry, or a physical science.

Although Management Analysts tend to be generalists, they might be given a task like looking into the funding possibilities for a particular program. Could the program be self-supporting? How much would citizens be willing to pay in fees? What kind of grant sources are available? Should money from existing departments be used? The Management Analyst typically would research all possible alternatives and write a report.

In addition, Management Analysts

- Review and analyze operating procedures
- Confer with staff to identify problems and needs
- Initiate special studies
- Determine the methods to be used in conducting studies
- Recommend changes in operations methods, procedures, and programs
- Compile various kinds of information for management use

Salaries

Salaries vary by education, experience, and size of the government entity. Generally, large entities pay more than smaller ones. Many positions pay in the $30,000 to $50,000 range. Management Analysts are often ranked by level: Management Analyst I, Management Analyst II, and so forth.

Employment Prospects

Employment prospects are good to excellent because local, state, and federal agencies are looking for ways to become more efficient. Opportunities for Management Analysts can be found at the local, state, and federal levels. If, however, a local entity is very small, such as a village, it probably won't need a Management Analyst.

Advancement Prospects

Advancement prospects are good to excellent, especially for entry-level positions. Individuals can rise from Management Analyst I to Management Analyst II, and so forth. From there, they might become a department head or assistant city manager.

Education and Training

A bachelor's degree or equivalent experience is generally required for entry-level Management Analyst positions in government. A master's degree in business, public administration, or a related field may substitute for required experience.

Experience, Skills, and Personality Traits

Strong analytical skills are a must for this position. Management Analysts gather and categorize information. Strong math skills help with the quantitative work. Management Analysts define problems, establish facts, and draw conclusions. Often they interpret complex and technical material. They need to be be able to make sound decisions.

Management Analysts also should be good communicators—both verbally and in writing. Management Analysts prepare reports that need to be concise and accurate. Individuals must be persuasive enough to gain acceptance for their projects. They need to be computer-literate and knowledgeable about the way government works. Management Analysts should be both self-starters and team players.

Unions and Associations

Management Analysts might be part of the bargaining unit of the National Association of Government Employees (NAGE) or another union representing professional, supervisory, or technical positions. Professional associations of interest to Management Analysts include the American Society for Public Administration and state municipal associations. Associations have been created specifically for municipal Management Assistants in Arizona, California, Colorado, Illinois, Ohio, and Texas.

Tips for Entry

1. Take courses involving qualitative and quantitative research methods.
2. Seek out an internship. Many internships open the doors to full-time employment.
3. Check "help wanteds" in a variety of places: local and state personnel offices, university career centers, newspaper classified ads, and state municipal associations.
4. Find out about conferences and other career-development opportunities offered by state municipal associations.
5. Consider getting a master's degree in public administration or a related field if you are interested in moving up to upper management in government or consulting positions in the private sector. Employers in the private sector generally look for Management Analysts with a master's degree in business administration or a related discipline.

PROGRAM MANAGER

CAREER PROFILE

Duties: Managing a particular program; acting as a liaison to other agencies; planning projects and activities

Alternate Title(s): Program Coordinator, Program Supervisor

Salary Range: $32,000 to $70,000

Employment Prospects: Good

Advancement Prospects: Good

Best Geographical Location(s): Large metropolitan areas, state capitals

Prerequisites:

   Education or Training—Two to five years relevant program experience

   Experience—Bachelor's or master's degree

   Special Skills and Personality Traits—Good communication, management, and organizational skills

CAREER LADDER

```
┌─────────────────────────────┐
│      Manager Director       │
└─────────────────────────────┘

┌─────────────────────────────┐
│      Program Manager        │
└─────────────────────────────┘

┌─────────────────────────────┐
│  Program Worker/Supervisor  │
└─────────────────────────────┘
```

Position Description

Program Managers do just as their title implies: They manage programs. The way they go about this, though, varies widely. Program Managers span the range of government programs. Just about any specialty can precede the word *Manager,* including arts, alcohol and drug rehabilitation, and transportation. The responsibilities of Program Managers depend largely on the needs of the particular agency. A Program Manager in health and human services might counsel clients and supervise staff, whereas someone with the same title in transportation might be heavily involved in public relations. Yet another Program Manager might coordinate activities ranging from holiday parties to special classes.

Many Program Managers act as liaisons for government, private, and nonprofit agencies. If, for instance, a state contracts out mental-health services to a private agency, a Program Manager might oversee training for the contracted employees.

Some positions are temporary, the result of grants. A state public health agency, for instance, might receive a grant to offer outreach services to citizens with infectious diseases. The position of Program Manager might go to someone with a master's degree in public health and a background in epidemiology. In some jurisdictions a Program Manager might be above a Program Coordinator, whereas in others one person handles all the responsibilities. Some Program Managers might also be called Analysts. In addition to being familiar with the nitty-gritty workings of the program itself, they need to be able to step back and look at the big picture. How many staffers are needed? How should they be trained? Is the department working within its budget?

Like many positions in government, those of Program Managers are ranked by level: Program Manager I, Program Manager II, and so forth. Typically, high-level Program Managers are more involved in management matters.

The larger the organization, the more complex the logistical issues. The Program Manager needs to grapple with a variety of questions: What's the best way to get out a message to 500 people? Is it best to arrange a meeting or send a memo? Does a particular problem need to be solved now, or can it wait until next week?

In addition, many Program Managers also

- Conduct surveys and studies
- Provide guidance and direction to staff
- Review, evaluate, and report on assigned program areas
- Maintain reports and records
- Attend agency planning sessions

Salaries

Salaries vary widely according to level and the nature of a program and its funding. Many salaries are in the $35,000 to $50,000 range.

Employment Prospects

Employment prospects are good. At the state level, for instance, most large agencies have programs that need to be coordinated and managed. Candidates should apply to agencies best suited to their backgrounds.

Advancement Prospects

Advancement prospects are good since one can move up the ladder to a higher-level Program Manager or management position. Program Managers hired on a contract basis, however, have more limited prospects since their work is time-limited. Once their contract is up, their work ends.

Education and Training

Educational requirements depend on the type of program being managed and he needs of the particular agency. A degree in accounting might be best for the department of revenue, social work for human services, physical science for an environmental agency, and so forth. A desired degree might substitute for a year or two of required experience. A master's degree in a particular program area can help Program Managers move up the career ladder.

Experience, Skills, and Personality Traits

Most positions require experience in the particular program area. For instance, a Program Manager for youth programs would typically have had experience as a youth worker, then as a program supervisor. Coordinating programs requires knowledge of not only the particular program but also general management skills: how to delegate responsibility, recruit workers, and motivate employees.

Unions and Associations

Program Managers might be part of the bargaining unit of the National Association of Government Employees (NAGE) or another union representing professional, supervisory, or technical positions. Professional associations of interest to Program Managers include the American Society for Public Administration and state municipal associations.

Tips for Entry

1. Determine your own area of interest. Which issues appeal to you most?
2. Volunteer or get an internship in your field of interest. In some fields, part-time or temporary positions offer a good foot in the door.
3. Check listings in a variety of places: newspaper help wanteds, college career offices, municipal association and state personnel websites. Browse job listings, checking to see whether or not you have the required education and experience for the position.

PUBLIC INFORMATION OFFICER

CAREER PROFILE

Duties: Disseminating information to the media; acting as a spokesperson; writing and producing materials; presenting information to the public

Alternate Title(s): Information Officer, Information and Communication Specialist

Salary Range: $25,000 to $65,000

Employment Prospects: Good

Advancement Prospects: Fair

Best Geographical Location(s): Capital cities and large metropolitan areas

Prerequisites:

Education or Training—College degree in journalism, communications, or a related field

Experience—Two years minimum in professional media or news setting

Special Skills and Personality Traits—Good writing skills; outgoing personality; resourcefulness; ability to establish professional rapport with the media

CAREER LADDER

```
┌─────────────────────────────────┐
│     Public Affairs Director     │
└─────────────────────────────────┘

┌─────────────────────────────────┐
│   Public Information Officer     │
└─────────────────────────────────┘

┌─────────────────────────────────┐
│ Writer/Reporter or Press Assistant │
└─────────────────────────────────┘
```

Position Description

Public Information Officers are the jacks-of-all-trades of government communications. They write press releases, gather information, prepare speeches, produce newsletters, and serve as the primary communicators for government agencies. PIOs, as they are called, often wear three different hats:

- Public relations: promoting the work of the government agency
- Public affairs: dealing with policy issues
- Public information: making information available to the public

How much time is devoted to each specialty depends largely on the nature of the government agency. A PIO for a government-run zoo, park, or museum, for instance, might be heavily involved in public relations. He or she needs to get out positive news to attract people to the site.

Sometimes all three specialties blend together in the course of one project. For instance, a PIO involved in an effort to promote the state parks might want to inform the public about their weaknesses (e.g., deteriorating condition) as well as their strengths in an effort to garner public support for increased funding. Proposals might be made, funding possibilities discussed. The PIO would then branch into the field of public affairs.

Public Information Officers have many of the same responsibilities as press secretaries, although they generally work for agencies rather than individuals. The Department of Environmental Management, for instance, might have a PIO, whereas the Governor has a press secretary. Typically, the PIO is a career employee and the press secretary is a political appointee. Both might call themselves "spokespersons." Others, though, might refer to them by more derogatory terms such as "flaks" or "spin doctors." Although such terms have negative connotations, PIOs acknowledge that "spin" can be a reality of the job. They need to make their government organizations "look good." To do this, seasoned PIOs emphasize the importance of well-reasoned decisions in their conversations with policy makers. Poor decisions don't spin well, they say.

Many PIOs have a background in news reporting, which helps them know how to pitch stories to the media. Is it a quirky story for radio? What might an editorial writer need to know? Could a feature accompany the news story? What kind of visuals are available for TV?

Public information is a field unto itself—not to be confused with information systems. Although both positions have "information" in their titles, an Information *systems* Officer deals more with the technical end of communications, such as computers and telecommunications. Public Information Officers, on the other hand, help governments communicate with the people, often via the media.

Typical responsibilities of PIOs include

- Conferring with government officials
- Attending and assisting at press conferences
- Overseeing websites
- Coordinating publicity
- Writing speeches (speechwriting is rarely a separate position)
- Directing multimedia projects such as public affairs announcements
- Developing posters, flyers, T-shirts, and so forth
- Managing a standardized policy for disseminating information

Work in this field can be stressful, particularly in agencies frequently involved in controversial issues. A government agency may be accused of wrongdoing, perhaps even be sued. Public Information Officers need to answer difficult questions such as, Why did your agency issue a permit for an industrial facility next to a school?

Such difficult assignments, though, can be rewarding, as PIOs facilitate communication with the public. Some PIOs work long hours, including nights and weekends. They are called out en masse to inform the public about emergencies such as hurricanes and earthquakes.

Salaries

Salaries depend largely on an individual's level of experience. A Public Information Officer might begin at about $25,000 but move up to a higher level after a few years on the job. Many PIOs make $35,000 to $40,000, according to industry sources. Pay classification usually coincides with the complexity of the work. Agencies dealing with complex issues generally pay the highest salaries.

Employment Prospects

Employment prospects are good because government, as does private industry, recognizes the importance of effective communication. Opportunities for Public Information Officers can be found in local, state, and federal government.

Current trends, too, contribute to the growth of the information industry. Public Information Officers are needed to deal with the public's increased demand for information, the expansion of the Internet, and the efforts of government to combat negative perceptions of its performance. Some individuals who see limited prospects in journalism are attracted to the more regular hours and higher pay of the field.

Advancement Prospects

Advancement prospects are fair because competition increases as one moves up the career ladder. In state government, for instance, only a few cabinet-level posts exist, thus making competition particularly intense. Some Public Information Officers move laterally to expand their base of knowledge and tackle new challenges.

Education and Training

Many Public Information Officers have bachelor's degrees in journalism, broadcast journalism, English, communications, or public relations. A master's degree in public administration can help individuals advance their careers.

Experience, Skills, and Personality Traits

Public Information Officers generally have some news experience, as being media-savvy is critical. Top-notch writing skills are a must. Individuals need to know how to organize and present information clearly and effectively. They also must be knowledgeable about the workings of government.

Being resourceful counts for a lot in this field. Public Information Officers need to dig up information quickly and communicate well with different types of people. Public Information Officers are always juggling multiple tasks, working against tight deadlines. When asked tough questions by the media, they need to respond professionally. This can be a high-pressure job.

Unions and Associations

Public Information Officers might belong to a variety of associations, including the National Association of Government Communicators (NAGC), the City-County Communications and Marketing Association (3CMA), and/or state organizations providing professional assistance to government communicators. NAGC deals with government communication at all levels of government—local, state, and federal. 3CMA, on the other hand, addresses issues at the local level and includes general government personnel such as City/County Managers as well as those involved specifically in communications.

Tips for Entry

1. Get media experience, preferably working for a newspaper. Many newspapers hire "stringers" to cover meetings. These part-time reporters gain the experience needed for full-time employment.
2. Seek an internship with a newspaper or other media outlet (e.g., TV, radio station, or public relations firm).

3. Scan government websites for openings. Check out state personnel or municipal association sites. Before applying for a position, familiarize yourself with the work of the particular agency.

4. Set up an informational interview with someone in an agency that interests you and ask to be apprised of future openings.

5. Attend events sponsored by professional associations.

LOCAL GOVERNMENT

LOCAL POLITICAL AIDE

CAREER PROFILE

Duties: Scheduling; answering the phone; writing; researching; attending meetings

Alternate Title(s): Mayor's Aide, Councilor's Aide, Executive Assistant, Executive Secretary

Salary Range: $25,000 to $35,000+

Employment Prospects: Fair

Advancement Prospects: Fair

Best Geographical Location: Larger cities

Prerequisites:

Education or Training—Bachelor's degree; master's degree preferred

Experience—Internship; political campaign work

Special Skills and Personality Traits—Loyalty; dedication; quick learner; team player; flexibility; willingness to work long hours

CAREER LADDER

```
┌─────────────────────────────┐
│                             │
│     Higher-level Staffer    │
│                             │
└─────────────────────────────┘


┌─────────────────────────────┐
│                             │
│       Political Aide        │
│                             │
└─────────────────────────────┘


┌─────────────────────────────┐
│                             │
│  Volunteer Campaign Worker  │
│                             │
└─────────────────────────────┘
```

Position Description

Local Political Aides assist mayors, city councilors, and other elected officials with scheduling, researching, answering the phone, and performing miscellaneous other tasks. In busy offices, where requests pour in for the elected official's time and attention, Local Political Aides serve as important buffers. Often elected officials want to be perceived as "nice" and so delegate the task of saying no to their Political Aides. When angry constituents call, Local Political Aides need to keep their cool and ask how they can help.

Turning down requests is a skill that requires both firmness and diplomacy. Local Political Aides must be sensitive to the needs of different groups. The Chamber of Commerce might have one set of needs, a community group another. Some requests involve funding. The Local Political Aide needs to say no to all inappropriate requests. Sometimes the Local Political Aide can refer the caller to another source of help. Many calls involve requests for the elected official's time. For instance, Can the elected official attend an event that day? The Local Political Aide might explain that scheduling is done weeks in advance.

Scheduling is also an important part of this job. Often, the elected official and the Local Political Aide have a weekly scheduling meeting. Time—a precious commodity in political life—needs to be scheduled wisely so all constituents are well-represented. Elected officials conserve time by delegating various responsibilities to their Local Political Aides. Aides often do the tedious but necessary work of digging through documents. For instance, they might find out which cities have curfews and which ones don't so the elected official can sound well-informed on the issue.

Local Political Aides assist with communications such as press releases and letters to constituents. Since some constituents frame letters from elected officials, Local Political Aides need to write accurately and grammatically. The Local Political Aide also might be included in strategy sessions. What's the best response to the budget crisis? How can he or she best support the elected official? The Local Political Aide might serve as a liaison to other political officials, perhaps those in state government.

Many Local Political Aides work long and irregular hours. They often attend meetings at night and/or on the weekends.

Salaries

Salaries generally range from $25,000 to $35,000 or more, depending on the size of the city. Smaller cities generally pay on the low end of the range.

Employment Prospects

Employment prospects are fair because there is a limited number of slots. The number of Mayors and City Councilors is relatively small. Elected officials in small towns generally lack the funding for Local Political Aides.

Advancement Prospects

Advancement prospects are fair since, again, the number of slots is limited. Some Local Political Aides move up to positions like chief of staff at the state level. Others run for political office themselves or move into allied fields such as consulting.

Education and Training

Generally, a bachelor's degree qualifies an individual for the position of Local Political Aide, although some elected officials might prefer someone with a master's degree. Often, Local Political Aides choose this position to get an inside view of the work of elected officials. From this, they can decide whether or not they want to continue to work in the field. Some Local Political Aides go on to law school or other graduate programs.

Experience, Skills, and Personality Traits

Although some Local Political Aides have advanced degrees and paid work experience, many others don't. A candidate can qualify for this position by volunteering on a political campaign or serving an internship. He or she should, however, already have strong writing and researching skills as well as good interpersonal skills. One of the top requirements of the job is being able to interact well with the public.

Local Political Aides need a sense of integrity to refuse perks offered in return for special favors. They should show maturity, reliability, and flexibility. Having a "can-do" attitude helps, as Local Political Aides often work under pressure.

Unions and Associations

Although no national association exists specifically for Local Political Aides, the American Society for Public Administration is a broad-based national organization representing individuals in public service. State municipal associations and political parties, too, deal with issues of concern to those in the field.

Tips for Entry

1. Volunteer to work on a political campaign.
2. Look into internship possibilities.
3. Become active in your local political party. Attend events to take advantage of networking possibilities.

RECREATION SUPERVISOR

CAREER PROFILE

Duties: Administering recreation programs by handling staffing, scheduling, and budgeting needs

Alternate Title(s): Recreation Coordinator, Athletic Supervisor

Salary Range: $20,000 to $40,000+

Employment Prospects: Good

Advancement Prospects: Good

Best Geographical Location: Municipalities

Prerequisites:

Education or Training—College degree, preferably in parks and recreation or leisure services management
Experience—Previous experience as recreation leader
Special Skills and Personality Traits—Leadership ability; management skills; strong interest in sports and leisure

CAREER LADDER

```
┌─────────────────────────────┐
│   Division Head or Director  │
└─────────────────────────────┘

┌─────────────────────────────┐
│    Recreation Supervisor     │
└─────────────────────────────┘

┌─────────────────────────────┐
│      Recreation Leader       │
│   or Program Coordinator     │
└─────────────────────────────┘
```

Position Description

Recreation is serious business for the Supervisor who oversees programs for a city or town. The Recreation Supervisor serves as a link between the Director of Parks and Recreation and the recreation leaders who organize and direct participants in sports, camps, and other activities.

America's health craze has contributed to an increase in recreation programs. People are living longer, healthier lives and looking for ways to channel their leisure time. Parents want positive activities for their children. Sports programs for girls as well as boys have mushroomed in recent years.

Recreation encompasses a wide array of offerings, including arts and crafts, competitive sports, and aerobics for senior citizens. In some communities, recreation and cultural events are combined. A recreation and cultural affairs department might oversee a food festival, balloon fair, ethnic heritage celebration, or other special event.

In small towns, Recreation Supervisors wear many hats. In addition to running recreation programs, they might lead an activity such as adult volleyball. They also might be responsible for park maintenance.

In a large city, the Recreation Supervisor might be in charge of just one facility, a skating rink, for example. Or he or she might be responsible for a particular activity, such as athletics, aquatics, performing arts, or outdoor programs. In a medium-sized community, the individual might be responsible for the gamut of recreation but not for parks as well.

Safety has become an increasing concern of recreation departments everywhere. To meet this need, professional associations offer certification in areas such as playground safety. On the job, Recreation Supervisors make sure that procedures are established and followed. For instance, ice packs must be easily accessible in case of injury.

Recreation Supervisors should be able to roll with the punches. Coin-operated lockers break down. Schedules change. Staffers fail to show up. Recreation Supervisors must deal with these kinds of situations without losing their cool. They also need to work while others play. Recreation Supervisors make sure that everything is going smoothly by making the rounds of programs, many of which take place at night or on the weekends. Since they are in charge of staffing, they have to watch their leaders in action.

Back in the office, Recreation Supervisors perform a variety of duties. These might include

- Writing press releases, brochures, and flyers
- Designing questionnaires so citizens can evaluate programs
- Reviewing the fee structure of various offerings
- Planning the annual budget

- Working out scheduling so different teams can practice and play at various times
- Interviewing prospective employees

Salaries

Salaries depend largely on the size of the community and the individual's level of experience. Salaries generally range from $20,000 to $40,000, although more senior Recreation Supervisors in larger communities could earn up to $60,000 or more a year.

Employment Prospects

Employment prospects are good. This is a field with an unusually large number of part-time, seasonal, and volunteer positions that provide a direct route to permanent employment. In some communities, the position of Recreation Supervisor is a part-time one.

Recreation is a growth field, as some staffers leave the public sector for commercial recreation and tourism management in the private sector. Positions in this rapidly growing field include camp directors, stadium managers, convention specialists, and resort services directors.

Advancement Prospects

Advancement prospects are good, although they vary with the makeup of the department. When people retire, those beneath them often move up the ranks. Generally speaking, the larger the department, the better the prospects of advancement. Some Recreation Supervisors advance their careers by moving to another community.

Education and Training

A college degree is usually required for this position. Most large universities offer baccalaureate degrees in parks and recreation or leisure studies. Programs typically include the history, theory, and philosophy of parks and recreation as well as management courses. Students can specialize in areas such as therapeutic recreation, park management, or commercial and industrial recreation. The National Recreation and Park Association accredits undergraduate programs and offers certification programs for specialists in the field.

Increasingly, Recreation Supervisors are earning master's degrees in parks and recreation or related disciplines. Some recreation administrators have backgrounds in social work, forestry, or resource management. Requirements for employment vary from community to community.

Experience, Skills, and Personality Traits

This field offers easy entry as a part-timer. Many college students who work as counselors or leaders decide to go into recreation as a profession. Experience in a particular field, such as athletics, is an asset for many positions. Some positions require certification in lifesaving, coaching, and/or another specialty. Activity planning calls for creativity and resourcefulness.

Working as a part-timer can help individuals decide whether or not they have the right temperament for the field. Recreation workers need to be outgoing and energetic. They should enjoy recreation and be comfortable interacting with the public.

Recreation Supervisors need to be sensitive to the needs and feelings of people in all age groups. They are in a service-oriented profession, which requires diplomacy. The Recreation Supervisor should be good at motivating others and delegating responsibility. Since recreation departments have a strong group focus, the Recreation Supervisor should have the mind-set of a team player.

Good administrative skills—knowledge of budgets, accounting, and, increasingly computers—are a must. Although Recreation Supervisors face many of the same budget constraints as other municipal workers, they often get satisfaction from using recreation to improve the quality of people's lives.

Unions and Associations

The National Recreation and Park Association (NRPA) is a national nonprofit service organization dedicated to promoting the importance of parks and recreation.

Tips for Entry

1. Work as a part-time employee or volunteer to gain experience in the field. Recreation has an unusually large number of part-time and seasonal jobs. Opportunities are plentiful for summer camp counselors, lifeguards, craft specialists, and after-school and weekend recreation program leaders.

2. Look into college programs in recreation and leisure studies. Most large universities offer this as a major. The NRPA accredits approximately 100 undergraduate programs in the field.

3. Check out ads in local newspapers for positions. Recreation Supervisor positions are usually listed under "Professional/Administrative."

4. Familiarize yourself with the field. The NRPA's website (*www.activeparks.org*) offers a good overview.

ASSESSOR

CAREER PROFILE

Duties: Identifying and evaluating taxable properties; collecting and analyzing data; preparing appraisal reports; testifying in court or defending assessments before appeals boards

Alternate Title(s): Appraiser, Assessment Commissioner, Valuator, Deputy Assessor

Salary Range: $17,000 to $120,000, full-time; $5,000 to $45,000, part-time

Employment Prospects: Good

Advancement Prospects: Good

Best Geographical Location: Large population centers, major cities

Prerequisites:
Education or Training—College degree desirable
Experience—Substantial experience in appraising and assessing
Special Skills and Personality Traits—Mathematical, statistical, and spatial-relations skills; technical aptitude; tact; good judgment; sense of fairness

CAREER LADDER

```
┌─────────────────────────────┐
│  Assessment Commissioner    │
└─────────────────────────────┘

┌─────────────────────────────┐
│   Appraiser/ Assessor       │
└─────────────────────────────┘

┌─────────────────────────────┐
│     Appraiser Trainee       │
└─────────────────────────────┘
```

Position Description

Assessors gauge the value of homes, golf courses, billboards, and other taxable properties. Local property taxes, based on these values, provide funding for municipal services such as police and fire protection, roads, and schools. Although taxpayers might disagree with their assessments, Assessors need to make sure that everybody pays a fair share of taxes.

The term *Assessor* usually refers to the chief elected or appointed officer, although he or she might also be called an Appraiser. Whether Assessors are elected or appointed varies from state to state: 21 states have elected Assessors; 18 states have appointed ones. The remaining 11 states have Assessors according to local option.

Elected Assessors tend to be less technically proficient than appointed Assessors. Often an elected Assessor appoints a Chief Deputy Assessor with more expertise in the field. Assessing offices vary widely in size, some staffed by one person, others by hundreds. In a small office, Assessors typically do all the appraisal work themselves.

Assessment work is complex, involving a combination of appraisal methodology, statistical analysis, and common sense. Assessors use a formula to calculate the tax burden of each property holder, multiplying assessed values by the municipal tax rate set by lawmakers to determine the amount of taxes owed. Because assessments are based on market values that change from year to year, Assessors appraise property annually.

Each year the Assessor prepares an annual assessment roll, which lists all properties in the district and their assessed values. Assessors and their staff evaluate "real property" (e.g., lands and buildings) and, in some places, "personal property" (e.g., crops, livestock, machinery). The assessment process typically involves

- Using special maps to locate and identify all taxable property in the jurisdiction; marking changes in the size and shape of each parcel as development takes place
- Making a property record of each parcel (e.g., photographs, soil samples, information about plumbing, electrical, and heating systems; the type of construction)

- Reviewing files from previous years to see whether or not a complete inspection is needed
- Noting street patterns, types of buildings, and other features of the neighborhood as a whole
- Collecting facts about recent sales prices, rents, and the costs of construction from deeds, property-transfer papers, and other resources

After analyzing all this information, Assessors estimate the market value of the property, which leads them to an assessment figure. Local clerks or Assessors mail the tax assessments to property owners.

Because taxpayers have the right to contest their assessments, Assessors must be prepared to defend their estimates and methods. They might hold meetings to answer questions or handle complaints. Action needs to be taken to recover delinquent taxes. Sometimes assessments result in lawsuits. The Assessor might have to testify in court or appear before an appeals board.

Assessment work can be stressful, as a great deal of money rides on the decision. Assessors usually work eight hours a day, 40 hours a week, although some positions, particularly in small towns, are part-time. The position of Assessor might also be combined with that of the Municipal Clerk.

Salaries

Salaries vary widely. Some Assessors—particularly in rural counties or small towns—are part-time and so earn considerably less than their full-time counterparts.

The annual starting salary for Assessors is about $27,000 a year. Earnings rise with experience and increased responsibility. After several years on the job, the average salary is about $36,000.

Assessors in large jurisdictions generally earn more than those in smaller ones. An Assessor in a county with millions of people, for instance, might make $100,000 a year. Management status, too, increases salaries.

Employment Prospects

Employment prospects are good because all towns and cities, regardless of size, have Assessors. Assessors can be either elected or appointed.

When the population of a region grows, the municipality may hire more Assessors. The chances for employment are greater in large population centers than in smaller ones.

Advancement Prospects

Advancement prospects are good. Some Assessors advance their careers by moving to areas of broader jurisdiction—from a town to a county, for instance. Skills developed in assessing are transferable to other jobs in business or industry. The banking industry, for example, uses independent property appraisals in making loans. Someone might work in both the public and the private sector.

Education and Training

Specialized training counts for a lot in this field. Most states have certification criteria for Assessors. Professional associations also offer certification programs.

Education programs cover assessment valuation and administration and local laws and regulations. Trainees who successfully complete their requirements can move up to professional positions. Those who pass examinations for one position can move up the career ladder to the next. Commercial Assessors, for example, require more specialized training than Residential Assessors.

Some courses help Assessors keep up with new trends, such as valuation of cellular towers or valuation of contaminated properties, and others provide the general skills necessary to be effective on the job, including public speaking and negotiation skills. Both types of knowledge are strongly required. Employers often pay tuition costs. Employees might get time off from work to attend classes.

Many state universities have programs of study for Assessors or offer them jointly with the government. A college degree or equivalent improves an Assessor's chances for advancement. Useful programs of study include urban studies, real estate, public administration, accounting, engineering, and business administration.

Experience, Skills, and Personality Traits

Assessing requires a combination of technical skills and interpersonal finesse. In addition to evaluating properties, Assessors need to talk to taxpayers who might object to their assessments.

On the technical end, Assessors should have an affinity for spatial relationships to mark accurately what goes where on specialized maps accurately. Other desirable qualities are working well with numbers; having an orderly, inquiring mind; and being able to make sound and objective judgments.

Assessors must be able to make technical information understandable to the general public. Some Assessors work in neighborhoods that require familiarity with another language. Assessors also need to communicate well with government officials involved in legislation, budget appropriations, building-permit data, and other matters of interest.

Because taxes are a sensitive subject for many people, Assessors need to be tactful and diplomatic. Taxpayers have a right to challenge their assessments. The Assessor might need to testify in court or appear before an appeals boards.

Unions and Associations

The International Association of Assessing Officers (IAAO) is a professional organization of Assessors. States, too, have organizations of assessing officers since state laws regulate this profession. The American Association of Certified Appraisers and the National Association of Independent Fee Appraisers are other organizations of Assessors.

Tips for Entry

1. Write to or call your local Assessor to make an appointment to discuss your interests.
2. Contact the personnel offices of municipal governments or the listings of municipal associations to ask about positions in assessment offices or related fields. Positions in local zoning offices and county courthouses sometimes provide transferable experience.
3. Tap into the resources of professional associations. If you have access to the Internet, check out the IAAO website at *www.iaao.org*. Ask professional associations about brochures or single-copy publications available to nonmembers.
4. Look into programs of study for Assessors offered by state universities or professional associations.
5. Become politically involved if you are interested in running for Assessor. Seek the endorsement of your political party.

HOUSING SPECIALIST

CAREER PROFILE

Duties: Screening prospective tenants; supervising properties; interviewing landlords; coordinating community outreach; writing grants; researching and reviewing policy

Alternate Title(s): Housing Development Manager, Section 8 Coordinator, HOPE VI Coordinator, Public Housing Manager, Contract Coordinator, Policy Analyst

Salary Range: $20,000 to $60,000

Employment Prospects: Good

Advancement Prospects: Good

Best Geographical Location: None

Prerequisites:

Education or Training—College degree generally required

Experience—Internship or experience in entry-level position

Special Skills and Personality Traits—Commitment to public housing and social change; ability to perform multiple skills; good communication skills; willingness to work hard

CAREER LADDER

```
┌─────────────────────────────────┐
│   Program or Agency Director     │
│   Housing Authority Director     │
└─────────────────────────────────┘

┌─────────────────────────────────┐
│       Housing Specialist         │
└─────────────────────────────────┘

┌─────────────────────────────────┐
│   Entry-Level Position or Intern │
└─────────────────────────────────┘
```

Position Description

Housing Specialists address a basic human necessity—the need for shelter. They can go about this in a number of different ways. Some Housing Specialists coordinate subsidized housing programs. Others apply for and administer grants. Still others do both, plus whatever else is required.

The federal department of Housing and Urban Development (HUD) allocates money to state governments for use by local housing authorities. Those authorities operate public housing developments and administer the Section 8 program, in which tenants rent from private landlords. Housing Specialists also tap into new HUD programs, which provide funding for development of rental and/or ownership properties.

Local housing authorities increasingly are being asked by the federal government to provide not only bricks and mortar but also social services to those who otherwise might fall through the cracks. Many of these residents need substantial help. Housing Specialists try not only to provide shelter but also to help residents help themselves. By pro-

viding access to job-training and other services, housing authorities work to encourage resident self-sufficiency.

Much has changed since public housing got its start shortly after World War II. Public housing was originally developed for veterans and working families. Over the years—and with scant policy review—this focus changed. Public housing developments shifted to housing the poorest of the poor, often with disastrous results. Many public housing developments became havens for crime and drug abuse. Sometimes, policy makers decide that the best thing to do is to tear down old housing developments and start again.

Public housing today stands at a crossroads. Federal legislation has deregulated certain housing policies, encouraging the development of more entrepreneurial programs linking the public with the private and nonprofit sectors.

On the local end, Housing Specialists need to know what works best for their communities. In small communities, Housing Specialists tend to be generalists. They manage finances, screen applicants for criminal records and/or other barriers to subsidized housing, organize residents' meetings, and oversee property maintenance. Because small organizations have fewer career rungs, Housing Directors might perform some of these responsibilities themselves.

Housing Specialists in larger housing authorities have more specialized jobs. One person might be in charge of the Section 8 program. Someone else might coordinate resident training. Another person might write grants. Yet another person might be in charge of monitoring federal legislation.

In many communities, housing and community development are linked—either formally under one department or informally through strong connections between the two. If, for example, a community sets a goal of creating more affordable housing, the Housing Specialist might team up with a private developer to come up with a site plan. How can the project address the safety concerns of the community? What are the needs of prospective residents? Community meetings are held, and plans take shape, perhaps calling for the inclusion of a community police office and recreational facilities. The Housing Specialist typically helps cobble together a funding plan: loans, tax credits, and the like. He or she might also take on the role of Project Manager.

To improve existing developments, Housing Specialists often apply for funding to improve services. The Department of Labor, for instance, administers Welfare-to-Work grants. Many grant writers also turn to private foundations for help. An arts grant, for example, might pay for music lessons for children in a public housing development.

Work in housing offers both challenges and rewards. Like any social service job, it can be satisfying but also frustrating at times. Many Housing Specialists work long hours, attending meetings at night and/or on the weekends.

Salaries

Salaries generally range from $20,000 to $60,000 and vary according to the area and the position in question. Larger housing authorities generally pay more than smaller ones. Salaries also rise with level of responsibility. Someone with five years of progressively responsible experience who manages a housing program might earn an annual salary of about $50,000.

Employment Prospects

Employment prospects are good because of the variety of positions. This is a relatively "old" industry. As employees retire, new positions open up. Internships help hook newcomers into the hiring network.

Advancement Prospects

Advancement prospects are good. Experience and training help advance careers. Promotion is possible for people who can prove themselves on the job and are willing to take the initiative to increase their skills. One also can become more marketable by taking courses in allied fields such as real estate. Increased education—a master's degree, in particular—helps Housing Specialists rise up the career ladder.

Education and Training

A bachelor's degree is generally required. Courses dealing with political science, public administration, business, and sociology help foster an understanding of the issues involved on the job. A master's degree, particularly in planning or public administration, may be required for upper management positions.

Experience, Skills, and Personality Traits

Midlevel jobs as a Housing Specialist generally require some experience in the field. Some housing authorities hire entry-level staffers right out of college. Those who have done internships have a particularly good chance of being hired.

People committed to social change do best in this position. Housing Specialists can be either liberal or conservative, since political ideology is less important than dedication and hard work. Strong analytical and communication skills are essential. Housing Specialists need to be detail-oriented to document the various procedures required by law.

The ability to keep information confidential is another must. Housing Specialists sometimes need to make difficult decisions involving people's access to shelter. Because public programs cannot accommodate everyone, individuals in this field sometimes need to turn down people in need of housing.

Unions and Associations

National associations involved in housing include the National Association of Housing and Redevelopment Officials (NAHRO) and the Public Housing Authorities Directors Association (PHADA).

Tips for Entry

1. Look into internship and work-study possibilities. These experiences often lead to full-time positions.
2. Volunteer with a local housing authority. Offer to assist residents or help out in the business office.
3. Get references from people you've worked with. Working well as part of a team helps in this field, as in many others.
4. Check out the websites of the National Association of Housing and Redevelopment Officials (www.nahro.org) and the Public Housing Authorities Directors Association (www.phada.org).
5. Consider graduate school if your goal is to reach the upper levels of management.

URBAN AND REGIONAL PLANNER

CAREER PROFILE

Duties: Analyzing trends in land-use, housing, transportation, and other community concerns; using computer planning tools; communicating graphically and verbally; touring sites; holding public hearings; mediating among conflicting groups; coordinating plans

Alternate Title(s): Town Planner, City Planner, Urban and Regional Planner, Planning Consultant

Salary Range: $26,000 to $65,000

Employment Prospects: Good

Advancement Prospects: Good

Best Geographical Location: Large cities, state capitals, rapidly growing communities

Prerequisites:

Education or Training—Master's degree in planning required for most positions

Experience—Internship; work experience preferred

Special Skills and Personality Traits—Self-motivated; able to think in terms of spatial relationships and physical design; well-organized, articulate, diplomatic

CAREER LADDER

```
┌─────────────────────────────────────┐
│  Planning Director, Executive Director, │
│    or Partner in Consulting Firm        │
└─────────────────────────────────────┘

┌─────────────────────────────────────┐
│     Planner II or Senior Planner        │
└─────────────────────────────────────┘

┌─────────────────────────────────────┐
│            Planner I                    │
└─────────────────────────────────────┘
```

Position Description

Urban and Regional Planners spend much of their time thinking about the future. They draw up plans for locations of houses and roads, taking into account factors such as zoning codes and population growth. Using maps, graphs, and other tools, Urban and Regional Planners help communities revitalize the old and make way for the new.

Planning is both an art and a science, combining design skills with technical knowledge. The road to a planning career often begins with a look around one's own environment. Urban and Regional Planners believe that communities large and small benefit from an organized approach to problem solving. They involve citizens, community groups, and public officials in the planning process.

For example, a Planner working to revitalize the downtown of an old industrial city might hold public meetings to discuss possibilities for development. He or she might conduct an analysis of existing conditions and possibilities for the future. The result is the Plan, a formal document presented to community officials, who review, revise, and adopt it for action. Once the document is adopted, the Planner's job is to implement it.

Urban and Regional Planners often act as boosters for their projects. They take potential investors and developers on tours of the site. Urban and Regional Planners also might need to mediate disputes among different interest groups.

Sometimes the process does not go smoothly, as different groups may want different things. Although the Urban and Regional Planner has professional expertise, officials, advocates, and citizens may feel that *they* are the experts and therefore ignore or reject outside advice. Planners need to be flexible enough to balance their ideal plan with the realities of their communities.

Heavy volume and tight deadlines can add to the pressures of the job. Although most Urban and Regional Planners are scheduled to work a 40-hour week, they frequently attend evening or weekend meetings with citizens' groups, which add to their time on the job.

Whereas in the past, Urban and Regional Planners generally chose between two options—public planning and private consulting—many are now finding new opportunities with nonprofit organizations. Sometimes government departments contract with private or nonprofit organizations for planning services.

Urban and Regional Planners also can choose to specialize. Areas of specialization include

- Historic preservation—blending design skills with an understanding of the economic and legal issues involved in preservation
- Transportation planning—designing new transportation facilities and increasing the efficiency of existing ones
- Policy planning and management—developing policies as part of the planning process, often for a city manager or other senior administrator
- Environmental planning—working on issues such as the preservation of wetlands, the implementation of air quality strategies, and the protection of natural areas
- Urban design—combining an interest in physical design with urban policy making
- International planning and development—examining strategies for regional and national development for less developed countries, U.S. agencies, and international organizations such as the United Nations

Salaries

Beginning Urban and Regional Planners generally earn between $30,000 and $40,000 a year, according to specialists. Planners with more than five years of experience earn considerably more than their less experienced counterparts. Some offices have increased salaries to attract better qualified Urban and Regional Planners. Consulting firms offer the prospects of higher salaries and ownership potential not available through public agencies.

Employment Prospects

Employment prospects are good for Urban and Regional Planners. Help wanted ads have grown steadily, reflecting new opportunities in the nonprofit, private, and public sectors.

A strong economy boosts opportunities for Urban and Regional Planners, who benefit from increases in residential construction, commercial development, transportation, and other activities. Many of the new planning positions are in affluent, rapidly growing communities. Job applicants open to a variety of possibilities have the best chances of landing a position.

Advancement Prospects

Advancement prospects are good for Urban and Regional Planners as they can move up in a variety of ways to a higher-level planning position in their own department, to a large municipality or region, or to a consulting or related position in the private sector.

Education and Training

Education is a key requirement for Urban and Regional Planners. Although some universities offer undergraduate majors in urban and regional planning, most programs are at the graduate level. Many agencies require a master's degree for advancement. Internships are becoming an increasingly common way to gain experience in the field.

Experience, Skills, and Personality Traits

Urban and Regional Planners must be able to think in terms of spatial relationships and physical design. Lower-level planning positions generally involve more technical, computer, and research skills than upper-level positions, which depend more on leadership and administrative know-how. Much of planning involves working with people, so good communication skills are a must.

Unions and Associations

The American Planning Association is a professional organization that offers professional-development resources and publicizes job listings. The Association of Collegiate Schools of Planning is a membership organization that includes most colleges and universities in the United States that offer planning programs.

Tips for Entry

1. Look into educational programs in planning by checking out resources available through the American Planning Association's Bookstore: *Guide to Graduate Education in Urban and Regional Planning* and *Guide to Undergraduate Education in Urban and Regional Planning*.
2. If already in a planning program, apply for an internship. For some individuals, an internship offers a direct line to a full-time career position. For others, an internship provides a chance to know what they do *not* want to be doing and so motivates them to strike out in a different direction.
3. Participate in community workshops/forums sponsored by local planning organizations.
4. Network with members of a student and/or professional planning association, and become active in your local chapter.
5. Prepare a résumé for each job type (e.g., Transportation Planner or Environmental Planner).
6. Write articles showing your knowledge of community projects.
7. Check help wanted ads in local newspapers as well as the Sunday editions of regional newspapers.
8. Travel to other cities and towns to see how *they* are organized. Speak to people; take pictures. The more you learn about the nature of planning, the less you need to reinvent the wheel.
9. Consult the American Planning Association's (APA's) magazine *JobMart* and/or job listings on the Internet. The APA lists jobs at its website *www.planning.org/jobs/all.asp*.

ECONOMIC DEVELOPER

CAREER PROFILE

Duties: Encouragement of business investment and job creation; marketing; strategic planning; project management; grant writing; and financial management

Alternate Title(s): Community Development Specialist, Economic Development Manager, Downtown Developer

Salary Range: $25,000 to $50,000

Employment Prospects: Fair to good

Advancement Prospects: Good

Best Geographical Location: Municipalities

Prerequisites:

Education or Training—Bachelor's degree; master's degree increasingly preferred

Experience—Usually a few years prior work experience in a related field such as planning, marketing, banking, or nonprofit management

Special Skills and Personality Traits—Professionalism; strong communication skills; ability to interact with businesses

CAREER LADDER

```
+-------------------------------------+
|             Director                |
+-------------------------------------+


+-------------------------------------+
|        Economic Developer           |
+-------------------------------------+


+-------------------------------------+
|  Position in Related Field or Assistant  |
+-------------------------------------+
```

Position Description

Economic Developers have a special mission: to build up the economic base of their communities. They do this by supporting new and existing businesses.

Economic development is a relatively new field. Often seen as an offshoot of urban and regional planning, economic development has come into its own in recent decades.

Much of the Economic Developer's job involves marketing. In much the same way a manufacturer sells a product to consumers, Economic Developers market a community to businesses, trying to convince them of the value of locating in a particular city or town. Businesses, though, may be skeptical of what the community has to offer. The business representative might worry that the neighborhood isn't safe enough, or that there's a lack of skilled workers, or that taxes are too high. The Economic Developer tries to help businesses meet their needs without jeopardizing the welfare of the community. For instance, he or she might tell business people about a local worker-training program. The business would get trained workers; the community, a new

supply of jobs. Communities want jobs that offer desirable wages and benefits for workers.

Economic Developers need to be familiar with a variety of funding possibilities, including revolving loan funds, loan guarantees, and venture and seed capital. They also need to know how to apply for and administer grants. For example, an Economic Developer might apportion a Community Development Block Grant to neighborhood groups.

The Economic Developer spends much of the time acting as a facilitator. The individual might, for instance, raise a business's concerns about safety with the appropriate municipal officials. An Economic Developer also might work to simplify the paperwork procedures for new businesses. The community might set up a "one-stop shop" where businesses can take care of all their permitting and licensing needs.

Often the Economic Developer coordinates the efforts of several different agencies and organizations. He or she might give out and manage grants, while the local Chamber of Commerce might provide more of the hands-on help to businesses.

The Economic Developer also works to retain or improve what's already in the community. An existing business might look to the Economic Developer to help it expand or to better market the community. The Economic Developer might market the community as a tourist destination, for instance, to generate more business.

Redevelopment is a subset of economic development. Many communities have their own redevelopment authorities. If a building has been abandoned, the Economic Developer might work to get an outside developer or public funds to renovate it.

The position of Economic Developer varies with the priorities of a community. One mayor might make economic development the centerpiece of his or her administration, whereas another goes about cutting back a department. A community might make a particular project—enhancing the arts, for instance—the centerpiece of its economic development program.

Like people in other fields, Economic Developers experience both successes and setbacks. One project might trigger the revitalization of a formerly rundown area. Another could result in a bitter clash between business people and environmentalists.

Economic Developers may work out of a planning department, office of community development, or organization or agency specifically set up for economic development. Some economic development offices are set up by the government as nonprofits to facilitate the use of both private and public funds.

Salaries

The Economic Developer's salary depends on the priorities of the community and the individual's level of responsibility. On the low end of the scale are starting positions (e.g., Assistant to the Economic Developer) in smaller communities. Salaries here range from $25,000 to $40,000. In the middle range ($35,000 to $50,000) are Economic Developers with a few years of work experience. Generally, the larger the city or district, the higher the salary. Economic Developers at the Executive Director level earn between $50,000 and $150,000.

Employment Prospects

Employment prospects are fair to good because, although economic development is a growing field, it also depends on the funding priorities of the community.

Advancement Prospects

Advancement prospects are good because there is a lot of movement in the field. Powerful links connect the public, private, and nonprofit sectors. Job climbers might need to move to a new city or town, however, to advance their careers.

Education and Training

A bachelor's degree or higher is required for this position. Many Economic Developers have master's degrees in public administration, urban and regional planning, or business administration.

Because they have a variety of different backgrounds, Economic Developers can demonstrate their mastery of skills by becoming certified through either of the two national professional associations. Certification is not a substitute for work experience, however. Economic Developers need to have some work experience in order to qualify for certification programs. Candidates need to pass both an oral and a written exam in order to be certified.

Experience, Skills, and Personality Traits

Many individuals become Economic Developers after working in a different but related field. Some have experience in marketing. Others have backgrounds in property development, banking, urban and regional planning, or some other field. Most have at least a couple of years of work experience before becoming Economic Developers because a certain level of professionalism is required.

Computers have transformed this field as they have many others. Increasingly, towns, cities, and regions are using the Internet to attract business. Some large economic development departments have created separate positions for Internet specialists. Experience analyzing data, too, is helpful.

Ideally, the Economic Developer excels at both analytical thinking and marketing, combining a feel for financial management with an outgoing personality. People with drive and enthusiasm do best in this position.

Economic Developers often work under pressure. Many businesses want quick answers to complex questions. Economic Developers who can think on their feet have a leg up in this position.

The Economic Developer needs to be able to move easily from one project to another, often with tight deadlines looming. Proposals for federal or state funding need to be completed, annual reports filed, and meetings with businesses and community groups attended while someone back in the office wants to know why a particular incentive went to one business and not another. The Economic Developer needs to be able to juggle a variety of tasks at once without dropping the ball.

Unions and Associations

The Council for Urban Economic Development (CUED) and American Economic Development Council (AEDC) are the two main national associations. Membership is open to college students. Members receive publications listing job openings.

Tips for Entry

1. Read up on the field of economic development. Start by checking out the websites of CUED (*www.cued.org*)

and AEDC *(www.aedc.org).* These websites inform readers about upcoming conferences, certification courses, and issues of interest to those in the field.

2. Check the course listings for your college or university. Many have courses in economic development in urban and regional planning or public policy. Take courses in business administration to get a better sense of how businesses work.

3. Do some sort of volunteer work to understand how communities work at the neighborhood level. Join a civic or neighborhood association. These often deal with economic development issues. Volunteer to teach at a job-training center, since employment training is a big area of economic development.

4. Make the most of your own work experience. Think in terms of the customer base in whatever line of work you do. Join a junior business group or some other business-related association.

5. Get your foot in the door by working as an intern or an assistant. Another possibility is to seek out a job in a related field such as banking, real estate, or marketing. Most Economic Developers have prior work experience.

6. Develop Internet and data-gathering skills. Large economic development offices often hire people specifically to perform these functions.

7. Become familiar with different communities. Pay attention to what works and what doesn't.

MUNICIPAL CLERK

CAREER PROFILE

Duties: Administering and facilitating open access to municipal records

Alternate Title(s): City Clerk, Town Clerk, Village Clerk, Borough Clerk, City Recorder, Clerk-Treasurer, Clerk-Administrator, Clerk-Analyst, City Secretary

Salary Range: $15,000 to $150,000

Employment Prospects: Good to excellent

Advancement Prospects: Good

Best Geographical Location: None

Prerequisites:

Education or Training—College degree recommended but not required

Experience—A few years in the field

Special Skills and Personality Traits—Organizational skills; facility for moving and formatting information; sensitivity to political relationships and the needs of citizens

CAREER LADDER

```
┌─────────────────────────────────────┐
│    Elected Official or City Manager  │
└─────────────────────────────────────┘

┌─────────────────────────────────────┐
│    Deputy Clerk or Municipal Clerk   │
└─────────────────────────────────────┘

┌─────────────────────────────────────┐
│ Other Position in Municipal Government│
│   or Record/Information Management    │
└─────────────────────────────────────┘
```

Position Description

Many people think of the role of the Municipal Clerk as a strictly clerical position. It's not. The name, though, can be misleading. Why work as a mere clerk, someone might ask, when, instead, you can become a mayor or a city manager? Because, insiders say, the position involves more than its name implies.

Although Municipal Clerks have talked over the years about changing their name to make it more attractive to new applicants, they have generally held on to it out of tradition. Many communities combine the old with the new by using a hyphenated title such as *Clerk-Treasurer* or *Clerk-Administrator*. The individual in this position might oversee everything from administering the cemetery to managing the budget.

Some 16 percent of Municipal Clerks are elected officials. As other politicians do, these Municipal Clerks need to campaign for office. The rest are appointed, usually by the Mayor, city council, or local government manager. Municipal Clerks have strong opinions about which status is better—appointed or elected. Elected Clerks argue that, because they are accountable to the citizens rather than the official(s) who appointed them, they can be more neutral.

Appointed Clerks, on the other hand, emphasize the advantages of being "professionals" rather than "politicians."

Many individuals become Municipal Clerks after graduation from college or work in a lower-level, often clerical, position in municipal government. Becoming a Municipal Clerk is a step up not only in salary but also in autonomy. The position is often what the individual makes of it. If, for example, a Municipal Clerk wants to be more involved in the community, he or she might organize a day at city hall for high school students. Municipal Clerks who prefer to stick close to the office, on the other hand, can spend more of their time on records management and other tasks.

The work of the Municipal Clerk varies widely from municipality to municipality, but many do the following:

- Swear in public officials
- Keep citizen records (e.g., birth, marriage, death)
- Provide information requested by citizens and public officials
- Send out public notices
- Assume responsibility for certain aspects of voter registration/elections

- Do research and translate new laws into municipal practices and procedures
- Conduct special projects and grant-administered programs
- Prepare agendas and be responsible for the accuracy of records of public meetings

Municipal Clerks need to be well-versed in parliamentary procedure to carry out their responsibilities in public meetings. If the discussion goes astray, they might interject with a point of business. This requires neutrality and diplomacy, as do many other aspects of the job.

A public official, for instance, might object to the way he or she was portrayed in the minutes, perhaps insisting that he or she never said what was recorded. A tape recorder could come in handy in an instance like this. Another possible scenario might find one faction of the council looking for "dirt" on the other. Or, perhaps, a citizen's group wants information to help oust the mayor. The Municipal Clerk needs to respond to legitimate requests but be neutral—no easy task.

Citizens and public officials go to the Municipal Clerk's office with myriad requests. One person wants a copy of a birth or marriage certificate. Someone else wants to research the history of a particular property. Still another person wants to know about a certain zoning code or who holds the contract for a particular parcel of land.

Even in this era of high technology, records are still kept in paper form. State law dictates how long original documents are held. Once the required date has passed, the document could end up on computer disk or in storage in someone's barn, depending on the municipality.

Day-to-day operations, too, vary from municipality to municipality. Certain election responsibilities may be handled by the Municipal Clerk or the registrar of voters, depending on the municipality. Office procedures, too, vary widely. Some Municipal Clerks require people to fill out Freedom of Information Act forms to get public documents. Others think such procedures are unnecessarily "bureaucratic" and so fill requests on the spot.

Some Municipal Clerks complain about the layers of regulation—filing dates, citizen mailings, county/state record keeping—that, if not followed to a tee, can result in penalties for the municipality and big problems for the Municipal Clerk. Individuals in this position also have to deal with citizens who are impatient or even rude.

New technologies and organizing systems have professionalized this position. Today Municipal Clerks may be responsible for overseeing such new technologies as cable-TV and/or Internet sites. Subordinates usually help out with some of the more routine tasks, but the Municipal Clerk is still responsible for massive amounts of paperwork.

Salaries

Salaries vary greatly, depending on the locale. A Municipal Clerk in a small town might earn $25,000 a year compared to a salary of $100,000 in a big city.

Employment Prospects

Employment prospects are good to excellent because competition is relatively low. Few people know about this position.

Advancement Prospects

Insiders say that advancement prospects are good because Municipal Clerks become familiar with all aspects of municipal operations. If they want to move up, they know what's available. People working in small towns, however, might need to move to advance their careers.

Education and Training

A college degree is generally recommended but not required. Large cities, however, have more stringent requirements—a minimum of a bachelor's degree, sometimes a master's degree preferred.

Experience, Skills, and Personality Traits

Many individuals become Municipal Clerks after working in other positions in local government or information and record keeping. Sometimes clerical workers rise to the position of Municipal Clerk. Promotions from deputy clerk to full clerk, too, are common. Familiarity with computer systems, particularly the Internet, can be a plus.

Municipal Clerks need to have a strong customer-service focus, thus making this position a poor choice for someone seeking glamour. Individuals must be extremely detail-oriented. A missed deadline can cost a municipality dearly. Municipal Clerks also need to be diplomatic, avoiding the temptation to be drawn into one political camp or another. Elected Municipal Clerks should be outgoing enough to campaign for office.

Unions and Associations

The International Institute of Municipal Clerks (IIMC) is a nonprofit membership association.

Tips for Entry

1. Decide what type of position you want. Sixteen percent of Municipal Clerks are elected to office and so need to campaign for their position.
2. Become familiar with what Municipal Clerks do by requesting a citizen's record or public document.
3. Get your foot in the door by working in a lower-level position in municipal government. Many Municipal Clerks have "migrated" up to their current positions.
4. Set up an informational interview with a Municipal Clerk to get more information about the position.
5. If you are considering running for Municipal Clerk, have a clear set of objectives for what you hope to accomplish. You will need to file papers and get signatures in order to run for office.
6. Learn more about local area practices and networks by contacting your State Municipal League for a referral to your state's association of Municipal Clerks.

ELECTION OFFICIAL

CAREER PROFILE

Duties: Maintaining certified voter-registration file; planning, developing, and implementing election day activities

Alternate Title(s): Registrar of Voters, Director of Elections, Commissioner of Elections, Election Manager, Election Supervisor, Election Official

Salary Range: $29,000 to $100,000

Employment Prospects: Fair

Advancement Prospects: Fair

Best Geographical Location: None

Prerequisites:

Education or Training—Bachelor's degree generally required

Experience—Five to 10 years for director-level positions; less for lower-level supervisory positions

Special Skills and Personality Traits—Well-organized; team player; detail-oriented; responsible; honest; able to work long, busy hours during election season

CAREER LADDER

```
┌─────────────────────────┐
│    Election Director     │
└─────────────────────────┘

┌─────────────────────────┐
│    Election Official     │
└─────────────────────────┘

┌─────────────────────────┐
│     Election Clerk       │
└─────────────────────────┘
```

Position Description

Election Officials compare the day the polls open to the Super Bowl. For months, they gear up for the big event. A successful election requires teamwork, much as a football game does.

Work in elections has definite peaks and valleys. Election Officials use the slow seasons to prepare for the next election. New voting machines need to be ordered. Employees need to be trained, the voting rolls updated. As the busy months approach, election departments transform themselves from small operations, with just a few full-time employees, to organizations overseeing hundreds, if not thousands, of poll workers. Recruiting, training, and coordinating these temporary employees are massive undertakings, similar to running a small business. Each individual needs a suitcase of supplies, which include lists of registered voters, instructions on how to open voting machines, and provisional ballots.

No amount of preparation, though, can guarantee complete success. Sometimes voting machines break down. The Election Official might respond by dispatching a courier with paper ballots. Election Officials need to respond quickly to whatever problem arises, often with TV news cameras on the scene.

Sometimes people who show up at the polls are not the registered voters they claim to be. Election laws prohibit underaged voting, registration in a community where one no longer resides, and various other practices. Penalties, such as fines, can be imposed.

Work in elections is exacting, as every procedure has a paper trail required by law. Usually, support staff help out with the more routine tasks.

One of the hottest issues in elections today is the potential use of the Internet for voting. Fans and foes of Internet voting disagree about whether or not this technology is "just around the corner." Insiders debate topics like how to protect against "hackers" and what to do about privacy.

Election Officials also orchestrate voter registration drives and other outreach work. While in the community, they scout around for polling places, looking for spots that are accessible for voters with disabilities or other special needs.

Back in the office, they update voter-registration lists, certify nomination papers and initiative petitions, analyze population trends, evaluate new technologies, and develop overall policy. Many communities, for instance, have loosened up their requirements for registration and voting.

Whereas once absentee ballots had to be witnessed and notarized, now they can be completed with a minimum of fanfare.

Some Election Officials work closely with legislators on policy issues related to voting. If, for instance, victims of domestic abuse are afraid to vote, the Election Official might work on a special law protecting the privacy of citizens with protective orders. As a result, these citizens might be able to vote without having their names printed on voter-registration lists.

Many municipalities split election responsibilities between departments. A city clerk's office, for example, might handle some responsibilities, the Election Official's the rest.

Election Officials typically work long hours during the weeks leading up to an election. It is not unusual for supervisors and staffers to work from 6:30 A.M. to 9:00 P.M. during this period. On the big day itself, Election Officials often work until the wee hours of the morning, staying until all the votes have been counted.

Salaries

Election Officials work at several levels, with salaries varying accordingly. Salaries are highest ($50,000 to $100,000) for the director-level positions, which go by a variety of different names, such as Registrar of Voters, Director of Elections, or Election Commissioner. Below these are the Deputy Directors ($40,000 to $60,000) and Election Managers ($29,000 to $39,500).

Employment Prospects

Employment prospects are fair because this is a very specific field with fairly low turnover. Many Election Officials stay in their jobs until they retire. However, opportunities in this field exist in all communities nationwide.

Advancement Prospects

Advancement prospects are fair for Election Officials because director-level positions are relatively scarce. Some individuals advance their careers by moving to a larger municipality or, perhaps, going from the local to the state level. Another possibility is to set one's sights on an elected office—secretary of state, for example.

Lower-level positions offer more possibilities for advancement because many offices offer the flexibility to grow with the job and thus be promoted. Election Clerks, for instance, might be able to get the position upgraded to the level of Manager and/or Supervisor.

Education and Training

Most supervisory positions require a college degree but do not specify a particular course of study. A background in business and/or political science, though, can be helpful.

Experience, Skills, and Personality Traits

Elections are a specialized field in which experience counts for a lot. Full-time positions are often difficult to obtain, so many in the field get experience by working as temporary and/or part-time staffers.

People in this field need to be team players, as successful elections depend on a coordinated group effort. Election Officials work closely with municipal clerks and assessors, as well as community groups. By understanding the needs of different groups of people, Election Officials can improve access to voting. The workload can be intense, particularly during the busy seasons, but Election Officials typically look forward to the adrenaline rush they get when the polls open.

Unions and Associations

The Election Center is a nonprofit organization of registration and voting officials.

Tips for Entry

1. Volunteer or work part-time in an election. Election offices often need extra help doing the "grunt work"—folding and stuffing ballots, receiving ballots by mail, and entering voters on data-entry lists.
2. Hone your computer skills. Candidates with technological expertise have an edge in this field.
3. Read up on elections and the democratic process—particularly Internet voting, one of the most controversial issues in the field. Check out the section on Internet voting on the Election Center website (www.electioncenter.com).
4. Register to vote, if you have not already. Being a registered voter might be a prerequisite of the job.

TOWN/CITY MANAGER

CAREER PROFILE

Duties: Directing daily operations of local government; implementing the policies of elected officials; preparing, submitting, and implementing the annual budget

Alternate Title(s): Town Manager, Local Government Manager, County Administrator, Chief Administrative Officer, Municipal Manager, Professional Manager

Salary Range: $44,000 to $153,000

Employment Prospects: Good to excellent

Advancement Prospects: Good

Best Geographical Location: Regions experiencing growth

Prerequisites:
  Education or Training—Master's degree preferred
  Experience—Five to 10 years of increasingly responsible management experience
  Special Skills and Personality Traits—Strong leadership qualities; good communication skills; high ethical standards; ability to work well under stress

CAREER LADDER

```
┌─────────────────────────────────┐
│       Town/City Manager         │
└─────────────────────────────────┘

┌─────────────────────────────────┐
│    Assistant Town/City Manager  │
└─────────────────────────────────┘

┌─────────────────────────────────┐
│       Management Analyst        │
└─────────────────────────────────┘
```

Position Description

Town or City Managers serve as all-around top administrators, much as corporate presidents do. They prepare budgets, hire and fire personnel, and direct the day-to-day operations of their organizations. But Town or City Managers differ from their corporate counterparts in one important way: They work specifically to complement the leadership of elected officials. Communities hire Town or City Managers for their administrative expertise in turning policies into action. In communities with a directly elected Mayor, the Town or City Manager may have fewer responsibilities than in municipalities with a council form of government.

Over the years, the number of Town or City Managers has grown in response to the increased complexity of government. Managers need to master a variety of new skills, including how to sell a bond issue, the best way to forecast revenues, and how to encourage citizens' involvement in the government process.

As the top administrator, the Town or City Manager oversees whatever needs to be done to make the community run smoothly. Typical responsibilities include

- Meeting with council members to discuss policies and issues of concern
- Preparing the annual budget, submitting it to elected officials for approval, and implementing it once it has been approved
- Managing personnel (e.g., hiring department heads, supervising top appointees)
- Soliciting bids from government contractors
- Investigating citizens' complaints and problems

The work itself varies from day to day. The Town or City Manager might go from attending a meeting with community groups or business leaders to soliciting of bids from government contractors to returning phone calls and completing administrative reports.

Local governments are under constant pressure to improve municipal services without increasing costs. Town or City Managers look into a variety of possibilities, such as privatization, performance reviews, and citizen input. They see to it that streets are plowed and potholes filled in a timely manner.

Many Town or City Managers see themselves as being in the forefront but not the limelight, a role often reserved for elected officials. The media often focus more attention on elected officials than on Town or City Managers.

Sometimes the line separating Town or City Managers from elected officials can be a blurry one. Take policy making, for example. Some insiders believe this is clearly the domain of elected officials; others say that Town or City Managers inevitably are involved. For instance, what if Town or City Managers believe that certain proposals are financially unsound? How can they *not* advise elected officials about something involving finances? Elected officials, however, might approve the proposal anyway. The Town or City Manager has little choice but to implement it. Because local Government Managers serve at the pleasure of the council, they can be dismissed at any time.

Tight deadlines and close public scrutiny, too, can add to the pressures. Town or City Managers typically work long hours, often during the evenings and weekends. They are invited—and often expected—to attend civic functions. They also need to be on call in order to handle emergencies.

Salaries

Salaries for Town or City Managers vary widely, depending on the population and demographics of the community. Managers who work in large municipalities generally earn higher salaries than those in small towns. The average for Town Managers is about $44,000, compared to about $153,000 for Town or City Managers in large cities. County Managers generally earn about $89,000 a year; Assistant Managers, about $56,000.

Town or City Managers serve at the pleasure of elected officials and so can be dismissed at any time. Individuals in this field are encouraged to have employment agreements that outline severance arrangements.

Employment Prospects

Employment prospects are good to excellent because many communities hire professional managers.

Advancement Prospects

Advancement prospects are good because many Town or City Managers are reaching retirement age, thus creating new opportunities for those already in the field to move to larger, better-paying positions.

Education and Training

Educational requirements have changed over the years. In the early years of the profession, many Town or City Managers had backgrounds in civil engineering to help with the community's infrastructure (e.g., bridges, roads, and water systems). Today, Town or City Managers generally have master's degrees in public administration or business. These programs typically offer courses in the financial and legal issues involved in public government—subjects relevant to Town or City Managers.

Experience, Skills, and Personality Traits

Few candidates are hired as Town or City Managers right out of college. Instead, most begin with an entry-level position as an administrative assistant, management analyst, or budget specialist. Any position in local government related to municipal administration is a good stepping stone toward the position of Town or City Manager. Experience at other levels of government (e.g., state, military) or as a manager in the private sector also can be helpful.

Town or City Managers need to have the right combination of professional skills and character traits. First, they should be dedicated to improving the quality of life in their communities. They should have high ethical standards, as they are held up to close public scrutiny. Practices censured by their peers include using public money for private use, contributing to political campaigns, and engaging in conflicts of interest. Town or City Managers need to enforce the policies and regulations of elected officials regardless of their own personal or political convictions.

As the local government's chief executive officer, the Town or City Manager must provide strong leadership and be able to work with all types of personalities. Self-confidence, dedication, and a willingness to work long hours can help. Because this position involves solving the problems of the community, good decision-making skills and sound judgment are key. So, too, is the ability to work under the stress of tight deadlines.

Unions and Associations

The International City/County Management Association is a professional organization for individuals in the field.

Tips for Entry

1. Participate in student government and community activities. Understanding the administrative process can help you decide whether or not a career in government is right for you.
2. Look into graduate programs in public administration or business. Check out graduate school directories and websites to get information about programs in your area.

3. Obtain an internship, if possible. This opportunity to gain practical experience can help launch a career.

4. Contact the personnel or human resource office of the town, city, or county where you would like to work and/or state municipal associations to find out about specific career opportunities.

5. Consider joining a professional association to receive membership publications and information about upcoming events. State municipal associations often run programs for staffers and prospective employees. Being hooked into a networking system can open up doors to employment.

LOCAL/STATE SPECIALISTS

EMPLOYMENT INTERVIEWER/COUNSELOR

CAREER PROFILE

Duties: Interview job applicants; refer applicants to prospective employers; contact employers to determine personnel needs and conduct follow-up

Alternate Title(s): Employment Specialist, Job Specialist

Salary Range: $18,000 to $35,000+

Employment Prospects: Good

Advancement Prospects: Excellent

Best Geographical Location: Branch or central offices of state employment agencies

Prerequisites:

    Education or Training—Bachelor's degree or equivalent

    Experience—One year as trainee or equivalent

    Special Skills and Personality Traits—Knowledge of interviewing and placement techniques and procedures; ability to associate with people from a variety of backgrounds; familiarity with counseling and testing; ability to communicate well and exercise good judgment

CAREER LADDER

```
┌─────────────────────────────┐
│    Recruiter or Manager     │
└─────────────────────────────┘

┌─────────────────────────────┐
│    Employment Counselor     │
└─────────────────────────────┘

┌─────────────────────────────┐
│    Employment Interviewer   │
└─────────────────────────────┘
```

Position Description

Employment Interviewers and Counselors are matchmakers of sorts, pairing job seekers with prospective employers. Unlike human resources managers who deal with hiring for government jobs, Employment Interviewers and Counselors provide career service to the general public. Many of these offices have incorporated "one-stop" into their titles, having consolidated and updated service from the day they were known as the "unemployment office" for their handling of unemployment claims. They list job openings for a wide variety of occupations: blue-collar, clerical, professional/managerial. Employers throughout the area place "job orders" for positions to be filled.

Employment Interviewers and Counselors might spend part of their time collecting job orders. They contact employers to determine their specific personnel needs. What type of education and training do applicants need? How is the particular job structured? Maintaining good relations with employers is an important part of the job since this helps assure a steady stream of job orders.

Besides helping firms fill job openings, Employment Interviewers and Counselors help individuals find jobs.

Many people are looking for jobs as a condition of collecting unemployment benefits; however, anyone can visit these offices.

The Employment Interviewer straddles the ladder between a clerk and a counselor. In clear-cut cases, the Employment Interviewer takes information about the applicant's work history and refers him or her to the appropriate job listings. Usually this can be done in a single interview. Sometimes, though, applicants are unsure about their choice of an occupation. Employment Interviewers listen for certain types of comments indicating the need for counseling:

"I need a job, and I'll take anything."
"I want to do something interesting, but I don't know what."
"I hate the work I do."
"I cannot stay on a job for more than a few months."

Employment Interviewers and Counselors work together as a team. Both conduct interviews, although those of the Counselors are less structured. Counseling may take place over a period of several weeks. Many applicants have a variety of problems, including limited education, drug or alcohol addiction, and a lack of marketable skills. Some have unrealistic expectations of the job market. Employment Counselors need to be empathetic and tactful but also persuasive and firm.

In the course of working with a particular applicant, an Employment Counselor might do vocational testing, make referrals to other agencies and/or programs, and assist with résumé-writing and interviewing skills. Many employment offices offer career-development workshops and classes to the public free of charge.

Salaries

Interviewers are below Counselors in the public employment office hierarchy and so earn lower salaries, although pay varies from state to state. An Employment Interviewer, for instance, might earn $24,000 to $28,000 compared to $26,000 to $30,000 for an Employment Counselor, a more skilled position. No national government organization keeps statistics on salaries for Employment Interviewers and/or Employment Counselors.

Employment Prospects

Employment prospects are good, as employment offices are typically scattered throughout a state. In some states, the offices are organized as public-nonprofit partnerships. Competition is stiffer for the more attractive locations. Being flexible about one's choice of location can enhance an individual's employment prospects.

Advancement Prospects

Advancement prospects are excellent as employees are commonly promoted from within.

Education and Training

A bachelor's degree is generally required. Requirements are less stringent for Employment Interviewers than for Employment Counselors. For the former, experience may substitute for a degree.

Experience, Skills, and Personality Traits

Employment Interviewers and Counselors are in a helping profession and so need to be sensitive to the needs of people whose race or background differs from theirs. Good listening skills are essential. Because employment specialists commonly refer clients for outside help, they need to be familiar with social-service agencies in the area. They should also be knowledgeable about the breadth of occupations in the world of work.

Employment Counselors need to be part cheerleader, part taskmaster. They must be positive and enthusiastic in order to motivate applicants to embark on a plan for career success, yet firm enough to enforce office rules when necessary.

Unions and Associations

The International Personnel Management Association (IPMA) is a professional association for public personnel professionals.

Tips for Entry

1. Visit a state employment office, which may be called a one-stop job or career center, in your area to become familiar with the services it offers.
2. Develop your "people skills." Employment Interviewers and Counselors need to have a good feel for all types of people.
3. Check out the IPMA website (www.ipma-hr.org). Go to the student center to get an overview of the field of human resources/personnel.
4. Get your foot in the door being willing to work part-time.
5. Try to arrange for an informational interview with a manager.
6. Consider graduate school if your goal is to advance to the levels of upper management. Many graduate programs in public administration offer a concentration in human resources.
7. Visit a library to check out books, journals, and articles about human resources and labor issues. Familiarize yourself with the wide world of work by perusing resources such as the U.S. Department of Labor's *Occupational Outlook Handbook*.

LABOR RELATIONS SPECIALIST

CAREER PROFILE

Duties: Dealing with contract negotiations, employee grievances, and other workplace matters; being up-to-date on labor law and bargaining trends; researching and writing

Alternate Title(s): Employee Relations Manager, Human Resources/Personnel Specialist

Salary Range: $25,000 to $55,000

Employment Prospects: Good

Advancement Prospects: Fair to good

Best Geographical Location: States with extensive unionization of public employees

Prerequisites:

Education or Training—Bachelor's degree required; master's or law degree preferred

Experience—Prior work experience in personnel/human resources department preferred

Special Skills and Personality Traits—Good listening and communication skills; patience; fair-mindedness

CAREER LADDER

Assistant Director of Labor Relations

Labor Relations Specialist

Personnel/Human Resources

Position Description

Labor Relations Specialists deal with the relationship between unions and management in government. Workers in local and state government are typically represented by several different unions—police, firefighter, and public service worker unions, to name just a few. The Labor Relations Specialist works on behalf of management to negotiate and enforce collective bargaining agreements with the unions. These agreements can be so complex that department managers need help understanding them. The Labor Relations Specialist provides the necessary help, serving as a sort of internal consultant.

On a typical day, a Labor Relations Specialist might field several different inquiries from department managers. Who gets the first pick of vacation? Can I require an employee to work at a certain location or time? Is everything in the workplace safe by federal standards? What does the contract say about promotion and seniority? What can I do about an attendance problem?

The Labor Relations Specialist also gets involved in problems that may or may not lead to a formal grievance. Someone in a department might be threatening or harassing someone else. Another employee might be introducing

longstanding personal problems to the workplace. Still another employee might complain that he or she was disciplined or fired unfairly. Typically, contracts call for managers and employees to try to work out their own problems. If, however, this is not possible, the Labor Relations Specialist becomes involved.

Sometimes, for example, an employee might refuse to take responsibility for his or her actions. Perhaps the employee had several vehicular accidents while on the job. The Labor Relations Specialist might recommend an employee assistance program or counseling. Sometimes an outside arbitrator is called in to resolve the problem.

Another problem might be that the manager is too authoritarian. The manager might be quick to yell but reluctant to listen. The Labor Relations Specialist might help the manager develop more effective supervisory skills.

Although the Labor Relations Specialist might at times act as an advocate for labor, he or she is the representative of management. Unions have their own representatives.

Relationships between unions and management in the past have been notoriously adversarial, with bitter disagreements costing taxpayer money. To prevent such problems, management has been forced to take a more collaborative stance. Labor Relations Specialists try to help managers and employees to work together.

Busy times generally occur around contract negotiations. Before contract negotiations, a Labor Relations Specialist might survey surrounding areas to see whether or not employee salaries are competitive. The Labor Relations Specialist could then use this information to bolster management's side in the contract negotiations. For example, he or she might argue that the 5 percent pay increase requested by the union is out of line and that a 2 percent increase would be sufficient.

Negotiations can be lengthy, often lasting into the night. Patience and good people skills are musts. Once an agreement is reached, the Labor Relations Specialist generally writes it out and explains it to managers.

Sometimes the Labor Relations Specialist holds training sessions for managers on topics such as what the contract says about promotion or dealing with difficult employees. Increasingly, innovative techniques, such as the Sexual Harassment Prevention Training Game, are being used to deal with sensitive workplace issues.

The job of the Labor Relations Specialist varies, depending on the size and locale of the office. In small towns, the individual tends to be a generalist. A Labor Relations Specialist in a large city or state, on the other hand, may be assigned to only one area, such as discipline, or a single collective bargaining unit.

Although Labor Relations Specialists deal primarily with the relationship between unions and management, they also become involved in federal and state regulations governing nonunion employees. Equal opportunity and workplace safety laws, for instance, cover all workers, not just those in unions. In cities and states (primarily in the South) where government workers are not unionized, the professional dealing with employment issues would probably be called a Human Resources/Personnel Manager rather than a Labor Relations Specialist.

Salaries

The size of the office and level of the candidate's experience help determine salary. In large urban areas with more than one Labor Relations Specialist someone recently out of college might earn $25,000, compared to $40,000 to $50,000 for a more experienced professional. Salaries in smaller jurisdictions generally range from $25,000 to $40,000.

Employment Prospects

Employment prospects are good because Labor Relations Specialists help government agencies resolve potentially costly labor disputes out of court. Employment prospects are solid and growing. Solid unionization in the public sector, too, makes for stability in the field. Labor Relations Specialists can be found in local, state, and federal government.

Advancement Prospects

Advancement prospects are fair to good, depending on the number of positions that are available at a higher level. Larger departments generally offer more opportunity for advancement. Directors and assistant directors often begin as Labor Relations Specialists.

Education and Training

Labor Relations Specialists can have either a background in liberal arts or a more specialized field of study such as industrial relations, human resources, business administration, public administration, or law. Different employers look for different backgrounds. A law degree can be particularly helpful for upper-level positions such as Labor Counsel.

Experience, Skills, and Personality Traits:

Labor relations is a specialized field in which employees learn largely by doing. Previous experience in employee relations helps in this middle-management position. Some Labor Relations Specialists have worked in other fields or been promoted from clerical positions. As in many careers, knowledge of computers and information systems is useful.

Being a good listener is crucial. The Labor Relations Specialist needs to be able to relate to a wide variety of people and deal with such sensitive workplace issues as dismissal and sexual harassment in an objective manner. Patience and empathy are important qualities. The position also requires good research and writing skills as well as some public speaking.

The Labor Relations Specialist works in a highly confidential environment and so should convey a sense of integrity and discretion. Knowing when to be persuasive and when to stand back is an important part of the job.

Unions and Associations

Associations of interest to Labor Relations Specialists include the National Public Employer Labor Relations Association (NPELRA), the International Personnel Management Association (IPMA); and the Society for Human Resources Management (SHRM).

Tips for Entry

1. Consider various courses of study for this interdisciplinary field. A combination of social sciences, business, and behavioral sciences can be particularly useful. Many graduate programs in public administration offer a specialty in human relations. Only a few universities offer programs specifically in labor relations.
2. Look into internship possibilities.
3. Be up-to-date on developments in labor law by following the news. Pay attention, in particular, to big-city newspapers since they are most likely to provide

comprehensive coverage of labor issues in a large unionized city.

4. Join a professional association dealing specifically with labor relations or the broader field of public administration.

5. Talk to people in labor relations. Ask to sit in on a contract negotiation or other type of meeting.

6. Ask about the possibility of a part-time position if the municipality lacks funding for a full-time Labor Relations Specialist.

ENVIRONMENTAL SPECIALIST

CAREER PROFILE

Duties: Conducts studies, inspections, and research projects; prepares reports; carries out or oversees programs to protect the environment

Alternate Title(s): Conservation Agent, Environmental Analyst, Environmental Health Manager, Environmental Manager, Environmental Planner, Environmental Engineer, Compliance Officer

Salary Range: $25,000 to $70,000

Employment Prospects: Good to excellent

Advancement Prospects: Good to excellent

Best Geographical Location(s): Varies by specialty (e.g., forestry in heavily wooded regions, coastal management by oceans); regulatory offices generally located in state capitals

Prerequisites:

Education or Training—Varies; graduate degree may be needed for advancement

Experience—Two years generally required

Special Skills and Personality Traits—Concern for the environment; desire to work indoors and outside; attention to detail; analytical skills; ability to interpret technical data and communicate results; willingness to work under pressure

CAREER LADDER

```
┌─────────────────────────────┐
│    Director or Consultant    │
└─────────────────────────────┘

┌─────────────────────────────┐
│   Environmental Specialist   │
└─────────────────────────────┘

┌─────────────────────────────┐
│      Intern or Student       │
└─────────────────────────────┘
```

Position Description

Environmental Specialists in government protect the environment in ways unimaginable only a few decades ago. Few fields have grown as quickly and dramatically as this one. Before 1960, the environmental field consisted mainly of park rangers, foresters, and a small number of public health officials. Then there occurred a massive shift in consciousness, as people began to realize that the Earth's resources were limited. The environmental movement was born. Two landmark events occurred in 1970: the creation of the Environmental Protection Agency (EPA) and the passage of the Clean Air Act. The Clean Water Act and myriad other initiatives followed.

Environmental Specialists in government encompass a variety of professionals (e.g., planners, pollution-control regulators, natural resource managers, educators, communicators), with some positions considerably more technical than others. A position monitoring air pollution might involve chemistry, engineering, and public health. Someone working to redevelop contaminated land, on the other hand, might need to know more about planning issues.

Environmental issues are often controversial, pitting one constituency against another, although sometimes different groups find common solutions. At the local level, for instance, a partnership might be formed between a municipality and a gas company to replace the old gas caps on citizens' cars. Citizens would get improved gas mileage and a reduction in air pollution. The oil company would improve its public image. Local initiatives also might include purchasing property for conservation purposes.

Large cities typically have environmental management departments headed by a Director. Underneath the Director might be Assistant Directors in charge of the following specialties:

- Air—helping communities stay within the ozone compliance levels stipulated by the Clean Air Act
- Water—preventing contamination of storm water and drinking water by pollution
- Land—redeveloping environmentally contaminated properties known as "brownfields" to prevent sprawl and encourage "smart growth"
- Solid waste—managing landfills and trash
- Recycling—establishing or operating efficient programs.

State environmental agencies tend to be involved more in regulatory matters as required by the federal Environmental Protection Agency. Over the years, many responsibilities for environmental protection have shifted from the federal government to the states. Each state also has a centralized operation for emergency management to respond to disasters ranging from floods and tornadoes to riots and terrorist attacks. Most environmental agencies either combine both regulatory and natural resource operations or focus on one of the two.

Of the two, regulatory jobs tend to be the more technical. State regulators inspect the property of different industries to make sure they are not harming the environment. A typical day might involve reviewing compliance data; determining what, if any, enforcement actions are needed; and participating in the development of regulations. The mix of engineering and science, on the one hand, and policy making and politics, on the other, depends on the position.

Natural resource agencies typically deal with biological, ecological, or forestry issues; environmental education; and environmental management. These individuals work as caretakers of the public lands. Some might, for example, coordinate a waterway program.

Environmental Specialists are often constrained in their decision making by technical information and the law. If, for instance, a factory with a wastewater discharge demonstrates through technical documentation that it can meet treatment requirements, the permit is issued even though citizens might object.

Local and state environmental agencies can, however, establish their own policies. A state might develop its own standards for companies exempted (under a "grandfather" clause) from the Clean Air Act or implement "burden reduction" techniques to make environmental protection more flexible and cost-effective. As a new era dawns for the environmental movement, emphasis is increasingly being placed on *preventing* pollution.

Salaries

Salaries vary according to an individual's level of responsibility. Although positions generally fall into the $25,000 to $70,000 range, someone in a small municipality might earn considerably less. Many positions are ranked by level—Environmental Specialist I, Environmental Specialist II, and so forth. Salaries increase with supervisory and management responsibilities. Many individuals start their careers in the $25,000 to $30,000 range and relatively quickly reach $43,000 to $47,000, then slow down before topping out in the $65,000 to $70,000 range, according to the Environmental Careers Organization.

Employment Prospects

Employment prospects are good to excellent because environmental work is a rapidly evolving field open to a variety of professionals: planners, educators and communicators, pollution-control specialists, and natural resource managers. Within these broad areas, individuals can choose from a number of specialties such as air, water, land and waste, fishery and wildlife, and coastal management. Jobs are becoming increasingly sophisticated.

Advancement Prospects

Advancement prospects are good to excellent because of the variety of agencies and organizations involved in the environment. Possibilities exist at the federal as well as the state and local levels, especially with a group of agencies collectively known as the Big Five: the U.S. Forest Service, National Park Service, Bureau of Land Management, Fish and Wildlife Service, and Environmental Protection Agency. Another federal agency involved in environmental issues is the Federal Emergency Management Administration.

As Environmental Specialists climb the career ladder, they become more involved in management and policy making. Environmental Specialists also work in the nonprofit and private sector.

Although Environmental Specialists often move from the public to the higher-paying private sector (causing employee retention problems for government agencies, insiders say), some individuals go in the opposite direction. Someone might change from working for a water or energy consulting firm, for example, to becoming the director of water conservation for a city.

Education and Training

Someone interested in a career related to the environment can choose from a variety of educational options. Interdisciplinary programs in environmental science have mushroomed over the past few decades at the associate's, bachelor's, and graduate levels. At the associate's degree level, many programs provide the training needed for the more technical aspects of environmental careers. Bachelor's degree programs in environmental studies combine science, engineering, government, law, and a variety of other disciplines.

As the field has become increasingly sophisticated, many people with bachelor's degrees are finding the need to continue their education to advance their careers. Graduate programs in environmental science are often linked to another specialty, such as public administration, public health, engineering, or urban and regional planning.

Educational requirements vary by position. Whereas a background in botany might be ideal for someone working on public gardens, a master's degree in public health would be better for an individual dealing with the health effects of air pollution. Positions with titles like *Planner* or *Engineer* might be open to candidates with a variety of educational backgrounds. Agencies set their own educational requirements.

Experience, Skills, and Personality Traits

A couple of years of experience in the field is highly desired. Internships, in particular, can open up doors to career-oriented positions. Backgrounds in science, statistics, and communication are useful. Environmental Specialists must have the analytical skills and attention to detail required to interpret data, prepare reports, and communicate results effectively.

On a more personal level, Environmental Specialists in government must be able to withstand the stress that results from dealing with controversial issues subject to criticism from the media and the public. Many Environmental Specialists work long hours under pressure.

Unions and Associations

Associations of broad interest include the Student Conservation Association, the National Associations of Environmental Professionals, and the Environmental Careers Organization.

An Environmental Specialist might also belong to the National Association of Local Government Environmental Professionals, the Environmental Council of the States, and more specialized organizations such as the Soil and Water Conservation Society or the Air and Waste Management Association.

Tips for Entry

1. Familiarize yourself with the role of government in environmental affairs. A good place to start is the Environmental Protection Agency website *(www.epa. gov/history)*. Many state and local governments also have websites for government agencies. Browsing these can help you pinpoint an area of interest.
2. Volunteer to work in your field of interest for an environmental agency.
3. Seek out opportunities for internships as well as seasonal or part-time employment. These opportunities are widely available, offering both paid and unpaid positions. Some are offered through professional associations such as the Student Conservation Association and the Environmental Careers Organization.
4. Look into environmental programs at the undergraduate and/or graduate level.
5. Check out environmental career websites, which include internships as well as regular job openings.
6. Look beyond city and county to regional entities such as regional planning commissions, solid waste planning districts, or water management districts. Ask someone in a local environmental department for leads in your area.

VICTIM ADVOCATE

CAREER PROFILE

Duties: Educating victims and witnesses about the rights and services available to them; informing them about the criminal justice proceedings; providing emotional support; acting as liaison with the prosecutor

Alternate Title(s): Domestic-Abuse Victim Advocate, Sexual-Assault Victim Advocate, Child Victim Advocate, Victim Assistance Specialist, Victim Witness Coordinator

Salary Range: $20,000 to $50,000

Employment Prospects: Good to excellent

Advancement Prospects: Excellent

Best Geographical Location: District attorney's offices nationwide

Prerequisites:
Education or Training—Bachelor's degree preferred
Experience—Two years related experience preferred
Special Skills and Personality Traits—Ability to develop rapport with others quickly; empathy; flexibility; interest in the legal system

CAREER LADDER

```
┌─────────────────────────────────┐
│   Director of Victim Advocacy    │
│      or Victim Specialist        │
└─────────────────────────────────┘

┌─────────────────────────────────┐
│          Victim Advocate          │
└─────────────────────────────────┘

┌─────────────────────────────────┐
│   Intern, Worker in Related Field │
│    (e.g., counseling, teaching)   │
└─────────────────────────────────┘
```

Position Description

Victim Advocates in District Attorney's offices guide victims and witnesses through the legal process. This relatively new position is part teacher, part counselor, and part legal specialist.

Until a couple of decades ago, victims of crime had few legal rights. Grieving relatives and victims themselves were kept out of the courtroom on the grounds that they might prejudice juries. Victims and witnesses received only a legal summons to court with no accompanying information or contact person to answer their questions. Prosecutors sometimes lost cases because they were too busy to prepare victims and witnesses adequately for trial.

Then the victim's rights movement arose. People began to talk openly about the impact of crimes such as rape, domestic violence, and child abuse. The federal government passed numerous bills, including the Victim and Witness Protection Act of 1982, the Victims of Crime Act of 1984, the Child Victims' Bill of Rights in 1990, and the Violence against Women Act of 1994. States began to require services for victims.

These new laws give victims legal rights in three basic areas:

- Information
- Notification
- Participation

Victim Advocates can now be found in virtually every District Attorney's office in the nation. They notify victims and advocates about upcoming hearings, inform them about victim compensation, and solicit their input in the case. As the prosecutor handles legal strategy, the Victim Advocate gives victims and witnesses the emotional support they need to get through the process. They help them apply for victim compensation and prepare them for questioning on the witness stand.

On a typical day, a Victim Advocate juggles ongoing cases with questions from new callers. A Victim Advocate might get a call from a woman who says her two grown children just told her they were abused by their grandfather. Do they need to speak to the police? Are they going to be cross-examined in court? Will their names be printed in the press? The Victim Advocate replies yes to the first two questions, no to the third. The names of sexual-abuse victims are generally kept out of the newspapers. Someone else might want to drop charges against the boy who stole her 12-year-old son's bicycle. The Victim Advocate replies that the court will take into account the woman's call for leniency but may proceed with the charges.

Other callers are reluctant to testify. They might have trouble getting transportation to the courthouse or worry about taking time off from work. Will they be reimbursed for their time and/or expenses (e.g., medical bills) related to the crime? The Victim Advocate may present some possibilities—restitution by the defendant, a local fund for victims—but emphasizes that there are no guarantees.

Many callers express cynicism about the criminal justice system. Why go forward when the defendant will just "cop a plea" or get a "slap on the wrist"? How can witnesses know that defendants won't go after them in retaliation? It is the Victim Advocate's job to explain that there are no guarantees, but, if the victim or witness does nothing, the defendant may continue committing crimes. Once the court process winds to a close, the Victim Advocate prepares the individual for what lies ahead.

Salaries

Salaries generally range from $20,000 to $50,000, with small districts on the low end of the scale and larger areas paying in the higher range. Salaries, too, increase with experience and promotion to program management positions.

Employment Prospects

Employment prospects are good to excellent because this is a rapidly growing field. Laws requiring victim services have led to the creation of new jobs across the country.

Advancement Prospects

Advancement prospects are excellent because Victim Advocates in a District Attorney's office can move in a variety of directions, including running for political office. The Washington State senator Jeralita Costa, for example, has an extensive background in victim advocacy.

Some Victim Advocates go on to law school. Others advance to supervisory positions within their own office or move to larger jurisdictions—from the district to the federal level, for instance. Still others take advantage of other opportunities dealing with victim issues, particularly in the nonprofit sector, including

- Speaking, training, and consulting
- Research/legislative efforts
- Program development
- Public awareness programs
- Prevention programs
- National victim organizations

Because this field is relatively young, new specialties are evolving. Some Advocates handle identity theft or cybercrimes. Other Advocates work with victims who do not speak English. A Victim Advocate knowledgeable about a certain specialty can carve out his or her own niche as an expert.

Education and Training

Victim Advocates have a variety of educational backgrounds. Many have bachelor's degrees in psychology or criminal justice. Some have graduate degrees. Others have an associate's degree.

New laws requiring victim services have prompted some jurisdictions to move existing personnel, such as secretaries, into the position of Victim Advocate. Because of this "training gap," states are moving toward certification for Victim Advocates. Supervisory positions may require a law degree.

Experience, Skills, and Personality Traits

Many Victim Advocates have a background in counseling, criminal justice, or a related field. Victim Advocates must be able to establish a rapport with others quickly, as usually their first contact with the people they serve is over the phone.

Many people have unrealistic ideas about victims; those who work with them understand that they are sometimes angry or difficult. Sometimes prosecutors, too, might have agendas that clash with those of Victim Advocates. If, for example, the prosecutor wants to plea bargain a case that the victim wants to put before a jury, the Victim Advocate might be caught in the middle.

Victim Advocates must have the "people skills" needed to defuse negative emotions such as anger, sadness, and outrage without dismissing them. Patience, empathy, and an ability to present information matter-of-factly help Victim Advocates be effective, as does a clear understanding of the legal system.

Unions and Associations

The National Organization for Victim Assistance is a private nonprofit organization of individuals involved in victim and witness rights and services. Other organizations dealing with victim issues include the Office for Victims of Crime and the National Center for Victims of Crime.

Tips for Entry

1. Take courses in counseling, criminal justice, law, psychology, and women's issues to become knowledgeable about the field.
2. Volunteer for a crisis hotline or intervention center that provides free training.

3. Get a job in a fast-paced, people-oriented field such as teaching or counseling.
4. Watch criminal trials to observe cross-examination and other experiences faced by victims and witnesses.
5. Browse the Internet, using the keyword *victim.* Use the same keyword to look for books, including first-person accounts by victims, in local libraries.

PUBLIC HEALTH PROFESSIONAL

CAREER PROFILE

Duties: Planning, designing, and administering public health programs; communicating with the public and the media; collaborating with others to provide health services

Alternate Title(s): Division Director, Program Coordinator, Epidemiologist, Policy Analyst, Health Agent

Salary Range: $27,000 to $68,000+

Employment Prospects: Good

Advancement Prospects: Good

Best Geographical Location: Nationwide, with more opportunities in large population centers

Prerequisites:

Education or Training—Master's degree required

Experience—Two to five years of graduate field experience

Special Skills and Personality Traits—Management skills; cultural sensitivity; analytical abilities; discretion in handling confidential information

CAREER LADDER

```
┌─────────────────────────────────┐
│   Senior Public Health Official  │
│         or Consultant            │
└─────────────────────────────────┘

┌─────────────────────────────────┐
│    Public Health Professional    │
└─────────────────────────────────┘

┌─────────────────────────────────┐
│        Graduate Student          │
│      or Program Assistant        │
└─────────────────────────────────┘
```

Position Description

Public Health Professionals are commonly asked one question: What, exactly, is the difference between "health" and "public health"? Health, they reply, deals with *individual* patients, whereas public health involves the needs of entire *communities*. Public Health Professionals plan, design, and administer an ever-changing array of programs to provide for the wellness of citizens. They assess the health needs of the community to answer questions like, Should funds be allocated for teen parenting, violence prevention, fluoridation, tuberculosis screening, or something else? What should their role be in immunizations? How can they collaborate with hospitals, health maintenance organizations (HMOs), nonprofits, and others in the community to assure that the health needs of all citizens are being met?

Increasingly, public health agencies are moving away from direct clinical care, following the general shift in government toward privatization and collaboration with other organizations. A Public Health Professional concerned about the high rate of diabetes among minorities, for example, might enlist the help of a prominent member of the clergy to publicize the problem. A city might go from immunizing patients to outsourcing to HMOs, while providing tracking and oversight.

Public Health Officials sometimes need to make quick decisions for the public welfare. How much of a risk does a mosquito-borne virus killing crows pose to humans? Is it enough to justify spending taxpayer money on spraying with insecticides? What can a community do to respond to someone who may have purposely been infecting others with the acquired immunodeficiency syndrome (AIDS) virus?

At the municipal level, Public Health Professionals often share decision making with a local board of health. If, for example, the Public Health Professional wants to implement an indoor smoking ban, he or she might have to go through the local board of health. In the case of the outbreak of a disease, on the other hand, the Public Health Professional might have the authority to act because of the risks involved in waiting to convene a board.

Local and state agencies vary in organization. In some states, top local Public Health Officials need to have a medical degree; in others, they don't. Environmental and public health might be combined into one department, typically called "environmental health," that addresses issues such as safe drinking water and air quality. Public health might also be a department of health and human services.

At the state level, Public Health Professionals head up a variety of programs. An individual might direct a program providing pregnant women and children access to health insurance, design and implement a community-based AIDS program for people recently released from correctional facilities and substance-abuse treatment centers, or conduct research analysis on the disease and mortality rates at hazardous waste sites.

In addition, Public Health Professionals

- Respond to state and federal mandates requiring the reporting of various diseases
- Speak to the media to inform citizens about public health concerns
- Prepare budgets, apply for grants, and award contracts
- Write reports
- Conduct statistical analyses
- Develop and conduct in-service training programs, workshops, and conferences
- Serve on advisory boards, coalitions, and commissions.

Salaries

Salary figures for Public Health Professionals in local and state government are difficult to pinpoint because of the lack of statistical information for various positions. According to the Association of Schools of Public Health, the salaries of Public Health Professionals in local/state government range from about $27,450 to $68,000.

Employment Prospects

Employment prospects are good because Public Health Professionals are needed in research, management, education, and policy making. Shortages of Public Health Professionals are expected to continue well into the 21st century, according to the Association of Schools of Public Health.

Opportunities exist at the local, state, and federal levels of government as well as in the private and nonprofit sectors. Among the trends responsible for creating an increased demand for Public Health Professionals are an increased reliance on managed care, which places greater emphasis on devising prevention strategies; infectious diseases such as acquired immunodeficiency syndrome (AIDS) and multidrug-resistant strains of tuberculosis, which require more surveillance, intervention, education, and research; and an aging population, increasing the demand for delivery of geriatric health care programs.

Advancement Prospects

Advancement prospects are good because of the variety of opportunities. Someone might go from the local or state level to a position with one of the three big federal agencies: the Centers for Disease Control and Prevention, the Health Resources and Services Administration, and the National Institutes of Health. An individual interested in public health policy might also become a congressional aide or other government staffer.

Public Health Professionals also can move between sectors. Someone might, for example, go from a position in government to one with a think tank, corporation, consulting firm, or nonprofit organization.

Education and Training

Although someone might get an entry level position with a college degree or less, many other positions call for a master's degree in either public health or public administration. Positions for top public health officials in some states call for a medical degree.

Public Health Professionals straddle the middle levels of the career ladder, taking part in program management, policy making, and other activities. Some positions might call for a background in public health, others in management. Many graduate programs in public health offer joint degree options in law, business, public administration, or some other discipline.

Experience, Skills, and Personality Traits

Public Health Professionals generally acquire experience in the field in graduate school and/or in lower-level positions. Many positions are ranked by level, such as Program Manager I, II, and II; higher level positions call for higher levels of experience and/or education.

Public Health Professionals wear a variety of hats: technical expert, communicator, data analyst, educator, policy maker, and manager. Individuals must be attentive to detail and government reporting requirements. Policy making requires political savvy. Whatever combination of hats one wears, having a firm commitment to public health, and government service in general, is vital.

Unions and Associations

Prominent organizations include the Association of Schools of Public Health, the National Association of County & City Health Officials, and the Association of State and Territorial Health Officials.

Tips for Entry

1. Explore the field of public health by volunteering or working in an entry-level position.
2. Look into graduate school options. Two places to begin: Association of Schools of Public Health

(www.asph.org) and the National Association of Schools of Public Affairs and Administration *(www.naspaa.org).*

3. Hone your political skills if you hope eventually to become a public health official, as top positions are commonly political appointments. Also, insiders add, legislation and programs often have political strings attached.

4. Browse the websites of local and state public-health agencies as well as those of the three major federal agencies: the National Institutes of Health *(www.nih. gov),* Health Resources and Services Administration *(www.hrsa.gov),* and Centers for Disease Control and Prevention *(www.cdc.gov).*

EMERGENCY MANAGER

CAREER PROFILE

Duties: Responsible for program administration and program development encompassing all phases of emergency management

Alternate Title(s): Mitigation Officer, Response/Recovery Officer, Emergency Management Coordinator, Training Officer, Antiterrorism Planner, Hazard Mitigation Specialist

Salary Range: $27,000 to $75,000

Employment Prospects: Good

Advancement Prospects: Good

Best Geographical Location(s): Positions throughout the nation

Prerequisites:

Education or Training—Four-year degree in emergency management or related field (e.g., public administration, planning) and/or field training; master's degree sometimes preferred

Experience—One to five years of related experience; field experience required for advancement

Special Skills and Personality Traits—Knowledge of principles, practices, procedures, and techniques of emergency management; ability to learn quickly; good people skills; coolness under pressure; willingness to be on call in case of emergency.

CAREER LADDER

```
┌─────────────────────────────┐
│          Director           │
└─────────────────────────────┘

┌─────────────────────────────┐
│     Emergency Manager       │
└─────────────────────────────┘

┌─────────────────────────────┐
│  Temporary Disaster Worker  │
│ or Member of Allied Profession │
│  (e.g., police, fire, military) │
└─────────────────────────────┘
```

Position Description

Emergency Managers coordinate programs to protect citizens from dangers ranging from hurricanes to terrorist attacks.

As the world grapples with a growing list of technological hazards, Emergency Managers have assumed new importance. Emergency Managers administer plans and services to help communities and states prepare for, respond to, and recover from both natural dangers and those caused by human beings.

This broad interdisciplinary profession combines elements of public safety with components of public administration, planning, environmental protection, and public health. Yet, as Emergency Managers draw from other professions, they also have carved out their own identity—more behind-the-scenes than first-line responders such as firefighters and police and more specialized than other public administrators.

Emergency Managers oversee the development of comprehensive plans to be followed in times of crisis. Such plans made it possible for officials to respond quickly to the terrorist attacks of September 11, 2001. Emergency Managers coordinated the steps needed to block off streets in the vicinity of the World Trade Center quickly because they knew whom to call for barricades, which intersections needed police, and how to initiate the paper trail needed to document that each task was completed.

Emergency Managers describe a four-step process needed to keep citizens safe:

- Mitigation
- Preparedness
- Response
- Recovery

Mitigation, the cornerstone of emergency management, involves the ongoing effort to lessen the impact of disasters on people and property. In this phase, Emergency Managers might propose initiatives such as modifying building codes to make houses more resistant to disaster. They also identify and assess the risks affecting the community.

Risk assessments vary from jurisdiction to jurisdiction. An Emergency Manager for a coastal community might identify hurricanes as a high risk, whereas a colleague in a highly industrialized city might be more concerned about chemical hazards posed by local factories. Still another Emergency Manager might take steps to safeguard the water supply and shopping mall because both serve large numbers of citizens.

Emergency Managers maintain comprehensive Emergency Operation Plans (EOPs), typically hundreds of pages long, outlining who is responsible for what during an emergency. For example, the EOP might detail the United States National Guard's responsibility for maintaining tankers of water for use in large-scale fire fighting.

During the preparedness phase, Emergency Managers provide the leadership and training needed to cope with disaster. State governments assist municipalities, which are responsible for most first-line activities for emergency preparation and response. Emergency Managers commonly hold exercises during which participants respond to a simulated emergency.

If a real emergency occurs, Emergency Managers follow agreed-upon procedures. They activate an Emergency Operations Center, which coordinates response to a crisis in much the same way that Mission Control orchestrates a space launch. The Emergency Manager responds to calls from the field. Volunteers are dispatched to wherever they are needed. Then, during the recovery phase, Emergency Managers work on getting all systems back to normal.

On any given day, an Emergency Manager might work on various parts of the four-step cycle. Risks are always being assessed and plans continually updated. Emergency Managers also

- Advise other agencies and organizations in the development and maintenance of their respective parts of the Emergency Operations Plan
- Establish and maintain the Emergency Operations Center on a continual basis
- Participate in in-state and interstate mutual aid programs
- Provide training in emergency planning as needed
- Attend meetings and give talks about emergency management to various civic fraternal, educational, religious, and other groups
- Respond to federal requirements

Salaries

Salaries vary according to the individual's level of experience and the size of the jurisdiction. Some communities rely largely on part-timers and/or volunteers for emergency management. Emergency Managers with limited experience, who work in relatively small communities, might earn around $27,000 compared to $75,000 for their more experienced counterparts in larger jurisdictions, specialists say. Salaries for Emergency Managers with the Federal Emergency Management Administration tend to be higher than those at the state level, which, in turn, tend to be higher than those at the local level.

Employment Prospects

Employment prospects are good because new threats to public safety have created a greater awareness of the need for emergency management. Industry experts predict an increase in the number of positions as policy makers earmark more time and money for emergency management. Because of the interdisciplinary nature of this field, large emergency management departments commonly hire individuals with a variety of backgrounds. Someone with a background in communications, for instance, might be hired as a Public Information Officer, and an individual with a background in human services might be in charge of relief work.

Emergency management positions can be found at the local, state, and federal levels. At the federal level, the Federal Emergency Management Administration hires not only full-time employees but also Disaster Assistance Employees paid by the hour for service during emergencies.

Each of the 50 states has an emergency management department, although it might be called by a slightly different name. State emergency management departments serve as conduits for information and resources from the federal government to municipalities. In an actual emergency, emergency management directors report directly to the Governor.

In a small state the Emergency Manager is likely to be a jack-of-all-trades, whereas in a larger state positions are more specialized. A position in mitigation or recovery dealing particularly with government grant programs and interagency planning might require a background in public administration, whereas a position leading preparedness exercises might be best suited for someone with a background in fire protection, law enforcement, emergency services, or the military.

At the local level, emergency management might be headed up by an Emergency Management Specialist or a sheriff, fire chief, or other public safety officer. Industry specialists expect the number of positions and departments devoted specifically to emergency management to increase in response to growing concern about technological hazards. A variety of departments, including zoning boards, public health departments, environmental agencies, police and fire departments, and 911 dispatch, are also involved in aspects of emergency management.

Advancement Prospects

Advancement prospects are good because of growth in this field. Some Emergency Managers advance their careers by moving from a small to a larger jurisdiction—from local to state government, for example. Others move into positions vacated by individuals reaching retirement age. Still others find opportunities outside government. Hospitals, universities, relief-oriented nonprofits, and private companies are among the groups offering positions in or related to emergency management.

Education and Training

Emergency Managers have a variety of backgrounds. Whereas some Emergency Managers have received most of their training on the job (e.g., fire protection, law enforcement, the military) and through professional-development courses, others hold undergraduate and/or graduate degrees. Some positions specify academic degrees in emergency management or allied fields such as public administration or urban and regional planning. A master's degree may be preferred. In addition to program management, Emergency Managers are commonly involved in public communication and human services, and some specialized positions are geared for individuals with backgrounds in those fields.

In the past 10 years, numerous colleges and universities have established specific academic programs in emergency management. The Federal Emergency Management Administration (FEMA) has encouraged the development of new academic programs to provide the growing sophistication needed for the profession.

According to FEMA's Higher Education College List of 2001, some 24 schools offer a certificate, diploma, or minor in emergency management; 11 schools offer associate degree programs; nine schools offer bachelor's degree programs; 17 schools offer master's degree programs; and six schools offer doctoral degree programs. Another 45 schools are investigating or developing programs in emergency management.

Programs vary in orientation: Some programs focus more on the technical aspects of emergency management; others, particularly at the master's level, are geared more toward public administration. An emergency management program might include classes such as introduction to crisis and emergency management, hazard mitigation, disaster recovery, and terrorism and emergency management. Courses related to emergency management are also offered through public health, environmental science, and other departments.

In addition to academic training, Emergency Managers who have the required years of work experience can seek professional certification. The International Association of Emergency Managers offers two levels of certification: Associate Emergency Manager and Emergency Manager.

Experience, Skills, and Personality Traits

Positions require different levels of experience, depending on the level of responsibility. Someone who has just graduated from an emergency management degree program might gain experience through an internship and/or a temporary position in the wake of a disaster. Supervisory positions generally require more extensive experience.

For success in this field, individuals must be cool under pressure. Calls come in from the field—a firefighter might be trapped in a building—and the Emergency Manager needs to know how to respond quickly and effectively. Individuals should understand how different key elements of the system (e.g., public works, fire department, and emergency medical services) work to hold duplication to a minimum.

Emergency Managers also must stay up-to-date on changes in technology and methodology. Individuals must be able to collaborate with others who might have the specialized information they need to keep citizens safe. Emergency Managers who have earned the trust of others are most successful on the job.

On a more personal level, Emergency Managers must be able to cope with the anxiety of facing a sudden crisis. Individuals are on call in case of emergency. Every time the phone rings, Emergency Managers must be prepared to respond to disaster.

Unions and Associations

The International Association of Emergency Managers represents professionals throughout the industry; the National Emergency Management Association is an organization for directors of state emergency management agencies.

Tips for Entry

1. Volunteer with the American Red Cross (www.redcross.org) or a government emergency management agency. The American Red Cross offers formal disaster training programs on a variety of subjects. Emergency Operations Centers activated during times of crisis also provide opportunities for volunteers.
2. Look into courses and programs in emergency management. The Emergency Management Institute of the Federal Emergency Management Administration (FEMA) lists programs in emergency management on its website (www.fema.gov/emi). The training office of your state emergency management agency also might provide courses.
3. View listings of emergency management jobs maintained by FEMA (http://www.fema.gov/career), the International Association of Emergency Managers

(www.iaem.com), and the National Emergency Management Association *(www.nemaweb.org).*

4. Check out internship opportunities with the Federal Emergency Management Association (FEMA) and other agencies.

5. Browse websites of FEMA *(www.fema.gov)* and state emergency management agencies to become familiar with the work done in this profession.

AUDITOR

CAREER PROFILE

Duties: Participating in audit planning; meeting with department managers being audited; conducting field-work; writing audit reports

Alternate Title(s): Program Auditor, Performance Auditor, Auditor I, Auditor II, and so on

Salary Range: $25,000 to $60,000+

Employment Prospects: Excellent

Advancement Prospects: Excellent

Best Geographical Location(s): Large cities and state capitals

Prerequisites:

Education or Training—Bachelor's degree; Certified Public Accountant (CPA) or other certification helpful

Experience—One year as trainee

Special Skills and Personality Traits—Business aptitude; ability to collect, compile, analyze, and interpret data; objective outlook; commitment to public service; strong writing and communication abilities

CAREER LADDER

```
┌─────────────────────────┐
│    Audit Supervisor     │
└─────────────────────────┘

┌─────────────────────────┐
│        Auditor          │
└─────────────────────────┘

┌─────────────────────────┐
│     Auditor Trainee     │
└─────────────────────────┘
```

Position Description

Auditors examine the records of government agencies and contractors to ensure that public funds are used properly and services performed appropriately. Although the term *Auditor* sometimes refers specifically to the top elected or appointed official, the title also encompasses the many staffers who carry out the actual work of gathering information, analyzing data, and writing reports to document financial improprieties, inefficiencies, and other problems. They also set forth steps to remedy the problems.

State auditing departments tend to be large operations, with some 200 to 800 Auditors of varying levels, whereas city agencies are smaller, averaging staffs of between 15 and 20, according to the National Association of State Auditors, Comptrollers, and Treasurers (NASACT). State and City Auditors commonly provide toll-free numbers for citizens to call with complaints of government wrongdoing.

Auditing is technically a subset of accounting, although, in government, it also draws heavily on the principles of public administration. Government auditors fall into two basic groups:

- Financial Auditors
- Performance Auditors

Insiders say that although a degree in accounting is generally required of Financial Auditors, it is not essential for Performance Auditors, whose work involves a broader range of responsibilities. Some Performance Auditors could also be called Program Evaluators. Performance Auditors evaluate an organization's operations with an eye toward making it work better, faster, and cheaper. Many audits involve a mix of financial and performance elements.

In a typical audit, Auditors work under the direction of a Supervisor or Manager, spending much of their time in the offices of the "auditee." For example, if a local Auditor is auditing the housing authority, he or she might spend 18 months at that assignment, working at a temporary desk.

The first phase of the work involves planning. Is the audit going to focus on the entire agency or one segment of its operations? What were the findings of the last audit? Should the audit be broken down into several small reports or one major report?

Next is a meeting known as an entrance conference with the managers of the agency being audited. During this conference, Auditors explain the scope of the audit and the access they will need to various records.

Then Auditors conduct their fieldwork. An Auditor with a nonaccounting background might be paired with a Certified Public Accountant on the auditing team so that each handles tasks within his or her areas of expertise. While the Accountant reviews financial records, the Auditor whose background is not in accounting might interview staff to find out about the flow of work in the department. What responsibilities need a supervisor's signature? Do any of these involve a duplication of effort? What kind of system is used for receiving and depositing checks?

In the course of their work, Auditors might find that checks are deposited only sporadically, costing the agency valuable money in lost interest. Auditors might then use data analysis techniques to calculate the amount of interest lost—perhaps a half million dollars a year. The Auditor might then illustrate his or her findings with the help of a computer spreadsheet.

Next, the Auditors would write their report, describing problems and recommending solutions. They might, for instance, recommend that an agency improve its finances by investing in a cash register, implementing a cash receipt system, and depositing checks in a timely fashion.

Finally, Auditors present their findings to agency managers in an exit conference. At this time, the managers might challenge their findings. Sometimes the manager's arguments have merit; at other times, they don't hold up against the Auditor's hard and fast data.

Once the audit is completed, its findings are released to the media and/or public. Then the cycle starts again, as Auditors periodically return to the sites of former audits to make sure that recommendations have been implemented.

Salaries

Salaries for Auditors generally range from $25,000 to $60,000. City Auditors generally earn $25,000 to $50,000, compared to $30,000 to $60,000 for private auditors, according to the NASACT. As a general rule, larger jurisdictions pay higher salaries than smaller ones.

Employment Prospects

Employment prospects are excellent because government competes with the private sector for Auditors. Because Auditors can choose either setting, those seeking positions in government usually find ample opportunities.

Public demand for accountability in government has, in some cases, sparked expansion of auditing staffs. If, for instance, the public becomes particularly concerned about the schools, the municipality might order a special audit. New interest in fraud detection and prevention, too, has led to the creation of positions for Forensic Auditors, who generally have acquired their expertise through exposure to cases on the job.

Advancement Prospects

Advancement prospects are excellent because Auditors can move up the career ladder in a variety of ways. As in many positions in government, Auditors are ranked by level of experience, rising in salary as they move up from Trainee to Manager to Deputy Auditor to City Auditor or State Auditor. Some use their auditing skills and contacts to become managers of other city or state agencies. An Auditor with a master's degree in public administration might, for instance, eventually become a City Manager. Another career track for someone with political aspirations but no auditing experience would be to run for City or State Auditor. Usually, in such cases, the Auditor hires a professional Auditor as a top manager. The majority of positions, however, are appointed rather than elected. Many top Auditors are Certified Public Accountants.

Opportunities for Auditors also abound in the private sector. Some government auditing departments contract out services to private firms, and businesses often hire staff Auditors.

Education and Training

Auditing combines two disciplines: accounting and social science. Although financial auditing requires a specific background in accounting, the broader field of performance auditing typically calls for a bachelor's degree or equivalent in business administration, accountancy, government, or public administration. Most auditing courses are offered through accounting or business departments, although a public administration program might include a class in auditing and/or offerings in financial and program management, industry sources say.

Many Auditors find that professional certification enhances their advancement prospects. The American Institute of Certified Public Accountants' designation of Certified Public Accountant (CPA) requires successful completion of a rigorous two-day examination; the Association of Government Accountants' designation of Certified Government Financial Manager (CGFM) is conferred on candidates who have passed a series of three exams and worked in government for two years.

A growing interest in fraud detection and prevention has also led to specialized training and certification. The Texas-based Association of Certified Fraud Examiners, or ACFE, offers a Certified Fraud Examiner designation. The American Board of Forensic Accountants offers its own Certified Forensic Accountant credential.

Experience, Skills, and Personality Traits

Typically Auditors begin as Auditor trainees. Auditors often work in teams of trainees paired with more senior staffers.

Some individuals enter the field through internships. In her article "Performance Auditing as a Public Administration Career Choice (Or Things They Never Taught Me in Graduate School)" published in the National Association of Local Government Auditors' newsletter, Amanda Noble recalled being introduced to the field through an internship that dispelled her notions of Auditors as strictly accountants.

Like accountants, however, Auditors must be detail-oriented and objective. Although performance auditing is broader in scope than financial auditing, it, too, requires an ability to analyze facts and figures quickly. Auditors must be good at working with people, including "auditees" who balk at the idea of being audited.

Unions and Associations

The National Association of State Auditors, Comptrollers, and Treasurers and the National Association of Local Government Auditors represent Auditors in state and local government.

Tips for Entry

1. Take a government accounting course. Government accounting differs from its counterpart in the private sector in that it deals with laws and regulations rather than net income.
2. Seek an internship with the State Auditor's Office.
3. Ask yourself whether you are a detail-oriented person, as this field requires meticulous attention to detail.
4. Browse the websites of the National Association of State Auditors, Comptrollers, and Treasurers *(www. nasact.org)* and the National Association of Local Government Auditors *(www.nalga.org)*.

ETHICS INVESTIGATOR

CAREER PROFILE

Duties: Contacting and interviewing respondents, complainants, and witnesses under oath; identifying, collecting, and evaluating documents; preparing comprehensive written reports for review by ethics commission members

Alternate Titles: None

Salary Range: $30,000 to $64,000

Employment Prospects: Poor

Advancement Prospects: Poor

Best Geographical Location(s): State Capitals

Prerequisites:

Education or Training—Bachelor's degree

Experience—Two to four years in a related field

Special Skills and Personality Traits—Investigative techniques; interviewing skills; analytical abilities; understanding of ethics rules and regulations; ability to maintain strict confidentially and communicate effectively orally and in writing

CAREER LADDER

```
┌─────────────────────────────────────┐
│      Senior Ethics Investigator      │
└─────────────────────────────────────┘

┌─────────────────────────────────────┐
│         Ethics Investigator          │
└─────────────────────────────────────┘

┌─────────────────────────────────────┐
│   Various Investigative Positions    │
│  (eg., insurance, child support)     │
└─────────────────────────────────────┘
```

Position Description

Ethics Investigators look into cases of possible government wrongdoing. Is an elected official misusing public funds? Has a lobbyist offered gifts to a state legislator? Has someone hired a relative? Any answer of yes to these questions could indicate a violation of state ethics laws.

Ethics Investigators differ from their counterparts in law enforcement in the way they go about their work. Because they are dealing with civil rather than criminal investigations, they do not carry guns or use fingerprints. Someone's name on an envelope is sufficient evidence for their purposes.

An Ethics Investigator spends much of his or her time writing reports for commissioners, who, in turn, decide whether or not to impose fines or other penalties. States determine the makeup of their own ethics commissions—how many members are appointed by the governor, who represents which political party, and so forth.

Often Ethics Investigators follow complicated paper trails. One time-consuming case in Seattle involved a money-laundering scheme in which a wealthy businessman had convinced eight different people to write checks to him in support of a ballot initiative. The Seattle Ethics and Elec-tions Commission subpoenaed bank records to trace the transactions. In another case in Seattle, the Ethics Investigator checked payroll records to see whether or not someone was getting paid overtime for time not worked. In yet another case, the Investigator tracked down lumber receipts to show the extent of illegal logging.

Although Ethics Investigators spend much of their time in the office, poring over records and writing reports, they also conduct interviews in the field, where they hear the respondent's side of the story and speak to witnesses. In the case of a public official accused of inappropriately using aides for personal chores such as baby-sitting, the Ethics Investigator might interview everyone involved in the situation. Did the aides feel pressured to help or did they do so willingly? What were the circumstances?

Setting up interviews can be a time-consuming process, as Ethics Investigators need to accommodate their sources but also keep travel expenses to a minimum. At the last minute, a source might decide to speak only if subpoenaed. The Ethics Investigator would then need to get a subpoena.

Sometimes cases are dismissed for lack of evidence at the end of an informal fact-gathering phase. Although such results might seem at first glance to be defeats, insiders say the investigative process of "nosing around" can prompt government officials to change their behavior.

Public scandal, too, can trigger change. Many state ethics commissions sprang up shortly after the Watergate scandal of the 1970s in response to the public's concern about government behavior. Not all states have Ethics Commissions, however. In a state without an ethics commission, the Attorney General or some other official would investigate cases of possible government wrongdoing.

The funding for state ethics commissions is controversial, as, in most cases, the budget is determined by elected officials who may be or have been investigated by the commission, thus posing a possible conflict of interest. The California Fair Campaign Practices Commission, however, is funded separately as a result of a citizens' initiative.

Responsibilities of Ethics Investigators have grown in response to the public's demand for government accountability. Common tasks of Ethics Investigators include

• Auditing political campaigns
• Attending public hearings
• Reviewing documents, tapes, transcripts, minutes of meetings, and other material
• Responding to questions from officials and employees about ethical matters
• Resolving ethical questions raised by the growing number of public/private partnerships.

Salaries

Salaries for Ethics Investigators generally range between $30,000 and $64,000, varying from state to state. Typically, Ethics Investigators gain more responsibility with experience. A senior Ethics Investigator's salary might be in the $50,000 to $75,000 range.

Employment Prospects

Employment prospects are poor because there are only a limited number of positions. Some states do not have ethics commissions. Ethics commissions generally have small staffs. Most ethics commissions are at the state, rather than the local, level.

Advancement Prospects

Advancement prospects are poor because of the small size of ethics commissions. If a state has the position of a *Senior Ethics Investigator*, it is likely to have only one. Ethics

Investigators may use their experience to move into another field such as law or investigation.

Education and Training

Criminal justice, paralegal, or legal training is preferred. Many four-year colleges have joined two-year colleges in adding such programs to their curriculums. Typically, these programs offer at least one course in interviewing techniques and investigation as well as internships offering practical experience in the field. Students learn how to ask questions, gather evidence, and testify. Advanced degrees may substitute for a year or two of required experience.

Experience, Skills, and Personality Traits

Individuals can get investigative experience in a variety of situations: law enforcement, the Internal Revenue Service, child-support investigations, insurance claims, for example. Journalism, too, can develop investigative and interviewing skills.

An Ethics Investigator needs to be open-minded and fair. Good listening skills are a must. Ethics Investigators also must be aggressive enough to pursue leads. They often deal with sensitive matters requiring tact and discretion.

Unions and Associations

The Council on Government Ethics Laws is a professional association of ethics professionals in government agencies.

Tips for Entry

1. Look into paralegal, criminal justice, and legal studies programs. Most offer courses in interviewing techniques and investigation.
2. Take advantage of internship possibilities. An internship need not be with an ethics commission, per se, to offer valuable investigative experience. Myriad private and public organizations—law enforcement, the Internal Revenue Service, child-support agencies, insurance companies—do investigative work.
3. Develop your interviewing and communications skills by taking an entry-level investigative position. Journalism experience, too, can be helpful.
4. Check help wanted ads in a variety of places, including local newspapers.
5. Visit government websites to read the home pages of ethics commissions and check out state personnel job listings.

ANTIDISCRIMINATION WORKER

CAREER PROFILE

Duties: Encouraging equal opportunity in obtaining government jobs and contracts; protecting citizens from discrimination in employment, housing, public accommodations, and other matters

Alternate Title(s): Investigator, Compliance Officer, Affirmative Action Officer, Diversity Coordinator, Equal Opportunity Administrator

Salary Range: $20,000 to $50,000+

Employment Prospects: Good

Advancement Prospects: Good to excellent

Best Geographical Location(s): State capitals

Prerequisites:

Education or Training—Bachelor's degree necessary; law degree for advancement

Experience—Entry level or two to five years related experience

Special Skills and Personality Traits—Commitment to equal opportunity; strong research/investigative skills; diplomatic personality; good analytical abilities

CAREER LADDER

```
┌─────────────────────────────────┐
│  Higher-Level Position in Private│
│  or Public Sector or Law Student │
└─────────────────────────────────┘

┌─────────────────────────────────┐
│    Antidiscrimination Worker     │
└─────────────────────────────────┘

┌─────────────────────────────────┐
│   Intern or Staffer in Related Field │
└─────────────────────────────────┘
```

Position Description

Individuals in this field know all about controversy. Every day, it seems, a new complaint or court challenge grabs headlines, raising new questions for Antidiscrimination Workers. How do threats of "reverse discrimination" affect policy making? What is a valid complaint of discrimination? How can governments handle the barrage of complaints dealing with sexual harassment, age discrimination, and other types of civil rights matters?

Antidiscrimination Workers in local and state governments deal with two pressing issues: (1) encouraging equal opportunity for government jobs and contracts and (2) protecting citizens from discrimination in employment, housing, public accommodations, and other matters. A complex patchwork of federal, state, and local legislation, along with judicial decisions, is constantly reshaping this field.

For instance, the Equal Employment Opportunities Act of 1972 set up a commission to enforce affirmative action plans, but, in 1978, the U.S. Supreme Court decided in the *University of California Regents v. Bakke* case that racial quotas constituted reverse discrimination. Meanwhile, state agencies investigating citizen complaints have broadened their definitions of discrimination to include not only concerns about race, religion, and ethnicity, but also the considerations related to age, harassment, sexual orientation, and disabilities.

Within government agencies, numerical quotas are out. Goal setting is in. Increasingly, the term *affirmative action* is giving way to *diversity* and *equal opportunity*.

Someone working in affirmative action/equal opportunity might set minority recruitment goals and sit in on job interviews to assure equitable hiring practices. Whereas affirmative action officers used to work largely on complaints of discrimination by government employees, they now take more of a proactive approach, leading employee training in diversity issues.

Staffers involved in a "set-aside" program for government contracts reach out to minority and small businesses. If, for instance, the department of corrections plans to buy new mattresses for inmates, an equal opportunity worker might give small businesses the information they need to apply for the contract.

Most states have commissions that investigate and address citizen complaints of discrimination in employment, housing, and other areas of concern. States determine the makeup of commissions, deciding, for instance, how many commissioners should be appointed by the Governor. Working with the commissioners are lawyers and investigators who research citizen complaints.

Take, for example, the hypothetical case of a complaint by a Latina woman who claims she was bypassed for a promotion because of her gender and ethnicity. The investigator might look into how many women held high-level positions in the company. Was there a pattern of denying advancement to women, or might the employee's performance explain why she was denied a promotion?

Some complaints are quickly dismissed; others are mediated or raised in a hearing of the commission. Investigators provide the information needed to help lawyers and commissioners decide which route to take.

Salaries
Industry sources say that salaries generally range from $20,000 to $50,000. An affirmative action officer for a mid-sized city, for instance, might earn in the $30,000 to $40,000 range.

Employment Prospects
Employment prospects are good because this is a rapidly growing and changing field with opportunities in all levels of government. Local agencies report to state agencies, which, in turn, report to federal agencies. A state agency dealing with employment discrimination, for instance, would report to the Equal Employment Opportunity Commission; one involved in housing discrimination, to the Housing and Urban Development Commission; and so on.

Whereas some areas, such as contract compliance, might be scaled back in response to court challenges, other areas promise steady growth. Diversity training, in particular, is "hot." Opportunities dealing with diversity also can be found in the private sector and in education.

Advancement Prospects
Advancement prospects are good to excellent because of the breadth of opportunities created by grappling with diversity in American society. Antidiscrimination Workers can move in a variety of directions. In addition to moving up within a government agency, Antidiscrimination Workers can move

from government into the private sector as well as to colleges and universities. Some increase their opportunities by becoming attorneys.

Education and Training
Industry sources recommend a bachelor's degree in political science, criminal justice, or a related discipline. Internships can be particularly helpful, giving students a hands-on introduction to work in the field. Some Antidiscrimination Workers advance their careers by earning a law degree.

Experience, Skills, and Personality Traits
Prior experience in a field involving employment issues, investigation, and/or statistical analysis can be particularly helpful. Because Antidiscrimination Workers deal largely with personnel issues, some agencies look for individuals with a background in human resources.

Many Antidiscrimination Workers enter the field because they believe strongly in equal opportunity and want to make a difference in the world. Some individuals, however, "burn out" because of the emotional nature of the work and the heavy workloads. State commissions are grappling with an ever-widening array of citizen complaints of discrimination, thus making for huge backlogs. Insiders say that Antidiscrimination Workers should be the type of people able to "calm the waters."

Unions and Associations
Individuals in this field might belong to the American Association for Affirmative Action and/or the National Association of Human Rights Workers.

Tips for Entry
1. Believe strongly in the policies you will be espousing. Individuals must be able to defend affirmative action and other controversial policies.
2. Stay current on the issues. Browse relevant websites, including the home pages of the United States Equal Employment Opportunity Commission (*www.eeoc.gov*), Diversity.com (*www.diversity.com*), and state commissions.
3. Look for entry-level jobs involving human resources, investigations, and/or social activism to make yourself a competitive candidate for jobs with state antidiscrimination commissions.
4. Seek an internship to gain hands-on experience in the field.

HUMAN SERVICES DIRECTOR

CAREER PROFILE

Duties: Overseeing the effective delivery of human services to clients by directing budgets, personnel, program development, and other areas of administration

Alternate Title(s): Area Director, Division Director

Salary Range: $45,000 to $110,0000+

Employment Prospects: Fair to good

Advancement Prospects: Fair

Best Geographical Location(s): Areas with a commitment to human services

Prerequisites:

Education or Training—Master's degree in public administration, public policy, business administration, public health, psychology, social work, or related field

Experience—Six to 12 years of increasingly responsible experience

Special Skills and Personality Traits—Vision, leadership, and a dedication to human services; ambition; good interpersonal skills; patience

CAREER LADDER

```
┌─────────────────────────────────────┐
│   Human Services Commissioner        │
└─────────────────────────────────────┘

┌─────────────────────────────────────┐
│   Human Services Director            │
└─────────────────────────────────────┘

┌─────────────────────────────────────┐
│   Human Services Program Manager     │
└─────────────────────────────────────┘
```

Position Description

Human Services Directors head up departments that provide child welfare, food stamps, Medicaid, and other help to those in need. Welfare reform and other legislative initiatives have spurred the creation of a more entrepreneurial, market-oriented environment for human services. Some state human service agencies have budgets on a par with those of Fortune 500 companies. Increasingly, human services once provided by local and state agencies are being contracted out to private and nonprofit organizations.

Human Services Directors enter this position from two basic directions: public policy or direct service. Many positions combine the two: Some positions fall more at the policy end of the spectrum, and others have more of a direct service orientation.

People on the policy end of the spectrum generally begin their careers in research-oriented positions, rising from program analyst to program manager to director. They ask questions such as, How well are Latino clients doing? How can services be improved?

Individuals with more of a direct service orientation often rise up the ranks from Human Services Worker to supervisor to program manager to Director. A Human Services Director who deals with issues of child abuse might chair a meeting to determine whether or not a child in foster care should be returned home. The caseworker, supervisor, and agency lawyer would contribute their input, and the Human Services Director would assume overall responsibility for the decision.

Each background—policy development or direct service—has its own set of perceived strengths and weaknesses. Someone with a policy background might be better at seeing "the big picture," whereas an individual with more direct service experience might be better at understanding the nitty-gritty realities of those in need.

Ideally, as individuals move up the ranks, they acquire the skills needed for the next level. By the time a mental health worker becomes a program manager, for instance, he or she should know about not only the day-to-day work of treatment, but also the setting of goals, development of policy, and motivating of others.

Typically, Human Services Directors provide leadership in five major areas

- Client services
- Budgets
- Personnel
- Program planning and development
- Public relations

A typical day might begin with reviewing reports. How much money is being spent on particular programs? How many children are being abused? What are the Governor's new policy objectives?

Then the Human Services Director might meet with Program Managers. How is everyone getting along in the office? Is a particular child in foster care doing better? Are all reports up-to-date?

Next up: more meetings. The Human Services Director might meet with administrators of state or private-sector agencies, talk to citizen advocates, or participate in a task force on a social program such as one related to teen pregnancy.

From there, the Human Services Director might return to the office to find numerous phone and e-mail messages waiting. A front-page news story might have portrayed the agency in an unfavorable light. The Governor wants a change in policy right away. The Human Services Director needs to drop everything and tend to the situation.

Human Services Directors commonly find themselves dealing with crises and emergencies. For instance, a fire in a foster home might result in two deaths. The Human Services Director would need to make a statement to the press and launch an internal investigation.

Personnel problems, too, might erupt. An employee with a drinking problem might not show up for work. A caseworker might accuse the supervisor of being a racist. The Human Services Director would be responsible for resolving such matters.

Because Human Services Directors spend so much time reacting to problems, they often find little time for developing new programs. The creative, innovative, "fun" part of the job is constantly preempted by day-to-day responsibilities. Such pressures notwithstanding, Human Services Directors can find satisfaction in helping to make the system work for those in need.

Salaries

Salaries vary according to the size of the jurisdiction and the level of responsibility. Human Services Directors at the local level might make $45,000 to $70,000, compared to $50,000 to $85,000 in midsized and $60,000 to $110,000 in large jurisdictions.

Employment Prospects

Employment prospects are fair to good. Privatization has created some new opportunities but scaled back others.

Some positions have been changed from overseeing staff to managing contracts. On the other hand, strong links exist among the public, private, and nonprofit sectors, creating opportunities for lateral and upward movement.

Advancement Prospects

Advancement prospects are fair. Human Services Directors can rise from a small jurisdiction, such as a city, to a larger one, such as a regional, county, or state agency. However, once they rise to the position of Human Services Director, they may find few positions above them: deputy commissioner, commissioner, secretary of human services, then, ultimately, governor.

Organizational structures vary from agency to agency, as some incorporate all services under one umbrella and in others specialties such as mental health, Medicaid, and substance abuse are more autonomous. Whether an individual is a specialist or a generalist might depend, in part, on the organization's structure.

Education and Training

Individuals can choose either a background in policy analysis/program administration or direct service/social work. For the first, degrees in public administration, business administration, and public policy are most helpful. For the second, degrees in social work, education, public health, and psychology are recommended. A law degree, too, can be useful.

Experience, Skills, and Personality Traits

Skills that make for an effective human services worker can backfire at the Director level. Whereas a clinician is trained to be empathetic and nondirective, a Human Services Director often needs to be tough and decisive. He or she should be willing to forge ahead with a plan even if others are trying to block it.

Human Services Directors need to have a vision and persuade others to share it. They must be tough negotiators and have a firm grasp of fiscal responsibility. They should be able to handle data analysis, complex problems, long hours, and high stress.

Unions and Associations

Associations that offer professional resources for Human Services Directors include the American Public Human Services Association and the National Association of Social Workers.

Tips for Entry

1. Determine your own area of passion. Are you passionate about social equity, public health, child welfare, or some other area of social concern?

2. Get experience in the field by working as a counselor, volunteer, or other human services worker. People in human services are generally expected to pay their dues by putting some time in "the trenches." Because human services worker positions constitute the majority of jobs in the field, they are often advertised in Sunday newspapers and college career offices.

3. Point yourself in the direction of "Director" by distinguishing yourself as a leader. Network, write, and do whatever else it takes to become visible. Attend summer institutes.

4. Ask yourself whether you're willing to put yourself forward and exercise influence in a public role or whether you'd rather work behind the scenes. If the latter, you might prefer to stay in a position like director of research.

5. Talk to professors in various graduate programs to explore your interest in the field and determine possible courses of study.

STATE/FEDERAL LEGISLATIVE STAFF

CONGRESSIONAL PAGE

CAREER PROFILE

Duties: Delivering correspondence, legislative material, and small packages; answering phones; preparing the Congressional Chambers; performing other assorted tasks as needed

Alternate Title(s): House Page, Senate Page

Salary Range: Pro-rated: based on annual salary of $15,500 for Senate Pages and $15,401 for House Pages

Employment Prospects: Poor

Advancement Prospects: Good

Best Geographical Location(s): Washington, D.C.

Prerequisites:

Education or Training—High school juniors with at least a 3.0 grade point average

Experience—Participation in extracurricular activities (e.g., student government, volunteer organizations)

Special Skills and Personality Traits—Good health; stamina; humility; strong interest in public service

CAREER LADDER

```
┌─────────────────────────────┐
│     High School Senior      │
└─────────────────────────────┘

┌─────────────────────────────┐
│     Congressional Page      │
└─────────────────────────────┘

┌─────────────────────────────┐
│    High School Sophomore    │
└─────────────────────────────┘
```

Position Description

Congressional Pages hold highly coveted positions living, working, and studying in Washington, D.C. In much the same way that pageboys in medieval times trained for knighthood by assisting their higher-ranked elders, high school juniors today can learn about the legislative process by working primarily as messengers for Congress. They see firsthand the lessons that they learned in history books about how a bill becomes law. Some members of Congress began their own careers as Pages.

To qualify for a position as a Congressional Page, individuals must be prospective high school juniors sponsored by a member of Congress. Congressional Pages are accepted for three sessions: fall, spring, or summer. During the academic year, members of the program attend the House or Senate Page School, where they take a standard high school curriculum, which includes English, math, science, and social studies. Congressional Pages attend classes only in the early morning, so they can spend the rest of the day on Capitol Hill. Those hired for the summer session do not attend school.

Easily recognized by their trademark uniforms, Congressional Pages typically begin the day by reporting to their supervisors. They work as a pool, rotating duties, rather than as staffers for individual members. Duties consist primarily of delivering correspondence, legislative material, and small packages, but Pages also answer phones, take messages, and staff the cloakroom.

On a typical day, the first order of business may be preparing the chambers for the day's proceedings. Congressional Pages lay out agendas, documents, and supplies such as water and pens. Then they begin their work as messengers. Pages deliver envelopes containing all sorts of news: good and bad, routine and history-altering. A Page might deliver notes to members from their office staff, flags from the flag room, and packages from the House to the Senate, and vice versa.

Congressional Pages sometimes work well into the night. If a session of Congress extends past 10 p.m., the next day's classes may be postponed.

Salaries

Pages are paid at an annual rate of $15,500 for Senate Pages, $15,401 for House Pages. Automatic deductions are made for federal and state taxes, social security, and residence hall fees. The cost of living in the residence hall is $450 a month for Senate Pages, $400 a month for House Pages. Most meals are included in the fee. Some Pages live with their parents or relatives.

Employment Prospects

Employment prospects are poor because of the highly competitive nature of this position and the limited number of openings. All applicants must be sponsored by a member of Congress. The number of more senior members wishing to sponsor a Page further limits the selection. Only 72 House Pages are chosen for more than 400 Representatives and 30 Senate Pages for 100 Senators.

The House and Senate programs are administered separately. The U.S. House of Representatives Page Board (made up of two members from the majority party selected by the Speaker, one member from the minority party selected by the minority leader, the clerk of the House, and the sergeant at arms of the House) administers the House Page Program.

On the Senate side, the U.S. Senate sergeant at arms administers the work and residential aspects of the Page Program; the Secretary of the Senate administers the educational component. The determination of which 30 of the 100 Senators is allowed to sponsor a Page is based on the patronage system of each party.

Advancement Prospects

Advancement prospects are good because a position as Congressional Page gives an individual valuable experience and personal contacts. Many individuals are impressed by a young person's experience as a Congressional Page. The position also offers excellent opportunities for making helpful contacts.

Education and Training

Page eligibility is limited to juniors in high school. All applicants must be 16 years old on the date they begin their Page term. There are no exceptions. Students must have at least a 3.0 grade point average to be eligible for the program.

In addition to their regular work and studies, Pages participate in a mandatory enrichment program. They attend field trips and lectures intended to give them a behind-the-scenes look at the way government works.

Experience, Skills, and Personality Traits

Participation in extracurricular activities related to public service can be helpful. Participation in student government and/or civic organizations such as the Boys or Girls Club, as well as strong recommendations from teachers, might help an applicant win sponsorship by a member of Congress.

For many young people, the opportunity to live, work, and study in the nation's capital is a dream come true. Boys and girls live on separate floors in dormitories supervised by proctors. "It's like summer camp," said one former Page about the residential aspects of the program.

Work as a Congressional Page requires stamina and maturity. The work tends to be fast-paced and physically taxing, with Pages on their feet, running messages all day long. They must be willing to follow direction and forgo activities such as family trips and proms if they occur during the school week and/or workweek.

Congressional Pages are expected to maintain a neat appearance and conservative hairstyle at all times and abide by the dress code. House Pages wear long-sleeved white shirts, navy blue blazers, and dark gray slacks (boys) or dark gray knee-length skirts without slits (girls). Senate Pages wear navy blue suits and white shirts. All Pages must wear solid black shoes.

Unions and Associations

Because of the strong educational component that accompanies the work, the House Page School and the Senate Page School serve as important organizations in lieu of traditional unions or associations.

Tips for Entry

1. Work on getting good grades, as Congressional Pages must have at least a B average.
2. Participate in extracurricular activities (e.g., student government, volunteer organizations) related to public service.
3. Think carefully about whether or not you are willing to sacrifice activities such as vacations and holiday plans if they interfere with school or work activities. The congressional calendar is subject to sudden change.
4. Write a letter to your Senator or Representative requesting consideration for the Page Program and asking what steps you should take in order to apply (e.g., a personal statement, description of extracurricular activities, high school transcript, birth certificate, and three letters of recommendation). Ask at your school or public library for addresses of members of Congress or search the webpages of the U.S. House (*www.house.gov*) and/or Senate (*www.senate.gov*).
5. Contact your state legislature to see whether it, too, has a Page Program. Program requirements concerning age, length of service, and other matters may be more flexible for state legislatures than for Congress.

LEGISLATIVE CORRESPONDENT

CAREER PROFILE

Duties: Opening, sorting, and routing mail; researching issues; formulating responses; initiating mailings to constituents on issues of importance

Salary Range: $19,000 to $27,000

Employment Prospects: Fair

Advancement Prospects: Excellent

Best Geographical Location: Washington, D.C.

Prerequisites:

Education or Training—College degree

Experience—None; generally considered an entry level position

Special Skills and Personality Traits—Good writing, research, and organizational skills

CAREER LADDER

```
┌─────────────────────────────────┐
│      Legislative Assistant       │
└─────────────────────────────────┘

┌─────────────────────────────────┐
│    Legislative Correspondent     │
└─────────────────────────────────┘

┌─────────────────────────────────┐
│        Student or Intern         │
└─────────────────────────────────┘
```

Position Description

Legislative Correspondents, as their name implies, write letters for busy members of Congress. They respond to hundreds, if not thousands, of pieces of mail a week. Many, but not all, members of Congress have Legislative Correspondents specifically for this purpose. In state legislatures, interns and Legislative Correspondents handle most of the mail.

On Capitol Hill, the workload of Legislative Correspondents rises and falls as "hot" issues generate huge volumes of mail. Some Legislative Correspondents sort their mail into categories, for example, issues, grants, visiting constituent, and invitations for the senator or representative. Legislative Correspondents also answer the phone and may do some photocopying or other tasks, if need be. Mostly, though, they open, sort, route, answer, fold, stuff, and send mail.

Legislative Correspondents commonly assign a code number to each letter, entering it on the computer system. People write to their senators and representatives to ask questions and express their points of view. How can a son or daughter find a job in Washington? What is the legislator's stand on a particular issue? Legislative Correspondents typically route some letters to fellow staffers and handle others themselves. Some letters are of the "I support" or "I don't like" variety. When a lot of mail is received on the same subject, the Legislative Correspondent responds with the appropriate preprogrammed issue paragraph.

More interesting tasks involve researching issues and generating responses. In some offices, the Legislative Correspondent is in charge of a particular issue and so can respond to mail directly related to it. If the supervisor is encouraging, the Legislative Correspondent can assume more responsibility with time. Still, this is a fairly low-level position. Legislative Correspondents become familiar with a wide range of issues and hone valuable writing skills. Legislative Correspondents can move up to positions such as legislative assistant, office manager, or press assistant.

Salaries

Salaries for Legislative Correspondents generally range from $19,000 to $27,000, according to the Georgetown University Career Education Center.

Employment Prospects

Employment prospects are fair because there are a limited amount of positions, and some are already promised to interns or individuals personally connected to legislators.

Advancement Prospects

Advancement prospects are excellent because individuals able to prove themselves in this difficult job may advance their careers. Legislative Correspondents can choose among three different tracks: legislative (e g., legislative assistant), administrative (e.g., office manager), or communication (e.g., press assistant). Insiders say that, of the three, the legislative track is the most common.

Education and Training

Legislative Correspondents need to have a college degree. Common majors are political science, economics, history, and English. Some Legislative Correspondents have advanced degrees.

Experience, Skills, and Personality Traits

Good writing skills are essential. Some Legislative Correspondents combine a background in journalism with an interest in politics. Because they respond to large amounts of mail, Legislative Correspondents need to be well-organized and efficient. They should care about the concerns of average citizens despite the lack of glamour associated with writing letters rather than hobnobbing with high-powered policy makers.

Some offices ask candidates for writing samples; others test their abilities by requiring them to respond to actual letters within a set amount of time. Excellent writing and research skills are required.

Unions and Associations

Legislative Correspondents might belong to the Congressional Legislative Staff Association or other organizations.

Tips for Entry

1. Look into internship possibilities. Many interns move directly to positions as Legislative Correspondents.
2. Call your U.S. senator's or representative's office to ask about possible positions.
3. Write for a student newspaper or something else that will give you writing samples to use in the application process.
4. Take advantage of central personnel services, such as the House and Senate job lines, but also leave your résumé with the chief of staff or whoever does the hiring for that office.
5. Check out classified ads in the two Capitol Hill newspapers, *Roll Call (www.rollcall.com)* and *The Hill (www.hillnews.com).*

DISTRICT AIDE

CAREER PROFILE

Duties: Maintaining the Legislator's visibility in the district; responding to constituent concerns; maintaining the Legislator's schedule; acting as liaison to central office

Alternate Title(s): Regional Assistant, Local Assistant, Administrative Assistant, Executive Assistant/Scheduler, Caseworker, Field Representative

Salary Range: $16,000 to $35,000+

Employment Prospects: Fair to good

Advancement Prospects: Fair to good

Best Geographical Location(s): Congressional districts

Prerequisites:
  Education or Training—Varies
  Experience—Campaign experience preferred
  Special Skills and Personality Traits—Outgoing; knowledgeable about local issues; flexible; loyal

CAREER LADDER

```
┌─────────────────────────────────┐
│   District Director or Position  │
│   in Member's Legislative Office │
│        or on Campaign            │
└─────────────────────────────────┘

┌─────────────────────────────────┐
│         District Aide            │
└─────────────────────────────────┘

┌─────────────────────────────────┐
│    Campaign Volunteer or Intern  │
└─────────────────────────────────┘
```

Position Description

District Aides deal with matters on the home-front for busy Senators or Representatives off in the capital tending to legislative business. Although the work of District Aides may lack some of the glamour of work in the capital, they are on the front lines of politics. District Aides serve as the "eyes and ears" of legislators. They help constituents, monitor issues, and provide feedback about the popularity (or lack thereof) of the lawmaker on the home turf.

All Members of Congress and about one-third of state legislators have offices in the district. Because most state legislators live in their districts, they have less need for district staff. Some use a secretarial pool for everything they cannot do themselves.

A State Legislator may use his or her home as a district office. In his book *Legislative Life,* Alan Rosenthal tells of one state legislator who, on getting a complaint from a constituent about overgrown weeds on the median strip of a local highway, packed up his lawnmower and cut down the plants.

Legislators in larger districts, though, may need district offices to keep in touch with constituents. In some states, Legislators have their main offices in the district because the legislature lacks sufficient office space. In others, when the legislative session ends, operations move back to the district.

Staffers in district offices at the state level deal with a variety of constituent issues, including requests for information (What are the state's laws on handguns?) as well as appeals for help (Can you cut through the red tape?). District Aides also schedule the legislator's local appearances and keep tabs on various issues. In California, for example, district offices are so well-established that District Aides might meet periodically with directors of state agencies.

All members of Congress have at least one district office, and many have more. The relationship between the Washington, D.C., office and the district office is sometimes strained as the two perform different functions. Central-office staffers dealing with legislative matters might consider questions from the district about constituent issues a nuisance.

District organization varies from one Member of Congress to the next. Some members have mobile offices, which travel from county to county. In such a case, locations might be announced on local radio stations.

In larger, more permanent offices, District Aides might include a mix of low-level and senior staffers. In some congressional offices, the chief of staff works out of the district, supervising lower-level District Aides, who do largely clerical tasks. Often, District Aides are divided into the following categories:

- Casework: handling constituent problems with federal agencies
- Scheduling: responding to invitations to the Senator or Representative
- Fieldwork: attending various functions, such as Chamber of Commerce meetings and Kiwanis Club dinners

District Aides work as ambassadors of sorts for senators and representatives. They may hand out literature or read a short statement from the Member. District Aides represent members of Congress but do not speak for them.

Because they work in the heart of the district, everyone they meet is a potential voter. District Aides make numerous calls to government agencies to straighten out constituent problems. A late Social Security check? Immigration problems? Trouble getting military benefits? The District Aide acts as a caseworker, explaining regulations to constituents and tracking down requests from different agencies.

On a typical day, the District Aide would check in with the Chief of Staff or the District Director to talk about the schedule. The District Aide might have meetings at the housing affairs office or school department. At the request of the Washington office, he or she might take an informal poll to find out what constituents think about a particular issue.

Often, District Aides accompany legislators on trips throughout the district. A District Aide responsible for scheduling might find out in advance what the legislator should wear and where he or she will sit.

Salaries

Salaries vary, depending on the size of the district and the level of responsibility. Only about one-third of state legislatures have district staffs, and salaries vary widely, according to the National Conference of State Legislatures. In some states, Legislative Assistants or part-timers staff the district office.

In congressional districts, salaries range from about $16,000 to $35,000+, according to the Georgetown University Career Education Center. Salaries are highest for senior-level positions in states with high standards of living.

Employment Prospects

Employment prospects are fair. Openings are limited, and individuals competing for this position may be up against others in the district with strong personal connections to the legislator.

Advancement Prospects

Advancement prospects are fair to good, depending on whether or not someone is willing to move to the state or federal capital. Someone in a small district office unable to relocate might find limited options.

Education and Training

District Aides have various educational backgrounds, depending on the requirements of the position. Whereas one District Aide might have little more than a high school diploma, another might have a law degree.

Experience, Skills, and Personality Traits

Some local political experience such as helping out on a campaign is generally preferred or required. District Aides must care about local people and issues. They should know who's who in the community. Former class presidents, who know and get along well with everyone in the community, make ideal field representatives, insiders say.

Major differences exist between district staffers, who focus on local matters, and central staffers, who work in the legislative arena. Because many District Aides have personal ties to the Legislator, they have a higher "loyalty quotient" than central staffers on the lookout for higher-level positions with other Members. Nevertheless, central staffers may regard their own policy work as more important than the District Aide's concerns about constituent issues. Some offices try to improve communication by hiring district staffers to work in the central office.

Unions and Associations

District Aides might be involved in the National Conference of State Legislatures or various other organizations. The nonprofit, nonpartisan Congressional Management Foundation provides information about and services for District Aides and other staffers.

Tips for Entry

1. Visit district offices to get a feel for the work they do.
2. Volunteer to work on a political campaign.
3. Take an interest in the community. Follow the issues and attend public meetings.
4. Begin with your own elected officials, since they represent your district. Contact the state director or chief of staff responsible for hiring

LEGISLATIVE ASSISTANT

CAREER PROFILE

Duties: Assisting the Legislator with bill processing and research, communication, and administrative support

Alternate Title(s): Legislative Aide, Legislative Clerk, Administrative Assistant, Administrative Aide

Salary Range: $20,000 to $50,000

Employment Prospects: Fair

Advancement Prospects: Good to excellent

Best Geographical Location(s): State legislatures, Congress

Prerequisites:

Education or Training—Bachelor's degree required; graduate degree preferred by some employers

Experience—Entry-level or some experience required

Special Skills and Personality Traits—Basic research, computer, and communication skills

CAREER LADDER

```
┌─────────────────────────────────┐
│ Committee Staffer, Legislative  │
│ Director, or Other Positions    │
└─────────────────────────────────┘

┌─────────────────────────────────┐
│      Legislative Assistant      │
└─────────────────────────────────┘

┌─────────────────────────────────┐
│ Legislative Correspondent,      │
│ Intern, Campaign Worker, or     │
│ Student                         │
└─────────────────────────────────┘
```

Position Description

Legislative Assistants help Senators and Representatives with everything from photocopying to bill drafting. Many recent college graduates drawn to the legislative arena's whirl of power and policy making set out for this highly coveted position. Few make a career of legislative work, however. The fast pace, long hours, and relatively low pay can take a toll. Still, even a year or two as a Legislative Assistant can propel one's career forward, opening up doors in the legislature, government agencies, lobbying firms, and other organizations. Often, too, Legislative Assistants leave to go back to school.

Although the job of Legislative Assistant might seem glamorous, it is often largely clerical—answering telephones, sorting mail, scheduling appointments, and working on constituents' problems. The volume of work can be overwhelming, insiders say.

Many Legislative Assistants start out performing mostly clerical tasks such as answering the phone and taking messages but, with time, do more research-oriented work. Legislative Assistants with a fair amount of responsibility work on legislation practically from start to finish. They draft it, work with committee consultants, gather information, round up supporters, and arrange for people to lobby on the bill's behalf. Along the way, they address questions like, How

might a particular bill affect the home district? What groups would be in favor of it? How do different legislators line up in favor of or against it?

The size of legislative staffs varies widely. Typically, Legislative Assistants report to a higher-level staffer such as a Legislative Director. Some state legislators lack their own staffs or have only part-time Legislative Assistants. Since Members of Congress work full time, their offices are better staffed than those of state legislators. Generally speaking, in Washington, D.C., Senate staffs tend to be larger than those of the House of Representatives, giving Legislative Aides more room for specialization. In many offices, work is divided by subject area. One Legislative Assistant might be involved in education, health care, welfare, and environmental issues; another, in a different set of issues. Each Legislative Assistant would then read—skim through—all the bills in those areas affecting the district, putting together a report on whatever is going to reach the legislative floor that day.

The Legislative Assistant involved in high-profile committee work holds an especially prized position. In the course of a legislative session, thousands of bills simply die. Those that the committee is actively considering, or "moving," stand the best chance of being passed into law. Depending on the organization of the office, committee work is handled by either Legislative Assistants or legislative directors. They participate in hearings and line-by-line drafting of the bill. Individuals involved in committee work try to incorporate their boss's ideas into the pending bill.

Legislative Assistants also commonly

- Meet with lobbyists
- Represent legislators at meetings and conferences
- Arrange committee and subcommittee hearings for Legislators' bills and activities
- Assist in developing legislation and amendments
- Respond to requests for information about legislators' bills and activities
- Prepare memos and reports based on completed research for Legislators

Salaries

Salaries for Legislative Assistants in state legislatures are considerably lower than for those in Congress. According to the National Conference of State Legislatures, many salaries for Legislative Assistants fall into the $25,000 to $35,000 range. In Congress, salaries are more likely to fall into the $30,000 to $40,000 range for the House of Representatives and the $40,000 to $50,000 range in the Senate, according to industry sources. Senators and Representatives determine their own staff salaries.

Employment Prospects

Employment prospects are fair for Legislative Assistants because there are a limited number of positions. On the plus side, these positions open fairly often because of high turnover. Few individuals stay more than a few years in a state legislature or Congress.

In state legislatures, more populous states have the greatest number of positions. Some small state legislatures, such as that of Wyoming, lack Legislative Assistants. Larger states break down the position into different levels—Legislative Assistant I, Legislative Assistant II, Senior Legislative Assistant, and so forth—creating room for advancement. On the national level, Legislative Assistant positions are generally easier to find in the U.S. House of Representatives, which has more members than the Senate. Salaries, however, tend to be higher in the Senate.

Advancement Prospects

Advancement prospects are good to excellent because Legislative Assistants make important personal contacts on the job, which come in handy for future job hunting.

Many Legislative Assistants are just "passing through," looking for a credential to put on their résumés. Some move up to central legislative agencies or committees. Others land higher-level positions with government agencies or private or nonprofit interest groups. A Legislative Assistant might become an analyst for a lobbying firm, for instance.

Education and Training

Usually positions specify a bachelor's degree or the equivalent of education and experience. Some Legislative Assistants leave to continue their education, perhaps entering law school or getting a master's degree in public administration.

Experience, Skills, and Personality Traits

Legislative Assistants should have excellent research and communication skills. They should be able to analyze information quickly and explain it clearly verbally or in writing, to various groups. Legislative Assistants also must be good at following directions. In state legislatures and Congress, the staffer's job is to be loyal to the legislator. Credit always goes to the Member, insiders say. Staffers need to be willing to put aside their own egos.

The volume of work in legislative offices can be enormous. Many staffers fall victim to boredom or burnout. A Legislative Assistant might be presented with three new projects when he or she already has a floor statement to write, a subcommittee meeting to attend, and four weeks worth of mail to answer. Although legislative staffers are notoriously overworked, they gain valuable experience on the job.

Unions and Associations

Legislative Assistants might be involved in the National Conference of State Legislatures, the American Society for Public Administration, or other organizations. The nonprofit, nonpartisan Congressional Management Foundation provides information about and services for Legislative Assistants and other staffers.

Tips for Entry

1. Begin with your own elected officials. Being a constituent offers you the hometown advantage.
2. Seek internship opportunities. Some colleges and universities have semester in Washington, D.C., programs.
3. Work on a Representative's or Senator's election campaign. Many campaign volunteers become paid staffers.
4. Realize that timing is crucial to landing a position as a Legislative Assistant. Find out when sessions begin, to take advantage of hiring possibilities presented by lawmakers who have not hired Legislative Assistants or have had a last-minute cancellation.
5. Read up on state legislators and members of Congress to see which ones share your political philosophy.

6. Look into central personnel services such as the job lines of the House Office of Human Resources (202-226-6731) and the Senate Employment Bulletin (202-228-5627), but also leave your résumé in members' offices and follow up periodically by phone or in person to take advantage of sudden openings.

7. Check out helpful websites, including that of the National Conference of State Legislatures *(www. ncsl.org)* as well as two Capitol Hill newspapers, *Roll Call (www.rollcall.com)* and *The Hill (www. hillnews.com)*.

RESEARCH ANALYST

CAREER PROFILE

Duties: Performing quantitative and qualitative analysis; analyzing policy questions and options; writing reports; responding to inquiries

Alternate Title(s): Legislative Analyst, Policy Analyst, Fiscal Analyst, Committee Staffer

Salary Range: $25,000 to $60,000

Employment Prospects: Fair

Advancement Prospects: Good to excellent

Best Geographical Location(s): State legislatures, Congress, other government entities

Prerequisites:

Education or Training—Graduate degree required or preferred

Experience—Varies by position

Special Skills and Personality Traits—Knowledge of research techniques; ability to summarize complex data orally and in writing; understanding of the legislative process

CAREER LADDER

```
┌─────────────────────────────────┐
│  Research Director or Other      │
│  Position with Government        │
│  Agency or Private or            │
│  Nonprofit Organization          │
└─────────────────────────────────┘

┌─────────────────────────────────┐
│      Research Analyst            │
└─────────────────────────────────┘

┌─────────────────────────────────┐
│     Research Assistant           │
│     or Graduate Student          │
└─────────────────────────────────┘
```

Position Description

Research Analysts provide the information and analysis that Legislators and other government officials need to make well-informed decisions. Research Analysts respond to complex questions like, What are the effects of welfare reform? and How can Social Security be improved?

Insiders say that Research Analysts involved in fiscal matters are particularly influential. Whatever the specialty, Research Analysts differ from librarians in that they provide not only answers but also in-depth analysis. Whereas a librarian might find out the gross domestic product in a particular fiscal year, a Research Analyst would compare the previous year's domestic product to the current year's and make an analysis. The chair of the health committee might ask a Research Analyst for the pros and cons of higher copayments for prescription drugs.

Much of this type of work originates in central agencies specializing in nonpartisan research. At the state level, agencies such as the Office of Legislative Research, the Senate Reference Bureau, and the Legislative Research Commis-

sion have sprouted up over the years. Often, staffers of these agencies are assigned to various committees. A Research Analyst might specialize in education, for example.

At the national level, the Congressional Research Service, a branch of the Library of Congress, provides information and analysis to expand or supplement research supplied by the Representative's or Senator's own staff. (Other congressional support agencies include the Congressional Budget Office and the General Accounting Office.) A sampling of Congressional Research Service reports includes "Decorum in House Debate," "Ideas for Privatizing Social Security," and "Russia's Presidential Election: Outcome and Implications."

Whereas these central agencies provide nonpartisan research, Research Analysts for caucuses or committees are more openly political. They analyze bills from a partisan perspective and research issues of special interest to the party.

Research Analysts are a notch above Research Assistants on the career ladder. Both groups are often ranked by level. The higher up the position, the more complex the research. Research Analysts commonly prepare reports with tables and charts. A Research Analyst might present flowcharts showing the differences between the House and Senate versions of a bill, for example. Many Research Analysts have a master's, Ph.D., or law degree. Research Directors are on the top rungs.

Although some Legislators have voracious appetites for research, many others want their information brief and to the point. A half-page memo might work better than a two-page brief. At the state level, opportunities for generating in-depth research are best during the interim when Research Analysts have the opportunity to do oversight studies.

Research Analysts at the state level tend to be more jacks-of-all-trades than their counterparts in a central federal agency such as the Congressional Research Service. When a state legislature is in session, the Research Analyst might arrive at 7:30 A.M. to meet with the chair and prepare for an 8:00 A.M. committee meeting. Materials would need to be organized, an agenda prepared. After sitting in on the committee meeting, the Research Analyst might write a report for an afternoon session of the House and Senate. Meanwhile, questions would have to be answered, legislation drafted, floor speeches written. They would also need to analyze legislation and coordinate administrative tasks such as scheduling and organizing hearings and meetings

During the interim, Research Analysts have more time to explore in-depth issues. Legislatures determine what issues should be studied during the interim. Perhaps, for example, the legislature calls for the creation of a task force to improve adult education in the state. The Research Analyst would then research types of programs, numbers of participants, possible improvements, prospective funding sources, and the like. The research group would solicit input from citizens' groups and education associations, hold public meetings, issue a report, and, finally, draft legislation. In Kentucky, this process resulted in legislation calling for a special council and new funding for adult education.

More generally, Research Analysts work on a variety of tasks, including

- Performing quantitative and qualitative research using library resources, Internet sources, information from policy centers, and other material
- Writing reports
- Responding to inquiries concerning an assigned subject area
- Conducting meetings to brief members of the House and/or Senate

Salaries

Salaries depend largely on the individual's educational background and level of experience. According to a salary survey by the National Conference of State Legislatures, average annual salaries for research staffers range from $25,689 for entry level positions with an undergraduate degree to $34,534 for a professional with a graduate degree

and one year's experience to $49,143 for a professional with 10 years' experience. At the national level, salaries in 2000 for Research Analysts at the Congressional Research Service ranged from $35,310 to $60,890.

Employment Prospects

Employment prospects are fair because the number of jobs in the legislative sector is fairly limited, although it varies from year to year. Someone with a master's degree might take a job as a Research Assistant with a prestigious government agency such as the Congressional Research Service with the hope of eventually moving up to Research Analyst.

Advancement Prospects

Advancement prospects are good to excellent because positions are ranked, thus creating ladders for advancement. Work as a Research Analyst for a state legislature or Congress may also open up doors with government agencies, interest groups, and various other employers. Links are strong among all the sectors, and many employ Research Analysts and similar staffers. Someone might move from a research position with a university, for example, to a higher-level position with the Congressional Research Service.

Education and Training

Positions typically call for graduate-level training, either a master's degree in public administration or a degree in a specialty such as international relations or education. Entry-level positions such as Research Assistant might call for only an undergraduate degree, but a graduate degree is needed for many other positions.

A Research Analyst working on social policy, for instance, might have a Ph.D. or equivalent doctoral degree in political science, public administration, public policy analysis, planning, or a related field. Many positions call for the kind of sophisticated quantitative analysis taught at the graduate level, such as how to "crunch numbers" and how to perform cost-benefit analysis. Attorneys are often sought for positions requiring a knowledge of the law.

Experience, Skills, and Personality Traits

A background in specific policy areas such as education, human services, or criminal justice can be helpful. The ability to work on multiple tasks in a fast-paced work environment is a must. Every phone call is different and each has potential for changing the whole day's schedule.

Research Analysts should be able to provide accurate and objective information while maintaining confidentiality. Many work as an integral part of a research team, in which good communication skills are required. The research process can be long and frustrating, so patience is important.

Unions and Associations

Research Analysts might belong to the National Conference of State Legislatures or the Congressional Research Employees Association. They also might belong to broad-based organizations such as the American Society for Public Administration or the American Political Science Association.

Tips for Entry

1. Plan to earn a graduate degree to better your chances in this field. Learn more about graduate school options by checking out the website of the National Association of Schools of Public Affairs and Administration *(www.naspaa.org)*.

2. Look into internship possibilities. Some colleges and universities have Semester in Washington, D.C., programs.

3. Realize that many highly educated people work in relatively low-level legislative jobs. It is not uncommon for a legislative assistant on Capitol Hill to have a graduate degree. A legislative assistant with a graduate degree might then become a Research Analyst.

4. Develop expertise in a particular area, such as education, international relations, or economics, by taking courses and working in the field. A background in quantitative research can be particularly helpful.

5. Browse the websites of the National Conference of State Legislatures *(www.ncsl.org)* and the Congressional Research Service *(www.loc.gov/crsinfo)*.

CHIEF OF STAFF

CAREER PROFILE

Duties: Acting as top administrator of legislative office by advising and supporting the Legislator as well as managing staff

Alternate Title(s): Administrative Assistant, Staff Director

Salary Range: $52,000 to $130,000

Employment Prospects: Poor

Advancement Prospects: Good

Best Geographical Location(s): Washington, D.C., or state capitals

Prerequisites:
Education or Training—Varies
Experience—Five to 10 years
Special Skills and Personality Traits—Management and leadership skills; good political instincts

CAREER LADDER

```
┌─────────────────────────────┐
│  High-Level Position in Public │
│     or Private Sector        │
└─────────────────────────────┘

┌─────────────────────────────┐
│       Chief of Staff         │
└─────────────────────────────┘

┌─────────────────────────────┐
│   Legislative Director,      │
│  Government Administrator,    │
│   or Campaign Manager        │
└─────────────────────────────┘
```

Position Description

The Chief of Staff is the top dog of the legislative staff—second only to the senator or representative. Although sometimes known by the alternative title of administrative assistant, the Chief of Staff is hardly the glorified clerical worker the former term might imply. Increasingly, offices are switching to *Chief of Staff* to reflect the stature of the position. The Chief of Staff is usually the most influential member of the Legislator's staff as well as his or her most trusted aide. The job of the Chief of Staff defies easy categorization, as the individual plays many different roles such as personnel director, budget administrator, conflict mediator, policy adviser, and counselor.

Senators and representatives lead such high-pressured, tightly scheduled lives that they need someone in the office to lean on—usually the Chief of Staff. Quarters are cramped, pressures high. Tempers flare. The Chief of Staff tries to do whatever it takes to keep the boss happy. Some Chiefs of Staff have been known to mediate disputes between legislators and their spouses.

Chiefs of Staff try to keep everyone on the staff marching in the same general direction. No one wants a legislative staff to be sidetracked by infighting. High-stakes decisions need to be made quickly, with the legislator able to trust the judgment of the Chief of Staff. The two work together so closely that the Chief of Staff often knows the boss's answers to questions without asking.

The Chief of Staff coordinates the "big picture" for the legislator, managing the often conflicting needs of three different worlds:

- The Campaign—getting the legislator reelected
- The District—dealing with constituents
- The Main Office—working on legislative issues

Because there is only one legislator, some function inevitably is deferred. The district office, for example, might want the Legislator to deliver the Kiwanis Club keynote address. The campaign, however, has received 18 breakfast invitations for that same morning. The Chief of Staff needs to make quick decisions. Which events will attract the most people? Are any being arranged by friends of the legislator? Have some groups been turned down before? Meanwhile, myriad other questions compete for attention. A reporter calls to ask about a false accusation. A local constituent threatens to withdraw support. Another office wants the legislator to cosponsor a bill. As these developments unfold, the Chief of Staff needs to see what legislation is on the floor for that day. If the legislator is out of the office, the Chief of Staff may need to make all the important decisions on the basis of his or her knowledge of the legislator's overall philosophy.

The Chief of Staff and legislator work together closely on policy issues. A bill on foreign trade, for example, might raise conflicting concerns. On the one hand, the legislator might oppose it because of the country's human rights record. On the other hand, the bill could be economically advantageous to the district.

The Chief of Staff would help the legislator weigh the options, then make a decision. If, for example, the legislator decided to vote against the bill, the Chief of Staff might come up with a plan to "neutralize" opposition in the district. Perhaps the Chief of Staff would have the Press Secretary write a piece highlighting the legislator's support of other protrade bills.

In addition, the Chief of Staff administers budgets and oversees long-term planning. When a staffer leaves, the Chief of Staff interviews and chooses a replacement. Other responsibilities include

- Setting goals for various areas of the office (e.g., administrative, legislative, press)
- Keeping the legislator involved in all areas of operation
- Representing the legislator at various meetings, strategy sessions, seminars, and social functions
- Writing speeches for the legislator
- Developing and enforcing procedures for quality control
- Organizing meetings, in which he or she acts as leader, moderator, and facilitator

Salaries

Salaries for legislative Chiefs of Staff tend to be lower in state legislatures than in Congress. According to the National Conference of State Legislatures, the average salary range for Chiefs of Staff is $52,097 to $77,984. In Congress, salaries for Chiefs of Staff generally range from $80,000 to $130,000, according to industry sources.

Employment Prospects

Employment prospects are poor because of the small number of positions.

Advancement Prospects

Advancement prospects are good because Chief of Staffs can advance their careers by moving in a number of different directions. Within the legislative sector, a Chief of Staff might move to a larger jurisdiction—from the House to the Senate, for example. Chiefs of Staff also can move from the legislative to the executive sector, in which they generally supervise more employees and earn higher salaries. A Chief of Staff for the secretary of the treasury might supervise 50,000 employees, compared to 18 in a congressional office.

In addition, Chiefs of Staff can move to high-level positions with political campaigns, lobbying and consulting groups, and fund-raising organizations.

Education and Training

This is a field in which experience counts far more than an advanced degree. Political science courses can be helpful, but an advanced degree without legislative experience won't do an individual much good. Experience is crucial. Most Chiefs of Staff have at least a bachelor's degree and substantial legislative experience.

Experience, Skills, and Personality Traits

Most Chiefs of Staff have substantial experience in legislative or government affairs. Some campaign managers, too, rise to Chief of Staff, as do individuals with a background in government management. A city manager, for example, might move to the Congress and become a Chief of Staff.

As a result, Chiefs of Staff have well-honed political instincts. These insights become so intuitive that some individuals believe they were born with them. People who see themselves as "political by nature" look at a set of circumstances and move toward wherever they want to go. They see the "knots" in any given situation and know how to cut through them while avoiding trouble.

Someone might be highly intelligent but lack good political instincts. In one actual case, a congressional staffer worried about an unfavorable press report bought the reporter a bottle of wine. The supervising Chief of Staff saw this as a case of bad political instinct and predicted that the reporter would criticize the staffer in the press for resorting to bribery, and that is exactly what happened. The staffer was eventually fired.

Ideally, the Chief of Staff and legislator develop a relationship based on mutual respect and trust. In some less fortunate cases, however, the legislator might try to micromanage the office, thus undercutting the authority of the Chief of Staff. Whatever the case, the Chief of Staff works long hours under extreme pressure.

Unions and Associations

Chiefs of Staff in the legislative sector might belong to organizations such as the National Conference of State Legislatures or the U.S. House of Representatives' Administrative Assistants Association. The nonprofit, nonpartisan Congressional Management Foundation provides services for and information about personnel on Capitol Hill, including Chiefs of Staff.

Tips for Entry

1. Get legislative experience. Individuals commonly rise up the ranks from legislative assistant to legislative or communications director to Chief of Staff.
2. Volunteer on a candidate's campaign. Some campaign workers become full-time staffers.
3. Pay attention to the personal styles of individuals in public office. Personalities can make or break the relationship between legislator and Chief of Staff.

OTHER STATE/FEDERAL POSITIONS

PARALEGAL

CAREER PROFILE

Duties: Performing legal research; interviewing clients, witnesses, and/or experts; conducting investigations; summarizing information; drafting legal documents, correspondence, and pleadings

Alternate Title(s): Legal Assistant, Paralegal Specialist

Salary Range: $22,000 to $50,000

Employment Prospects: Excellent

Advancement Prospects: Excellent

Best Geographical Location(s): Washington, D.C.; state capitals; major urban areas

Prerequisites:
    Education or Training—Bachelor's degree and/or certificate
    Experience—Entry-level or relevant experience
    Special Skills and Personality Traits—Detail-oriented; analytical; willing to learn and adapt to new technologies; interested in legal issues

CAREER LADDER

```
┌─────────────────────────────────────────┐
│   Law Student or Paralegal Coordinator   │
└─────────────────────────────────────────┘

┌─────────────────────────────────────────┐
│                Paralegal                 │
└─────────────────────────────────────────┘

┌─────────────────────────────────────────┐
│             Student/Trainee              │
└─────────────────────────────────────────┘
```

Position Description

Paralegals play a role in law similar to that of nurses in medicine. Just as nurses care for patients but cannot prescribe medication, paralegals can assist with cases but must refrain from the actual practice of law, which includes presenting cases in court. Nevertheless, Paralegals are responsible for substantive tasks such as interviewing experts, analyzing documents, and drafting pleadings and motions. Because Paralegals can perform many of the same duties as lawyers for considerably less money, they are in great demand by both government agencies and private law firms seeking to boost efficiency. The U.S. Department of Labor expects the Paralegal profession to be one of the fastest-growing occupations in the decade ahead.

Individuals typically become Paralegals because they are interested in legal issues but uncertain about or disinclined toward going to law school. Some individuals want to get a close-up look at the legal environment before deciding to invest considerable time and money in law school. Others find that the increasingly substantive nature of Paralegal work makes it a career unto itself rather than a mere stepping stone to a law practice.

Some government agencies, including the U.S. Department of Justice and the Federal Trade Commission, offer temporary positions of particular interest to individuals pondering whether or not to attend law school. Permanent positions in government draw candidates from a variety of educational and career backgrounds, including career changers and entry-level professionals. Most Paralegals start out doing the "grunt work," sorting through boxes of information, coding documents, and checking copies for accuracy.

As Paralegals gain more experience, they do more research, interviewing, and report writing. Often, they review documents for relevant material or evidence—the so-called smoking gun. The everyday vocabulary of Paralegals includes words like *interrogatories, motions,* and *pleadings,* in reference to the various processes of the legal system.

Responsibilities for Paralegals in government agencies often fall into two main areas: investigation and court preparation. A Paralegal might investigate possible cases of fraud, which, if confirmed, are then raised in administrative hearings.

Paralegals might interview clients, sources, and/or experts. A Paralegal for the Federal Trade Commission, for instance, might look into possible antitrust statute violations by interviewing corporate executive officers from competing companies. What kind of impact has a particular merger had? Has their own business been harmed? What kind of market is there for the product?

Paralegals also commonly

- Review relevant case law
- Participate in pretrial conferences
- Initiate searches for supportive materials
- Prepare reports, exhibits, and statistical analyses
- Draft and edit legal and nonlegal materials

Salaries

Industry sources say that salaries for Paralegals in government generally range from $22,000 to $50,000, varying according to education, experience, and the size of the agency. According to the U.S. Department of Labor's *Occupational Outlook Handbook,* the median salary for Paralegals in the federal government is reported as $43,900; in local government, $32,200; and in legal services, $30,300.

Employment Prospects

Employment prospects are excellent because Paralegal work is a relatively new and rapidly growing field. The U.S. Department of Labor expects rapid growth in the decade ahead as Paralegals increasingly take on tasks formerly carried out by lawyers.

Advancement Prospects

Advancement prospects are excellent because Paralegals can move in a variety of directions. Some Paralegals leave their jobs to enter law school, attend law school at night, or apply to graduate programs in other fields such as business or public administration.

Others stay in the field, either in government or in private law firms, rising to positions like senior paralegal or paralegal administrator. Some fields, such as patent law, are particularly lucrative. Paralegals also commonly move into an administrative position in the courts, such as that of a court clerk. Still others use their knowledge of Paralegal work to branch off in new directions in the private sector. A Paralegal might become a recruiter for a temporary employment agency specializing in paralegal work. Or an individual might join a software company that trains Paralegals to use new computer programs.

Education and Training

Requirements for education and training vary from position to position. Over the past few decades, paralegal education has evolved from the in-house training of the 1960s to the master's degree programs of the 1990s. Educational options include

- Two-year associate's degrees
- Four-year baccalaureate degrees in paralegal/legal studies
- Postbaccalaureate certificate programs
- Master's degree programs

Paralegals disagree among themselves about how much and what type of education should be required. Currently there are no uniform standards for Paralegals. Some insiders oppose standardizing educational requirements; others believe that Paralegals should have a minimum of a baccalaureate degree.

Many universities and colleges offer majors in paralegal or legal studies, which include courses in legal research and writing, criminal law, and civil procedure. Another path for candidates, increasingly favored by employers, is an undergraduate major in a liberal arts field such as English or history followed by a postbaccalaureate certificate program.

Industry specialists recommend a combination of general education, legal specialty, and professional ethics requirements. Foremost among the liberal arts is English composition/grammar because Paralegals spend a fair amount of time writing. The American Bar Association approves (but does not accredit) paralegal education programs that seek its recognition.

Both the National Association of Legal Assistants and the National Federation of Paralegal Associations provide professional certification to individuals who meet their educational/experience requirements and pass a qualifying exam. Although the terms *Paralegal* and *legal assistant* are often used interchangeably, the designation of Registered Paralegal indicates higher educational attainment than that of Certified Legal Assistant because the National Federation of Paralegal Associations, unlike the National Association of Legal Assistants, requires candidates to hold a baccalaureate degree.

Experience, Skills, and Personality Traits

Many Paralegal programs provide experience through internships. The University of Massachusetts legal studies program, for instance, has an internship arrangement with the Massachusetts Commission against Discrimination. Internships can provide the practical experience needed to answer questions like, Would law school be worth the time and money? Is Paralegal work challenging enough? Which areas of specialization are most interesting? Whatever the specialty, Paralegals need to be detail-oriented. As one Paralegal put it, "You have to look out for crossing the *t*'s and dotting the *i*'s."

Paralegals must also have the analytical abilities needed to grasp the "big picture" and be willing to adapt to new technologies such as animated databases, scanning, and imaging. These days, court exhibits often are loaded directly onto CD-ROMs.

Temperament, too, might come into play. Some individuals may become Paralegals because they thrive behind the scenes rather than out front, arguing in the courtroom.

Unions and Associations
Professional associations representing Paralegals include the National Association of Legal Assistants and the National Federation of Paralegal Associations. The American Association of Paralegal Education and the American Bar Association's Standing Committee on Legal Assistants are involved in educational programs for Paralegals.

Tips for Entry
1. Research Paralegal programs. Industry specialists recommend baccalaureate or postbaccalaureate programs.
2. Join a Paralegal association to take advantage of networking opportunities.
3. Read up on the field by checking out books and/or the trade journal *Legal Assistant Today*.
4. Check out the U.S. Office of Personnel Management's website *(www.usajobs.opm.gov)* to look for opportunities for Paralegals.

GOVERNMENT LAWYER

CAREER PROFILE

Duties: Enforcing and administering the nation's systems of law and justice, which entail research, litigation, and other forms of legal practice

Alternate Title(s): Attorney, Counsel

Salary Range: $30,000 to $95,000

Employment Prospects: Good

Advancement Prospects: Good

Best Geographical Location(s): Positions at all levels of government (e.g., local, county, state, federal)

Prerequisites:

Education or Training—Law degree; necessary to pass bar exam in state where you plan to practice

Experience—Varies by level

Special Skills and Personality Traits—Interest in and commitment to public-sector law; excellent writing and speaking abilities; skill in analysis, and logic; perseverance

CAREER LADDER

```
┌─────────────────────────────────────┐
│  Lawyer in Private Practice or Judge │
└─────────────────────────────────────┘

┌─────────────────────────────────────┐
│         Government Lawyer            │
└─────────────────────────────────────┘

┌─────────────────────────────────────┐
│           Law Student                │
└─────────────────────────────────────┘
```

Position Description

Government Lawyers draft, analyze, and defend the laws of the land. Since law provides the framework for our nation, it should come as no surprise that Government Lawyers play an important role in all branches and levels of government. They interpret statutes for regulatory agencies, draft legislation for Congress, argue cases in criminal court, and act as advocates and advisers on virtually every issue of government concern, from drug trafficking to water rights. Government Lawyers often work closely with public officials, many of whom also hold law degrees.

Despite the wide variety of positions, Government Lawyers share a keen interest in public service, according to Lisa L. Abrams, J.D., author of *The Official Guide to Legal Specialties*. They want to make a difference by grappling with issues of concern to all citizens, not just paying clients. Some Government Lawyers—prosecutors of high-profile crimes like murder and kidnapping, for instance—grab the public spotlight; others toil behind the scenes.

At the municipal level, Government Lawyers, who may be called City Solicitors, are constantly answering questions from public officials, department heads, and other staffers. They grapple with questions such as the legal issues involved

in a particular plan for land development or the city's response to a possible lawsuit.

At the state level, a Government Lawyer might work in an executive agency involved in regulatory matters. If, for instance, a citizen files a complaint against a licensed professional, the Government Lawyer might help decide whether or not the person is guilty of fraud or misconduct.

Government Lawyers at the federal level work for a number of different agencies, including the Department of Justice, which is supervised by the U.S. Attorney General. Among other responsibilities, the Department of Justice deals with civil rights issues and defends the United States when it is sued. For instance, the attorney might handle a case involving the access of disabled people to public accommodations or defend the United States in a suit involving an accident on federal property.

In the legislative sector, Government Lawyers work in offices of members of Congress, legislative committees, and organizations providing special legal services such as bill drafting, policy advising, and legal oversight. An attorney involved in a committee dealing with health-care oversight, for example, might be involved in questions related to Medicaid fraud. What types of cases are investigators handling?

Are certain policies leaving programs vulnerable to fraud and abuse? How might these problems be best addressed? Another Attorney might work on bill drafting to make sure all proposed legislation meets legal standards.

In the criminal justice system, Government Lawyers work as state attorneys general, prosecutors, and public defenders. Prosecutors, who represent the people of the United States against suspected criminals, sometimes run for elected positions such as district attorney or attorney general. On the other side of the court are the public defenders, who represent defendants unable to afford a private attorney. Many cases are resolved by plea bargain rather than taken to trial.

Because of the wide variety of positions, government law attracts both individuals seeking a long-term niche and those looking for a stepping stone. Many Government Lawyers move into the private sector, where they can earn higher salaries but often have to work longer hours. Some, though, return to the public sector, where they can represent the issues of all citizens without having to worry about such private-practice concerns as generating "billable hours" or "making partner."

Salaries

Government Lawyers generally earn less than attorneys in private practice. According to the Department of Labor's *Occupational Outlook Handbook,* median annual salaries for Government Lawyers were recently about $66,000 at the local level, $64,000 at the state level, and $87,000 at the federal level. Salaries were lower for entry-level Government Lawyers and higher for those with considerable experience.

Employment Prospects

Employment prospects are good because all levels and branches of government employ Lawyers. About 13 percent of law school graduates take jobs with the government, according to the National Association for Law Placement. Areas of pressing concern, such as health care, intellectual property, international law, elder law, environmental law, and sexual harassment, offer particularly good opportunities.

Insiders say that the government provides a greater degree of security and better working hours than private practice. On the other hand, the financial rewards of private practice can be much greater as top salaries in the private sector exceed those in government.

Advancement Prospects

Advancement prospects are good because government practice gives Lawyers two important assets: expertise in a particular field of law and personal contacts valuable for networking. Some individuals continue to work in government, perhaps advancing to administrative positions. Others enter private practice, in which hours may be longer and financial

rewards greater, or the nonprofit sector, which puts a similar emphasis on the public interest. For example, someone might go from being a prosecutor for the government to working as an attorney for a women's advocacy group.

Education and Training

Becoming a lawyer generally requires seven years of post-secondary education. Although some colleges and universities offer courses in legal studies or criminal justice, industry sources say there is no one recommended "prelaw" major. Many majors, including English, political science, and history, can be useful, as they help students develop proficiency in researching, writing, and thinking logically—skills needed to succeed in both law school and the profession.

Individuals applying to law school face stiff competition, especially for the most prestigious schools. All law schools approved by the American Bar Association require students to take the Law School Admission Test (LSAT). Some law schools offer joint programs, such as in law and business or public administration, which usually require an additional semester or year.

For the first year or so of law school, students generally take core classes in topics such as constitutional law, contracts, property law, torts, civil procedure, and legal writing. Later, they can take more specialized courses to investigate fields of interest such as criminal or labor law. Clinical programs, clerkships, and internships help students decide what kind of practice best suits them. Law school graduates receive the degree of juris doctor (J.D.) but must pass a written bar examination to practice in any state or other jurisdiction.

Experience, Skills, and Personality Traits

Government Lawyers share many traits with other attorneys but also possess one special characteristic—a commitment to public service. They want to represent all citizens rather than a select group of clients. Many become interested in public-sector law through clinical programs in law school or clerkships for judges.

Under the broad umbrella of government law, skills vary by position and field of specialization. Those who appear frequently in court must be able to think quickly and speak with ease and authority. Negotiating skills are particularly important for resolving cases through plea bargains.

Most Government Lawyers spend the majority of their time outside the courtroom, interviewing clients and witnesses and handling other details in preparation for trial—tasks that require a combination of interpersonal and organizational skills. Lawyers must be able to persevere in the face of legal problems and win the respect of others to succeed on the job. Because Government Lawyers handle complex cases, they must be able to think logically and write clearly. Legal writing must be precise to prevent potential misinterpretation and, hence, lawsuits.

Unions and Associations

Associations of interest include the National Association for Law Placement and the American Bar Association.

Tips for Entry

1. Participate in debating or other activities to hone public-speaking skills for the courtroom.
2. Check out guides to law schools. The websites of the American Bar Association *(www.abanet.org)* and the National Association for Law Placement *(www.nalp.org)* also provide useful information.
3. Look into working as a law clerk for a judge after graduation from law school. These positions provide an excellent credential as well as firsthand exposure to the judicial system.
4. Arrange for informational interviews with Government Lawyers as part of your career planning. Respect the busy schedules of individuals by offering to limit interviews to 10 minutes.

POLICY ANALYST

CAREER PROFILE

Duties: Using various analytical tools to prepare reports, conduct briefings, and perform other duties that advise decision makers about policy options

Alternate Title(s): Budget Analyst, Program Analyst

Salary Range: $25,000 to $80,000

Employment Prospects: Fair to good

Advancement Prospects: Good

Best Geographical Location(s): Varies by state

Prerequisites:

Education or Training—Master's degree in public policy, public administration, or public affairs
Experience—Internship recommended
Special Skills and Personality Traits—Understanding of decision making, budget, and legislative processes as well as analytical techniques and particular area of public policy (e.g., health care, education); excellent communication and interpersonal skills; ability to think logically

CAREER LADDER

```
+-----------------------------------+
|  Policy Maker, Think Tank Analyst |
+-----------------------------------+

+-----------------------------------+
|         Policy Analyst            |
+-----------------------------------+

+-----------------------------------+
|        Graduate Student           |
+-----------------------------------+
```

Position Description

Policy Analysts trace their roots back to the experts of ancient times who advised princes and kings. Yet despite such links to the past, the modern profession of policy analysis dates back only to the second half of the 20th century. An outgrowth of the economic techniques of the 1960s, policy analysis changed dramatically in the following 40 years, according to Beryl Radin, author of *Beyond Machiavelli: Policy Analysis Comes of Age.*

Gone are the days when Policy Analysts hatched new government programs in isolation. Such programs suffered unexpected political and practical problems, as formal analysis alone was not enough. Decision makers began looking for newcomers with program expertise and master's degrees in public policy instead of economics. These days, Policy Analysts generally specialize in a particular area, such as housing or child care, working collaboratively with other specialists inside and outside government.

Increasingly, long reports have given way to pithy papers and briefings. Policy Analysts have lost some of the clout they had in the old days but gained a wider range of responsibilities. These days they focus not only on the development of programs but also on their implementation and evaluation. Some Policy Analysts also produce "quick and dirty" analyses to help public officials respond immediately to topical issues or bad press.

Policy Analysts use techniques such as program analysis and cost estimates to advise policymakers. Eugene Bardach describes the classic approach in *The Eight-Step Path of Policy Analysis: A Handbook for Practice:*

- Define the problem
- Assemble some evidence
- Construct the alternatives
- Select the criteria
- Project the outcomes
- Confront the trade-offs
- Decide
- Tell your story

In the real world of government, however, Policy Analysts often follow a less formal route that is based on the needs of decision makers. For example, a short briefing might consist of only two steps, compared to all eight for a full-length strategic or annual performance plan. Ultimately, the decision maker determines which of the Policy Analyst's recommendations are accepted.

Increasingly, Policy Analysts wrestle with such political issues as ideological differences and budget limitations. For instance, a Policy Analyst working on a plan to expand a block grant program for child care might lead focus groups to gauge public reaction to various proposals. How might the proposal win the broadest possible public support despite probable opposition from stay-at-home parents? Would interest groups in favor of child care find the proposal too weak? Might opposition arise in other departments within the agency?

As do traditional bureaucrats, Policy Analysts spend much of their time attending meetings and responding to correspondence. Yet they also introduce a certain logic to the messy business of government decision making. In the end, the role of Policy Analyst depends on the needs of the agency.

Salaries

Salaries generally range from $25,000 to $80,000. On the low end of the scale are states with relatively low costs of living. On the higher end are upper-level positions in the federal government. In the federal government, positions are "stepped," with earnings recently ranging on the government pay scale from a GS-9 level of $33,254 to a GS-15 of $79,710.

Employment Prospects

Employment prospects are fair to good. The downsizing of the federal government and devolution of responsibilities to the states have eliminated some positions and created others. Because not all states have positions for Policy Analysts, the types of analytical tasks they perform may be incorporated in other positions, such as program manager. Positions with the federal government have become increasingly competitive. As a result, insiders recommend that individuals take advantage of internship possibilities, particularly the Presidential Management Internship, to get a foot in the door.

Advancement Prospects

Advancement prospects are good because entry into the profession opens up doors. Once individuals find their first jobs, they can move in a variety of directions, either within government or to think tanks, advocacy groups, or other organizations.

Policy Analysts work in a variety of settings. Someone might, for example, leave a Policy Analyst position with the federal government to become director of policy for an advocacy group. Another possibility is staying within government but moving into a decision-making rather than an advising role.

Education and Training

Graduate programs in public policy, public administration, and public affairs serve as common training grounds for individuals in the field. These programs train students in the tools of the trade, such as program analysis, budget projections, implementation analysis, and evaluation.

Experience, Skills, and Personality Traits

Internships provide an excellent way to get a foot in the door. Insiders recommend that individuals use the time between college and graduate school to gain experience (either through an internship or in an entry-level position) in a particular area of policy. Someone interested in child care policy, for instance, might work as a research assistant for an interest group such as the Children's Defense Fund.

Policy Analysts must be able to draw on a variety of quantitative and qualitative analytical techniques. Computers have revolutionized this field, as they have many others. Policy Analysts increasingly are expected not only to be good writers and analysts but also to be experts in a particular field of policy.

Although trained to be objective observers, they must also be savvy about the inner workings of politics and government. They commonly meet with others in government and special interest groups to discuss policy issues. Increasingly, Policy Analysts are expected to make short, pithy summaries for busy decision makers. One big challenge for Policy Analysts is finding time to reflect on ways to improve and initiate programs.

Because Policy Analysts advise but do not make policies, their job can be frustrating at times. For example, a long report might be used only for fine-tuning a program, not structuring it, the decision maker's role. Some Policy Analysts act not only as objective observers but also as advocates in their area of expertise. Ultimately, Policy Analysts must decide for themselves what their expectations should be.

Unions and Associations

Policy Analysts belong to a variety of associations, including the Association for Public Policy Analysis and Management (APPAM), National Association of Schools of Public Affairs and Administration, American Political Science Association, and American Society for Public Administration.

Tips for Entry

1. Look into graduate programs in public policy, public administration, or public affairs; many Policy Analysts are graduates of these programs. The website of the National Association of Schools of Public Affairs and Administration (www.naspaa.org) provides helpful links.

2. Focus on a particular policy area in keeping with your own interests. Increasingly, this is a field of specialists.
3. Seek out internship programs and/or entry-level positions between college and graduate school to develop expertise in a particular area of policy. Insiders recommend the Presidential Management Internship program as a foot in the door to competitive positions in the federal government.

4. Check out the federal government's personnel website *(www.usajobs.opm.gov)* to learn more about the Presidential Management Internship program.
5. Create your own internship program by offering to work for the head of policy for an agency or organization of interest.

PRESS SECRETARY

CAREER PROFILE

Duties: Disseminating information to the media; advising and counseling public officials

Alternate Title(s): Media Adviser, Public Information Officer

Salary Range: $25,000 to $60,000

Employment Prospects: Good

Advancement Prospects: Good

Best Geographical Location(s): Large metropolitan areas, state capitals

Prerequisites:

Education or Training—College degree

Experience—Media experience preferred

Special Skills and Personality Traits—Articulate; able to create good writing; energetic; outgoing; creative; willing to work long hours

CAREER LADDER

```
┌─────────────────────────────┐
│      Chief of Staff         │
│ or Communication Director   │
└─────────────────────────────┘

┌─────────────────────────────┐
│      Press Secretary        │
└─────────────────────────────┘

┌─────────────────────────────┐
│ Campaign Worker, Writer/Reporter, │
│   or Press Assistant        │
└─────────────────────────────┘
```

Position Description

Press Secretaries combine the personal loyalty of political aides with the communications savvy of public information officers. Their job is helping government officials maintain a positive public image, largely through the media. Press Secretaries spend much of their time disseminating information to reporters and editors as well as responding to questions about specific issues. As do Public Information Officers, they often have backgrounds in journalism. Having first-hand experience helps Press Secretaries know how to pitch stories to the media.

Press Secretaries generally work for individuals rather than agencies. This one-on-one relationship gives them some unique responsibilities. A Press Secretary might write a short biography of the public official for the Internet or oversee a newsletter for constituents.

The Press Secretary is often a part of the politician's inner circle. This exposure to day-to-day operations helps Press Secretaries understand the issues well enough to communicate them effectively to the media. Once the public official takes a stand, the Press Secretary monitors public reaction.

As an adviser, the Press Secretary counsels the public official on the likely reactions of different constituencies. Who, for example, might object to a new manufacturing plant? Environmental groups? Neighbors? The last thing the public official wants is for an unexpected source of opposition to make itself known at the last minute.

Press Secretaries often need to answer difficult questions from reporters. Certain techniques can either score points or backfire. An off-the-cuff emotional response, for instance, might generate more press coverage than a bland statement, but it also might reflect negatively on the government official and hurt the Press Secretary's own career.

Being proactive, rather than reactive, can make the Press Secretary more effective. Seasoned Press Secretaries know that three things can quell a crisis—speed, facts, and focus. They have an action plan prepared so they can quickly disseminate the facts and get back to business.

Pressure can be intense in this deadline-driven field. Press Secretaries often wear beepers to respond to reporters under deadline. If the Press Secretary releases information too late, the public official might lose out on much-needed exposure.

Press Secretaries also commonly

• Monitor the media
• Give staff oral and written briefs
• Analyze the attitudes and opinions of the public
• Advise the politician on appropriate responses to questions
• Prepare information on key projects or policy for the public
• Write speeches

Salaries

Salaries vary greatly, as smaller entities generally pay on the lower end. Officeholders decide the salaries of their Press Secretaries. If they consider the Press Secretary an entry-level position, they pay less than if they look at it as a senior-staff job. Many salaries fall into the $30,000 to $50,000 range, according to the National Association of Government Communicators.

Employment Prospects

Employment prospects are fair to good because positions with elected and administrative officials can be found at the local, state, and federal levels. Opportunities are generally best during an election cycle. In smaller entities such as local government, the Press Secretary might work as a general aide as well as a media adviser.

Advancement Prospects

Advancement prospects are good because Press Secretaries can advance their careers in a few different directions. Some stay with an elected official but move up the ranks to a position such as chief of staff. Others move laterally in government. Still others go into private consulting.

Education and Training

A degree in English, journalism, political science, communication, history, or public policy is helpful in this field. A master's degree in a field such as political science might help a candidate land certain positions.

Experience, Skills, and Personality Traits

Often Press Secretaries have a media background or experience in campaign work, public relations, or research. Certain skills, though, are acquired on the job. In this quick-paced field, individuals need to "hit the ground running." Time is precious, and events occur at a moment's notice. Press Secretaries must be able to communicate well, both verbally and in writing, under pressure.

Individuals need to have a good understanding of the media, public opinion, and current issues. Good research skills are important. The ability to spot an issue before it becomes a problem is a definite plus. Press Secretaries also should be well-organized, persuasive, and able to handle stress.

Unions and Associations

The National Association of Government Communicators is a professional association that hosts a yearly conference for individuals in the field. Press Secretaries also might be members of the American Society for Public Administration, state municipal associations, and other organizations.

Tips for Entry

1. Volunteer on a political campaign.
2. Get an internship, if possible. Internships can open doors to full-time positions such as Press Assistant, which, in turn, can lead to assistant press secretary or Press Secretary.
3. Offer to help a school board or other organization with press releases and/or brochures.
4. Become active in a political party to take advantage of important networking opportunities.
5. Check listings for Press Secretaries and related positions at university career centers. Sometimes entry-level jobs such as press assistants are available.

SPEECHWRITER

CAREER PROFILE

Duties: Meeting with public officials; writing speeches, position papers, analyses, and other special projects

Alternate Title(s): Special Assistant, Communication Officer, Writer

Salary Range: $40,000 to $100,000+

Employment Prospects: Poor

Advancement Prospects: Good

Best Geographical Location(s): Washington, D.C.

Prerequisites:

Education or Training—Bachelor's degree required; master's degree sometimes preferred

Experience—Five to 10 years

Special Skills and Personality Traits—Quick thinking; computer literacy; creativity; willingness to let credit for one's work go to the boss

CAREER LADDER

```
┌─────────────────────────────────┐
│    Communication Director        │
│    or Corporate Speechwriter     │
└─────────────────────────────────┘

┌─────────────────────────────────┐
│         Speechwriter             │
└─────────────────────────────────┘

┌─────────────────────────────────┐
│    Public Information Officer    │
└─────────────────────────────────┘
```

Position Description

Individuals who work exclusively as Speechwriters are a rare breed. Most speeches are written by staffers and public officials themselves, who juggle a variety of responsibilities. Individuals who hold the title of Speechwriter work primarily for high-level politicians such as the president, the vice president, cabinet secretaries, and some members of Congress, administrative officials, U.S. governors, and mayors of large cities.

Many speechwriting jobs go to insiders who are at the right place at the right time. Typically they have worked their way up a communication track, although sometimes expertise in a particular field, such as foreign policy, opens doors to a position as Speechwriter. Positions often include other types of writing, such as articles and policy papers, as well as special projects such as drafting the greeting for Christmas cards.

Speechwriting has long been shrouded in mystery to assure that credit goes to those who utter the words rather than those who write them. Although Presidents as far back as George Washington have sought help with their speeches, they have done so under the guise of policy advice. President Washington turned to his secretary of the treasury, Alexander Hamilton; Abraham Lincoln, to his sec-

retary of state, William Seward. Everyone knows that U.S. Presidents and other key officials are too busy to write all their own speeches from scratch. In the 20th century, speechwriting gained some recognition. By the 1970s, the White House had established an Office of Speechwriting. The former presidential Speechwriter Peggy Noonan writes openly about how she, not President George Bush, created such memorable lines as "a thousand points of light" and "read my lips."

The way Speechwriters go about their work depends largely on the needs of their bosses. Whereas some public officials draft most of their own speeches, others depend more heavily on Speechwriters. Seasoned Speechwriters know how to dig down into the experiences, personalities, and passions of their bosses to create phrases that "sound" like those of the speaker. In the process, they ask themselves questions like, Who is the audience? Which key issues should be addressed?

Usually the Speechwriter and public official meet to discuss what should be included in the speech. Because speeches can make or break the speaker's reputation, speechwriting is often done "by committee." Drafts of the speech are often given out to various advisers for comment. One of President Jimmy Carter's Speechwriters compared his role to that of a trauma surgeon: He was the one who did the suturing, stitching together everyone else's input.

An important speech might go through more than a dozen drafts as speaker and Speechwriter fine-tune the text. Does the beginning effectively set the tone? Is the speech "punchy" enough? Does one section lead naturally into the next? Will people with short attention spans want to listen to the whole speech?

One veteran Speechwriter, Warren Anderson, formerly of the army and the Joint Chiefs of Staff, compares the relationship between speaker and Speechwriter to a two-career marriage: First, the two depend heavily on each other even though they see little of one another. Second, interference from outsiders can put an undue strain on the relationship. And, third, the initial excitement of the pairing often wears off with time.

Not surprisingly, there are a lot of "divorces." But legendary pairings like that of President John F. Kennedy and his Speechwriter, Theodore Sorenson, result in words that can capture and define an era. Speechwriters often come and go with administrations. Once an elected official is voted out of office, the Speechwriter might be out of a job.

Salaries

Salaries range widely, from $40,000 to $100,000 or more, according to industry sources. Speechwriters working on the national level tend to make higher salaries than those at the state or local level. Some Speechwriters work on a freelance basis. The general rule of thumb is to allow one hour of work for every minute of speech. In the private sector, freelance Speechwriters can make more than $100 an hour, according to the newsletter *The Executive Speaker.*

Employment Prospects

Employment prospects are poor because of the scarcity of positions devoted exclusively—or even primarily—to speechwriting. However, political positions turn over fairly quickly, thus creating the need for new Speechwriters, especially during an election cycle. Speechwriters also can lose their jobs because of shifts in administration. Presidential candidates, for example, hire Speechwriters, but, if the candidate loses the election, the Speechwriter is out of work.

Advancement Prospects

Advancement prospects are good because writing speeches for well-known officials can open up doors. Speechwriters can move in a variety of directions. In addition to advancing in government, they can get into media or corporate communication. Many become corporate Speechwriters. Some open up their own communication businesses.

Education and Training

A bachelor's degree is required, and graduate work in communication or a related field may be helpful. At many universities, communication programs offer courses in public relations that address speechwriting. The Accrediting Council on Education in Journalism and Mass Communications maintains a list of all currently accredited journalism and mass communications programs with links to program websites.

Experience, Skills, and Personality Traits

Speechwriters generally have several years of experience. Many begin writing speeches after working in journalism, then in government communication. Communication staffers commonly write speeches as well as press releases, position papers, and the like. By the time someone becomes a Speechwriter, he or she should have well-developed political instincts as well as a feel for the power of the spoken word.

Speechwriters try to coin memorable phrases. Often they use symbols and metaphors as shorthand representations of more complex ideas. In an article in *Writer's Digest,* Speechwriter Mike Brake describes how, in a speech to the legislature to urge reform of state purchasing regulations, he chose a symbol—a box of staples—to illustrate how complicated the old spending rules were.

Many Speechwriters use split screens and other computer techniques in their work. Computer literacy can speed up the work, and, in speechwriting, time is of the essence. A Speechwriter might be told at 4 P.M. that the boss is going to be on the six o'clock news.

Because credit for speeches generally goes to the speaker, not the writer, Speechwriters need to be willing to subordinate their own egos to those of their bosses. As one veteran speechwriter put it, "You need a pretty good ego."

Unions and Associations

Speechwriters might belong to the National Association of Government Communicators, the Public Relations Society of America, Inc., or a variety of other organizations dealing with communication.

Tips for Entry

1. Join a public speaking or debating club.
2. Check out books on speechwriting and anthologies of speeches at the library. Pay attention to political speeches and addresses on television.
3. Volunteer to write speeches for a community or charity group. Keep a copy of the text for your portfolio and list the project on your résumé.

INTERNATIONAL AFFAIRS

UNITED NATIONS HEADQUARTERS INTERN

CAREER PROFILE

Duties: Assisting with preparation for meetings, conducting research, drafting papers, attending meetings, and becoming familiar with United Nations (UN) operations

Alternate Title(s): Intern, Secretariat Intern

Salary Range: None

Employment Prospects: Fair to good

Advancement Prospects: Good to excellent

Best Geographical Location(s): Interns come from a variety of locations to work at UN Headquarters in New York City

Prerequisites:

Education or Training—Graduate school

Experience—Volunteer work and travel abroad recommended

Special Skills and Personality Traits—Good academic and analytical skills; language abilities; excellent communication and interpersonal skills

CAREER LADDER

```
┌─────────────────────────────┐
│     Various Positions in     │
│    International Affairs     │
└─────────────────────────────┘

┌─────────────────────────────┐
│    UN Headquarters Intern    │
└─────────────────────────────┘

┌─────────────────────────────┐
│      Graduate Student        │
└─────────────────────────────┘
```

Position Description

United Nations Headquarters Internships expose graduate students to the inner workings of a legendary institution. However, anyone expecting to go directly from a UN Headquarters Internship to paid employment with the United Nations is bound to be disappointed. UN Headquarters Interns are prohibited from seeking employment with the United Nations for six months after completion of their internships. Because employment at the United Nations is highly competitive—partly as a result of a geographical quota system, partly because of the UN's need for highly trained personnel—the six-month rule was developed to dissuade applicants from thinking of the internship as an automatic "door opener."

UN Headquarters Interns work in the Secretariat, the main administrative body of the United Nations. Internships are generally two months long, although they can be extended, with sessions in the fall, spring, and summer. Applicants must submit an application, résumé, and short (150 to 250 words) essay stating their reasons for wanting to be in the program. Selected candidates are expected to work five days a week from 9 A.M. to 5 P.M.

The UN Headquarters Internship program combines job responsibilities with educational activities. For instance, a Headquarters Intern might be asked to sit in on a session of the General Assembly and report on it to his or her department. Headquarters Interns commonly conduct research, participate in preparation for meetings, draft papers, and attend briefings about the UN system and its goals. They also usually have the opportunity to meet with the Secretary-General for a photo shoot.

The United Nations assigns Headquarters Interns to 11 different departments:

1. Executive Office of the Secretary General
2. Office of Internal Oversight Services
3. Office of Legal Affairs
4. Department of Political Affairs
5. Department of Disarmament Affairs
6. Department of Peacekeeping Operations
7. Office for the Coordination of Humanitarian Affairs
8. Department of Economic and Social Affairs
9. Department of General Assembly Affairs and Conference Services
10. Department of Public Information
11. Department of Management

When applying for internships, applicants indicate their top three areas of interest. The Internship Coordinator takes these choices into consideration when making assignments. Each Intern is then assigned to a supervisor, who provides a written description of responsibilities during the first week of the internship.

A typical day usually begins when Interns check in with their supervisors. From there, the Intern might go to the UN library to gather data, then return to the office to assist with tasks such as preparing agendas and contacting individuals abroad for an upcoming meeting or conference such as the World Summit on Sustainable Development.

The Intern might also help draft a major document, update the department's webpage, and perform some clerical tasks. In the afternoon, the Intern might attend an informational meeting about the responsibilities of another department. The day usually ends when the Intern follows up with his or her supervisor. At the end of the session, the Intern receives a certificate signed by the Secretary-General.

Salaries

UN Headquarters Interns are not paid. Because their schedules do not allow for other work, UN Interns must be prepared to pay an estimated $2,500 a month to live in New York City.

The majority of Interns—60 to 75 percent—receive either full or partial funding from educational institutions or organizations, according to the Internship Coordinator. Some Interns receive funding from their governments. The rest pay their own expenses.

Most students choose to share apartments. The average studio apartment rents for $700 to $1,700 per month, according to the UN Headquarters Internship website. The Internship program provides a list of accommodation possibilities to all selected candidates.

Employment Prospects

Employment prospects are fair to good because, although internships are competitive, they are offered three times a year, in the fall, spring, and summer. About 15 percent of applicants are accepted for 120 to 150 slots per session, according to the Internship Coordinator Rene Moller. Applicants indicate their top three fields of interest, but certain areas—including peacekeeping, humanitarian, social, and political affairs—are particularly popular and so more competitive.

The UN Headquarters Internship is just one of several internships offered within the highly decentralized UN system. Affiliated specialized agencies or programs with separate internship programs include the UN Development Program, UN Children's Fund (UNICEF), International Labor Organization (ILO), and UN Institute for Training and Research. Although there is no one listing of all UN-affiliated internships, all offices are linked to the UN's website (*www.un.org*).

Advancement Prospects

Advancement prospects are good to excellent because, even though internships do not lead directly to employment with the United Nations, they nevertheless open a variety of doors. Some UN Headquarters Interns find mentors who take an interest in their career goals. UN Interns commonly move on to positions with intergovernmental organizations (e.g., The North Atlantic Treaty Organization [NATO]); nongovernmental organizations (e.g., the International Red Cross), and the private sector (e.g., international finance). More than 1,500 nongovernmental organizations have "consultative status" with the United Nations. Some former Interns are hired at the UN after working in nonprofits or other types of organizations for a few years.

Although an internship does not ensure entry, it can give a qualified candidate an advantage over another applicant who is equally qualified. The UN Headquarters Internship Coordinator estimated in 2002 that 5 percent of Headquarters Interns are eventually hired by the United Nations.

Education and Training

To qualify for a UN Headquarters Internship, a student must be enrolled in a degree-granting graduate program. Relevant fields of study include, but are not limited to, diplomacy, international affairs, business administration, economics, law, political science, and peace studies. However, no restrictions are placed on the fields of study of prospective Interns.

Experience, Skills, and Personality Traits

Many UN Headquarters Interns have lived or studied abroad and worked as volunteers. Any work experience that involves dealing with a wide variety of people is helpful, as the United Nations is a culturally diverse environment.

The United Nations looks for applicants with good academic and analytical skills, good language skills, and excellent communication and interpersonal skills. Knowledge of one or more languages is helpful. Successful Interns tend to be self-starters who have the patience needed to work within a bureaucracy, according to Helen Anderson, Director of Internships for the Fletcher School at Tufts University.

Unions and Associations

There are no unions or associations for UN Headquarters Interns. Graduate students, though, can turn to their schools' career counselors for professional guidance.

Tips for Entry

1. Study or live abroad.
2. Participate in volunteer activities.
3. Choose a graduate program in your field of interest. To qualify for the UN Headquarters Internship program, you must be a graduate student.

4. Browse the UN website *(www.un.org)* for information about the UN Internship program (click on *About the United Nations*) and links to other internship programs within the highly decentralized UN system. Other internship programs include those of the UN Children's Fund (UNICEF), the UN Development Program, the International Labor Organization, and the UN Institute for Training and Research.

5. Seek the help of graduate school career counselors. They might be able to put you in touch with alumni who work at the UN and can help you get the most out of your internship experience.

FOREIGN SERVICE OFFICER

CAREER PROFILE

Duties: Advocating and advancing U.S. policy interests and protecting the welfare of U.S. citizens abroad in embassies throughout the world

Alternate Title(s): Junior Officer, Professional Diplomat, Consular Officer, Administrative Officer, Economic Officer, Political Officer, Public Diplomacy Officer

Salary Range: $32,000 to $62,000

Employment Prospects: Fair

Advancement Prospects: Good

Best Geographical Location(s): U.S. embassies throughout the world

Prerequisites:

Education or Training—Generally bachelor's degree or higher; passing grade on the foreign service examination

Experience—Varying requirements; age between 20 and 59 years

Special Skills and Personality Traits—Availability for worldwide assignments and sometimes hardship; willingness to learn a foreign language; strong interpersonal and communication skills; good problem-solving and decision-making abilities; uncommon commitment

CAREER LADDER

```
┌─────────────────────────────────────┐
│   Senior Foreign Service Officer     │
└─────────────────────────────────────┘

┌─────────────────────────────────────┐
│   Junior Foreign Service Officer     │
└─────────────────────────────────────┘

┌─────────────────────────────────────┐
│     College or Graduate Student      │
└─────────────────────────────────────┘
```

Position Description

Foreign Service Officers represent the interests of the United States abroad. From their posts in embassies throughout the world, they promote U.S. foreign policy, administer U.S. immigration and nationalization laws, assist Americans overseas, and explain American objectives and cultures to the people of other countries. Foreign Service Officers report to policy makers in Washington, D.C., about everything from routine tasks to earthquakes, coups, or terrorist attacks.

As professional diplomats, Foreign Service Officers hold front-line positions under the embassy's top official, the Ambassador. Embassies generally include five sections corresponding to the career paths of Foreign Service Officers:

- Consular (e.g., visa processing, assistance to American citizens)
- Administrative (e.g., management of budgets, personnel)
- Economic (e.g., trade agreements, U.S. business)
- Political (e.g., human rights issues, political parties)
- Public diplomacy (e.g., public information, cultural programs)

Foreign Service Officers generally begin their service in the Consular Division. In addition to interviewing applicants applying for visas to visit the United States, consular officers protect against visa fraud and prevent potentially dangerous individuals from entering the United States. They also serve as a "life raft" for American citizens in the host country. If an American tourist loses his or her passport, the consular officer replaces it. Or, perhaps, an American is arrested abroad, runs out of money, or needs help in the event of a disaster—all responsibilities of the consular officer.

After completing their consular assignments, Foreign Service Officers generally enter into long-term service in their chosen career path. Individuals who serve as Administrative Officers provide the management expertise needed for the smooth and efficient operations of the post. They locate housing for incoming staff, hire support staff, order supplies, and perform other administrative tasks.

Foreign Service Officers in the Economic Division deal with trade policy and other business matters. They might participate in trade negotiations between countries that involve months of detailed point-by-point debate. In addition, economic officers are commonly involved in tracking significant economic developments in the host country, offering assistance to U.S. business representatives, and providing support for specific U.S. trade promotion programs.

Political officers, as their title implies, monitor political events within the host country and advocate U.S. political interests. In the case of an upcoming election, the political officer might spend months preparing for it, perhaps working with government officials to invite international observers to certify the fairness of the election. Political officers might also launch projects such as voter-education drives using sketches and storyboards to educate a largely illiterate population about voting procedures. Political officers also are commonly involved in tracking the development of new and existing political parties and reporting on human rights issues.

The final career path—public diplomacy—involves building bridges of communication between the United States and the host country. Foreign Service Officers in the Public Diplomacy Division combine press-related functions with cultural-exchange responsibilities. They serve as spokespersons for the United States and coordinate people-to-people exchanges, including the Fulbright program, which administers programs of study in the United States and overseas.

Whatever the career path, Foreign Service Officers must commit to a life-style, not just a job. Foreign Service Officers generally spend more than half of their careers overseas and the rest on domestic assignments in Washington, D.C., or occasionally in other parts of the United States on special assignment. Many oversee posts are in small or remote countries where American-style amenities are unavailable

Salaries

Salaries for Foreign Service Officers vary according to levels of education and experience. Currently, the entry-level salary for all candidates without a college degree is $30,719, compared to $34,575 for candidates with a bachelor's degree in any field and $38,675 for candidates who have a master's degree, a law degree, or both, and $41,030 for candidates with a doctorate or a master's degree in law. Within each grouping, salaries vary according to experience. Most applicants find their starting salary to be in the high $30,000s.

In addition, Foreign Service Officers receive a package of benefits and a system of allowances that supplement the basic salary. This includes free housing while serving overseas, overseas moving expenses, hardship allowances, danger pay up to a total of 40 percent of one's salary, educa-

tional expenses overseas for dependents, home leave travel, and, in some posts, rest and recuperation travel.

Employment Prospects

Employment prospects are fair because, although the United States State Department recently increased the number of entry-level Foreign Service Officers from about 250 to 466 a year in 2001, the application process for Foreign Service Officers is rigorous, demanding, and highly competitive.

Entry-level applicants are required to take both a written and an oral exam. Between 10,000 and 15,000 applicants take the Foreign Service Written Exam each year, according to ACT Inc., the government contractor that administers the exam. Individuals who do well on the written exam are invited to take the oral assessment. The application process is a lengthy one, about 18 months from start to finish.

The political and public diplomacy career paths tend to be particularly competitive because of the large numbers of candidates who apply. The U.S. State Department has indicated a greater recruitment need for administrative and consular officers, and to a lesser degree, economic officers but discourages applicants from choosing one career path with the intention of switching to another one.

The U.S. Department of State also recruits and hires individuals for the related positions of foreign service specialist and Civil Service employee. Foreign service specialists are hired for their technical or administrative expertise in fields such as information management and security engineering. Unlike Foreign Service Officers, foreign service specialists do not need to take the Foreign Service Written Exam, although they must have an oral assessment and agree to worldwide availability. Civil service employees serve in Washington, D.C., and regional offices.

Advancement Prospects

Advancement prospects are good because the Foreign Service offers promotion opportunities from junior to mid-level to senior officer. Like teachers and professors, Foreign Service Officers are eligible for tenure. Junior Officers must serve at least one term as consular officers and demonstrate proficiency in a foreign language in order to qualify for tenure after three years of duty. If they are not successful, they are considered again one year later. Tenure is required for continued service.

Most of a Foreign Service Officer's career is spent, after gaining tenure, at the midgrades. Experienced Foreign Service Officers can eventually compete to become members of the Senior Foreign Service, a small group of officers who fill the most demanding and sensitive positions in the Foreign Service. Members of the Senior Foreign Service formulate, organize, direct, coordinate, and implement U.S. foreign policy. Entry into the Senior Foreign Service is highly competitive.

Education and Training

No specific educational background is required for Foreign Service Officers, although most have at least a college degree. Many hold advanced degrees in international relations, economics, business administration, law, journalism, or other areas. A recent Foreign Service Officer class included the following educational categories: B.A. (18), J.D. (3), M.A. (20), M.B.A. (1), Ph.D. (4).

Aptitude for the Foreign Service is gauged through a rigorous testing process. Candidates for the Foreign Service must register for the written exam, which includes three multiple-choice sections and an essay writing exercise. Only candidates who pass the multiple-choice segments have their essays scored.

The multiple-choice sections include job-related knowledge, English expression, and a biographical inventory. The job-related knowledge section tests a candidate's understanding of a variety of subjects, including international affairs, U.S. history, and basic economic principles. The English expression section gauges knowledge of correct grammar, organization, spelling, and punctuation as well as the ability to express ideas clearly and accurately, to correct sentences, and to read with comprehension. The biographical inventory measures the candidate's skills, previous experience, and achievements in school, employment, and other activities.

The oral assessment is a day-long set of exercises, which measure skills such as judgment, planning, and working with others. Candidates participate in a group exercise during which they must present a prospective project and debate how best to allocate limited U.S. government funds. Next are individual exercises, including a series of hypothetical questions (e.g., How would you handle a case involving an American student caught with illegal drugs?).

Incoming Foreign Service Officers begin their career with a seven-week orientation class focusing on foreign affairs responsibilities and the life of the diplomat abroad. Once Foreign Service Officers are assigned to a specific post, they receive additional training, including language instruction and specific skills needed to perform effectively in the country or region to which they have been assigned.

Experience, Skills, and Personality Traits

Candidates for the Foreign Service must be U.S. citizens between the ages of 20 and 59 and available for worldwide assignment. The average age of Foreign Service Officers is around 30. Individuals with a variety of backgrounds join the Foreign Service. A recent Foreign Service orientation class included individuals with experience as Peace Corps Volunteers, business/financial consultants, lawyers, and teachers as well as a bartender and a state senator.

Before joining the Foreign Service, individuals must agree to be available for worldwide assignment. Many overseas posts are in areas that lack American-style amenities and pose heath and safety hazards. Cases of bombings and kidnappings involving embassy personnel have prompted the U.S. State Department to devise safety plans, including, if necessary, evacuation of the post.

Although the life-style of Foreign Service Officers offers the occasional glamour of state receptions, individuals spend much of their time working behind the scenes, laying the groundwork for future agreements. Foreign Service Officers must be interested in living in new and different cultures and willing to learn at least one language, if not several. Foreign Service Officers must have well-developed problem-solving skills to resolve whatever comes their way.

Anyone who receives a conditional offer of employment must be investigated for security clearance. Issues that could delay issuance of security clearance include a current or past history of drug or alcohol abuse, credit problems, foreign contacts, and/or a foreign-born spouse. Although such issues might not ultimately preclude security clearance, they lengthen the time required to complete the clearance process.

Unions and Associations

The American Foreign Service Association is an organization dedicated to maintaining a strong, effective Foreign Service.

Tips for Entry

1. Spend time living, working, or studying in another country. Get to know people from different cultures.
2. Learn as many languages as possible.
3. Check out the U.S. State Department's Foreign Service website (*www.foreignservicecareers.gov*). This website provides information about student positions as well as registration and preparation for the Foreign Service written exam.
4. Browse the website of the American Foreign Service Association (*www.afsa.org*), publisher of the booklet "Inside a U.S. Embassy: How the Foreign Service Works for America."
5. Prepare for the Foreign Service Written Examination (FSWE) by taking courses and/or brushing up on English grammar, international affairs, and U.S. history. The Foreign Service website (*www.foreignservicecareers. gov*) includes suggested courses and reading material as well as information about the FSWE Study Guide. Individuals also can obtain the FSWE Study Guide by contacting the contractor, ACT, Inc., at (319) 337-1429.

INTELLIGENCE OPERATIVE

CAREER PROFILE

Duties: Acting as liaison between policy makers and overseas operatives; providing support for operatives abroad, and/or working on espionage cases in foreign countries

Alternate Title(s): Professional Trainee (PT), Clandestine Service Trainee (CST), Operations Officer, Field Officer, Staff Operations Officer, Collection Management Officer, Spy, Officer (Central Intelligence Agency)

Salary Range: $39,000 to $60,000+

Employment Prospects: Fair to good

Advancement Prospects: Good to excellent

Best Geographical Location(s): Washington, D.C.

Prerequisites:

Education or Training—3.0 grade point average; background in Central Eurasian, East Asian, or Middle Eastern language a plus

Experience—Foreign travel; previous residency abroad; and/or military experience helpful

Special Skills and Personality Traits—Willingness to learn a foreign language; patriotism; resourcefulness; well-developed interest in foreign affairs; successful completion of background investigation and polygraph exam; ability to keep secrets

CAREER LADDER

```
┌─────────────────────────────────┐
│  Senior Officer or Branch Chief  │
└─────────────────────────────────┘

┌─────────────────────────────────┐
│     Intelligence Operative       │
└─────────────────────────────────┘

┌─────────────────────────────────┐
│            Trainee               │
└─────────────────────────────────┘
```

Position Description

Intelligence Operatives participate in activities related to espionage, the practice of spying. Although the word *spy* might bring to mind images of James Bond jetting around the world as Agent 007, real operatives in the Central Intelligence Agency (CIA) lead considerably less glamorous lives. They spend more of their time digging for information than chasing villains. They rarely carry guns or ride around in expensive cars. Indeed, glamour seeking is counterproductive. Real operatives try to fit in to maintain their cloak of secrecy. Operations that are *clandestine,* meaning "secret, covert, or hidden" have long been controversial. In the 1970s, the CIA was under fire for its involvement in assassination attempts, coups, and other paramilitary operations. Stricter regulations and prohibition of assassinations followed.

The Clandestine Service is part of the CIA's Directorate of Operations, which is involved in the collection phase of the intelligence cycle. After information is collected, it is analyzed by experts and disseminated to policy makers. Technological advances in intelligence gathering by electronic and satellite photography have not eliminated the need for what the CIA calls HUMINT, human intelligence.

The CIA's Clandestine Service offers two training programs. The first, the 18-month Professional Trainee (PT) Program, gives newcomers an introduction to the field. The second, the Clandestine Service Trainee (CST) Program, which many individuals enter on completion of their 18-month training, prepares trainees specifically for overseas operations. Some applicants are accepted directly into this more advanced program.

Individuals in the Professional Trainee Program provide support to their colleagues overseas and act as liaisons between U.S. policy makers and officers in the field. If, for example, an officer in the field has questions about a possible informant, the Trainee might do background research. Or, perhaps, the officer abroad needs to obtain supplies or talk to a highly skilled technical person. The Trainee would make the necessary arrangements.

In addition, Trainees convey requests from policy makers to officers in the field. If, for instance, the policy maker has a question about the nuclear capabilities of a particular country, the Trainee might notify the field officer to contact an informant working as a nuclear engineer. Informants—not the field officers themselves—are known as agents.

At the end of the 18-month period, the Trainee should have a better idea of the type of assignments he or she would like to pursue. Trainees who are more interested in research and case management in Washington, D.C., than in gathering intelligence overseas might become Staff Operations Officers. Those more interested in working overseas apply for the Clandestine Service Trainee (CST) Program.

This more specialized training takes place at the CIA's training facility, known as The Farm, outside Washington, D.C. Trainees learn how to detect whether they are being trailed and how to communicate secretly in countries where phones are tapped and their movements monitored. They might send messages in code or develop other modes of clandestine communication such as "dead drops," a system that involves leaving packages of information in predetermined locations. Trainees also gain the language skills they need for assignments in the field.

Individuals who successfully complete the Clandestine Service Trainee Program are then chosen for assignments. CIA Operatives work undercover and might use assumed names. Much of their time is spent cultivating and meeting with sources. In some cases, informants have later turned out to be double agents working for the other government.

Intelligence Operatives, over the years, have participated not only in information gathering but also in political and economic actions, propaganda, and paramilitary activities. Although the exact nature of CIA operations is classified information, details culled from declassified documents and books by former Intelligence Operatives provide a sampling of activities:

- Interrogating unwilling sources
- Providing financial support to political contacts
- Training forces involved in battling the opposition
- Participating in the capture of suspected terrorists

Some assignments are more dangerous than others. The cold war has given way to threats from new enemies—terrorists, drug lords, and weapon dealers, among them. Intelligence Operatives face the challenge of penetrating this new world. As one former CIA official told *The New York Times,* "It's like dining with the devil."

Salaries

Salaries vary with levels of experience; Trainees earn less than officers. Salaries for members of the Professional Trainee Program start at around $39,000. Entry level salaries for intelligence operatives in the Clandestine Service range from about $43,000 to $60,000. Within each pay level, individuals receive step increases as they gain experience.

Employment Prospects

Employment prospects are fair to good. As widely reported in the media, the CIA in recent years has increased the size of its Clandestine Service. The application process, however, is highly competitive. Applicants must pass a rigorous screening process, which includes a polygraph exam and security clearance.

The CIA is organized into four teams: the Directorate of Operations, the Directorate of Science and Technology, the Directorate of Intelligence, and the Directorate of Administration. The Directorate of Operations, which includes the Clandestine Service, is probably the best known of the teams. Information gathered by the first two teams is then turned over to the Directorate of Intelligence, the analytical department, which interprets it and writes the finished product. The Directorate of Administration is in charge of managing resources for the agency.

Career tracks for analysts are separate from those for Clandestine Service Officers, according to the CIA. Analysts are usually specialists with advanced degrees. An analyst might be an expert in either a particular country or region or field such as chemical weapons. The CIA offers a summer internship in intelligence analysis focusing on international affairs, languages, economics, or engineering for graduate students.

Advancement Prospects

Advancement prospects are good to excellent because individuals are screened carefully for suitability for the job. Applicants accepted into entry-level positions generally have the skills needed to advance in the CIA. Individuals can move up in either foreign or domestic positions. Individuals who choose to serve abroad can advance either as senior officers or in managerial positions such as branch chief or deputy director.

Not everyone, however, stays with the CIA. Some Officers have left disillusioned with the CIA's objectives and/or methods. Several have written articles, books, and/or speeches critical of their former employer.

The field of intelligence is a broad one, extending well beyond the confines of the CIA to include defense and law enforcement agencies as well as private corporations. The Federal Bureau of Investigation (FBI) differs from the CIA in that it has a law enforcement function (see the profile of

FBI Special Agent in Facts On File's *Career Opportunities in Law Enforcement, Security, and Protective Services).*

Education and Training

To be eligible for the CIA's training programs, applicants must be recent college or graduate school graduates with at least a 3.0 grade point average. Foreign language proficiency and a graduate degree are pluses. Degrees and experience in international business, finance, or relations; physical science; computer science; or nuclear, biological, chemical engineering are preferred. The CIA is particularly interested in candidates with backgrounds in Central Eurasian, East Asian, and Middle Eastern languages.

Some colleges, military schools, universities, and graduate programs offer courses specifically in intelligence, commonly through political science or international affairs departments. The Association of Former Intelligence Officers *(www.afio.com)* provides a listing of these courses, including some syllabuses, through the *Academic Exchange Program* section of its website. Course titles include Intelligence: Process, Policy, and Management (University of Oklahoma, Fall 2001), National Strategic Intelligence (California State University, Spring 2001), and Intelligence and Foreign Policy (Columbia University, School of International and Public Affairs, Fall 2001).

Experience, Skills, and Personality Traits

Individuals who have traveled or lived abroad have valuable experience for positions with the CIA, especially if they have become fluent in a foreign language of strategic importance to the agency. Military experience, too, can be helpful. Other work experience also can provide a background for undercover work abroad.

The application process for the CIA is a rigorous one. The CIA looks at an individual's background to determine, for example, whether he or she would be good at keeping secrets. Someone with a history of seeking public acclaim, for instance, might be deemed unsuitable because covert operations require relative anonymity.

To determine suitability for employment, the CIA examines the applicant's life history, trustworthiness, reliability, and soundness of character. Abuse of drugs, including marijuana, is one of the common reasons applicants are denied a security clearance. Individuals with foreign contacts also may experience security delays while they are investigated for their loyalty to the United States. All applicants must take a polygraph exam.

Although the day-to-day operations of Intelligence Operatives are considerably less glamorous than those of fictional spies, real-life operatives must cultivate some of the same personality traits as their screen counterparts: an adventurous spirit, ingenuity, and resourcefulness. Intelligence Operatives must be able to deal with fast-moving, ambiguous, and unstructured situations.

Unions and Associations

The Association of Former Intelligence Officers is an organization dedicated to fostering, through education programs and publications, public understanding of the role of intelligence in serving U.S. national interests.

Tips for Entry

1. Spend some time abroad to gain an understanding of foreign policy issues.
2. Look into the CIA's employment opportunities for college students. As outlined on the CIA's employment website *(www.cia.gov/cia/employment),* the agency offers three programs: Undergraduate Student Trainee (Co-op), Internship Program, and Graduate Studies Program. The first two are for undergraduate students. The third is for graduate students interested in the CIA's analytical career track.
3. Browse the CIA's website *(www.cia.gov).* In addition to information about employment, the site includes a section for kids, with spy games and an intelligence book list. A book list for adults, *Intelligence Literature,* is included in the *Publications* section of the main website.
4. Read up on intelligence by searching public libraries, magazine, and Internet databases using keywords such as *spy* or *strategic intelligence.*
5. Refrain from any activities that might jeopardize your acceptance. Candidates for the CIA must pass medical and polygraph examinations as well as a background investigation.

PART III
ACTIVISM

NONPROFIT ADVOCACY AND ADMINISTRATION

PROGRAM ASSISTANT

CAREER PROFILE

Duties: Assisting with communication, conference planning, and fund-raising; answering phones; maintaining databases; providing general clerical/administrative support

Alternate Title(s): Administrative Assistant, Marketing Assistant, Fund-Raising/Development Assistant

Salary Range: $20,000 to $30,000

Employment Prospects: Good

Advancement Prospects: Good

Best Geographical Location(s): Major cities

Prerequisites:

Education or Training—Bachelor's degree
Experience—Entry level
Special Skills and Personality Traits—Basic office skills; attention to detail; excellent oral and written communication skills; ability to juggle multiple tasks; belief in the mission of the organization; willingness to learn

CAREER LADDER

```
┌─────────────────────────────┐
│    Program Coordinator      │
└─────────────────────────────┘

┌─────────────────────────────┐
│     Program Assistant       │
└─────────────────────────────┘

┌─────────────────────────────┐
│     Student or Intern       │
└─────────────────────────────┘
```

Position Description

Program Assistants get an entry-level introduction to the world of nonprofit organizations. They assist higher-ups with everything from clerical tasks to fund-raising, research, and writing. They are constantly juggling tasks, such as answering the phones, sending faxes and contacting other organizations. In an age of e-mails and websites, they're often the ones behind the computer, updating news and notifying members.

Often, individuals become Program Assistants because they are drawn to the idealism of the nonprofit sector. Nonprofit organizations allow people to pursue their passions, whether saving the whales or feeding the poor. Someone interested in the fields of education, public policy, and law, for instance, might become a Program Assistant for an educational advocacy group. Someone else might do outreach work for a community-development group. Yet another individual with an interest in writing might look for a communication-oriented position that involves, among other things, preparing the organization's newsletter. Program Assistants who prove themselves on the job often are given increased responsibility.

Typically, organizations are made up of two parts:

• Program staff: carry out the mission of the organization

• Administrative staff: perform tasks such as fund-raising and public relations in support of the organization

In organizations whose program personnel have specialized education and training in fields such as social work, environmental science, and law, the administrative route offers the best opportunities.

Responsibilities of Program Assistants vary according to the needs of the particular nonprofit organization. A Program Assistant for a professional association might work on logistics for the annual conference. Which rooms are available? What is a prospective speaker's availability? Should members be notified by e-mail or snail mail? Because Program Assistants are usually fairly low on the totem pole, they often clear final decisions with higher-ups in the organization.

Typical responsibilities of Program Assistants include

• Acting as liaison with outside agencies
• Preparing basic correspondence
• Tracking and analyzing data
• Answering phones
• Maintaining databases
• Implementing special projects

- Assisting with the writing of articles, grants, and training materials
- Providing general administrative support

Salaries

Salaries generally fall into the $20,000 to $30,000 range, according to industry experts. Large organizations generally pay more than small ones. Salaries in nonprofit organizations tend to be relatively low compared to those in the government and in the private sector. According to Ron Krannich and Caryl Rae Krannich, Ph.D.s, authors of *Jobs and Careers with Non-Profit Organizations,* jobs paying $40,000 a year in government or business may pay only $25,000 to $30,000 in a nonprofit organization.

Employment Prospects

Employment prospects are good because of the large number of positions. Managers in nonprofits need the assistance of entry-level staffers to keep the organization running smoothly.

Advancement Prospects

Advancement prospects are good because Program Assistants get valuable work experience that helps them move up within their own organization or to a larger nonprofit. Many individuals also move from nonprofit organizations to government or business. These positions often serve as training grounds for staffers who want to grow with the organization. As one insider put it, "They learn what flies and what doesn't."

Sometimes, though, advancement requires additional schooling or outside experience. This is particularly true in specialized areas such as international development that require individuals to have advanced degrees.

Education and Training

Program Assistant positions generally require a bachelor's degree. Industry specialists see many Program Assistants with liberal arts degrees in majors such as English, history, or political science. A graduate degree is particularly helpful for advancement into some upper-level positions. Many colleges and universities offer graduate level programs in nonprofit management.

Experience, Skills, and Personality Traits

Program Assistant positions are generally entry-level but may require some experience in the nonprofit sector and/or related fields. As does any field, the nonprofit sector has both positives and negatives. Nonprofit work can be an excellent "fit" for someone who cares passionately about a particular issue. Many nonprofit organizations dedicate themselves to pressing social and political issues such as the environment, community development, and civil rights.

On the negative side, nonprofit workers tend to earn low salaries, work in cramped quarters, and endure high levels of uncertainty, industry sources say. Unlike in the private sector, in which results are measured by bottom-line profits, in nonprofit organizations outcomes are less measurable.

When the pros outweigh the cons, individuals can gain valuable experience. Program Assistants are always juggling a variety of tasks and therefore need strong organizational skills. Positions generally call for basic office skills, which include competency with computers. Often, the Program Assistant acts as a liaison for the organization, linking the main office to members and outside agencies. Being able to get along well with others is crucial. As one insider says, "They [Program Assistants] need to build bridges between people."

Unions/Associations

Program Assistants might belong to the Office and Professional Employees International Union.

Tips for Entry

1. Read books about the nonprofit sector to help pinpoint your areas of interest as well as skills you would like to develop. Jobs in this field abound, so it is helpful to know your own goals.
2. Go in willing to learn. This may be your most important asset on the job.
3. Practice prioritizing. Program Assistants must be able to juggle multiple tasks.
4. Think in terms of lightening someone else's load. Managers hire Program Assistants to make their own lives easier.
5. Volunteer at a nonprofit organization in your area.

PROGRAM DIRECTOR

CAREER PROFILE

Duties: Implementing programs; supervising staff; managing budgets; planning and monitoring program activities

Alternate Title(s): Program Manager, Program Coordinator, Director of Programs

Salary Range: $30,000 to $65,000

Employment Prospects: Fair

Advancement Prospects: Good

Best Geographical Location: Major cities

Prerequisites:

Education or Training—Bachelor's degree required; master's degree preferred

Experience—Three to five years

Special Skills and Personality Traits—Capacity to make sound decisions, communicate well, and build coalitions; ability to manage people, budgets, and events

CAREER LADDER

```
┌─────────────────────────────┐
│    Program Director for      │
│    Larger Organization       │
└─────────────────────────────┘

┌─────────────────────────────┐
│      Program Director        │
└─────────────────────────────┘

┌─────────────────────────────┐
│    Program Coordinator       │
│    or Field Organizer        │
└─────────────────────────────┘
```

Position Description

Program Directors head a particular area of a nonprofit organization. Unlike executive directors, who are responsible for everything from satisfying board members to making sure everyone gets a paycheck, Program Directors focus on one specific area. Someone in an environmental organization, for instance, might be a Program Director in charge of saving the rain forest. The executive director, on the other hand, would be in charge of budgets, staff, and issues for the entire organization.

Usually Program Directors work for organizations large enough to justify Directors in addition to a chief executive. Program Directors carve out one area of expertise, whether it be providing relief to Bosnia or providing preventive health care for children and families. Yet within that one area, Program Directors juggle numerous different tasks. Is the program meeting its timeline? Which strategies are most effective? How can the Internet be used to communicate a particular message?

Positions vary according to the needs of a particular organization. Someone working to save the rain forest might spend part of the time raising money for the project and the rest doing research in the fields of Central America. A Program Director involved in social services might visit corpo-

rations to get their support in providing jobs to youth, and someone directing a block watch program might work at developing leadership within the community. Someone working for legislative change, in turn, might research the issue, draft legislation, drum up grass-roots support, and meet with the media.

Common responsibilities of all Program Directors include

• Implementing programs
• Hiring, training, and supervising staff
• Monitoring program activities
• Preparing reports, proposals, and budgets
• Writing and speaking in public
• Building coalitions
• Working closely with the executive director on plans

Whatever the type of organization, Program Directors are forever asking themselves one crucial question: Is the program accomplishing its goal, often referred to as its "mission"? If, for example, the mission is to build a better life for children in developing nations, the Program Director should be asking, What have I done today to save the children?

Salaries

Salaries generally fall into the $30,000 to $65,000 range and are commensurate with experience according to industry experts. A small organization that hires Program Directors with a bachelor's degree would generally pay considerably less than a large nonprofit looking for an experienced professional with a master's degree in a field such as social work or international affairs.

Employment Prospects

Employment prospects are fair because some organizations have consolidated positions. One Program Director might oversee two or three different programs. Opportunities are somewhat linked to political tides. When a particular area is threatened, organizations gear up to address it.

Advancement Prospects

Advancement prospects are good because Program Directors acquire skills readily transferred to larger organizations. They might advance within their organization, move to another group, or even use their skills to move into the private sector.

Education and Training

Often Program Directors have a graduate degree in a particular area of expertise such as social work, business, or environmental science. Experience in the field, though, may substitute for a graduate degree.

Experience, Skills, and Personality Traits

By the time individuals become Program Directors, they have shown an interest and expertise in a particular program area. They need one additional trait, however, to be effective Program Directors: strong leadership skills. Insiders look for a track record of teamwork and managerial skill.

In addition to leading a staff, Program Directors must also communicate the program's message to the outside world. Often, this involves turning complicated data and information into simple and persuasive messages.

Unions and Associations

Many Program Directors belong to associations in their particular field of expertise, whether it be the environment, social work, or international affairs, as well as to organizations such as the Society for Nonprofit Organizations that deal with issues of concern to the nonprofit sector.

Tips for Entry

1. Take stock of your own interests. Program Directors need to be dedicated to a particular area of concern.
2. Get the required experience. Program Directors generally start out in lower-level positions such as field organizer or program assistant before moving up to management-oriented positions such as program coordinator or Program Director.
3. Ask yourself whether you have the combination of expertise in a discipline and ability to lead and manage that is required of this position.
4. Browse nonprofit websites such as Idealist.org (*www.idealist.org*) to read job ads for Program Director.

FUND-RAISER

CAREER PROFILE

Duties: Coordinating fund-raising drives (e.g., locating new donors, encouraging existing donors to give more) and related public relations and marketing activities

Alternate Title(s): Development Officer, Director of Development, Campaign Director, Large Gift Director, Director of Planned Giving, Event Coordinator, Grant Writer, Director of Mailing and Direct Marketing, Canvassing Supervisor

Salary Range: $25,000 to $90,000

Employment Prospects: Excellent

Advancement Prospects: Good

Best Geographical Location(s) for Position: Metropolitan areas

Prerequisites:
   Education or Training—Bachelor's degree required; master's sometimes preferred for upper-level positions
   Experience—Two to four years
   Special Skills and Personality Traits—tenacity, dedication, ability to handle rejection, confidence, good writing and research skills, attention to detail, and belief in the cause

CAREER LADDER

```
┌─────────────────────────────┐
│    Development Director      │
└─────────────────────────────┘

┌─────────────────────────────┐
│        Fund-raiser           │
└─────────────────────────────┘

┌─────────────────────────────┐
│      Related Career          │
│ (e.g. business, public relations, │
│   education) or Volunteer    │
└─────────────────────────────┘
```

Position Description

Fund-raisers can be lifesavers for nonprofit organizations. Without funding, nonprofit organizations would be hard pressed to feed the hungry, advocate for their causes, and perform countless other good works. Competition for the tax-deductible dollar has spawned the need for increased sophistication in an industry that has its own terminology. Contributors are "donors," the money they contribute is a "gift."

Contrary to what some people might think, grants from foundations and government agencies make up only a small share of the philanthropic pie. By far the largest percentage—approximately 75.6 percent—comes from private individuals, according to the Association of Fundraising Professionals.

In small nonprofits, Fund-raisers generally combine a variety of fund-raising strategies, whereas in larger nonprofits they are more apt to specialize. Fund-raisers raise money in five basic ways:

- Asking for large gifts from individual donors
- Soliciting bequests
- Hosting special events
- Applying for grants
- Launching phone, letter, or canvassing appeals

A large organization might have a large-gift director who looks for "big money"; a director of planned giving who specializes in helping people make charitable endowments and bequests; an event coordinator who plans and executes the organization's annual benefit and other major events; a grant writer who seeks money from foundations and government agencies; and a director of mailing and direct marketing who sends letters and makes phone calls to potential donors. In addition, many grassroots organizations canvass door-to-door, with the supervisor performing a role similar to the Fund-raiser in charge of volunteers.

Organizations generally work from one event or campaign to the next. Event coordinators, for instance, organize fund-raising functions such as celebrity galas, black-tie dinners, walkathons, charity bowling tournaments, and other social gatherings to raise money for an organization. In the process, they manage every detail of the event, from the invitations and speeches to the refreshments and seating.

Grant writers, in turn, write proposals describing why the organization they work for needs money and exactly how it would be spent. They search databases of foundations and government grant-making agencies to find organizations that fund the nonprofit's areas of concern.

In small organizations, fund-raisers generally juggle a number of responsibilities—annual drives, capital campaigns, and special events, among them—carefully planning each campaign or project. Experts note that fund-raisers are allowed few shortcuts. Hours of painstaking research and planning go into each solicitation. How can the organization find new donors? How can it encourage existing donors to be more generous?

Fund-raisers set dollar goals and timetables, prepare feasibility studies, train workers and volunteers, and organize events to kick off their campaigns. Everyone needs to be committed, enthusiastic, and ready to go.

Organizers generally work from the inside out, soliciting board members and other reliable sources of support before moving on to other donors. If, for example, the organization provides educational programs for children, the Fund-raiser might solicit parents. Past donors, too, are likely sources of contributions. In the process of raising money, Fund-raisers often embark on various public relations and marketing projects—T-shirts bearing the group's logo, for example—to get the organization in the public eye.

Salaries

Salaries vary by the size and type of organization, ranging from $25,000 to $90,000. Small grassroots groups pay lower salaries than large, established organizations. Salaries for mid-sized organizations generally fall into the $40,000 to $50,000 range, according to the Association of Fundraising Professionals.

Employment Prospects

Employment prospects are excellent because the demand for Fund-raisers exceeds the supply. Opportunities for Fund-raisers abound.

Advancement Prospects

Advancement prospects abound because Fund-raisers can easily move from small to larger organizations or climb the hierarchy within their own organization. Many successful Fund-raisers advance to become directors of development or vice presidents.

Education and Training

An explosion of workshops, seminars, and undergraduate and graduate programs has created new opportunities for learning about fund-raising. Although Fund-raisers still learn informally from mentors on the job, they also can take advantage of more formal programs.

Colleges and universities throughout the United States offer courses dealing with fund-raising and other financial matters. Some universities offer on-line courses. Indiana University has its own fund-raising school, which offers a certificate program with credits applicable to a master of arts in philanthropic studies or a master of public affairs in nonprofit management. Other universities offer courses in nonprofit management that deal with topics such as fundraising.

At the graduate level, 86 programs in the United States offer a concentration (three or more courses) in nonprofit management, according to a recent study supported by the Kellogg Foundation. Often these courses are part of a program leading to a master's degree in public administration.

Many continuing education programs, too, offer courses in fund-raising and related subjects. Professional associations such as the Association of Fundraising Professionals provide not only classes but also certification programs for Fund-raisers.

Experience, Skills, and Personality Traits

Fund-raisers commonly have backgrounds in such fields as marketing, business, or education. Many individuals become Fund-raisers for nonprofit organizations because they want to make a difference.

Asking people for money, however, is no easy task. In addition to sex, politics, and religion, money is a contentious subject. People are taught not to discuss it. The mere mention of money is considered rude. As a result, Fund-raisers are often viewed with suspicion.

Successful Fund-raisers, though, believe deeply enough in what they are doing to challenge social conventions regarding the discussion of money. They see themselves not as beggars but as dedicated professionals. Instead of taking rejection personally, they keep moving ahead, inspiring others to want to help.

Unions and Associations

The Association of Fundraising Professionals is a professional organization of nonprofit Fund-raisers. Other organizations include the Association for Healthcare Philanthropy and the National Committee on Planned Giving.

Tips for Entry

1. Get your foot in the door by volunteering or interning for a nonprofit. Join a fund-raising committee or help plan a special event.

2. Ask about courses in nonprofit studies at your local college or university.

3. Look into on-line courses in fund-raising offered by universities such as Case Western Reserve University, George Mason University, and the Indiana University Center on Philanthropy. For more information, visit the "educational opportunities" section of the Association of Fundraising Professionals website (*www.afpnet.org*).

4. Consult trade publications such as the *The Chronicle of Philanthropy* (*www.philanthropy.com*), *The Non-Profit Times* (*www.nptimes.com*), and *Grassroots Fundraising Journal* (*www.chardonpress.com*) for listings of fund-raising workshops and employment opportunities.

5. Be prepared to learn on the job. Very few individuals enter the field with the perfect set of skills. Many individuals learn from a development director who acts as a mentor.

COMMUNICATION DIRECTOR

CAREER PROFILE

Duties: Directing public relations for an organization by overseeing projects such as press releases, brochures, websites, and newsletters

Alternate Title(s): Public Relations Director, Public Information Director, Communication and Marketing Director, Communication Coordinator, Communication Manager

Salary Range: $25,000 to $100,000

Employment Prospects: Good

Advancement Prospects: Fair

Best Geographical Location(s): Major cities

Prerequisites:

Education or Training—Bachelor's degree; master's degree sometimes preferred

Experience—Five years related experience

Special Skills and Personality Traits—Excellent writing, verbal, and interpersonal skills; media savvy; interest in and commitment to the issues

CAREER LADDER

```
┌─────────────────────────────────┐
│   Communication Director        │
│   for Larger Organization       │
└─────────────────────────────────┘

┌─────────────────────────────────┐
│   Communication Director        │
└─────────────────────────────────┘

┌─────────────────────────────────┐
│   Communication Assistant,      │
│   Writer, or Reporter           │
└─────────────────────────────────┘
```

Position Description

Communication Directors act as modern-day messengers. They deliver an organization's message to its members as well as to the public and the media. In an increasingly competitive and technologically sophisticated world, they must work hard to ensure that their messages are not drowned out by the din of others.

Communication Directors work closely with executive directors, who handle the overall direction of the group. In many small organizations, the executive director acts as de facto Communication Director, conveying the mission of the organization to the outside world. In organizations with both positions, the Communication Director generally focuses on such public relations tasks as producing press releases, brochures, a website, newsletters, and other items.

Many Communication Directors have more than one responsibility. Communication, or public relations, as it is often called, might be linked to another specialty such as fund-raising, marketing, or general administration, with positions bearing titles such as Director of Communication and Marketing. Communication Directors face special challenges, as many people have only a limited understanding of what nonprofit organizations do. Unlike private companies that produce and sell products like cars and videocassette recorders (VCRs), nonprofit organizations peddle something more difficult to measure—programs.

Organizations themselves are sometimes unsure about how best to communicate their message. Should Communication Directors promote programs for the public good in the same way merchants sell their wares, or should they take a more low-key approach? Although good deeds have long been performed with great modesty, nonprofit organizations increasingly are adopting private-sector techniques to raise public awareness of important issues such as poverty, homelessness, and acquired immunodeficiency syndrome (AIDS).

Sometimes Communication Directors are torn between the organization's desire to put its best foot forward and the public's need for openness and disclosure. For example, the organization may be reluctant to list the salaries of top executives on its website for fear that the public will think the figures too high since charity has long been associated with great personal sacrifice.

Communication Directors are constantly juggling tasks. They might go from returning calls from the media, hiring printers, and assigning stories, to meeting with staff to gather input for the next edition of the newsletter. How are various programs doing? Any noteworthy developments? How can members help?

Although organizations commonly use terms familiar only to those in the field, Communication Directors strive for words and phrases that are widely understood. Passages full of acronyms, for instance, can baffle readers.

Communication Directors commonly prepare brochures and other publications to generate public involvement in the organization. An advocacy group, for instance, might prepare a list of ways individuals can get involved (e.g., writing to members of Congress, joining the organization).

Other responsibilities of Communication Directors include

- Developing strategy to enhance the visibility of the organization and respond proactively to negative exposure
- Organizing and participating in events and briefings
- Enlisting reporters, editors, and others to cover stories or issues
- Writing and editing publications
- Evaluating communication efforts
- Identifying target audiences and most effective modes of communication (e.g., press releases, public service announcements)

Salaries

Communication Directors in the nonprofit sector generally earn $25,000 to $100,000, industry sources say. Small organizations tend to pay lower salaries than their larger counterparts.

Employment Prospects

Employment prospects are good because of the rapid growth of the nonprofit sector and the importance of communication.

Advancement Prospects

Advancement prospects are fair because upward mobility generally, although not always, depends on moving from a smaller organization to a larger one. New openings depend on turnover, which can be low in organizations with dedicated Communication Directors. A new job also might entail a move to another city. Sometimes a Communication Director moves up to the post of executive director.

Education and Training

Insiders recommend a bachelor's degree in journalism, English, communication or a related discipline. A master's degree in one of those areas can help with advancement.

Experience, Skills, and Personality Traits

Communication Directors typically have several years of related experience. Some have worked in journalism and are knowledgeable about how reporters and editors develop and place stories. An individual may, for example, move from a newspaper to a nonprofit organization, where he or she gains important experience in how to use communication techniques to advance social change. Within an organization, a writer or editor or communication assistant typically acquires experience and supervisory skills before moving up to a management position such as Communication Director.

Organizations look for individuals with a proven track record in communication. In addition to being able to communicate well verbally and in writing, Communication Directors should have a good visual sense to give publications a high-quality look. Communication Directors must be able to write for a number of different audiences, including the public, prospective funders, and the media.

Unions and Associations

Communication Directors might belong to the Public Relations Society of America, the Society for Nonprofit Organizations, or various other organizations.

Tips for Entry

1. Get as much writing experience as possible, starting with school publications. Organizations often ask for writing samples when hiring a Communication Director.
2. Volunteer for an organization in your field of interest.
3. Check directories of nonprofit organizations in public libraries and career centers.
4. Browse the web, using keywords (e.g., *environment, human rights*) in line with your own issues of concern to lead you to websites, an increasingly important responsibility of Communication Directors.

DIRECTOR OF VOLUNTEERS

CAREER PROFILE

Duties: Designing and implementing volunteer programs; recruiting, training, and supervising volunteers; recognizing the efforts of volunteers

Alternate Title(s): Volunteer Coordinator, Recruitment and Recognition Manager, Community Outreach Coordinator; other titles that vary by setting

Salary Range: $12,000 to $100,000

Employment Prospects: Fair

Advancement Prospects: Good

Best Geographical Location(s): Good

Prerequisites:

Education or Training—Varies by setting; college degree or higher

Experience—Volunteer experience generally required

Special Skills and Personality Traits—Enjoyment of working with people; ability to speak well in groups; energy; flexibility; positive outlook

CAREER LADDER

```
┌─────────────────────────────────────┐
│   Position with Larger Organization  │
│         or Related Specialty         │
└─────────────────────────────────────┘

┌─────────────────────────────────────┐
│        Director of Volunteers        │
└─────────────────────────────────────┘

┌─────────────────────────────────────┐
│              Volunteer               │
└─────────────────────────────────────┘
```

Position Description

Directors of Volunteers manage a resource worth million of dollars—America's cadre of unpaid workers. Schedules need to be juggled, logistics coordinated. Although some organizations still assign responsibilities for volunteers to staffers on top of their regular responsibilities, many are creating specific positions as Director of Volunteers.

Individuals may work in a variety of settings: professional associations, advocacy organizations, and social-service agencies, to name just a few. Programs span the gamut. Some use volunteers to provide clerical support to paid staffers; others, to supplement social services; still others, to advocate for a cause. Someone involved in managing volunteers for a designated-driver program, for example, might be involved in everything from advertising for volunteers to maintaining the database needed to match volunteer drivers to those needing a ride.

Directors of Volunteers do many of the same tasks as personnel officers involved in recruiting and interviewing staff with one major difference: they must find ways to motivate people without the use of a paycheck. Within the organiza-

tion itself, they often need to act as in-house educators to dispel notions of volunteers as "second best."

Directors of Volunteers manage programs from start to finish, in a process that involves a number of steps:

- Program planning
- Recruitment
- Screening
- Training
- Recognition

Typically, program planning begins with assessing the organization's need for volunteers. The Director of Volunteers might design a questionnaire or survey to determine areas where assistance is needed. What tasks need to be done? Should volunteers work independently or assist paid staff? How can positions be designed to appeal to the needs of volunteers?

Once the program has been established, Directors of Volunteers recruit, screen, and train volunteers. The Director of Volunteers might contact community leaders and design ads and flyers for volunteers. Screening might involve conducting background checks to prevent inappropriate candidates from having contact with vulnerable individuals. The Director of Volunteers then trains volunteers and supervises them in their progress.

Finally, the Director of Volunteers recognizes the efforts of volunteers and others within the organization. He or she might plan a formal recognition ceremony, present volunteers with small gifts as tokens of appreciation, and/or issue awards.

In addition, Directors of Volunteers

- Meet the needs of an increasingly diverse pool of volunteers (e.g., students required to do community service, court-ordered appointments)
- Keep up-to-date on new technologies such as virtual volunteering (e.g., offering services such as editing or counseling on-line)
- Act as liaison between paid and volunteer staff

Salaries

Salaries vary widely, depending on the individual's level of experience and the size of the organization. The Director of Volunteers for a small organization might earn $12,000, compared to $100,000 for someone at a large international organization. Titles vary by setting, as do salaries. In the hierarchy of volunteer administration, a coordinator or manager might work under a Director of Volunteers. According to a 2001 *Nonprofit Times* salary survey quoted by the Association for Volunteer Administration, the average annual salary for a Director of Volunteers is $35,285, compared to $59,220 for a Director of Development, a top fund-raising position.

Employment Prospects

Employment prospects are fair because although this is an emerging profession, some organizations place volunteers rather than paid staff in the position of Director of Volunteers.

Advancement Prospects

Advancement prospects are good because individuals can either advance within volunteer administration or move into related fields such as human resources, special events work, development, and public relations. Positions coordinating volunteers can be found in all sectors. In the private sector, for example, a large company might have a volunteer program for employees as part of its human resources department.

Education and Training

Requirements for education and training vary widely by setting. Although some positions might require a specific degree in a field such as social work or nonprofit management, many others are more interested in practical experi-

ence and knowledge of the field. Some community colleges, colleges and universities, and graduate schools offer courses in nonprofit management addressing issues of volunteer administration. The Association for Volunteer Administration provides professional credentialing leading to the designation of Certified in Volunteer Administration (CVA). Candidates must have the equivalent of three years of full-time experience in volunteer management, which can include both salaried and nonsalaried positions.

Experience, Skills, and Personality Traits

Many Directors of Volunteers start out as volunteers, a role that can help them better understand the people they are coordinating. Directors of Volunteers should enjoy working with people and be good at motivating them. They spend much of their time acting as cheerleaders of sorts, offering encouragement in the place of a paycheck. Directors of Volunteers also work closely with paid staffers, who are sometimes ambivalent about the use of volunteers. As the liaison between the two groups, the Director of Volunteers should have good mediation skills. For example, if work space is tight, the Director of Volunteers might help paid and unpaid staff find ways to share the quarters.

Unions and Associations

The Association for Volunteer Administration is an international professional association for individuals committed to effective leadership of volunteer efforts.

Tips for Entry

1. Participate in volunteer programs as a student. Options abound not only for hands-on service such as tutoring, but also for coordination of events involving other volunteers such as book drives. Many student organizations are involved in service to the community.
2. Offer to work as a volunteer or intern for the Director of Volunteers of an organization of interest to you.
3. Browse the Internet, using the keywords *Volunteer Management*. Two websites, Energize, Inc. *(www.energizeinc.com)* and the Association for Volunteer Administration *(www.avaintl.org),* provide job listings and other resources.
4. Look into educational opportunities in nonprofit management by checking the website maintained by Seton Hall University *(www.shu.edu).*
5. Check the white pages of your phone book for a listing for "Volunteer Center," as many major cities have one. If yours doesn't, call your local United Way to learn more about organizations in your area of interest.

PROGRAM OFFICER, FOUNDATION

CAREER PROFILE

Duties: Investigating and evaluating grant proposals and/or implementing in-house projects

Alternate Title(s): Program Associate

Salary Range: $18,000 to $132,000

Employment Prospects: Poor

Advancement Prospects: Fair

Best Geographical Location(s): Major cities (with some exceptions)

Prerequisites:

Education or Training—Master's degree preferred, usually in the foundation's field of interest

Experience—One to 10 years in the foundation's area of interest

Special Skills and Personality Traits—Strong oral and written communication skills; critical thinking and good judgment; interest in program area(s) funded by foundation

CAREER LADDER

```
┌─────────────────────────────────┐
│  Associate Director, Foundation  │
└─────────────────────────────────┘

┌─────────────────────────────────┐
│   Program Officer, Foundation    │
└─────────────────────────────────┘

┌─────────────────────────────────┐
│ Nonprofit Activist or Administrator │
└─────────────────────────────────┘
```

Position Description

Program Officers help philanthropic foundations decide which organizations and/or individuals should receive grants. Unlike many of their peers in the nonprofit world who are struggling to *raise* funds, foundations are in the enviable position of having money to give away.

Philanthropic foundations serve as society's research and development arm—providing funds for education, public health, the arts, social services, and numerous other program areas. In the competitive world of philanthropy, foundations receive many more requests for funding than they can possibly meet.

Program Officers sift through the proposals to decide, first of all, which fall within the general scope of the foundation. A foundation that deals primarily with the environment, for example, probably would reject a request for arts funding. The Program Officer would then notify the grant seeker that the proposal had been denied.

If, however, the proposal fits within the parameters of the foundation, the Program Officer analyzes it further. The Program Officer might determine what percentage of the grant would be spent on costs such as equipment, staff, and build-ing construction. Who would benefit from the grant? Does the grant seeker have the expertise needed for the project?

Take the hypothetical example of a proposal from a hospital for a new day care center. The Program Officer would find out whom the new day care center would benefit: families of patients or the hospital's own employees? The foundation might give a higher priority to families of patients, deciding that the hospital itself could fund day care for its own employees.

Next, the Program Officer would rank the proposal against others that address the same general topic. In the case of the hospital proposal, the Program Officer might need to compare it to a plan by an existing day care center for a new playground. Which is more important for the foundation to fund? Then the Program Officer would rank all of the proposals that are up for that funding cycle, which could be annual, quarterly, or based on another period.

The Program Officer might then present his or her findings at a preliminary meeting where others in the foundation could raise questions of concern. Why is the hospital asking for $100,000 when a similar project funded last year cost only $50,000? What is the reputation of the agency affiliated with the day care center? Would each plan be financially feasible?

To follow up, the Program Officer might schedule site visits. He or she might interview individuals involved with the proposals, tour the sites, and more thoroughly research the grant seekers. Has the foundation ever funded other projects undertaken by either of these organizations? If so, what were the results?

Finally, the Program Officer would write summaries of the competing proposals for a presentation before the foundation's chief executive officer and/or board of directors. The decision makers would make the final determinations. The Program Officer would then notify each of the grant seekers of the results.

As Program Officers gain experience, they might be given additional decision-making responsibilities. A foundation might allow experienced Program Officers not only to analyze incoming proposals but also to develop their own projects. A Program Officer might see a need for a particular type of research, for example. The Program Officer would then write a proposal and work with an organization involved in that line of research.

Program Officers in foundations might also

- Analyze conditions and trends in the program area
- Work with research teams to measure the program's effectiveness and impact in the field
- Conduct grant workshops
- Track grants and progress reports

Salaries

Salaries are linked largely to the size and type of foundation. Types of foundations include

- Community foundations, which must raise funds publicly
- Family, which are run by family members who serve as trustees or directors of foundations on a voluntary basis
- Independent, which are private like family foundations but are not controlled by a benefactor or the benefactor's family

According to the Council on Foundations, Program Officers for community foundations earn $18,333 to $93,178; for family foundations, $28,500 to $131,785; and for independent foundations, $19,750 to $127,500. The median salary for Program Officers is $44,133 for community foundations, $73,522 for family foundations, and $76,900 for independent foundations.

Employment Prospects

Employment prospects are poor because of the desirability of this position versus the relatively small number of jobs. Competition is stiff because many people see foundation

work as a way to make a difference without having to raise money. According to the Council on Foundations, one job ad might attract 300 applicants. A few large foundations, including the Ford and Kellogg Foundations, provide the majority of jobs in the foundation world. A small foundation might use part-time Program Officers.

Advancement Prospects

Advancement prospects are fair because most foundations have only a small number of positions above the level of Program Officer. To advance, an individual might need to move to another foundation. A very large foundation, however, might have a couple of tiers of Program Officers.

Some Program Officers leave philanthropic foundations to pursue other interests. For example, an individual might leave a foundation to run a nonprofit agency or go into private consulting.

Education and Training

Foundations generally look for expertise in whatever program areas the foundation serves. A foundation involved in social-service projects, for example, might look for someone with a background in social work, whereas one involved in the environment might prefer someone with a degree in ecology. An advanced degree in a particular discipline might substitute for a certain number of years of work experience in the field.

Experience, Skills, and Personality Traits

Often individuals have worked in one of the program areas funded by the foundation. For instance, the executive director of a social-service agency might become interested in working for the foundation that funded one of its projects.

Program Officers must be able to communicate well verbally and in writing. They often write summaries and give oral presentations. Good analytical skills and a sense of fairness are important.

Although working for a grant-giving organization might seem stress-free compared to doing the usual fund-raising of the nonprofit world, foundation workers face a special kind of pressure: always being asked for money. Foundations receive many more proposals than they can approve. Insiders say that Program Officers run the risk of succumbing to arrogance and cynicism unless they have the ability to empathize with grant seekers.

Unions and Associations

The Council on Foundations is a professional association of grant-making organizations. Foundation professionals also come together through affinity groups representing a variety of different issues and population groups. Examples listed on the Council on Foundations' website include the Association of Black Foundation Executives, Disability Funders Network, Funders for Lesbian and Gay Issues, and Grantmaker Forum on Community and National Service.

Tips for Entry

1. Look into internships with foundations as a way to get a foot in the door.
2. Find a field of interest about which you are passionate. Foundation workers typically have work experience and/or education in a particular area such as public health, the environment, social services, or the arts.
3. Browse the website of the Council on Foundations *(www.cof.org)* for job postings and information about affinity groups.
4. Check your school or local library for *The Foundation Directory* by the Foundation Center staff. Also browse the Foundation Center's website *(www.foundationcenter.org)* to view listings of foundations by program area and geographical location.

FOUNDER, NONPROFIT ORGANIZATION

CAREER PROFILE

Duties: Articulating the purpose of the organization; recruiting supporters; formulating operating expenses; filing for tax-exempt status

Alternate Title(s): President, Social Entrepreneur

Salary Range: $0 to $120,000

Employment Prospects: Fair

Advancement Prospects: Fair

Best Geographical Location: Nationwide

Prerequisites:
   Education or Training—Varies
   Experience—Helpful but not required
   Special Skills and Personality Traits—Passionate; socially savvy; proficient in communication skills

CAREER LADDER

```
┌─────────────────────────────┐
│     Executive Director       │
└─────────────────────────────┘

┌─────────────────────────────┐
│          Founder             │
└─────────────────────────────┘

┌─────────────────────────────┐
│      Previous Career         │
│ (e.g., teacher, social       │
│  worker, student)            │
└─────────────────────────────┘
```

Position Description

Founders of start-up organizations are the entrepreneurs of the nonprofit world. Some call themselves social entrepreneurs, eschewing words like *charity* and *philanthropy* for private-sector terms such as *results-driven management* and *quarterly goals*. They know that good intentions, alone, are not enough to guarantee success in the competitive world of the 21st century.

Young idealists are turning to nonprofits in much the way their parents flocked to government programs like the Peace Corps in the 1960s. New community service programs have sprouted up around the nation, introducing high school and college students to the nonprofit sector. Some graduates of these programs have decided to create their own nonprofit organizations. An individual who tutored in college, for example, might found an organization to boost the academic skills of inner-city children.

Others become Founders after scoring big profits in the private sector and deciding they want to "give something back." Still others draw on their professional backgrounds, lifelong interests, or personal experiences with disease, trauma, or some other life-altering situation. A small, local group might catapult into the national spotlight if it hits just the right public nerve. Mothers against Drunk Driving, for example, quickly became successful, as did the United Way and the Make-a-Wish Foundation.

Although no one can predict exactly how well an idea will catch on, careful planning and research can help prospective Founders decide whether or not to take the plunge. Resources for prospective Founders abound, including websites, books, and start-up manuals. As a first step, insiders say, Founders should turn their idea into a statement of purpose or "mission" by asking a number of questions: What service will the nonprofit provide? Is it needed? How many people will use it? From this statement of purpose, the Founder can move on to a business plan. What kind of operating expenses are needed? How big a staff? How much time and money will be spent on lobbying?

Founders typically delegate some of their responsibilities to a planning committee and/or board of directors. Sometimes, after researching the organizational landscape, the group decides not to move forward. If, however, the Founder's original idea gains acceptance, the next step is to establish a structure. Organizations usually choose representatives—typically a board of directors—to make decisions for the group. Once the structure is chosen, the group can write its bylaws (in keeping with the specific requirements of the secretary of state's office).

An organization need not incorporate—a group of friends can form a self-help group and call themselves a nonprofit—but, if the organization remains an informal group, the Founder assumes financial liability and the group lacks certain privileges. Organizations register for incorporation with the state's secretary of state or secretary of commerce.

Next is filing for tax-exempt status. People commonly refer to nonprofits as (c)(3)'s or (c)(4)'s, abbreviations used by the Internal Revenue Service. The difference between them is the amount of lobbying they can do. Both are tax-exempt organizations (they need not pay corporate income taxes on their money), but only (c)(3) organizations can offer donors a tax deduction. In return, (c)(3)'s must limit the amount of lobbying they do. A (c)(4) organization can make lobbying its primary activity but loses the opportunity to offer donors a tax break.

Once the paperwork is done, the Founder can celebrate the birth of a new nonprofit organization. The hardest part of the job, however, is keeping the organization alive. Often the Founder also becomes the organization's executive director. He or she runs the organization, chairing meetings, setting goals, and motivating others to achieve them. *Running* an organization can be very different from *founding* it. Some high-profile Founders have been fired by the board of directors. Once a Founder has established an organization, it can live on without him or her to lead it.

Salaries

Often it takes more than a year for the Founder to start earning a salary. Money needs to be put into the organization before it can be taken out. Start-up expenses include filing costs, office expenses, and often legal fees exceeding $500. If a nonprofit generates an income of less than $25,000, it need not file with the Internal Revenue Service. In these cases, the Founder may receive only token pay.

Employment Prospects

Employment prospects are fair. Some 29,000 new nonprofits are started every year, according to the Society for Nonprofit Organizations. Because the number of nonprofits has doubled in the past few decades, organizations face stiff competition. No longer is a nonprofit likely to be "the only game in town."

Industry sources sometimes advise prospective Founders to collaborate with existing organizations rather than to strike out on their own. For example, a group organized to help middle-class disaster victims might partner with a local chapter of the Red Cross, with the latter acting as a financial sponsor.

Advancement Prospects

Advancement prospects are fair because many nonprofits "limp along" for years because they lack the skills, talent, and resources to flourish, industry sources say.

Education and Training

Education and training vary widely because, in this field, personal experience can count for more than a degree. Someone might, for example, draw on experiences as a welfare recipient to teach self-sufficiency skills. A medical doctor, on the other hand, might build on years of formal education and training to start an organization providing health-related services overseas.

Experience, Skills, and Personality Traits

Founders draw on a variety of experiences, both formal and informal. Someone whose child suffers from a particular disease might found a nonprofit organization to help other parents cope with the problem. An art lover might start a small museum even though he or she has no formal experience in the field. Often, though, Founders *do* have a background in their organization's area of expertise. For example, a group of human service workers might leave their old employer because of philosophical differences and form their own nonprofit organization.

Although many people see Founders as risk takers, insiders dispute this notion, saying that success depends largely on careful planning to *minimize* risk. Founders need to go out and sell their ideas. Excellent communication skills are a must.

Unions and Associations

Founders might belong to the Society for Nonprofit Organizations or other organizations that provide resources to nonprofits. The National Council of Nonprofit Associations is a network of 39 state and regional associations of nonprofit organizations.

Tips for Entry

1. Ask yourself whether you are motivated by the right reasons. Industry sources advise against forming a nonprofit organization to address personal problems such as workplace unhappiness or general malaise.
2. See whether your state has an association of nonprofit organizations. One place to look is the website of the National Council of Nonprofit Associations (*www.ncna.org*).
3. Read about starting a nonprofit organization. Check out library books. Scan the Web for sites (e.g., *www.helping.org*) that provide numerous links.
4. Check state regulations by contacting the offices of the attorney general and the secretary of state.

EXECUTIVE DIRECTOR

CAREER PROFILE

Duties: Lead organization; evaluate programs; raise funds; work with board of directors; build alliances; act as chief spokesperson of the organization

Alternate Title(s): President

Salary Range: $35,000 to $150,000

Employment Prospects: Good

Advancement Prospects: Good

Best Geographical Location: Major cities

Prerequisites:

Education or Training—Graduate degree or special training in nonprofit management preferred

Experience—Five years of related experience

Special Skills and Personality Traits—Committed; persuasive; diplomatic; politically savvy; organized; flexible; resilient; visionary

CAREER LADDER

```
┌─────────────────────────────────┐
│   Executive Director of Larger  │
│   Organization or Consultant    │
└─────────────────────────────────┘

┌─────────────────────────────────┐
│      Executive Director         │
└─────────────────────────────────┘

┌─────────────────────────────────┐
│   Management-Level Position or  │
│     Founder of Organization     │
└─────────────────────────────────┘
```

Position Description

Executive Directors are the nonprofit sector's equivalent of corporate executive officers. As the person at the top, the Executive Director sets the tone for the organization, serving as chief advocate and administrator. Individuals assume responsibility for not only long-term planning but also day-to-day operations—everything from payroll to program evaluation. Most important, they communicate the organization's message to the outside world.

Whether an organization is fighting for human rights, lobbying for government reform, or working to improve the community, the Executive Director must communicate its "mission" to the public. Certain words crop up repeatedly in talk about successful Executive Directors, *passion, vision,* and *leadership,* among them. The Executive Director serves as the driving force, the figurehead, and the voice of the organization.

He or she acts as the "point person" for the organization, handling problems and complaints. Often different groups have different needs. Take, for example, the various funding priorities of the following three groups:

- Board of Directors—cut costs
- Staff—raise salaries
- Public—beef up programs

Forging a consensus is no easy task. Since the board of directors (made up of volunteers) usually has the power to hire and fire the Executive Director, the relationship between the two can make or break a career.

Executive Directors spend their days making difficult decisions. Are programs running smoothly? What kind of resources are necessary for improvement? Should the organization take a firm stand or be willing to compromise?

For years, Executive Directors kept quiet about the difficulties of their jobs. Few wanted to risk being seen as incompetent. But, as word of the difficulties spread, attention shifted from the shortcomings of individuals to the difficulties of the position itself. Management consultants became involved, offering new help for Executive Directors in the form of books, articles, and workshops such as the Management Center's aptly titled Executive Director 101.

Advice givers encourage Executive Directors to find ways to lighten their loads. New strategies include delegating responsibility for internal matters to an associate director and working out barter-type arrangements with other organizations. For instance, the Executive Director of a small organization might arrange for a larger group to do its payroll in return for certain services.

A typical day for an Executive Director might include

- Touching base with key personnel
- Strategizing with the Board of Directors
- Reviewing reports and data to improve programs
- Attending meetings in the community
- Participating in alliances with other organizations
- Raising money and overseeing finances

Salaries

Salaries range widely, depending primarily on the type of organization, according to the Society for Nonprofit Organizations. An Executive Director for a small community-based nonprofit might earn $35,000 to $50,000 compared to $60,000 to $90,000 for a midsized group and $80,000 to $150,000 for a large national organization.

Employment Prospects

Employment prospects are good because of the variety of nonprofit organizations. Turnover at the top, too, makes for openings. Insiders emphasize that prospective Executive Directors should "know what they're getting into." Executive Directors may spend much of their time fund-raising to enable the organization to survive.

Advancement Prospects

Advancement prospects are good because Executive Directors can either grow with the job, move to a larger organization, or branch off in other directions. According to the study "Leadership Lost" by CompassPoint Nonprofit Services of San Francisco, California, many individuals decide against taking another position as Executive Director because of the long hours, often 80 hours a week or more, and high stress levels. Some Executive Directors go into consulting or other endeavors in the private sector.

Education and Training

Education and training have become especially important because of the increasingly complex and competitive nature of the nonprofit sector. Programs in nonprofit management are offered through professional organizations and universities, including Harvard University's JFK School of Government, the Indiana University Center on Philanthropy, and Syracuse University's Maxwell School. In some fields, such as social work, a specialized graduate degree may be required.

Experience, Skills, and Personality Traits

Most Executive Directors have previous management experience, but, even so, this position can be daunting because of the multitude of responsibilities. Executive Directors must listen to the needs and wants of staff, board members, and the public, ultimately deciding what is best for the organization. As one insider says, "There are quite a number of balls to juggle."

Outside forces can add to the pressure. As trends change, a group that was the nonprofit sector's "flavor of the year" may lose its appeal. Funds may dry up as a result, posing new challenges for the Executive Director. Many Executive Directors work long hours because they believe deeply in the mission of their organizations. They must possess stamina and patience.

Unions and Associations

Executive Directors belong to a variety of organizations, including the Society for Nonprofit Organizations, the American Society of Association Executives, and the Alliance for Nonprofit Management.

Tips for Entry

1. Volunteer for an organization that deals with your own areas of interest.
2. Become a member of the board of directors.
3. Read professional journals such as *Nonprofit World* and *Nonprofit Times*.
4. Look into educational programs in nonprofit management.
5. Take a professional approach. *Wanting* to "do good" is not enough. Individuals must also know *how* to do so.

PUBLIC INTEREST

CANVASSER

CAREER PROFILE

Duties: Going door-to-door to conduct membership drives and educate citizens about issues of concern to the organization

Alternate Title(s): Activist

Salary Range: $15,000 to $22,000

Employment Prospects: Good

Advancement Prospects: Good

Best Geographical Location(s): Major cities

Prerequisites:

Education or Training—Training provided

Experience—Prior community experience a plus

Special Skills and Personality Traits—Outgoing; personable and optimistic; interested in issues; enthusiastic about making a difference

CAREER LADDER

```
┌─────────────────────────────┐
│   Director of Canvassing     │
└─────────────────────────────┘

┌─────────────────────────────┐
│         Canvasser            │
└─────────────────────────────┘

┌─────────────────────────────┐
│         Student              │
└─────────────────────────────┘
```

Position Description

Canvassers get a valuable foot in the door of activism. This entry-level position generally involves going door-to-door to raise funds for an organization and educate citizens about issues of concern. The Public Interest Research Group (PIRG) and Clean Water Action use canvassers extensively, as do other groups, both locally and nationally based. Canvassing can be done on the phone as well as in person.

Those who canvass door-to-door generally work in the late afternoon and early evening hours, when most people are home for dinner. They typically visit between 30 and 100 homes a night, depending on how far apart the buildings are spaced. Canvassers might have a petition to sign or postcards for citizens to send to lawmakers. They provide ways for citizens to get involved.

Canvassers often work in teams headed up by supervisors. A talented Canvasser might be in charge of mapping out an area and supervising others. Because people may be unfamiliar with the term *Canvasser,* organizations often use the more general title *Activist* for this position.

Salaries

Salaries for full-time Canvassers generally range from $15,000 to $22,000, according to industry sources. The pay structure varies from group to group, as some organizations link salaries closely to performance. A high-performing Canvasser may be given supervisory responsibilities and extra pay. Some organizations hire Canvassers on a part-time basis, paying $7 to $12 an hour.

Employment Prospects

Employment prospects are good because positions are widely available. Many organizations rely heavily on Canvassers to build the kind of grass-roots support they need to survive. Positions that turn over need to be quickly refilled, presenting a steady stream of opportunities.

Advancement Prospects

Advancement prospects are good because organizations often promote Canvassers to other positions. A Canvasser might be given supervisory responsibilities and be promoted to a position such as Canvassing Director or Field Organizer. Canvassing gives individuals valuable experience in communication and fund-raising—skills needed in many positions. Some Canvassers branch into related endeavors such as running an initiative campaign or helping a political candidate. Others leave canvassing to attend law school or other graduate programs.

Education and Training

Organizations generally provide their own training to familiarize Canvassers with the art of talking to people about the issues. Many Canvassers are college students who see canvassing as a temporary, part-time job.

Experience, Skills, and Personality Traits

Canvassing can be a difficult job, as some people resent strangers' knocking on their doors. Because Canvassers are dealing directly with the public, good communication skills are essential. Canvassers should be outgoing, personable, and engaging. Insiders say that having a sense of optimism is particularly important. Enthusiasm is contagious, they say; a Canvasser's excitement about the work of the organization can make others more willing to get involved. Canvassers with an upbeat attitude who believe that change is possible do best in this job. They should care deeply about the issues.

Unions and Associations

There are no unions or associations specifically for Canvassers, insiders say, but individuals might belong to organizations in their field(s) of interest.

Tips for Entry

1. Check help wanted ads in newspapers and notices around town. Positions are often posted on lampposts or bulletin boards in cafes and other gathering spots.
2. Cultivate a positive attitude. Believing that change is possible can help motivate others to get involved.
3. Expect some rejection. Canvassers should not fall apart if someone closes the door in their face. Having a "thick skin" helps.

ENVIRONMENTAL ACTIVIST

CAREER PROFILE

Duties: Advocating for the environment; developing strategies to encourage public action; building coalitions

Alternate Title(s): Program Coordinator, Campaign Coordinator, Organizer, Program Officer, Campaign Manager, Community Organizer

Salary Range: $15,000 to $44,000

Employment Prospects: Fair to good

Advancement Prospects: Fair to good

Best Geographical Location(s): Washington, D.C.; San Francisco; Boston; Seattle

Prerequisites:

Education or Training—Bachelor's degree or higher generally preferred

Experience—Two to five years

Special Skills and Personality Traits—Dedication; aggressiveness; creativity; energy.

CAREER LADDER

```
┌─────────────────────────────┐
│     Executive Director       │
└─────────────────────────────┘

┌─────────────────────────────┐
│   Environmental Activist     │
└─────────────────────────────┘

┌─────────────────────────────┐
│ Volunteer, Intern, or Canvasser │
└─────────────────────────────┘
```

Position Description

Environmental Activists defend what cannot speak for itself—the natural world around them. Environmental Activists are involved in a dizzying array of activities, from counting killer whales off the coast of Alaska to promoting citizen awareness of safe drinking-water standards to addressing the issues of global climate change. Environmental nonprofit organizations abound, numbering in the thousands. Many, though, are largely volunteer operations. The number of environmental staffers in nonprofits, as opposed to government or private industry, is relatively small.

Nevertheless, their influence has been enormous. Nearly every major environmental victory of our time can be traced to the leadership or involvement of nonprofit groups, according to the Environmental Careers Organization, a national nonprofit based in Boston, Massachusetts, dedicated to helping people pursue careers related to the environment.

Although environmentalists of the late 1960s and early 1970s were often dismissed as eccentrics or radicals, many environmental groups have become well-established and highly professional over the years. Some groups link environmental and consumer issues, while others are devoted to a particular environmental cause such as animal rights. Still

others focus on a particular strategy such as lobbying or direct action. Well-known environmental groups include the Appalachian Mountain Club, the Audubon Society, Clean Water Action, the Defenders of Wildlife, the Environmental Defense Fund, the National Wildlife Federation, the Nature Conservancy, the Public Interest Research Group, the Rails to Trails Conservancy, the Sierra Club, and the World Wildlife Fund.

New grass-roots organizations, meanwhile, have sprouted up, giving rise to the "environmental justice" movement. According to the Environmental Careers Organization, the environmental justice movement began in 1987 with the publication of a landmark study finding that, nationwide, communities with two or more hazardous waste sites have three times the percentage of minorities among their population as those with no waste sites. Community groups arose to address their own issues of concern. After some success, a group might decide to become permanent and hire its own staff.

Generally speaking, activism falls under the umbrella of "environmental education and communication." Strategies differ from group to group. Some adopt a more confrontational approach than others. But all share the same basic goal: to communicate the importance of environmental issues in ways that educate the public and encourage action.

If, for example, an organization is trying to draw attention to air pollution caused by fossil fuel use, the Environmental Activist needs to explain the problem clearly and succinctly to the average person. Why should someone care about fossil fuels? What can he or she do to make a difference? Should he or she sign a petition? Join a campaign? Next, the Environmental Activist sizes up the power structures involved. Who are the main players in the corporate arena? Who are the decision makers at the federal level? How should the group go about gaining their support?

Environmental Activists know from experience that there is power in numbers. To increase their strength, they commonly build coalitions with other groups. Then they work tirelessly to achieve their goals. One day might involve community meetings and phone calls; another, research and lobbying. Whether an Environmental Activist gravitates more toward street theater or press conferences depends in large part on the goals of the organization.

This is not, by any stretch of the imagination, a 9 to 5 job. Environmental Activists often work nights and weekends. If a group is arranging a headline-grabbing event such as a protest, demonstration, or boycott, an Environmental Activist is likely to be working late at night confirming last-minute details.

A typical day for an Environmental Activist in a state capital might include

- Reading the newspaper to see how the organization's issues are playing out in the press
- Seeing what is happening in the state legislature that day
- Meeting with the communication staff to plan a special event (e.g., a public gathering on the state house steps)
- Testifying before a legislative committee
- Meeting with legislative staff to lobby on behalf of issues
- Answering correspondence of citizens and members
- Attending a night meeting to organize people in a neighborhood that needs support

Salaries

Usually an individual has worked as a volunteer or an entry-level staffer before arriving at this middle rung on the career ladder. Salaries for full-time Environmental Activists generally fall into the $15,000 to $44,000 range, and relatively large organizations generally pay more than smaller ones. Salaries for Environmental Executive Directors range from the low to mid-$30,000s to more than $100,000, according to the Environmental Careers Organization.

Employment Prospects

Employment prospects for this midlevel position are fair to good. Opportunities are much better lower down on the career ladder, as opportunities for volunteers and canvassers abound. Canvassing involves knocking on a lot of doors—typically 75 in a particular neighborhood per night—to explain issues and solicit funds for the organization. Anyone willing to endure the rigors of door-to-door campaigning can find excellent prospects as a Canvasser. Good Canvassers are often promoted to field organizers or hired for mid-level positions as Environmental Activists.

Mid-level positions, however, can be hard to find because many groups rely heavily on volunteers and part-timers. Nevertheless, people with passion, persistence, and a well-developed array of skills can find jobs as Environmental Activists. New groups continue to form, although paid staffs tend to be small.

Advancement Prospects

Advancement prospects, too, are fair to good. Upper-level positions in nonprofit activism tend to be relatively low-paying. An executive director of a nonprofit might earn less than a midlevel staffer in a government agency or private company. Job satisfaction, though, can be high, thus compensating for the long hours and relatively low pay.

Opportunities are best for individuals willing to explore a variety of possibilities. One of the fastest growing environmental fields is "green-products" marketing, which, although in the private sector, shares the idealism of nonprofits. Opportunities to market solar energy, recycled paper, and other green products are commonly listed in environmental magazines and on websites.

Education and Training

No one educational background is recommended for Environmental Activism, as requirements vary from job to job. Some insiders caution against making long-term educational plans without first exploring the field as a volunteer, intern, or staffer.

Organizations vary so much in scope that one group may want an attorney, another an economist, and yet another a naturalist fluent in Japanese. Still, generalists, too, are in demand. Being a quick learner is always a plus.

Experience, Skills, and Personality Traits

Most Environmental Activists enter the field as a calling rather than a job. Many start out as volunteers. Nonprofits are known for their flexibility and high level of personal involvement. Offices tend to be small, allowing individuals to exercise a variety of skills. Staffers commonly do a little of everything, from creating websites to taking out trash.

Chronic underfunding and understaffing, though, can take a toll. Often it is difficult to achieve goals. Environmental Activists commonly need to do some fund-raising. Passion and boundless energy are required, but increasingly organizations also are looking for solid skills in areas such as program management and fund-raising.

Unions and Associations

The Student Conservation Association, the Environmental Career Center, and the Environmental Careers Organization offer professional guidance and development to individuals interested in the field. Environmental Activists might also belong to the National Association of Environmental Professionals or one of a variety of more specialized organizations.

Tips for Entry

1. Volunteer, intern, or work part-time. Begin by checking out the websites of organizations such as the Student Conservation Association *(www.sca-inc.org)*, the Environmental Careers Organization *(www.eco.org)*, and the Environmental Career Center *(www.environmentalcareer.com)*.

2. Participate in a campaign involving either a candidate or an issue to develop your political savvy for the job.

3. Bypass the large, brand-name organizations for the medium to small ones. Competition can be fierce for jobs at the larger organizations. Smaller organizations can offer the best opportunities for self-starters.

4. Browse the abundant supply of environmental resources on the Internet. One good place to start is Southampton College Library's Environmental Resources on the Internet *(www.southampton.liu.edu/library/environ.htm)*, which has links to on-line publications such as *Conservation Ecology* and *E Magazine,* as well as to myriad environmental organizations. Surf organizational webpages for a wealth of information: a detailed description of the organization and its programs, its publications, the names and responsibilities of key staffers, and perhaps even a list of current job openings. EnviroLink *(www.envirolink.org)* and the Amazing Environmental Organization Web Directory *(www.webdirectory.com)* also offer numerous links.

5. Check out job listings on environmental employment websites as well as in environmental publications.

6. Read books and articles on the environmental field. Search for books, magazines, and articles, using the keyword *Environmental*.

CONSUMER ACTIVIST

CAREER PROFILE

Duties: Investigating suspected consumer problems; publicizing findings; and advocating for change

Alternate Title(s): Project Director, Research Associate, Consumer Advocate

Salary Range: $15,000 to $100,000

Employment Prospects: Good

Advancement Prospects: Good

Best Geographical Location(s): Washington, D.C., state capitals; and major cities

Prerequisites:

Education or Training—College degree, with courses in history, political science, and journalism helpful

Experience—Volunteer experience or internship recommended

Special Skills and Personality Traits—Strong research and writing skills; public-speaking abilities; media savvy; understanding of government and political processes; tenacity

CAREER LADDER

```
┌─────────────────────────────────────┐
│  Position with Larger Organization   │
└─────────────────────────────────────┘

┌─────────────────────────────────────┐
│         Consumer Activist            │
└─────────────────────────────────────┘

┌─────────────────────────────────────┐
│         Volunteer or Intern          │
└─────────────────────────────────────┘
```

Position Description

Consumer Activists advocate for goods and services in the public interest. Often they fight for the "little guy" against powerful corporations or interest groups. Over the years, Consumer Activists have pushed for—and won—legislation affecting such areas as housing, health care, utility rates, and food labeling. As other activists do, they generally perform a combination of research, public education, and lobbying.

Much of the growth in this field has resulted from the activism of Ralph Nader, who founded a variety of consumer organizations in the 1970s. Many of these, including the Public Interest Research Group, remain active today.

Some groups, including large organizations such as Consumers Union, Public Citizen, and Consumer Federation of America, cover a wide variety of issues. Others focus on single issues such as food safety, health care, or privacy on the Internet. Often, consumer groups form alliances with other organizations. A group dealing with Medicare reform, for example, might enlist the support of those who work with the elderly.

Consumer Activists generally work in cycles by project. The cycle typically begins with research. Because certain techniques, such as direct questioning, are often ineffective when exploring controversial issues, Consumer Activists must use other strategies to get the information they need.

For instance, someone investigating suspected nursing home abuse might use the Freedom of Information Act to research a government inspection database. Another possibility is for the Consumer Activist to go undercover, pretending to be the child of a nursing-home patient.

After investigating the problem, the Consumer Activist tries to publicize and address it. The Consumer Activist who works undercover might write a report documenting his or her experiences. He or she might release a report to the media and try to appear on radio or television talk shows.

The next step involves advocating for change. The Consumer Activist might form alliances with other groups to lobby. Together they might work with an executive agency involved in nursing home regulations. They might propose new legislation. Successes result, as do setbacks, as one cycle gives way to the next.

In addition, Consumer Activists might be involved in

- Community organizing
- Fund-raising
- Program management
- Statewide coordination

Salaries

Salaries vary with the experience of the individual and the size of the organization. Someone in an entry-level position with no prior experience might make $15,000 a year compared to $100,000 or more for someone in a large organization with several years' experience.

Employment Prospects

Employment prospects are good. Industry specialists describe the field as stable: neither expanding nor contracting.

Advancement Prospects

Advancement prospects are good because Consumer Activists who prove themselves on the job tend to move up the career ladder. However, insiders caution that the job can be difficult. In order to be successful, a Consumer Activist must develop the kind of media and political savvy needed to promote institutional change.

Education and Training

A college degree is generally required, although no one particular major is recommended. Courses in history, political science, and journalism can be helpful.

Experience, Skills, and Personality Traits

Many individuals break into consumer activism through internships or volunteer work, although this type of experi-ence is not always required. Journalism experience also can be useful, as Consumer Activists must be able to research the "who, what, where, when, and why" of a topic; write in simple, declarative sentences; and know how to communi-cate with the media.

Whereas an entry-level position might be suited for someone right out of college, a program manager position generally requires some experience. Often, organizations give Consumer Activists a great deal of autonomy, thus requiring the individual to be a self-starter. Being able to cultivate alliances with other groups and overcome frustra-tion is also important. Above all, Consumer Activists must believe in their cause.

Unions and Associations

The Consumer Federation of America is an advocacy, edu-cational, and membership organization comprising more than 285 organizations throughout the nation.

Tips for Entry

1. Volunteer to work for a consumer organization. Many volunteers are hired for paid positions.
2. Look for an internship.
3. Check nonprofit directories, journals, and websites for consumer organizations and/or jobs. *Consumer Protection* is a common subject heading.
4. Submit op-ed pieces and/or letters to the editor for publication. Because writing skills are important to this position, having samples of your work can be helpful in the job-search process.

GOVERNMENT REFORM ACTIVIST

CAREER PROFILE

Duties: Researching, lobbying, community organizing, and educating the public to improve government and the political process

Alternate Title(s): Political Organizer, Legislative Advocate, Democracy Advocate, Program Manager, Policy Analyst

Salary Range: $25,000 to $50,000

Employment Prospects: Good

Advancement Prospects: Good

Best Geographical Location: Washington, D.C.

Prerequisites:

Education or Training—Bachelor's degree required; master's or law degree sometimes preferred

Experience—Three to four years

Special Skills and Personality Traits—Commitment to public-interest issues; familiarity with government processes; excellent communication skills; political contacts

CAREER LADDER

```
┌─────────────────────────────────────┐
│   Executive Director or Lobbyist     │
└─────────────────────────────────────┘

┌─────────────────────────────────────┐
│    Government Reform Activist        │
└─────────────────────────────────────┘

┌─────────────────────────────────────┐
│  Legislative Staffer or Staff Assistant │
└─────────────────────────────────────┘
```

Position Description

Government Reform Activists work to improve the democratic system by championing a variety of measures: campaign finance reform, increased citizen involvement, and new election laws, among them. Individuals ask themselves questions like, How responsive is the political system to the needs of the people? Should political ads be regulated? Would same-day voter registration do more to boost citizen participation or increase the chances of fraud?

Government reform organizations overlap with research institutes (e.g., think tanks), which also take an interest in the way government operates. But whereas a think tank's work ends with the release of a written report, government reform advocacy groups move on to the next step of fighting for change.

Over the past couple of decades, government reform issues have grabbed front-page headlines. Presidential candidates in the 2000 election, for instance, made campaign finance reform a rallying cry of their campaigns, spawning new organizations and revitalizing old ones.

Government Reform Activists take part in four major activities: research, lobbying, community organizing, and public education.

The percentage of time devoted to each activity depends on the orientation of the group. Whereas some groups make lobbying their primary activity, others take a more varied approach in keeping with their tax-exempt status. Individuals can be hired primarily for one task—lobbying or grassroots organizing, for instance—or a mix.

Organizations vary greatly in size. Common Cause, for instance, has not only a national headquarters but also a network of state offices covering a wide range of issues. Other groups, for instance, U.S. Term Limits, focus on a specific area of concern.

Organizations span the political spectrum, commonly describing themselves as "nonpartisan" even though certain issues may attract more members of one political party than another. The nonpartisan Council for Government Reform, for instance, appeals to fiscal conservatives with its message of limited government.

Government Reform Activists typically research issues and convey them to members. If, for example, a bill for campaign financing reform is before Congress, they might analyze the pros and cons, deciding to compromise on some points but not others.

Common responsibilities of Government Reform Activists include

- Researching and analyzing issues
- Lobbying (e.g., testifying at hearings, providing information)
- Acting as spokesperson and media contact
- Organizing phone banks, events, rallies, and other activities
- Preparing newsletters and other publications

Salaries

Salaries for Government Reform Activists generally range from approximately $25,000 to $50,000, Executive Directors earn $45,000 to $120,000, according to industry sources. Small grass-roots organizations, though, might pay considerably less—in the $15,000 to $25,000 range. Salaries are generally commensurate with experience.

Employment Prospects

Employment prospects are fair to good. Rapid growth of new organizations during the past two decades has resulted in numerous positions, but industry specialists are uncertain about whether or not this trend will continue.

Advancement Prospects

Advancement prospects are good because Government Reform Activists make important contacts, opening doors to future advancement. Individuals can either move up to management positions within their organizations or advance in an area of specialization such as lobbying or communication.

Education and Training

A bachelor's degree is generally a minimum in this field. Insiders recommend a degree in political science, journalism, or another major concerned with public-policy matters.

A law degree or a master's degree in public policy or administration or political science can be helpful for advancement.

Experience, Skills, and Personality Traits

Individuals in this field tend to be civics buffs. Positions that involve lobbying generally call for prior legislative experience because of the importance of personal contacts. Someone who has worked for a high-ranking member of Congress, for example, would be "golden."

Other positions look for backgrounds in organizing or communications. Government Reform Activists must be persuasive both verbally and in writing. They should be able to structure their arguments soundly to combine public policy with advocacy.

Unions and Associations

Individuals might be members of the American Political Science Association, the American Society for Association Executives, and/or the American Society for Public Administration.

Tips for Entry

1. Familiarize yourself with the Constitution of the United States. One good secondary source about the document is *The Federalist Papers,* the classic writings of Alexander Hamilton and others in favor of the Constitution. As one insider states, "If you can read the Constitution and not be moved to be a political activist, you should not be one."
2. Volunteer in a political campaign and/or community activity.
3. Check employment websites (e.g., *www.idealist.org*) and books such as *Good Works: A Guide to Careers in Social Change,* edited by Donna Colvin, with a preface by Ralph Nader, for organizations dealing with government reform.
4. Get legislative, campaign, media, and/or organizing experience to enhance your chance of getting hired.

PUBLIC INTEREST LAWYER

CAREER PROFILE

Duties: Arguing cases in court; providing legal services for underrepresented or poor populations; performing law-related tasks such as lobbying and policy analysis

Alternate Title(s): Staff Attorney, Litigation Counsel, Community Lawyer, Legal Director

Salary Range: $30,000 to $85,000+

Employment Prospects: Fair

Advancement Prospects: Good

Best Geographical Location(s): Large cities; rural areas

Prerequisites:

Education or Training—Law degree; passing of bar exam

Experience—Entry-level to several years, depending on the position

Special Skills and Personality Traits—Dedication to equal justice; sound legal skills; ability to assume responsibility quickly; knowledge of a second language helpful

CAREER LADDER

```
┌─────────────────────────────────┐
│     Lawyer for Private Firm      │
└─────────────────────────────────┘

┌─────────────────────────────────┐
│     Public Interest Lawyer       │
└─────────────────────────────────┘

┌─────────────────────────────────┐
│      Law School Student          │
└─────────────────────────────────┘
```

Position Description

Public Interest Lawyers represent clients and causes that are often not served by private law firms. Over the years, Public Interest Lawyers have fought for—and won—victories in areas such as racial justice, women's rights, and environmental protection. The work of Public Interest Lawyers varies by organization: some groups represent individual clients; others deal more with policy issues.

Often, though, the two overlap. An organization that represents a particular group of clients, for instance, might challenge a city's policy on an issue of concern. Harvard Law School's *Public Interest Job Search Guide* describes a variety of settings in which Public Interest Lawyers work, including

- Client-oriented public interest organizations
- Organizations involved in international affairs
- Labor unions
- Legal services offices
- Policy-oriented public interest organizations

Client-oriented public-interest organizations, such as the Washington Legal Clinic for the Homeless and the AIDS

Legal Council of Chicago, represent individuals with problems in the office's area of specialization. A client faced with possible eviction, for example, might turn to the organization for help. One Public Interest Lawyer profiled in a Harvard publication described his office as a "legal emergency room."

Casework in client-oriented public interest organizations commonly involves not only litigation (court proceedings) but also strategies such as writing letters on the client's behalf, holding legal rights seminars for clients, and contacting government agencies. Sometimes Lawyers for these organizations are also involved in tracking of legislation, lobbying, and public advocacy.

Other Public Interest Lawyers work for international organizations, labor unions, or legal services offices. The latter provide free or reduced-fee assistance for low-income clients. These community or neighborhood-based groups generally deal with civil, as opposed to criminal, cases in areas such as family, housing, and consumer law. Public Interest Lawyers in legal services offices have close client contact and substantial caseloads.

Policy-oriented organizations employ a variety of strategies to accomplish their goals. Some groups, such as the

American Civil Liberties Union and the National Association for the Advancement of Colored People (NAACP) Legal Defense and Education Fund, rely largely on class action suits and other legal strategies. Others combine legal strategies with social action. Still others focus primarily on research, analysis, and dissemination of information.

Common responsibilities for Public Interest Lawyers in policy-oriented organizations include

- Litigating in state and federal courts
- Analyzing pending legislation and government initiatives
- Coordinating efforts of volunteer attorneys, law students, and other volunteers
- Engaging in public speaking at conferences and other events
- Participating in education and outreach efforts

Salaries

Salaries for Public Interest Lawyers generally range from $30,000 to $85,000, industry sources say. The median salary of Public Interest Lawyers six months after graduation was $34,000 in 2000, according to the U.S. Department of Labor's 2002–2003 *Occupational Outlook Handbook.* Salaries are higher for Public Interest Lawyers with more experience.

Although salaries for Public Interest Lawyers are considerably lower than those of attorneys in private practice, many take advantage of financial-assistance programs. A growing number of law schools offer public service scholarships and/or loan forgiveness programs. Fellowships, grants, and public service programs also provide funding for public interest law.

Employment Prospects

Employment prospects are fair because opportunities are linked to government and charitable funds, which are limited. In addition, many nonprofit organizations lack the resources of private firms for recruiting. As a result, law students often need to work harder to find jobs as Public Interest Lawyers than they would to find positions in private law firms.

Advancement Prospects

Advancement prospects are good because Public Interest Lawyers can find opportunities in a variety of settings. Some Public Interest Lawyers advance to positions such as senior counsel or director of litigation within the world of nonprofits, and others move into government or private practice. The American Bar Association recommends that all private law firms provide some legal services on a pro bono basis at no cost to clients. Some private law firms handle a substantial number of cases with broad social, political, or economic impact. Common areas of concern include employment discrimination, civil rights, and immigration law.

Education and Training

Since the 1960s, law schools around the nation have incorporated public interest issues into their courses and fieldwork. Most law schools offer students the choice of a public interest track, according to Equal Justice Works (formerly the National Association of Public Interest Law). In choosing a law school, Equal Justice Works recommends that students

- Examine the course catalog for relevant offerings.
- Look for schools with law clinics and/or pro bono programs offering students the opportunity to practice law.
- Ask about summer and term-time externships (a term commonly used for credit-granting internships).
- See whether any student groups (e.g., Environmental Law Society, Black Law Student Association) deal with issues of public interest concern.
- Find out about career services for students seeking public interest careers. Some schools have public interest coordinators and sponsor job fairs, panels, and other educational programs for students interested in working in the field.

Experience, Skills, and Personality Traits

Legal clinics and pro bono programs give law students valuable hands-on experience in public interest law. Programs such as Equal Justice Works' national service program, funded by the National Corporation for Public Service, also provide opportunities for law students and lawyers. Volunteer and community work in a nonlegal setting or capacity can also be helpful.

Public Interest Lawyers must be committed to the cause of equal justice. Because most public interest organizations are short-staffed, Public Interest Lawyers assume high levels of responsibility early in their careers. They should be able to "hit the ground running." Public Interest Lawyers also should have excellent research, writing, and interpersonal skills. The work is typically fast-paced, and many Public Interest Lawyers work long hours.

Unions and Associations

Equal Justice Works is an organization dedicated to mobilizing lawyers and law students to work in the public interest. The American Bar Association's pro bono section also represents Public Interest Lawyers.

Tips for Entry

1. Volunteer for a legal services organization. Consult the yellow pages of your local phone book under *Legal Services* to find organizations in your area.
2. Look for a part-time or summer job doing research or office work in a law firm or law-oriented nonprofit organization to see whether you like the field well enough to attend law school.

3. Attend career fairs, panel discussions, and other events sponsored by law schools and/or professional associations.

4. Read more about careers in public interest law. Good resources include the website of Equal Justice Works *(www.equaljusticeworks.org)* and Harvard Law School's annual *Public Interest Job Search Guide,* which can be ordered by Internet *(www.law.harvard. edu/students/opia),* e-mail *pia@law.harvard.edu),* phone (617-495-3108), or fax (617-496-4944).

COMMUNITY, SOCIAL, AND INTERNATIONAL ISSUES

COMMUNITY ORGANIZER

CAREER PROFILE

Duties: Researching issues; talking to people; attending meetings; communicating with the media

Alternate Title(s): Grassroots Organizer, Field Organizer, Campus Organizer, Political Organizer, Activist, Advocate

Salary Range: $15,000 to $40,000

Employment Prospects: Good

Advancement Prospects: Good

Best Geographical Location(s): None

Prerequisites:

Education or Training—Bachelor's degree sometimes preferred, but not always required

Experience—Organizing experience preferred

Special Skills and Personality Traits—Passionate; patient; outgoing; resourceful; motivated; committed to social change; knowledge of Spanish a plus

CAREER LADDER

```
┌─────────────────────────────────────┐
│  Program Director or Public Official │
└─────────────────────────────────────┘

┌─────────────────────────────────────┐
│        Community Organizer           │
└─────────────────────────────────────┘

┌─────────────────────────────────────┐
│     Student, Volunteer, or Intern    │
└─────────────────────────────────────┘
```

Position Description

Community Organizers work on the front lines to persuade others to take up their cause. Organizing is so fundamental to social change that some call it the backbone of activism. The two functions often are joined in one heading: Activism/Organizing.

Whether advocating for affordable housing, utility-rate fairness, voter registration, or something else, Community Organizers rely largely on the power of persuasion. They need to listen as well as talk. They must connect with others in order to mobilize them into action.

Typically, Community Activists champion the cause of "social and economic justice." They fight for the underdog—the poor and powerless. They organize against wealthy, powerful foes because they believe there is strength in numbers.

The work of Community Organizers falls roughly into three areas: research, fieldwork, and meetings. A Community Organizer involved in welfare-to-work issues, for example, might follow the issue in the media and summarize legislation, producing fact sheets and other information. Next, the Community Organizer might go around to area businesses to inform them of training options. Finally, he or she might raise a proposal before the city council.

Increasingly, groups representing low- and moderate-income citizens are forming coalitions to increase their influence. A few neighborhood groups, for instance, might join to form their own nonprofit organization and hire a Community Organizer. Or a group working for social change might launch a variety of campaigns: a petition drive to prevent public hospitals from converting to for-profit status, an educational campaign to help Native American schools, and a housing initiative to promote resident councils.

Whereas Community Organizers often deal with grassroots neighborhood efforts, many groups use similar organizing strategies, hiring individuals as

- Campus Organizers—to form student chapters of national organizations such as the Public Interest Research Group
- Political Organizers—to build support for referendum and candidate campaigns, voter-registration, and other issues
- Field Organizers—to mobilize support for issues on a regional level

Whatever the focus of the group, Community Organizers work to get their issues in the spotlight. They organize news conferences, write press releases, prepare flyers, and generate opinion pieces and letters to the editor. They might also coordinate a grass-roots letter-writing campaign to public officials.

Organizing strategies vary from group to group. Community Organizers advocating for a new school, for example, might spend much of their time talking to parents at playgrounds. Many Community Organizers knock on doors to discuss issues, recruit new members, and identify potential leaders. They also spread the word by sending e-mails, making countless phone calls, and coordinating headline-grabbing events such as demonstrations and marches. Often Community Organizers work to nurture leadership in the community. By identifying and training grass-roots leaders, the organization builds a stronger base of support.

As Community Organizers gain experience, they often seek new challenges, moving into more policy-oriented and supervisory roles. Many seek new challenges by taking a higher position within the organization, accepting a job with another organization, or running for political office.

Salaries

Salaries for Community Organizers tend to be low, because there is an abundance of part-time, temporary, and volunteer positions. Large, well-established organizations tend to pay higher salaries than small, start-up groups. Still, no one makes an enormous salary as a Community Organizer. The salary of a long-time Community Organizer might top out at around $40,000.

Employment Prospects

Employment prospects are good because numerous types of organizations hire Community Organizers, including environmental groups, women's organizations, and antipoverty groups. Many grass-roots organizations are forming coalitions to increase their strength, pooling their resources for Community Organizers.

Advancement Prospects

Advancement prospects are good. A Community Organizer might branch into a related activity, such as running for city council or becoming a political aide, or move up within the organization or to a slightly different position in activism. Someone might, for example, move from community to union organizing.

Although some Community Organizer positions are temporary, others provide more stability but are nevertheless subject to economic ebbs and flows. Many longtime Community Organizers have worked for organizations that no longer exist.

Education and Training

Some positions call for a bachelor's degree; others do not. In this field, drive, passion, and resourcefulness count for more than a formal degree.

Nevertheless, many universities offer undergraduate and/or graduate degrees in subjects related to community organizing such as social work, human services, public policy, and urban affairs. Graduate students in public policy at the University of California at Berkeley, for example, can take advantage of its affiliation with the Institute for the Study of Social Change.

Other institutes and organizations offer nonaccredited programs in organizing and activism. Training programs for community organizers include the Social Action and Leadership School for Activists (SALSA), offering classes in Washington, D.C.

Experience, Skills, and Personality Traits

Community Organizers often have experience as volunteers working for social and/or political change. Many have grown up seeing injustice in their own lives and the world around them. Such sensitivity can be an asset on the job, as are the two *ps*—passion and patience. Community Organizers also need to be hard-working, dependable, and accepting of diversity. Knowledge of another language, such as Spanish, is a plus.

Community Organizers are likely to encounter disagreements within the group and between organizations. Hours can be long, and the work frustrating and stressful. Community Organizers commonly work nights and weekends. On the plus side, work environments are often close-knit and casual.

Unions and Associations

The National Organizers Alliance is a group of people working for social, economic, and environmental justice. The Center for Campus Organizing is a national organization dedicated to building progressive movements on college campuses. Community Organizers also commonly participate in local alliances (e.g. D.C. Cares) or issue-based coalitions (e.g., Colorado Environmental Coalition).

Tips for Entry

1. Get involved in your community. Often volunteer positions lead the way to paid employment.
2. Browse the National Organizers Alliance website (*www.noacentral.org*)
3. Browse Internet job sites such as Idealist.org (*www.idealist.org*) to get an overview of positions in the field.
4. Check listings for paid internships and other temporary positions. Community organizing is a field that lends itself to internships and other temporary employment opportunities.
5. Work for more than one organization to get a sense of the differences in organizing strategies and to learn as much as possible.

COMMUNITY DEVELOPMENT ASSOCIATE

CAREER PROFILE

Duties: Participating in a variety of tasks, such as organizing meetings, obtaining permits, and securing financing, related to the development of housing and/or other revitalization projects

Alternate Title(s): Development Assistant, Real Estate Associate, Community Development Corporation (CDC) Organizer, Housing Counselor, Job Developer, Assistant Property Manager, Training Program Coordinator, Program Associate

Salary Range: $25,000 to $35,000

Employment Prospects: Good

Advancement Prospects: Good

Best Geographical Location(s): Large urban areas

Prerequisites:

Education or Training—Bachelor's degree or equivalent required; master's degree preferred

Experience—Two to three years' volunteer, internship, or other experience

Special Skills and Personality Traits—Commitment; resilience; problem-solving, communication, and analytical skills; familiarity with low-interest financing programs

CAREER LADDER

```
┌─────────────────────────────────────┐
│ Higher-Level Position with Community │
│   Development Corporation (CDC)      │
│  or Allied Organization; Consultant  │
└─────────────────────────────────────┘

┌─────────────────────────────────────┐
│  Community Development Associate     │
└─────────────────────────────────────┘

┌─────────────────────────────────────┐
│         Volunteer or Intern          │
└─────────────────────────────────────┘
```

Position Description

Community Development Associates participate in revitalization efforts that combine the passion of a movement with the entrepreneurial savvy of an industry.

From its early days in the 1960s and 1970s, the community development movement has flourished, giving rise to thousands of locally based nonprofits known as Community Development Corporations, or CDCs. These organizations develop housing, commercial space, jobs, and a variety of community services.

Most CDCs focus their revitalization efforts on a place—an inner city neighborhood, a deteriorating suburb, a rural community, or another geographical area—but some organizations form to serve a group of people such as Hispanics, senior citizens, or Vietnamese immigrants. CDCs, which might also be called by other names such as neighborhood housing services or community-based development groups, range in size from a couple of staffers to hundreds of employees. According to the National Congress for Community Economic Development (NCCED), the average size of a CDC is six staffers, comprising entry-level Associates, midlevel project managers, and an executive director.

Initially, CDCs focused primarily on real estate development and renovation. Over the years, however, CDCs have established programs in other areas, including human services, the arts, urban gardens, and economic and workforce development. For example, to develop entrepreneurial jobs, a CDC might launch a commercial cleaning cooperative to help low-income residents with equipment costs, marketing, and other services needed for successful small business ownership. However, as Paul C. Brophy and Alice Shabecoff observe in *A Guide to Careers in Community Development,* CDC jobs involved in real estate development continue to outnumber those in other areas.

Many Community Development Associates get their start as volunteers or interns. From there, they might land an entry-level position as an Associate, an umbrella term that covers a variety of positions. A Community Development Associate might be either a jack-of-all trades staffer or an assistant to a project manager in a particular area. The jack-of-all trades Community Development Associate might help organize community meetings, prepare funding applications, and contact contractors while assisting with a commercial development project one day and a plan for affordable housing the next.

Some staffers in CDCs work primarily as community organizers. Unlike other groups that use community organizers primarily to get outside powers to fix a problem, CDCs can often act autonomously. The CDC Organizer, for instance, might help residents and merchants participate in a plan to develop vacant lots and buildings.

Other entry-level positions are more specialized, depending on the needs of the organization, industry sources say. For example, a CDC might need a training program coordinator for a new computer center, a job counselor to help residents through the job-hunting process, a housing counselor for a program for first-time home buyers, a program associate for after-school activities, or a job developer for a new employment program encouraging businesses to hire neighborhood residents. Some CDCs also hire property managers, caseworkers, researchers, writers, and/or fund-raisers.

Although staffing varies from organization to organization, many individuals who start in entry-level jobs move up to increasingly complex and responsible positions involving project management. A project manager in housing, for instance, might be involved in the following duties:

- Obtaining zoning and building permit approvals for project development
- Performing financial feasibility analyses
- Preparing applications for financing
- Working with the community to assess housing needs and develop support for projects
- Monitoring construction during development
- Researching possible sites for new projects

Salaries

Salaries for Community Development Associates and other entry-level positions in CDCs generally range from $25,000 to $35,000, according to the National Conference for Community Development; project managers and other midlevel staff in CDCs might earn $35,000 to $45,000. Individuals with master's degrees often start at higher levels than those with bachelor's degrees, industry specialists say.

Employment Prospects

Employment prospects are good because community development is a growing field that provides a variety of opportunities. New CDCs have formed, and older ones have expanded their array of services. However, financial pressures offset expansion, as some CDCs are unable to raise the funds needed to survive.

Advancement Prospects

Advancement prospects are good because community development is a field with a lot of different paths for advancement. Within the world of community development corporations, individuals commonly advance to higher levels of responsibility either within their own organization or in another CDC. One Community Development Associate might decide to become a specialist in a project area such as housing renovation or commercial development and others to set their sights on the position of the top generalist—the executive director—who nurtures the talents of all those involved in the different activities of the organization. A Community Development Associate might become executive director of a small CDC in three to five years or, after learning the ropes, leave to start his or her own CDC, insiders say

In addition to CDCs, the vast and interconnected network of community development settings includes

- National and regional community development organizations
- Government agencies
- Foundations and other funders
- Community-oriented businesses and nonprofits
- Policy, advocacy, and trade organizations
- Consulting firms

Many individuals advance their careers by moving from community-based to regional or national organizations, known as intermediaries, that provide technical and financial assistance to CDCs and other community-based groups. National intermediaries include the Neighborhood Reinvestment Corporation, the Local Initiatives Support Corporation (LISC), and the Enterprise Foundation.

Other CDC staffers move into positions with government agencies, foundations, banks, private developers, think tanks, human service organizations, chambers of commerce, or consulting groups. Someone, for example, might become an economic developer for a city, a research associate for a think tank, or a partner in a consulting group.

Education and Training

A college degree or equivalent in experience usually qualifies individuals for entry-level positions in community development. Internships are highly recommended. Because the field of community development encompasses a variety of disciplines, some specialists recommend working in the field for a couple of years to pinpoint areas of interest for further education, including a master's degree in public administration or policy, urban and regional planning, social work, architecture, or business administration.

A master's degree can help individuals start at a higher level or advance their careers. For instance, someone who wants to advance to a position as program manager might find it helpful to earn a master's degree in urban planning or public administration. Someone more interested in direct service, on the other hand, might pursue a master's degree in social work.

Training programs, too, have developed to provide the technical skills and knowledge needed for this rapidly evolving field, sometimes constituting an alternative to further academic schooling. Practitioners often turn to training programs to update their knowledge of specialized areas such as housing finance as well as more general concepts and strategies.

Experience, Skills, and Personality Traits

Many Community Development Associates get their start through grass-roots volunteering, internships, or other work related to improving community life. An entry-level position may require a few years of unpaid or paid experience. Volunteering at a food bank or working on a church program, for instance, might provide relevant experience.

Community development requires many of the same skills needed to succeed in advocacy and business. Community Development Associates must have a keen interest in improving local communities and the entrepreneurial skills needed to get the work done.

Primarily, Community Development Associates must be problem solvers. In the course of a typical day, a Community Development Associate might tackle a problem like getting housing rehabilitated on a tight budget or getting zoning approved for a new building.

Good communication skills, too, are a must, as Community Development Associates often write reports, make presentations, and interact with a variety of people, including low-income residents, architects, contractors, public officials, and bankers.

Strong analytical skills are also important. Many positions in community development involve work with spreadsheets, or asset management or at least some familiarity with financial programs and practices in order to solve problems like what to do if the property insurance is canceled.

On a more personal level, Community Development Associates must be able to weather the ups and downs of the field. They face the challenge of overcoming the cycle of poverty, which can often overwhelm even the best efforts. Disappointments are inevitable, although they are often softened by the satisfaction that results from improving lives and neighborhoods. Many Community Development Associates work long hours, including nights and weekends.

Unions and Associations

The National Congress for Community Economic Development (NCCED) is the advocacy and trade association for the community-based development industry. Community Development practitioners are also organized into state associations, which are linked through the *associations* link of NCCED's Website *(www.ncced.org)*.

Tips for Entry

1. Read more about careers, internships, and education in community development. Helpful resources include A *Guide to Careers in Community Development* by Paul C. Brophy and Alice Shabecoff (Island Press, 2001) and the website of the National Congress for Community Economic Development *(www.ncced.org)*.

2. Look into internship possibilities. For example, the National Congress for Community Economic Development, in partnership with the Association for Public Policy Analysis and Management, places graduate students studying public policy or urban planning in paid summer internships with CDCs.

3. Take courses in urban and regional planning, government, and related disciplines.

4. Contact your city's community development department to find out about CDCs in your area. Attend a CDC meeting and volunteer to help out with activities such as renovating buildings or serving on the board of directors.

5. Volunteer for a national organization such as Habitat for Humanity or a local church, synagogue, or other faith-based group involved in helping to improve the lives of community residents.

6. Explore the AmeriCorps program (see the entry in the Service Programs section) if you are interested in a national service program that places volunteers with community development corporations and other nonprofits.

WOMEN'S RIGHTS ACTIVIST

CAREER PROFILE

Duties: Vary by position but may include policy work, advocacy, research, and/or direct services as well as administrative support

Alternate Title(s): Regional Organizer, Advocate, Program Specialist, Policy Associate, Research Specialist, Government Relations Director

Salary Range: $20,000 to $60,000

Employment Prospects: Good

Advancement Prospects: Fair to good

Best Geographical Location(s): Major cities

Prerequisites:

Education or Training—Bachelor's or graduate degree

Experience—Entry level or two to five years

Special Skills and Personality Traits—Commitment to women's rights; excellent verbal and written communication skills; critical thinking; computer literacy; willingness to work long hours

CAREER LADDER

```
┌─────────────────────────────────┐
│      Executive Director          │
└─────────────────────────────────┘

┌─────────────────────────────────┐
│    Women's Rights Activist       │
└─────────────────────────────────┘

┌─────────────────────────────────┐
│  Student, Intern, or Volunteer   │
└─────────────────────────────────┘
```

Position Description

Women's Rights Activists fight for gender equality on a number of different fronts: legal, political, and economic, to name just a few. From winning the right to vote in 1920, Women's Rights Activists have fought for—and won—the Equal Pay Act, abortion rights, seats in Congress, sports programs for girls, and prohibitions against sexual harassment. Now Women's Rights Activists are trying to appeal to a new generation of women, many of whom may be reluctant to call themselves "feminists." Some bristle at the word itself, which they see as overly strident. Others believe that women already have equal rights.

In a recent article in *Ms.* magazine, the well-known Women's Rights Activist Gloria Steinem responds to the question, Where are all the young feminists? She answers that, whereas males tend to be rebellious when young and more conservative with age, women often start out conservative but get radicalized by experience. Problems at home and/or in the workplace spur many women to activism.

Over the past few decades, the feminist movement has branched out to include a variety of causes and agendas. Women's Rights Activists differ on answers to questions like, Should men be included in the organization?, What should the mission of the organization be?, and Which is more important—the economic concerns of the general public or the agenda of longtime members?

Women's Rights Activists say that gender discrimination has become more subtle and complex over the years. For example, although men and women must be paid the same wages for *equal* jobs, they can be paid different salaries for *equivalent* work. Activists believe that maids are paid less than housemen in the hotel industry because women's labor is valued less than men's. They also speak about a "glass ceiling," a level above which few professional women are able to rise.

Since the 1970s, myriad organizations have sprouted up to advance the causes of women. Insiders says that categories of women's rights organizations include

- Legal advocacy
- Single issue constituency
- Multiissue advocacy
- Research and think tanks
- Political advancement
- Direct service

The first category, legal advocacy groups (e.g., the National Women's Law Center, Women's Equal Rights Advocates), litigate cases to change laws and break new legal ground. Next are the groups that deal with either a single issue (e.g., Planned Parenthood) or a particular constituency (e.g., Black Women United for Action).

Third on the list: multiissue advocacy groups such as the National Organization for Women (NOW), the largest feminist organization in the country, and umbrella groups such as the National Council of Women's Organizations. Smaller, grassroots groups also advocate for women, as do organizations not specifically devoted to gender such as labor unions and antipoverty groups.

Fourth are research institutes or think tanks, such as the Institute for Women's Policy Research and the Center for Advancement of Public Policy, that conduct studies on issues such as violence against women and affirmative action. Next on the list: political advancement groups (e.g., the National Women's Political Caucus, the Women's Campaign Fund) that help women get elected to office and make political progress. Finally, direct service organizations, such as local women's shelters and youth organizations, provide hands-on care to clients as well as outreach work and advocacy.

Women's rights activism is such a broad field that responsibilities vary with the nature of the position. Someone working in a local women's shelter, for example, is bound to perform a different array of tasks than a project manager for a large national organization.

Such differences notwithstanding, Women's Rights Activists often do policy work, advocacy, research, and some lower-level administrative tasks. For example, someone working on the pay gap between men and women might do research and organize support for a bill to change it. In addition to doing electoral and lobbying work, a Women's Rights Activist might write press releases and coordinate headline-grabbing events such as marches, rallies, and/or pickets.

Salaries

Salaries generally fall into the $20,000 to $60,000 range, rising with levels of experience and responsibility. In a large organization such as the National Organization for Women, a program assistant would work under a Program Coordinator, who, in turn, would work under a Director.

Employment Prospects

Employment prospects are good because of the vast number of nonprofit organizations devoted to women's issues. Positions are somewhat dependent on political times, as new jobs are created in response to perceived threats to women's rights. A threat to abortion rights, for example, is likely to trigger activity in the field.

Nonpaying and part-time opportunities also abound. Insiders say that many feminists view activism as a state of mind rather than a career choice. They help the women's movement with organizing and other activities while bringing a "feminist consciousness" to whatever they do to make a living. A museum curator, for example, might organize an exhibit on textiles to highlight the lives of the women who made them.

Advancement Prospects

Advancement prospects are fair to good. As one moves up the career ladder, prospects get tighter. Insiders say that many top leaders, particularly founders of organizations, stay in their positions for a long time.

On a more positive note, the variety of positions within the women's movement creates opportunities for growth. As Women Rights Activists gain experience, they may advance to management positions. Someone with a long history of women's rights activism, for example, might become political director of a large group such as the National Organization for Women.

Another possibility is using women's rights activism as a stepping stone to a related career. For instance, someone might go from researching women's issues to working for a think tank involved in a broader array of issues. Similarly, a Women's Rights Activist might decide to run for political office.

Education and Training

Many Women's Rights Activists have taken courses dealing with the influence of gender in society. Since the early 1970s, the number of women's studies programs in colleges and universities has mushroomed. Women's studies programs vary from college to college but typically draw on a variety of disciplines, including anthropology, sociology, economics, and history.

Although supporters praise these programs for filling a gap in education, some skeptics fault them for being more about camaraderie than about scholarship. Decades of criticism, though, have not slowed the growth of women's studies. From 78 women's studies programs, centers, or departments in 1973, the number today has grown to some 736, according to a recent article in *Newsweek*. Some programs include a volunteer component, introducing students to a variety of women's rights organizations.

But individuals need not major in women's studies to embark on a career in the field. Other liberal arts majors, such as English, history, or political science, are also useful. Any discipline that trains students to think critically and analytically provides a good background for work in social change, insiders say.

Some positions in women's rights activism call for graduate-level training. A position in legal advocacy, for example, might call for a law degree; a think tank, a graduate degree in public policy or a related field; and direct service, a degree in social work.

Experience, Skills, and Personality Traits

Because the field of women's rights is so broad, experience, skills, and personality traits depend largely on the nature of the position in question. Someone counseling clients, for example, needs a different set of skills than someone managing projects. Direct service positions may require knowledge of Spanish, and a lobbying position might call for political or legal experience. An organizing position, in turn, may call for a few years of grassroots experience.

A belief in social change is crucial for anyone interested in women's rights activism. Also important: excellent oral and written communication skills, because whether one is helping victims of domestic abuse or lobbying Congress on employment issues, one needs to be able to connect with others. Computer skills have become increasingly important, as "virtual organizing" by Internet now links activists around the world. Political savvy, too, comes in handy whether one is looking for increased funding for a women's shelter or advocating for reproductive freedom.

Unions and Associations

Individuals might belong to the National Council of Women's Organizations, a bipartisan organization of more than 100 women's organizations, or the National Organization for Women, the largest feminist organization in the nation, with more than half a million contributing members. The National Women's Studies Association represents colleges, universities, and others involved in feminist education.

Tips for Entry

1. Determine your own areas of interest and skills to give to a job. Are you concerned about economic equity, domestic violence, electoral politics, or something else? Do you want to work on the front lines or behind the scenes? What type of skills (e.g., writing, counseling, organizing) would you like to develop?
2. Read books and articles about the women's movement. Browse directories of women's organizations in libraries and on-line.
3. Volunteer for a local women's organization.
4. Look into college and graduate programs in women's studies and related fields.

PEACE WORKER

CAREER PROFILE

Duties: Policy research; lobbying; public education; petitioning and protest action; community service; intercultural "citizen-to-citizen" diplomacy

Alternate Title(s): Program Assistant, Grassroots Organizer, Peace Educator

Salary Range: $12,000 to $40,000

Employment Prospects: Fair to good

Advancement Prospects: Fair to good

Best Geographical Location(s): Washington, D.C., New England; Philadelphia; Northern California; and major cities

Prerequisites:

Education or Training—College degree or higher

Experience—Entry-level or some experience

Special Skills and Personality Traits—Research, writing, administrative, and grassroots organizing skills; strong sense of commitment to world peace

CAREER LADDER

```
┌─────────────────────────────────────┐
│  Position with Larger Organization   │
└─────────────────────────────────────┘

┌─────────────────────────────────────┐
│            Peace Worker              │
└─────────────────────────────────────┘

┌─────────────────────────────────────┐
│         Intern, or Volunteer         │
└─────────────────────────────────────┘
```

Position Description

Peace Workers advocate nonviolent solutions to conflicts between nations. Although they work for organizations that vary in focus, they share a common idealism. Peace Workers give a high degree of commitment to their jobs, which tend to be relatively low-paying, if they pay at all, since much of the work in this field is done by volunteer activists. A church-sponsored organization, for example, might offer a Peace Worker room and board in place of a modest salary.

The jobs of Peace Workers vary somewhat from organization to organization. A peace organization in Washington, D.C., for example, might focus on lobbying Congress, whereas one elsewhere might devote more attention to educational activities.

Most peace organizations, though, combine a variety of activities, as staffers generally do a little of everything:

• Producing posters and newsletters
• Organizing protests
• Arranging lobbying activities
• Holding meetings
• Doing mailings for fund-raising and other activities

Someone just starting out might do more knocking on doors and stuffing envelopes than someone in a midlevel position, although both would have a combination of responsibilities. Someone in a higher-level position would be involved in overseeing the budget and developing strategy. For example, he or she might organize a campaign to block development and deployment of a new nuclear missile, an activity that would necessitate lobbying, petition drives, press conferences, and demonstrations.

Salaries

Salaries range from about $12,000 to $40,000. Many positions in the $12,000 to $15,000 range are with religious-based peace organizations that provide room and board in a communal house to supplement salaries. Midlevel positions pay about $20,000 to $25,000, compared to $30,000 to $40,000 for senior-level positions with peace groups, which may have both national offices and local branches.

Employment Prospects

Employment prospects are fair to good. Although the number of salaried jobs is relatively small because of the high reliance on volunteers, jobs open up regularly, creating opportunities for newcomers. Peace Workers tend to be young people who leave after a few years to continue their education or seek other positions. Many who work for peace see themselves as part of a movement for social change involving issues such as poverty and hunger as well as war. Some Peace Workers go on to law school or other graduate training.

Advancement Prospects

Advancement prospects are fair to good. Although there are not many senior-level positions in the field, the types of advocacy skills one acquires in peace organizations are valued in other settings. A Peace Worker might move on to a public interest group or humanitarian-aid organization, for example.

Education and Training

Students interested in peace can major in a traditional discipline such as political science or opt for one of more than 100 undergraduate degree or certificate programs specifically in peace studies. This relatively new discipline emerged as a scholarly reaction to World War I and World War II, according to the Five College Program in Peace and World Security Studies (PAWSS), based at Hampshire College in Amherst, Massachusetts. Peace studies take a widely interdisciplinary approach, drawing on the social sciences, liberal arts, and international relations. Over the years, the discipline has evolved to include discussion of not only peace but also issues such as poverty and oppression underlying human conflict. Many people in the field of peace studies share an interest in such related topics as environmental studies, women's studies, human rights, religion, ethics, international law, and social movements.

Programs in peace studies often begin with the teachings of such well-known proponents of nonviolence as Mohandas Gandhi and Martin Luther King, Jr. Courses also examine past international efforts to prevent war and promote peace, including the League of Nations and the United Nations, and assess possible new approaches to peacemaking. Many programs also place particular emphasis on the principles and methods of conflict resolution, encouraging students to participate in workshops and training sessions in negotiation and mediation. Programs in peace and conflict studies reflect this growing trend.

Most programs in peace studies extend beyond the classroom. Programs typically sponsor lecture and seminar series and encourage students to assume more active roles as citizens.

At the graduate level, programs fall into six broad areas: peace and justice in the religious context, general peace and conflict studies, mediation and conflict resolution, citizen participation in socioeconomic development, arms control and international security, and/or public interest law and alternative dispute resolution. Many programs combine two or more areas. Traditional graduate programs in international relations, economic development, political science, sociology, psychology, and other relevant fields also address issues related to peace.

Experience, Skills, and Personality Traits

Many individuals become involved in the peace movement by attending a protest rally, lecture, or seminar. From there, they might volunteer at a local peace organization, then become a member of the staff. Peace Workers commonly move from local to national organizations.

As do other positions in activism, peace work calls for a variety of skills—researching, writing, fund-raising, grass-roots organizing, and lobbying. Peace Workers pore over government documents and data, produce newsletters and press releases, raise funds and manage budgets, and organize activities and lobbying campaigns.

Insiders say that Peace Workers should have a strong degree of commitment because many jobs are unpaid or poorly paid. Peace Workers derive their motivation less from a paycheck than from a common desire to prevent war, create a more democratic and equitable society, and promote human rights and economic well-being around the world. Peace Workers, though, can feel overwhelmed by the enormity of the challenge. Gains are often followed by setbacks. One war ends, and another begins. Funding is scarce. Instead of trying to solve all the world's problems at once, Peace Workers should be able to divide up their work into discrete tasks and believe in the long-term importance of what they are doing.

Unions and Associations

Peace Workers might belong to the Peace Studies Association and/or the Consortium on Peace Research, Education, and Development (COPRED).

Tips for Entry

1. Volunteer for a local peace group. Check out college bulletin boards, area chapters of the American Friends Service Committee or Peace Action, or local notices to find out about ways to get involved.
2. Check out listings of organizations and peace studies programs on the "students" section of the website of the Five Colleges Program in Peace and World Security Studies (http://pawss.hampshire.edu).
3. Look for peace-oriented positions on employment websites (e.g., www.idealist.org or www.accessjobs.org) specializing in the nonprofit sector.
4. Browse the website of the U.S. Institute for Peace (www.usip.org), established by the U.S. government in 1984 to support research and education on peace studies.

CONFLICT RESOLUTION SPECIALIST

CAREER PROFILE

Duties: Communicating with disputants; developing and maintaining relationships with referring agencies; supervising volunteer mediators; managing cases; fostering public awareness of conflict resolution

Alternate Title(s): Intake Coordinator, Case Manager, Program Coordinator, Director of Training

Salary Range: $14 to $15 an hour to $32,000+ a year

Employment Prospects: Fair to poor

Advancement Prospects: Fair

Best Geographical Location(s): States with a high degree of commitment to community mediation (New York, North Carolina, California, and Oregon)

Prerequisites:
　　Education or Training—Forty hours of training and/or academic degree in conflict resolution or peace studies
　　Experience—One year as volunteer mediator
　　Special Skills and Personality Traits—Nonjudgmental attitude; good listening and communication skills; comfort with situations characterized by conflict; commitment to peacemaking

CAREER LADDER

```
┌─────────────────────────────────────┐
│   Executive Director or Consultant   │
└─────────────────────────────────────┘

┌─────────────────────────────────────┐
│    Conflict Resolution Specialist    │
└─────────────────────────────────────┘

┌─────────────────────────────────────┐
│         Volunteer Mediator           │
└─────────────────────────────────────┘
```

Position Description

Conflict Resolution Specialists provide an alternative to settling disputes through force or legal action. Unlike the traditional, adversarial "win-lose" approach to settling disputes, conflict resolution relies on a "win-win" model to arrive at a mutually beneficial solution. The term *conflict resolution* encompasses a variety of methodologies (including mediation, conciliation, and arbitration) used in school and community programs throughout the nation. Many students are introduced to peer mediation in elementary schools, thanks, in part, to the support of community mediation centers. Since the early 1990s the number of community mediation centers has mushroomed from about 150 to more than 550, according to the National Association for Community Mediation.

Much of this growth, however, has created opportunities for volunteers rather than paid staff. Usually trained volunteers conduct the actual mediations. Paid staffers do all the preparation work and follow-up. They set up the sessions, schedule and train volunteers, manage cases, do community outreach, and administer programs. Many cases are referred to community mediation centers by the police, courts, or other agencies such as the housing authority or human rights commission. Community mediation centers deal with conflicts ranging from mild disagreements to assaults, threats, and harassment. They address landlord/tenant, consumer/merchant, family/custody, and various other types of disputes. For instance, someone might call the police to complain about the noise next door. The next-door neighbors, however, insist that they were not being noisy. The two parties might be referred to mediation.

The National Association for Community Mediation describes the typical community mediation program as having 30 Volunteer Mediators and 1.5 paid Staff (often a full-time executive director and part-time intake coordinator or case manager). Other common staff positions include project managers and trainers. Specialists say that each mediation session involves about six hours of preparation.

Most Conflict Resolution Specialists begin their careers as volunteer mediators. After a year of mediating cases, a volunteer may be offered a paid position, as a part-time or full-time employee, depending on the organization of the center. Common responsibilities include

- Case management
- Volunteer management
- Outreach

Conflict Resolution Specialists spend much of their time on the phone, talking to clients and handling referrals. They schedule mediations and answer questions from disputants like, What will this [the mediation] mean for my court case? Often mediation takes the place of prosecution, although that is not always the case. Conflict Resolution Specialists serve as liaisons between the center and referring agencies. They also prepare statistical and program reports on matters such as caseload, the volunteer mediator pool, referral sources, and the outcome of cases.

In their responsibilities for volunteer management, Conflict Resolution Specialists schedule volunteer mediators and "debrief" them after sessions to find out about how the matter was resolved. They also recruit, train, and supervise Volunteers. If, for instance, the community has a large Spanish population, the Conflict Resolution Specialist might recruit bilingual volunteers.

Conflict Resolution Specialists also commonly do outreach work. In this capacity, they promote mediation to community groups, develop and maintain relationships with new and existing referral agencies, and foster public awareness of conflict resolution. As Conflict Resolution Specialists gain experience, they may be given additional responsibilities involving fiscal and program management.

Many community mediation centers provide not only mediation but also other forms of conflict resolution such as arbitration and conciliation. For example, community mediation centers might be responsible for arbitrating cases involving the state's lemon law. An independent arbitrator would listen to both sides in the dispute and render a decision much as a judge would. Conciliation (comparable to "shuttle diplomacy") is used when one disputant cannot meet with the other; facilitation involves resolving conflicts among a group of people.

Salaries

Salaries range from $14 to $15 an hour to about $32,000 a year, industry sources state. Many positions are part time as a result of financial constraints. Full-time positions below the level of Executive Director commonly pay in the mid-$20,000s to low $30,000s, according to the National Association for Community Mediation. Executive directors might earn in the $60,000 range. Because community mediation centers provide low- or no-cost services to the public, they rely largely on Volunteers and relatively low-paid staffers. Some centers, however, have larger budget: A community mediation center that receives state subsidies and/or provides fee-for-service training might have a large enough budget to hire several staffers.

Employment Prospects

Employment prospects are fair to poor because of the relative scarcity of full-time paid positions. However, individuals committed to conflict resolution can, with time, establish careers in the field. Many Conflict Resolution Specialists have worked their way up from volunteer to part-time to full-time positions. Others have entered the field after working in other nonprofit organizations. Someone who ran a women's shelter, for example, might have important nonprofit management skills for a community mediation center. Usually these individuals, too, are trained in conflict resolution and work as volunteers before joining the staff.

Advancement Prospects

Advancement prospects are fair because Conflict Resolution Specialists can move in a variety of directions. Rather than move up to the level of executive director, a Conflict Resolution Specialist might leave a community mediation center to begin private practice and/or consulting.

Conflict Resolution Specialists in private practice have a variety of backgrounds, including law and social work as well as community mediation. A divorce mediator, for instance, might have a background in law. Many private practitioners combine a variety of endeavors related to conflict resolution, including designing programs, providing training, writing, and teaching. One former executive director of a community mediation center, for instance, is a consultant on training matters. Another consultant recently traveled to Cambodia to help develop a system for resolving land disputes.

Other Conflict Resolution Specialists move into higher-paying positions in the private sector. Many large corporations incorporate conflict resolution practices and/or programs in their personnel departments, as do federal agencies. Yet another possibility is to work for an organization, such as the United Nations, that addresses wide-scale, rather than community-based, conflicts.

Education and Training

Conflict resolution has blossomed as an area of education and training. The majority of Conflict Resolution Specialists have completed a basic 40-hour training program. Family mediators often have 40 to 60 hours of special family training. Training programs are offered by a variety of sources (e.g., nonprofit organizations, professional associations) throughout the nation. The National Association for Community Mediation, for instance, provides conflict resolution training at its regional institutes.

At colleges and universities, the number of academic programs in conflict resolution (often in conjunction with peace studies) has grown steadily since 1980. Programs offered include

- Undergraduate classes, concentrations, and/or degree programs in peace resolution programs
- M.S. or M.A. degree programs in conflict resolution or in peace studies (with some conflict resolution)
- Graduate certificate programs in conflict resolution
- Ph.D. programs in conflict resolution

Some programs are particularly well known. Among them are the Institute on Conflict Analysis and Resolution (ICAR) at George Mason University, the Program in the Analysis and Resolution of Conflict (PARC) at Syracuse University, the Kroc Institute of International Peace Studies at Notre Dame University, and the Program on Negotiation at Harvard University.

In addition, some professional schools (law, business, education) offer specialization in conflict resolution. Peer mediation programs, too, have become increasingly common at colleges and universities, as have internship programs that give students hands-on experience in conflict resolution.

Experience, Skills, and Personality Traits

Most Conflict Resolution Specialists have acquired at least a year of volunteer mediating experience. Working as a volunteer mediator can help individuals discover whether or not they are comfortable in situations that entail conflict. What might seem a frivolous matter to outsiders is likely to be a grave concern to the disputants. Conflict Resolution Specialists must be able to suspend judgment. They should be good listeners who are willing to let disputants reach their own agreements. Perhaps most important of all, Conflict Resolution Specialists should be committed to the peacemaking process.

Unions and Associations

The National Association for Community Mediation and the Association of Conflict Resolution are the two main professional associations representing professionals in this field. Conflict Resolution Specialists also might be involved in the Consortium on Peace Research, Education, and Development or the Peace Studies Association.

Tips for Entry

1. Look into academic programs in conflict resolution and peace studies. Internet directories of undergraduate and graduate programs include the student section of the Five College Program in Peace and World Security Studies *(www.pawss.hampshire.edu)* and CRInfo, the Conflict Resolution Information Source *(www.crinfo.org)*. Another source of information is the *Global Directory of Peace Studies and Conflict Resolution Programs* (2000 edition), published by the Consortium on Peace Research, Education, and Development.
2. Become a volunteer mediator. If you are a student, look into peer mediation programs in your school or college. To receive the necessary 40-hour training for community mediation, check the website of the National Association for Community Mediation *(www.nafcm.org)* or look in the yellow pages of your phone book under *Mediation* to contact local centers.
3. Browse the job openings listed on the National Association for Community Mediation website.
4. Attend conferences and gain additional training in conflict resolution to develop your skills.

HUMAN RIGHTS ADVOCATE

CAREER PROFILE

Duties: Participating in human rights efforts such as organizing public education campaigns and fact-finding missions; conducting research; coordinating services for affected groups; monitoring legislation

Alternate Title(s): Human Rights Assistant, Development Associate, Program Coordinator, Campaign Coordinator, Program Manager, Program Director, Executive Director

Salary Range: $18,000 to $75,000

Employment Prospects: Fair to good

Advancement Prospects: Fair to good

Best Geographical Location(s): New York; Washington, D.C.; Minneapolis; other major cities; various locations abroad

Prerequisites:

Education or Training—Bachelor's degree or higher

Experience—Two to four years

Special Skills and Personality Traits—Passion and commitment; strong research, writing, and communications skills; familiarity with human rights mechanisms and processes; ability to build and sustain coalitions; knowledge of second language and willingness to travel or live abroad sometimes required

CAREER LADDER

```
┌─────────────────────────────────┐
│   Consultant, Lawyer, or Position │
│    with Related Organization      │
└─────────────────────────────────┘

┌─────────────────────────────────┐
│      Human Rights Advocate        │
└─────────────────────────────────┘

┌─────────────────────────────────┐
│    Volunteer, Intern, or Fellow   │
└─────────────────────────────────┘
```

Position Description

Human Rights Advocates promote equality and justice for people around the world. Since the United Nations's passage of the Universal Declaration of Human Rights in 1948, hundreds of nonprofit human rights groups have sprung up to further the cause. Human Rights Advocates like Jody Williams, the Nobel Prize–winning leader of the nonprofit International Campaign to Ban Landmines, have spurred initiatives leading to the adoption of international treaties. The continually evolving field of nonprofit human rights groups includes

- Multi-issue research and advocacy groups, (e.g., Amnesty International, Human Rights Watch)
- Relief and development organizations (e.g., CARE, Oxfam America)
- Legally oriented organizations (e.g., Center for Constitutional Rights, Center for Justice and Accountability)
- Organizations focused on a particular issue (e.g., Center for Victims of Torture, American Refugee Committee)
- Organizations focused on a geographical region (e.g., Kurdish Human Rights Project, Resource Center of the Americas)

Although the modern human rights movement has its roots in law and diplomacy, insiders have seen a general broadening of the field since the early 1990s to include more positions for nonlawyers. Many organizations that once focused primarily on civil and political rights have expanded their agendas to address social, cultural, and economic rights both at home and abroad.

Proponents of this new holistic approach to human rights explain that complex problems like discrimination cannot be solved through such strategies as lawsuits alone. New human rights groups and programs have formed to promote human rights education in U.S. schools, reform the World Trade Organization, protest U.S. business connections to sweatshops abroad, assess human rights in the United States, and link human rights to the women's movement and various other causes. Because the field is so broad, many Human Rights Advocates specialize in a particular issue or geographical region.

Human Rights Advocates commonly refer to their employers as nongovernmental organizations (NGOs) to distinguish them from intergovernmental organizations (IGOs) such as the United Nations. As do other nonprofits, these NGOs generally employ fund-raisers and other administrative staffers as well as Human Rights Advocates involved in the organization's programs.

Entry-level staffers, who might be called assistants or coordinators, are commonly involved in general constituency outreach and education. Often groups sponsor events such as lectures and film screenings to raise public awareness of human rights issues. If the organization offers services to refugees or other clients, the assistant or coordinator might arrange for translators, doctors, attorneys, and/or other professionals to help. Entry-level staffers also commonly do research, maintain websites, work on membership, assist with fund-raising, and coordinate Volunteers.

Human Rights Advocates in a higher-level position, such as program manager and division director, are more likely to be involved in lobbying and traveling abroad. In some organizations, policy and lobbying staffers are a group unto themselves, whereas in others they are under the direction of a program manager. Some organizations look for Human Rights Advocates knowledgeable about a particular region—such as Latin America or the Middle East—to work from offices either in the United States or abroad. A Human Rights Advocate in the United States might coordinate fact-finding missions and other research-oriented activities, whereas someone abroad would compile information from the field. Positions also vary according to the orientation of the group, whether it be research, organizing, economic development, social service, legal advocacy, or a combination of strategies.

A typical day for a mid- to upper-level staffer in a human rights group might involve going to the state legislature to lobby for funds related to human rights (e.g., services for new immigrants), conducting research, and writing reports. Other common responsibilities include

- Collaborating with affected communities to highlight grass-roots concerns
- Developing plans for organizing campaigns, fact-finding missions, and other activities
- Writing fact sheets, press releases, and other public education materials
- Fostering and maintaining relationships with related organizations to build coalitions
- Preparing budgets, fund-raising proposals, and other material

- Working with lawyers or other service providers
- Promoting awareness of the organization through public speaking, radio interviews, and other activities
- Monitoring legislation and advocating for alternative policies

Salaries

In the field of human rights, many positions are unpaid or part-time. In general, internships are unpaid and fellowships offer a stipend or part-time wage of $8 to $10 an hour. Salaries for full-time positions vary by level of experience and education. Entry-level staffers generally earn in the $18,000 to $25,000 range, compared to $25,000 to $35,000 for midlevel and $40,000 to $75,000 for upper-level Human Rights Advocates, according to industry experts.

Employment Prospects

Employment prospects are fair to good. Although the field of human rights is expanding, the number of full-time salaried positions is limited because organizations rely heavily on unpaid staffs and pro bono assistance. On the plus side, volunteer positions, including summer internships and unpaid activism, often involve high degrees of responsibility, allowing individuals to gain valuable experience.

Advancement Prospects

Advancement prospects are fair to good because Human Rights Advocates can move in a variety of directions. Some enter law school to become better qualified for legal work in human rights. Others, who may already have advanced degrees, move to higher-level positions in larger organizations or start their own private or nonprofit organization. Still others find positions with a variety of related organizations, including

- Consulting groups involved in human rights
- Charitable foundations that fund human rights work
- Research-oriented human rights centers, think tanks, and academic programs
- Intergovernmental organizations such as the United Nations
- Governmental organizations, including congressional committees involved in human rights

Education and Training

A bachelor's degree is generally required for entry-level positions. A law degree or master's degree in international relations, education, economics, human rights, public policy, or a related discipline is often recommended or required for mid- to upper-level positions. In some cases, a law degree is required. In other cases, particularly in grassroots-organizing groups, experience is generally more important than an advanced degree, industry insiders say. Other individuals enter human rights work from a clinical background in social work, public health, or a related field, which qualifies them for positions such as working with refugees. Requirements vary from organization to organization.

Courses in human rights are becoming increasingly common at all levels of education, as some elementary and secondary schools are incorporating human rights into social studies, language arts, and other curriculums. Increasingly, colleges and universities are offering classes, self-designed majors, or entire programs in human rights. Courses in human rights generally introduce students to four documents known collectively as the International Bill of Human Rights.

Graduate programs in human rights are generally offered through law schools or schools of international relations. These include, but are not limited to, law school programs at American University, Harvard University, Yale University, and the University of Minnesota; master's degree programs at the University of Chicago and the University of Denver; and both law school and master's degree programs at Columbia University.

At the undergraduate level, colleges and universities offering programs in human rights listed on the Derechos Human Rights website include Bard College, Colby College, Purdue University, Trinity College, Tufts University, the University of Chicago, and Webster University. Many other colleges and universities offer courses or self-designed majors in human rights.

Internships are a common way to acquire hands-on experience in human rights. Many internships offer high levels of responsibility, as human rights organizations rely heavily on unpaid staff. Fellowships offering part-time pay are also common in this field.

Experience, Skills, and Personality Traits

Human rights organizations often look for volunteer or intern experience as an indication of passion and commitment. As mentioned earlier, human rights organizations depend heavily on volunteers and interns, often giving them high levels of responsibility. Interns and volunteers are commonly involved in grassroots organizing, human rights education, fact-finding efforts, and various other leadership-building responsibilities. Human rights work introduces newcomers to everything from the plight of the Kurds in Iran to the business practices of corporate America.

In the field of human rights, research and writing skills are important, as individuals must be able to craft a message that is both knowledgeable and convincing. Many positions in human rights require a solid knowledge of complex government procedures and practices. For example, someone working for a group to prevent the sexual exploitation of children might be involved in monitoring the implementation of an international plan that calls for, among other things, promoting extradition and other arrangements to curb sex tourism. In the course of their work, Human Rights Advocates need to know when to compromise and when to hold firm. Knowledge of a second language is sometimes required, particularly in positions abroad. Many relief and development organizations, for instance, hire individuals to work in the field.

Like other activists, Human Rights Advocates must be willing to weather tough battles that may end in defeat. Arguing for immigrant rights, for example, can be difficult in a time of increased national security. The breadth and depth of the work can sometimes be overwhelming. Human Rights Advocates should value making a contribution to social justice over monetary gain, as pay in this field is relatively low.

Unions and Associations

Industry insiders know of no professional association specifically organized for Human Rights Advocates. Internet-based organizations such as Derechos Human Rights (www.derechos.org) and the Human Rights Internet (www.hri.ca) serve as clearinghouses for the broad human rights community, providing information about internships, jobs, and the issues.

Tips for Entry

1. Look into courses or programs in human rights. If your school does not offer one, research a human rights topic for a paper or design your own major, combining courses from a variety of disciplines, including political science, economics, anthropology, and law or legal studies.

2. Pinpoint an area in human rights most in line with your own interests. Browse the University of Minnesota's Human Rights Center library (www.umn.edu/humanrts) and/or Derechos' (www.derechos.org/links) listing of issues—children's rights, reparations, torture, and so on—and geographical areas—countries, regions, and so on.

3. Find out about volunteer jobs, internships, and fellowships, as well as paid positions, in human rights. Helpful websites include the University of Minnesota's Human Rights Center (www.hrusa.org), Derechos Human Rights (www.derechos.org), ReliefWeb (www.reliefweb.int), One World.net (www.oneworld.net), and the Human Rights Internet (www.hri.ca).

4. Study a foreign language or two. Insiders recommend languages spoken by large numbers of people, including French, Spanish, Chinese, Russian, and Arabic.

5. Get involved. Volunteer opportunities in this field abound.

LOBBIES, UNIONS, AND ASSOCIATIONS

LOBBYIST

CAREER PROFILE

Duties: Researching and analyzing legislation and/or regulatory proposals; attending legislative hearings; providing information; building support for issues of concern

Alternate Title(s): Government Affairs Representative, Government Relations Manager, Legislative Associate

Salary Range: $30,000 to $250,000+

Employment Prospects: Good

Advancement Prospects: Good

Best Geographical Location: Washington, D.C., state capitals

Prerequisites:

Education or Training—Bachelor's, master's, or law degree

Experience—Three to five years of legislative experience

Special Skills and Personality Traits—Strong public-speaking skills; energy; charisma; connections

CAREER LADDER

```
┌─────────────────────────────┐
│   Partner; Government        │
│   Relations Director         │
└─────────────────────────────┘

┌─────────────────────────────┐
│   Lobbyist                   │
└─────────────────────────────┘

┌─────────────────────────────┐
│   Legislative Staffer or     │
│   Government Relations Coordinator │
└─────────────────────────────┘
```

Position Description

Lobbyists get their name from their practice of buttonholing lawmakers in the lobbies of state legislatures and Congress. All sorts of organizations—trade and professional associations, labor unions, public interest groups, corporations, even state, local, and foreign governments—hire Lobbyists to advocate for their points of view. Lobbyists battle for or against handguns. They skirmish over smoking, foreign trade, and oil rights.

Although some people might think Lobbyists spend most of their time talking to lawmakers, such exchanges represent only a small part of the job, according to the American League of Lobbyists. Instead, Lobbyists spend the bulk of their time researching and analyzing legislation, attending congressional or regulatory hearings, working with coalitions interested in the same issues, and educating others about the implications of various changes.

Lobbyists can work either for a professional lobbying firm that represents a variety of clients or for a particular organization. In the first case, the Lobbyist acts as a "hired gun" on an issue of concern to the client. In the second, he or she works on public-policy issues of concern to the organization. The lobbyist might have a title like government relations manager rather than Lobbyist when working for an organization.

Lobbying can be either direct or indirect, and many positions entail both. In direct lobbying, Lobbyists focus their efforts on influencing government decision makers. In indirect lobbying, also known as grassroots lobbying, Lobbyists organize others, often volunteer activists, to write letters, sign petitions, attend meetings, join protests, and otherwise speak out on issues of concern. Because government officials often lack the resources to do their own in-depth research, they commonly turn to trusted Lobbyists for information. Lobbyists compile information, often including charts, data from polls, and reports, on how government policies will affect their organizations.

Few fields have generated more controversy. Some lobbying activities, such as testifying before a legislative committee, occur in the open, whereas others take place in private, raising ethical questions. Depending on one's point of view, a Lobbyist is either an unscrupulous "influence peddler" or a hardworking "activist." In keeping with America's tradition of free speech, any citizen—rich or poor, liberal or conservative—can lobby the government.

Paid Lobbyists typically keep fast-paced schedules. Many in Washington, D.C., have offices on K Street, a location that allows them to bound over to Capitol Hill quickly if a busy member of Congress has a few free minutes. At any given time, Lobbyists know the status of bills affecting their issues. Which ones are before a committee? Which ones are up for a floor vote? Lobbyists testify before committees, distribute press releases, chat with reporters, and try to meet with politicians and aides.

A Lobbyist representing a business interest, for instance, might want to meet with senators and representatives whose districts employ a lot of people in that industry. If a particular regulation goes through, the Lobbyist might argue, thousands of people in the district could lose their jobs.

Back in the office, Lobbyists research issues and phone staffers to check Legislators' positions on various bills. They work on strategies. A grassroots Lobbyist might collect signatures on a petition in favor of certain legislation. If the Lobbyist can produce thousands of signatures, the legislator is bound to take notice or risk the possibility of losing valuable votes come election time.

Salaries

Salaries vary greatly, as well-funded private industries pay considerably more than nonprofit advocacy groups. Someone with limited experience working for a small organization might earn $30,000, compared to more than $100,000 for someone with a few years of Capitol Hill experience, according to the Center for Responsive Politics.

Legislative staffers who have worked in high-profile positions, such as on the appropriations committee, generally earn more than those who have less visible jobs. Lawyers, too, are often in demand, as are individuals who have held political office.

In Washington, D.C., well-connected members of Congress who go into lobbying might earn $500,000 to $1 million a year, according to the Center for Responsive Politics. Individuals who have established visible careers on Capitol Hill can skip the middle rungs of the career ladder, jumping right to partner or head of their own lobbying firms. Some Lobbyists are paid a straight salary; others work on a contract or commission basis.

Employment Prospects

Employment prospects are good because of the variety of organizations—professional and trade associations, corporations, and public interest and nonprofit groups—that hire Lobbyists. In Congress, Lobbyists need to register with the Senate Public Records Office and/or the House Legislative Resource Center.

Advancement Prospects

Advancement prospects are good because turnover creates new opportunities. Some individuals leave lobbying to prac-

tice law, take high-level government positions, or retire, enabling others to rise to higher-level positions within their organizations.

Education and Training

Educational requirements vary, depending on the firm or group. Professional lobbying firms dominated by lawyers usually require law degrees for top positions. Most other positions require at least a college degree, with experience on Capitol Hill a definite plus. Political science courses are useful, as are new programs in political management. Such programs include the Lobbying Institute, a two-week intensive course offered twice a year by the Center for Presidential and Congressional Studies at American University in Washington, D.C.

Experience, Skills, and Personality Traits

Many Lobbyists have held positions such as legislative aide, committee staffer, or chief of staff in the legislative sector. Because Lobbyists must thoroughly understand the legislative process, employers often look for experience on Capitol Hill.

Some individuals, though, become Lobbyists without such experience. In the world of trade and professional associations, for example, an individual might rise up the ranks from government relations coordinator to government relations director. An activist involved in lobbying can advance similarly in his or her organization.

In this personality-driven field, it helps to have charisma. Lobbyists need to be confident and persuasive enough to convince people to do what they want them to do. Yet, they should be low-key enough that Legislators feel informed and persuaded rather than coerced and threatened by their actions. Insiders say that a "soft sell" approach works better than a "hard sell." Legislators want information from Lobbyists to be reliable even if it is favorable to a particular point of view.

Unions and Associations

Associations of interest to Lobbyists include the American League of Lobbyists, the American Society of Association Executives, and the American Association of Political Consultants.

Tips for Entry

1. Hone your public-speaking skills by joining a debate team or otherwise developing ease in talking about political issues.
2. Get legislative experience to develop an insider's knowledge of lawmaking. Capitol Hill experience is particularly useful.

3. Develop grassroots lobbying skills by working as a canvasser, or field organizer, or campaign volunteer. These entry-level positions help individuals hone the basic persuasive skills needed by Lobbyists.

4. Volunteer to work on a political campaign. Lobbying and mobilizing support for a candidate or issue require similar skills.

LABOR UNION ORGANIZER

CAREER PROFILE

Duties: Educating workers about their rights; explaining the union organizing process; recruiting, developing, and mobilizing worker organizing committees; developing and carrying out plans for union campaigns

Salary Range: $22,000 to $70,000

Employment Prospects: Excellent

Advancement Prospects: Excellent

Best Geographical Location: None

Prerequisites:

Education or Training—Various backgrounds

Experience—Six months preferred

Special Skills and Personality Traits—Commitment to workers' rights; energy and enthusiasm; leadership qualities; good listening and communication skills; willingness to work long and irregular hours

CAREER LADDER

```
┌─────────────────────────────┐
│       Lead Organizer        │
└─────────────────────────────┘

┌─────────────────────────────┐
│    Labor Union Organizer    │
└─────────────────────────────┘

┌─────────────────────────────┐
│   Recent College Graduate   │
│      or Union Member        │
└─────────────────────────────┘
```

Position Description

Labor Union Organizers help groups of workers, ranging from janitors to airplane pilots, obtain union representation to improve their working conditions.

After years of declining membership due to America's shrinking industrial base, unions are looking beyond the traditional "men in hard hats" to recruit new members. Hotel and restaurant workers, health care workers, government employees, and, most recently, doctors are joining unions, changing the face of American labor.

The vast majority of groups are affiliated with the American Federation of Labor and Congress of Industrial Organizations (AFL-CIO), an umbrella organization of 65 unions. The rest are independent. Whether working for an independent union or an AFL-CIO affiliate, the Labor Union Organizer has the same basic role of educating and mobilizing workers.

Labor Union Organizers begin their careers in different ways: Some workers become activists on the job; other individuals become Labor Union Organizers after being exposed to labor issues through campus activities and/or jobs in activism. Someone might, for example, be a community organizer involved in a "living-wage" campaign. From there, the individual might hear about a national union looking for Organizers or apply to the AFL-CIO's Organizing Institute.

An individual's first assignment might involve a local organizing drive lasting a few months. Typically, a drive begins after someone has called the union to complain about working conditions. Perhaps salaries have been cut or benefits revoked. The new Organizer might begin by calling the person who lodged the complaint. Can he or she find five fellow workers to take to an organizing meeting? Because Labor Union Organizers are usually not allowed in the workplace, they meet with workers outside the facility or at their homes.

Much of the work of Labor Union Organizers involves listening to and encouraging workers. Often new Labor Union Organizers are paired with more experienced Lead Organizers, who accompany them to house meetings. As the campaign develops, Labor Union Organizers might prepare and distribute leaflets, meet with workers in their homes, and lead organizing meetings.

The next step is to persuade one-third of workers to sign union cards. Once that is accomplished, the Labor Union Organizer can petition the National Labor Relations Board for an election. Often management opposes the drive. Workers initially favorable to the campaign might back away from the union, afraid of losing their jobs or seeing conditions worsen in a heated battle.

Each campaign presents its own challenges. Labor Union Organizers often need to devise innovative strategies to mobilize workers and hold employers accountable. In a restaurant in Las Vegas, for example, Labor Union Organizers orchestrated a "sip-in," during which members took over a restaurant, ordering nothing but water for three hours before tipping the servers and leaving. Such actions may result in victories for the union that occur after months, if not years, of uphill battles.

Salaries

Salaries for Labor Union Organizers generally range from $22,000 to $70,000, according to industry sources. Labor Union Organizers for low-paying industries like farmwork pay less than those for high-paying ones like aviation.

Employment Prospects

Employment prospects are excellent because, after years of decline, the labor movement is trying to attract new members. As a result, many unions are creating new positions for Labor Union Organizers. The Service Employees International Union, the fastest-growing union in the AFL-CIO, is a prime example.

Advancement Prospects

Advancement prospects are excellent because Labor Union Organizers can rise to higher levels of pay and responsibility within the labor movement. Many Labor Union Organizers move up to positions like lead organizer after a year on the job. The lead organizer makes key decisions and supervises others. Some individuals become long-time organizers while others choose a variety of paths, including jobs in politics and social justice.

Education and Training

Labor Union Organizers have a variety of backgrounds, as on-the-job experience can be as valuable as a college degree. Many college graduates learn the ropes of organizing workers through union-sponsored training programs. Some unions conduct their own training, but many of the 65 unions under the AFL-CIO umbrella refer individuals to the organization's Organizing Institute.

The AFL-CIO's Organizing Institute includes classroom training, field training, and job placement. Individuals accepted into this paid training program begin with a three-day weekend training session. Those who do well go on to a paid 10-day orientation and then three months of fieldwork. Field training offers a weekly salary, housing, transportation, and health insurance. Those who successfully complete the program are placed in permanent positions.

Labor Union Organizers also take other paths. Someone who has worked as a community organizer, for example, might be a good candidate for a union looking for roughly equivalent skills. Someone else might have a master's degree in labor studies. Still another candidate might be a rank-and-file worker who assumed leadership as a shop steward while still drawing a paycheck from the company. A variety of backgrounds and experiences can help someone become a successful Labor Union Organizer.

Experience, Skills, and Personality Traits

Labor unions generally look for individuals with organizing experience, either with a labor union or in a comparable group. Student and community organizing may satisfy experience requirements. Individuals also can gain experience by volunteering or participating in training programs such as the AFL-CIO's Organizing Institute.

Union organizing is anything but a 9-to-5 job. Individuals must be prepared to work long and often irregular hours. They often meet with workers in the evenings and at the beginnings or ends of shifts. Many Labor Union Organizers spend much of their time on the road, traveling from one campaign to another.

Although some think of Labor Union Organizers as individuals who make speeches, insiders say that Union Organizers spend much more of their time *listening* than *talking*. They work with diverse groups of people and should be sensitive to their concerns.

Labor Union Organizers also should have a strong commitment to social and economic change, as campaigns can be long and heated. Unions are controversial, criticized by some people as too big and powerful. To hold their own, Labor Union Organizers must have energy and enthusiasm, leadership qualities, resourcefulness, and strong communication skills. Being bilingual can be a plus.

Unions and Associations

The AFL-CIO is an umbrella organization of 65 unions, which trains individuals through its Organizing Institute. Some Labor Union Organizers also belong to the National Organizers Alliance.

Tips for Entry

1. Participate in a student group dealing with issues like opposition to tuition hikes or sweatshops. Many student groups deal with economic and labor issues.
2. Check out Internet websites for job postings. Several sites dealing with the nonprofit sector list union organizing jobs; one site in particular—*www.unionjobs.com*—specializes in the area.
3. Get at least six months of union organizing experience. Candidates can gain experience through opportunities provided by the AFL-CIO's Organizing Institute or union drives looking for temporary or Volunteer Organizers.
4. Read up on the labor movement. Helpful resources include the Labornet website (*www.labornet.org*).

MEMBERSHIP DIRECTOR, ASSOCIATION

CAREER PROFILE

Duties: Identify and acquire new members; retain existing members; manage membership database

Alternate Title(s): Recruitment Director, Retention Director, Membership and Marketing Director, Membership Service Representative

Salary Range: $35,000 to $75,000

Employment Prospects: Excellent

Advancement Prospects: Good

Best Geographical Location: Washington, D.C.; state capitals

Prerequisites:

Education or Training—Bachelor's degree

Experience—Two to five years

Special Skills and Personality Traits—Understanding of marketing tasks such as public relations, advertising, and copywriting; ability to communicate well with members; belief in and commitment to the association

CAREER LADDER

```
┌─────────────────────────────────┐
│   Position with Larger Association │
│      or Executive Director       │
└─────────────────────────────────┘

┌─────────────────────────────────┐
│      Membership Director         │
└─────────────────────────────────┘

┌─────────────────────────────────┐
│    Entry Level in Related Field  │
└─────────────────────────────────┘
```

Position Description

Membership Directors head up efforts to recruit new members and retain the old, knowing that the larger the membership, the more powerful the association.

An association is basically a club organized to promote the interests of members, often through lobbying. Some 70 percent of all Americans belong to at least one association, according to Ronald Krannich and Caryl Krannich, Ph.D.s, authors of *The Complete Guide to Public Employment.* Employers belong to associations, as do members of various professions and charitable groups; as a result, associations are important special interest groups.

Associations vary by orientation. Trade associations such as the National Automobile Dealers Association are made up of businesses that meet to share information about legislation and trends affecting their industry. Professional associations, on the other hand, represent individuals in a particular field, such as doctors or teachers, concerned about professional standards and practice. In addition, there are a number of philanthropic and charitable associations such as the National Society to Prevent Blindness and the American Cancer Society.

Membership Directors keep constant watch on their numbers. How many memberships have been renewed? Is the association losing or gaining members? What kind of message might appeal to specific types of members? For example, the Membership Director of an association dealing with vocational education might launch a recruitment drive by replacing the word *vocational* with *vocational/technical* to update the group's image.

Members of associations vary in their levels of involvement. Some attend conferences and set policy; others do little more than read notices, which, in itself, can be a challenge in this age of "information overload." For example, Membership Directors ask themselves, Does anyone read membership-renewal letters? To reach individuals who might not have the time to read a letter, an association might attach a gummed notice on the invoice for renewal.

The number of hats a Membership Director wears depends largely on the size of the organization. In a large organization, a Membership Director might be involved in a specific activity, such as recruitment or retention. In a small organization, on the other hand, the Membership Director might also be involved in a host of other activities such as meetings and training.

Common responsibilities of Membership Directors include

- Implementing a membership campaign, using direct mail, telemarketing, and other techniques
- Promoting the annual conference
- Developing new-member orientation programs
- Providing information about the profession or trade
- Conducting surveys, evaluations, and needs assessments
- Resolving member inquiries and concerns

Salaries

Salaries for Membership Directors in associations range from $35,000 to $75,000, according to industry sources. Large organizations generally pay higher salaries than smaller ones. Salaries also tend to be higher for trade and professional associations than for charitable or philanthropic groups.

Employment Prospects

Employment prospects are excellent because associations are membership-based organizations in which Membership Directors play a key role. Nonprofit charitable organizations (e.g. YMCA) also hire Membership Directors.

Many individuals take jobs with associations without setting out to make a career of association management. Either they become involved in an association in their line of work or they take a job with an association, find they like it, and move up to increased responsibility from association to association, finding that, accidentally, they've developed a career.

Advancement Prospects

Advancement prospects are good because Membership Directors can move from smaller to larger associations and/or to higher-level positions such as executive director.

Education and Training

A bachelor's degree in communication, marketing, or a related field works well for positions as Membership Director. As the nonprofit sector has grown, new programs have sprung up in nonprofit management, primarily at the graduate level, through public administration or business administration departments.

The American Society of Association Executives (ASAE) identifies core competencies leading to the designation of Certified Association Executive (CAE). To qualify,

individuals must have three to five years of experience in associations, complete 75 hours of continuing education or professional development, and pass a written examination.

Experience, Skills, and Personality Traits

Because Membership Director is a management position, most individuals have at least a few years in the field. Some Membership Directors have held positions in allied fields, such as marketing and direct mail, before becoming involved with an association.

Membership Directors must be willing to listen to members. If, for example, members of a professional association want to change their certification process, the Membership Director should be willing to listen. Flexibility counts for a lot in this field. Times change, technology changes, and so, too, do member needs. Membership Directors should be well-organized and able to roll with the punches. Believing in the work of the association also leads to success in this field.

Unions and Associations

The American Society of Association Executives (ASAE) represents Membership Directors as well as other association executives.

Tips for Entry

1. Get in where you can. An entry-level job as a Membership assistant or in a research department, for example, can help someone get on a career path in associations leading to a position as Membership Director.
2. Take stock of your interests. If, for example, you care about health, you may want to work for an association representing doctors, nurses, or others in the industry.
3. Check out the website of the American Society of Association Executives *(www.asaenet.org),* which lists jobs and provides information about careers.
4. Browse through one of the two directories, *National Trade and Professional Associations of the United States* by Columbia Books or *Encyclopedia of Associations* by Gale Research, widely available in public libraries to research the activities of associations and see what interests you.
5. Find associations in your local area by checking your phone book under the listings *American, Association, International, Society,* and/or *United.* The names of many associations begin with these words.

POLITICAL ACTION COMMITTEE (PAC) PROFESSIONAL

CAREER PROFILE

Duties: Conducting fund-raising and recognition drives; filing compliance reports; researching political issues; educating members; performing various other government relations tasks

Alternate Title(s): Government Relations Manager, Political Education Manager, Political Involvement Director, Grassroots Manager

Salary Range: $25,000 to $100,000+

Employment Prospects: Good

Advancement Prospects: Good

Best Geographical Location(s): Washington, D.C., and other cities.

Prerequisites:

Education or Training—Bachelor's degree in government, political management, political science, or related field

Experience—Entry-level or one to three years' experience on Capitol Hill or with political campaigns

Special Skills and Personality Traits—Enthusiasm; ability to motivate others; engaging personality; belief in the issues; interest in the political process

CAREER LADDER

```
┌─────────────────────────────────┐
│      Lobbyist or Government      │
│       Relations Director         │
└─────────────────────────────────┘

┌─────────────────────────────────┐
│  Political Action Committee (PAC)│
│          Professional            │
└─────────────────────────────────┘

┌─────────────────────────────────┐
│ College Student or Legislative Staffer │
└─────────────────────────────────┘
```

Position Description

Political Action Committee (PAC) Professionals help businesses, associations, labor unions, and other interest groups raise funds to channel into political campaigns.

Most PACs represent business, labor, or ideological interests. Both liberal and conservative groups, including well-known organizations such as the Sierra Club and the National Rifle Association, operate PACs, as do some congressional and party leaders. PACs typically get their money from individuals who are employees or members of the group that formed the PAC.

Usually, according to PAC consultant Peter Kennerdell, PAC positions fall under the broader heading of government relations, and individuals assume responsibilities aside from those directly related to the PAC. In addition to administering the PAC, many Political Professionals are involved in grassroots lobbying.

The PAC part of the job involves asking people to donate money. The grassroots component involves motivating people to donate time. Grassroots lobbyists encourage members to participate in activities such as writing letters, making phone calls, and sending telegrams. Fund-raising and grassroots lobbying constitute political involvement. Both entail mobilizing customers, members, and/or supporters to take action.

PACs are permitted under federal law to make larger contributions than individuals to political candidates: Individuals may donate no more than $1,000 to any single candidate, whereas a PAC may donate up to $5,000. PACs, like lobbies, are often controversial, as opponents contend that PACs allow interest groups to influence politicians unfairly with large contributions. Supporters, on the other hand, argue that PACs represent the legitimate role of business, labor, and/or ideological interests in the political process.

Because PACs are regulated by the government, PAC Professionals spend at least part of their time keeping records and filing reports. Much of their time also goes to planning and conducting fund-raising drives. In addition to direct-mail and e-mail campaigns, PAC Professionals organize raffles, auctions, booths at annual conventions, cocktail parties, and other fund-raisers intended to make the process fun for prospective donors.

Insiders say that fund-raising is closely linked to political education because prospective contributors are more willing to donate money if they understand the issues involved. A PAC Professional might edit a newsletter to keep members politically informed and give talks such as "The Political Realities of the Upcoming Year."

PAC Professionals also conduct research, which insiders call political intelligence. They review voting records and other matters of importance to determine which political officials are "friends" and which are "foes." Individuals then communicate their findings to PAC Board Members, who ultimately decide which candidates are deserving of funds. In addition, PAC Professionals plan recognition events and awards for donors. For instance, the PAC might buy small gifts for contributors.

In addition, PAC Professionals commonly assume other government relations responsibilities such as coordinating a letter-writing drive as part of a grassroots lobbying effort. PAC Professionals range in levels of responsibility from fairly low-level employees responsible for bookkeeping or compliance reporting to high-level political managers. As PAC Professionals gain experience, they generally become more involved in formulating political strategy.

Salaries

Salaries vary according to the type of organization and the PAC Professional's level of responsibility. Entry-level PAC Professionals earn about $25,000, whereas individuals in high-level positions may earn $100,000 or more.

Employment Prospects

Employment prospects are good because this is a field with a lot of movement, which creates opportunities for newcomers. Depending on the level of the position, a PAC Professional may be a recent college graduate or have a background in a related field such as marketing or legislative affairs. Prospects may be particularly good for someone with Capitol Hill experience.

Advancement Prospects

Advancement prospects are fair to good. Although PAC Professionals are often involved in lobbying, they are sometimes not regarded as real lobbyists, especially if they lack experience on Capitol Hill, insiders say. However, individuals who prove themselves on the job often move up. Often, PAC Professionals with associations move to higher-paying positions with corporate PACs.

Education and Training

A bachelor's degree in any field generally qualifies individuals for positions with PACs. Courses in government and political science can be particularly useful in familiarizing individuals with the political system within which PACs operate. The relatively new academic field of political management also deals with issues of concern to PACs.

Experience, Skills, and Personality Traits

Because this field relies heavily on social contacts, some employers look for experience on Capitol Hill; others, however, are willing to hire an enthusiastic college graduate with limited experience. Volunteering on a political campaign can be helpful, as campaign volunteers learn the skills needed to motivate people to donate money and/or time. PAC Professionals must have a sales-oriented personality. Vibrant, charismatic people do best in this field.

Unions and Associations

The National Association of Business Political Action Committees (NABPAC) is an organization representing PAC Professionals in business. The American Society of Association Executives deals with PACs in trade and professional associations. The American Federation of Labor and Congress of Industrial Organizations (AFL-CIO) is an umbrella organization representing labor unions, many of which have PACs.

Tips for Entry

1. Ask yourself whether you are interested in fund-raising. If so, this might be a good position for you.
2. Browse the Center for Responsive Politics website (*www.opensecrets.org*) to view PAC listings by category such as *Ideological/Single Issue, Labor,* and *Miscellaneous Business.* Another resource for PAC listings: the *Almanac of Federal PACs* by Edward Zuckerman, available in some large public libraries and many college libraries.
3. Volunteer to work on a political campaign, particularly in a fund-raising capacity.
4. Focus on the largest PACs since these offer the most opportunities for employment. The Federal Elections Commission (*www.fec.gov*) lists the nation's top 50 PACs.
5. Check the *career* section of the American Society of Association Executives (ASAE) website (*www.asae.org*) for information about positions with associations. The *Encyclopedia of Associations,* commonly available in public libraries, is another helpful resource for people interested in association PACs.
6. Look for PACs in your state by checking with the secretary of state's office, which may list PACs on its website.

SERVICE PROGRAMS

PEACE CORPS VOLUNTEER

CAREER PROFILE

Duties: Living in another country for three months of training and two years of service; learning another language; becoming part of another culture; working in one of a variety of fields such as education, health, or environment to improve the human condition at the grassroots level

Salary Range: Stipend to cover basic necessities such as food, housing, and local transportation; readjustment allowance of $225 for each month served—$6,075 for completion of the full three months of training and two years of service

Employment Prospects: Excellent

Advancement Prospects: Excellent

Best Geographical Location: Volunteer positions are located in countries throughout the world: Africa, Inter-America and the Caribbean, the Pacific, Europe and the Mediterranean, Central and East Asia

Prerequisites:

Education or Training—Most assignments call for a bachelor's degree; more specialized assignments require a master's degree and/or three to five years of related work experience; all Volunteers receive three months of preservice training

Experience—Volunteer experience as a tutor, clinic worker, or other worker, for most positions; more extensive background for specialized positions

Special Skills and Personality Traits—Determined; self-motivated; patient; self-sacrificing; creative; compassionate; resourceful; well-organized

CAREER LADDER

```
┌─────────────────────────────────┐
│  Educator or Peace Corps Recruiter │
└─────────────────────────────────┘

┌─────────────────────────────────┐
│     Peace Corps Volunteer        │
└─────────────────────────────────┘

┌─────────────────────────────────┐
│    Recent College Graduate,      │
│  Entry or Midlevel Employee,     │
│         or Retiree               │
└─────────────────────────────────┘
```

Position Description

The Peace Corps bills itself as "the toughest job you'll ever love." Peace Corps Volunteers leave behind the comforts of their American life-style to help people in developing nations build a better future for themselves, their children, and their communities. In the process, many Volunteers find that they receive as much as they give. Peace Corps Volunteers not only get the adventure of world travel but also discover strengths they never knew they had.

Over one-third of Peace corps Volunteers—the largest single category—work as educators. Many teach English as a foreign language to give people around the world access to the global economy. As the primary language of the Internet, English has become an important asset worldwide. Other Peace Corps programs include environment, health, business, and agriculture.

In addition to their primary assignment, Peace Corps Volunteers take on a secondary project of their own choosing. An English teacher, for example, might organize a sewing coop for local women or start a baseball league for area children. Each Volunteer's experience is unique.

Peace Corps Volunteers without specialized training typically work in a field in which they've been volunteers for at least three months. Someone who worked at an acquired immunodeficiency syndrome (AIDS) clinic in college, for example, might qualify as a Health Educator with the Peace Corps.

Applying to the Peace Corps is a lengthy process. Applicants need to write personal essays, gather up educational transcripts, detail their work histories, and provide three references. Usually within a month of sending in their applications, applicants are interviewed by a Peace Corps recruiter. At this point, the recruiter may advise the applicant to get additional volunteer experience to become better qualified for the Peace Corps.

Once an individual's skills match a Volunteer opening, the Recruiter "nominates" the applicant for an assignment, pending legal and medical clearance. Assignments are based primarily on where the applicant's skills are most needed, although the Volunteer's preferences are taken into consideration.

Peace Corps Volunteers settle into their new countries with three months of training in language, cross-cultural understanding, and practical skills. Many stay with host families during this training period.

Once their assignments begin, Peace Corps Volunteers need to be flexible and resourceful, as commercial supplies such as textbooks tend to be in scant supply. Sometimes the efforts of Peace Corps Volunteers are greeted with indifference or misunderstanding. Patience and creativity can help Volunteers succeed in their assignments.

For example, a Peace Corps Volunteer in the classroom might use games like Simon Says and Bingo to teach English skills. Peace Corps Volunteers work closely with local teachers to develop teaching materials. They also promote adult literacy and improve education for women and girls. If need be, Peace Corps Volunteers might build schoolhouses and find books to stock libraries.

The skills of a good Peace Corps Volunteer—resourcefulness, flexibility, and patience—translate readily to many other positions. Because the program is highly regarded by employers in various fields, serving in the Peace Corps can further one's career. Former Peace Corps volunteers include the former Health and Human Services Secretary Donna Shalala (Iran, 1962 to 1964), the Connecticut Senator Christopher Dodd (Dominican Republic, 1966 to 1968), and the television personality Bob Vila (Panama, 1969 to 1970).

Peace Corps Volunteers typically work long hours. During their stays, they learn to do without many of the things they have come to take for granted. In villages without refrigerators, for instance, Volunteers need to adjust to life without cold drinks. Some Volunteers live in rural communities, hours or even days away from the nearest Peace Corps worker.

Salaries

The Peace Corps provides a stipend for basic living expenses, such as food, housing, and transportation, so Volunteers can live at the same level as the people they serve in their communities. Stipends vary from country to country. Peace Corps Volunteers receive a readjustment allowance of $6,075 at the completion of their three months of training and two years of service.

Employment Prospects

Employment prospects are excellent because of the revolving nature of the work. New Volunteers are constantly needed to replace those who have completed their assignments. Although the Peace Corps tries to accommodate the requests of applicants, it cannot guarantee placement in any specific country or region. Applicants are encouraged to be flexible, so the Peace Corps can place Volunteers in the countries where their skills are most needed.

Advancement Prospects

Advancement prospects are excellent because service in the Peace Corps helps a résumé to be noticed. The flexibility and resourcefulness a Volunteer learns in the Peace Corps are valuable in any career. Fluency in a foreign language and cross-cultural knowledge are especially valuable in certain fields. The Peace Corps' Office of Returned Volunteer Services provides career counseling and publishes a newsletter featuring employment opportunities for returned Volunteers.

Education and Training

Most assignments require at least a college degree and some volunteer experience, but the Peace Corps also takes into account an applicant's life experiences, community involvement, and hobbies. Because the Peace Corps provides intensive language instruction during its preservice training, applicants need not be fluent in a foreign language. Some Volunteers combine international service with graduate school through admission to the Master's International Program, a partnership between the Peace Corps and more than 20 schools offering master's level studies.

Experience, Skills, and Personality Traits

Peace Corps Volunteers need to demonstrate maturity, adaptability, and flexibility to succeed in their assignments. Applicants should want to join the Peace Corps for the right reasons—to serve others, to make a difference, to change the world for the better.

Unions and Associations

Peace Corps Volunteers are non–Civil Service government employees. The National Peace Corps Association is a nonprofit organization dedicated to teaching Americans about other cultures through the Peace Corps.

Tips for Entry

1. Read up on the Peace Corps to find out about the programs where you would best qualify. Contact a local university or the Peace Corps regional office or website *(www.peacecorps.gov)*.
2. Volunteer in any capacity: as a tutor, a member of a student group, or in another activity.
3. Take courses in foreign languages.
4. Make sure the lengthy application process is as smooth as possible by checking to see that all forms and recommendations have been sent, but be prepared to wait six months to a year for a final decision.
5. Meet a Peace Corps regional recruiter to discuss ways of enhancing your application.

AMERICORPS MEMBER

CAREER PROFILE

Duties: Participating in programs that tutor children, build affordable homes, respond to natural disasters, and otherwise improve communities throughout the United States

Alternate Title(s): Americorps*VISTA (Volunteers in Service to America), Americorps*NCCC (National Civilian Community Corps)

Salary Range: Monthly living allowance; education award at end of service

Employment Prospects: Excellent

Advancement Prospects: Excellent

Best Geographical Location(s): Programs located throughout the United States

Prerequisites:

Education or Training—Varies by program; training provided

Experience—Varies by program; volunteer or work experience required or preferred

Special Skills and Personality Traits—Commitment to national service; dedication; drive; good communication skills; flexibility; resilience

CAREER LADDER

```
┌─────────────────────────────────┐
│   College or Graduate Student or │
│ Position in Education or Other Career │
└─────────────────────────────────┘

┌─────────────────────────────────┐
│        AmeriCorps Member         │
└─────────────────────────────────┘

┌─────────────────────────────────┐
│ Student, Recent College Graduate, │
│ Entry-Level or Midlevel Employee, │
│             Retiree              │
└─────────────────────────────────┘
```

Position Description

AmeriCorps is often called "the domestic Peace Corps." While Peace Corps Volunteers travel to countries around the world, AmeriCorps Members serve in intensive, results-driven programs throughout the nation. They tutor children, clean up the environment, build affordable houses, respond to natural disasters, and empower communities to help themselves.

AmeriCorps exemplifies the recent resurgence of community service. Young people may be cynical about politics and politicians, observers say, but they are passionate about helping others. Unlike their predecessors of the 1960s, who sought to *change* the world, participants today today are looking for ways to *improve* it.

AmeriCorps Members give a year of their lives to one of four areas of national concern: education, the environment, public safety, and health and other human needs. Programs are initiated by sponsors—nonprofit organizations like the American Red Cross or Habitat for Humanity, the mayor of a city, a local organization, or someone else—but, in order

to be approved, they must live up to AmeriCorps' results-driven philosophy of "getting things done."

Founded in 1993 by the National Community Service Trust Act, AmeriCorps encompasses hundreds of projects, including two preexisting programs: Volunteers in Service to America (VISTA) and the National Civilian Community Corps (NCCC).

VISTA is the older of the two, established in 1965 as part of President Lyndon Johnson's "war on poverty." Throughout the 1960s, VISTA helped develop some of the first Head Start programs and Job Corps sites. Unlike other AmeriCorps programs, VISTA requires a college degree or at least a few years of work experience, pays relocation expenses, and offers the option of a monthly salary instead of an education award. AmeriCorps*VISTA Members develop projects that can continue after they complete their service. They act more as organizers than as direct care providers, often grooming citizens for leadership roles in keeping with VISTA's emphasis on community self-empowerment. A VISTA Member involved in an after-school tutoring program, for instance, might tutor one or two students but spend most of the time recruiting, training, and supervising volunteers.

Unlike VISTA, which has no upper age limit, the National Civilian Community Corps (NCCC) requires participants to be between the ages of 18 and 24. With its team spirit and hands-on approach to service, NCCC harks back to the Civilian Conservation Corps (CCC) of the Great Depression. Members live and work as teams assigned to five regional bases—Denver, Colorado; Charleston, South Carolina; San Diego, California; Perry Point, Maryland; and Washington, D.C.—but spend much of their time traveling to service sites around the nation. NCCC appeals to young people with a thirst for adventure. An individual assigned to the base in Charleston, South Carolina, might tutor children on-site, then go on the following assignments:

- Five weeks of building houses in rural Georgia for Habitat for Humanity
- Six weeks of providing hurricane relief in Puerto Rico
- Eight weeks of clearing trails for a state park

Some AmeriCorps programs combine the hands-on work of NCCC with the permanence of VISTA. AmeriCorps encompasses thousands of opportunities, including an AmeriCorps Promise Fellows Program for individuals with demonstrated leadership and community service skills. Individuals of all backgrounds can search for AmeriCorps programs by subject area and location. If, for example, a prospective AmeriCorps Member wants to work in health in California, he or she could choose from programs such as health education, immunization outreach, and infant-mortality prevention.

Salaries

AmeriCorps Members receive a modest living allowance. After completing a 10-month to one-year term of service, AmeriCorps members receive a $4,725 education award to help pay for school tuition or student loans.

AmeriCorps Members who serve part-time get a portion of the amount, and those in Volunteers in Service to America (VISTA) can opt for a cash payment of $100 per month of service instead of the education award. All other AmeriCorps Members are eligible only for the education award. A few programs, such as the National Civilian Community Corps, provide housing, but most programs are nonresidential. Applicants who already have demonstrated leadership and community service skills can apply for the Americorps Promise Fellows Program, which offers a $13,000 living allowance and other benefits.

Employment Prospects

Employment prospects are excellent because AmeriCorps encompasses hundreds of programs throughout the nation.

Over 40,000 Americans serve a year in AmeriCorps programs, which have garnered broad bipartisan support.

Some AmeriCorps programs are more competitive than others. The National Civilian Community Corps, for example, receives many more applications than it can accept because of its popularity among young people eager to travel. AmeriCorps Recruiters advise applicants to be flexible about their choice of program rather than "put all their eggs in one basket."

Advancement Prospects

Advancement prospects are excellent because experience in AmeriCorps helps individuals develop skills needed for success in almost any field: teamwork, dedication, and flexibility, among them. AmeriCorps experience can be helpful on employment forms and college applications.

Education and Training

Although some assignments require a bachelor's degree or related experience, many others require only motivation and commitment. All AmeriCorps programs provide training. Because AmeriCorps Members receive funds for college tuition or student loans at the end of their service, the program combines national service with education.

Often, individuals choose AmeriCorps as a way to experience something new before going on to college, graduate school, or a career. Someone interested in medicine, for instance, might take an assignment in Appalachia to learn about the health needs of rural America before applying to medical school. Other AmeriCorps Members want to do something totally outside their field of interest.

Experience, Skills, and Personality Traits

Although some AmeriCorps programs call for specialized experience, many others require only commitment and a desire to serve. AmeriCorps includes people from a variety of backgrounds. Individuals, though, must be committed to national service. They should believe in making personal sacrifice for the common good. AmeriCorps Members transcend the parochialism of their own lives to experience, up close, the needs and promises of the nation. Programs can be challenging, so dedication and resourcefulness are vital

Specific requirements vary from program to program. Volunteers in Service to America (VISTA), for instance, must be patient enough to work on a project that might not quickly produce visible results. To see whether an individual is right for the program, VISTA asks, "Are you an organizer, a resource-builder, a self-starter?"

The National Civilian Community Corps (NCCC) appeals more to young people who thrive on variety. Participants live in dormitories, wear uniforms, and travel from site to site, always doing something different: clearing trails, renovating housing, tutoring kids. Individuals should be between the ages of 18 and 24 years old and enjoy active assignments.

Whatever the program, all AmeriCorps Members take the same pledge at the start of their service. New recruits must dedicate themselves to strengthening communities, building common ground, and taking action to "get things done." AmeriCorps Members pledge: "Faced with apathy, I will take action. Faced with conflict, I will seek common ground."

Unions and Associations

The Corporation for National Service oversees AmeriCorps as well as Learn and Serve America and the National Senior Service Corps. The Corporation for National Service has state offices, and most states have Governor-appointed commissions for national service that administer local programs. Former AmeriCorps Members might belong to AmeriCorps Alums.

Tips for Entry

1. Learn more about AmeriCorps by browsing its website *(www.americorps.org)*.
2. Get involved in your community by volunteering.
3. Find the right service program for you. Do you prefer variety or consistency? Hands-on work or empowerment of others? Would you like a little of each? An AmeriCorps recruiter in your area can help you get the most out of the program.
4. Request an application packet by calling 1-800-942-2677 or download one off the website *(www.americorps.org)*.
5. Be sure to convey your motivation and commitment on the application.

APPENDIXES

APPENDIX I
FREQUENTLY ASKED QUESTIONS ABOUT THE CIVIL SERVICE AND FEDERAL EMPLOYMENT

1. WHAT IS THE CIVIL SERVICE?

The term *civil service* generally refers to nonmilitary employment in nonelective office in the executive branch of government.

In the United States, the civil service was developed in the 19th century in response to widespread public dissatisfaction with political patronage. In 1881, an unsuccessful candidate for a federal post assassinated President James Garfield. Two years later, Congress passed the Civil Service Act.

2. ARE ALL GOVERNMENT JOBS CIVIL SERVICE?

No. Some jobs are classified as *excepted,* meaning that agencies set their own qualification requirements. The word *exempt* is sometimes used synonymously with *excepted.* Many specialists, however, prefer the term *excepted* because *exempt* often applies specifically to overtime regulations.

Federal agencies in the civil service are required by law to post their vacancies with the Office of Personnel Management (OPM), although OPM is much less of a central control agency than it used to be. Many vacancy announcements refer applicants directly to the agency with the opening, and job seekers interested in working for a particular agency can often find helpful information on its website. State and local jurisdictions vary widely in their definitions of those jobs covered by the civil service. For example, a relatively newly created position such as management analyst might be outside the realm of the civil service in one jurisdiction but covered by it in another.

Civil service regulations stipulate that applicants and employees receive fair and equal treatment. For example, if an election creates a shift in administration, civil service employees cannot be replaced by new hires, whereas political appointees—legislative assistants, for example—can.

Agencies maintaining excepted positions are allowed to set their own qualification requirements and are not subject to the appointment, pay, and classification rules established for the civil service. Some federal agencies, including the Central Intelligence Agency, have only excepted service positions. In other instances, certain groups of jobs within an agency may be excepted from civil service procedures. Some individuals enter government through special programs, such as the Pres-idential Management Internship, which put them on a fast track to higher civil service status.

3. IS THE EMPLOYMENT PROCESS DIFFERENT FOR CIVIL SERVICE POSITIONS AND EXCEPTED POSITIONS?

Yes, in general, civil service positions are listed centrally and excepted positions are handled directly by the agency or the individual doing the hiring. However, many agencies allow applicants to contact the agency directly for job information and application processing. At the federal level, all civil service positions are listed through the Office of Personnel Management's USA Jobs database. The Office of Personnel Management's website *(www.usajobs.opm.gov)* also provides links to excepted agencies.

4. DO ALL CIVIL SERVICE JOBS REQUIRE A STANDARDIZED TEST?

No. Although civil service exams are still common for some jobs—such as for police and firefighters—many professional positions do not require them. Personnel specialists observe that qualifications for professional positions are particularly difficult to measure through standardized tests.

At the federal level, most standardized written tests have been eliminated, according to the Office of Personnel Management. Positions are filled, much as they are in the private sector, by assessing the individual's personal, educational, and work-history qualifications. One exception is the Foreign Service, which requires applicants to take a comprehensive written exam.

State and municipal personnel agencies, too, have been moving away from standardized written exams. States that once tested for positions such as public information officer might now gauge candidates simply by evaluating their educational backgrounds and experience.

5. HOW WILL I KNOW WHETHER A PARTICULAR POSITION REQUIRES APPLICANTS TO TAKE A TEST?

The position description, also known as the "vacancy announcement," will describe the requirements. For instance, a position may require applicants to write an essay in response to a particular question rather than take a standardized exam.

6. IF NO TEST IS REQUIRED, HOW ARE APPLICANTS RANKED?

Agencies generally rank applicants by assigning point values to their qualifications, with more points assigned to "direct" than "indirect" experience. Someone with a degree in journalism and experience as a newspaper reporter, for example, would have more direct experience for the position of public information officer than a fellow applicant who majored in music and worked as a bike messenger.

Federal vacancy announcements commonly include a section on KSAs, the Knowledge, Skills, and Abilities an applicant should possess. The applicant then addresses these KSAs in an essay accompanying his or her application. A recent KSA for the position of human resource specialist, for example, asked applicants, "Describe the variety and types of staffing, pay issues, and federal recruitment and/or special emphasis programs with which you have experience."

7. ARE APPLICANTS FOR CIVIL SERVICE POSITIONS STILL PUT ON A REGISTER OF "ELIGIBLES" AND REQUIRED TO WAIT FOR A POSITION TO OPEN IN THEIR JOB CATEGORY?

At the federal level, the Office of Personnel Management has eliminated the register system. Job seekers apply directly for a specific position instead of an entire category of jobs.

Personnel policies vary at the state and municipal levels. A state personnel agency may, for example, rank applicants for eligibility by job grouping but allow certain positions to be filled without use of a register, specialists say. Municipalities, in turn, may contact state personnel agencies for lists of "eligibles" for some but not all jobs.

8. IS IT BEST TO APPLY FOR A SPECIFIC POSITION OR JUST SEND IN A RÉSUMÉ OR COMPLETED APPLICATION TO AN AGENCY OF INTEREST?

In general, it is best to apply for a specific position or group of positions rather than to send out a résumé or application and hope that it will be kept on file. Agencies may lack the resources to accept applications for positions for which they are not actively recruiting.

9. WHAT IS THE FEDERAL GOVERNMENT'S OUTSTANDING SCHOLAR PROGRAM?

The Outstanding Scholar Program is for college graduates who have maintained a grade point average (GPA) of 3.5 or better on a 4.0 scale for all undergraduate course work or who have graduated in the upper 10 percent of their graduating class or major university subdivision such as the School of Business Administration. Outstanding Scholar positions are offered through the federal government at the GS-5 through GS-7 levels in a variety of career fields, including economics, foreign affairs, intelligence, paralegal specialist, personnel staffing, program management and analysis, and public affairs. Positions are posted through USA Jobs (www.usajobs.opm.gov).

10. WHAT IS THE PRESIDENTIAL MANAGEMENT INTERN PROGRAM?

The Presidential Management Intern (PMI) Program was established in 1977 to attract outstanding graduate students to federal service. Presidential Management Interns must have completed a master's degree in public administration, public policy, or a related field and been nominated by their schools. Individuals in this paid internship program receive an initial two-year appointment to an excepted service position in the federal government. They are hired at the GS-9 grade level (currently $36,000 range per year) but, on completion of the program, may be converted to a permanent GS-12 grade level (currently $53,000 range per year). The PMI Program places a strong emphasis on career development, offering seminars, briefings, conferences, and at least one rotational assignment. Students apply for the PMI from mid-September through October 31 of their final year of graduate school. Applications are available from graduate schools and the USA JOBS (www.usajobs.opm.gov) website.

11. WHO QUALIFIES FOR POSITIONS CATEGORIZED BY THE FEDERAL GOVERNMENT AS ENTRY-LEVEL PROFESSIONAL?

Applicants who hold a bachelor's degree, one year of professional experience, or three years of general experience are eligible for Entry-Level Professional positions, which start at around $22,000 to $39,000. Applicants can browse positions by the following job types: Engineering, Architecture, and Transportation; Medical and Health; Financial and Budgeting; Administrative; Social Science and Welfare; Legal, Investigative, Law Enforcement, and Safety; Computers and Mathematics; Physical and Biological Sciences; and/or All. The federal government uses the same categories for professional positions, which require higher levels of education and experience.

APPENDIX II
FEDERAL PAY SCALE

Federal salaries vary according to the qualifications of applicants. The general qualifications needed are as follows, but job seekers should also check the specific education and experience requirements for desired positions listed on the Office of Personnel Management's (OPM's) USAJOBS website *(www.usajobs.opm.gov)*.

$14,000 to $20,000—Three months of general experience or a high school diploma (including or equivalent to GS-1 through GS-2)

$17,000 to $22,000—Six months of general experience or one year of education beyond high school (including or equivalent to GS-3)

$19,000 to $25,000—One year of general experience or one year of education beyond high school (including or equivalent to GS-4)

$22,000 to $39,000—Three years of general experience or at least one year of professional experience or a bachelor's degree (including or equivalent to GS-5 and GS-8)

$33,000 to $62,000—One or more years responsible and independent experience related to the job or a master's or higher degree (including or equivalent to GS-9 through 12)

$57,000 to $88,000—One or more years highly responsible and independent experience directly related to the job to be filled (including or equivalent to GS-13 to GS-14)

$79,000 or more—More than one year of highly responsible and independent experience directly related to the job to be filled; supervisory or managerial skills frequently required

APPENDIX III
FEDERAL GOVERNMENT AGENCY
ORGANIZATIONAL CHART

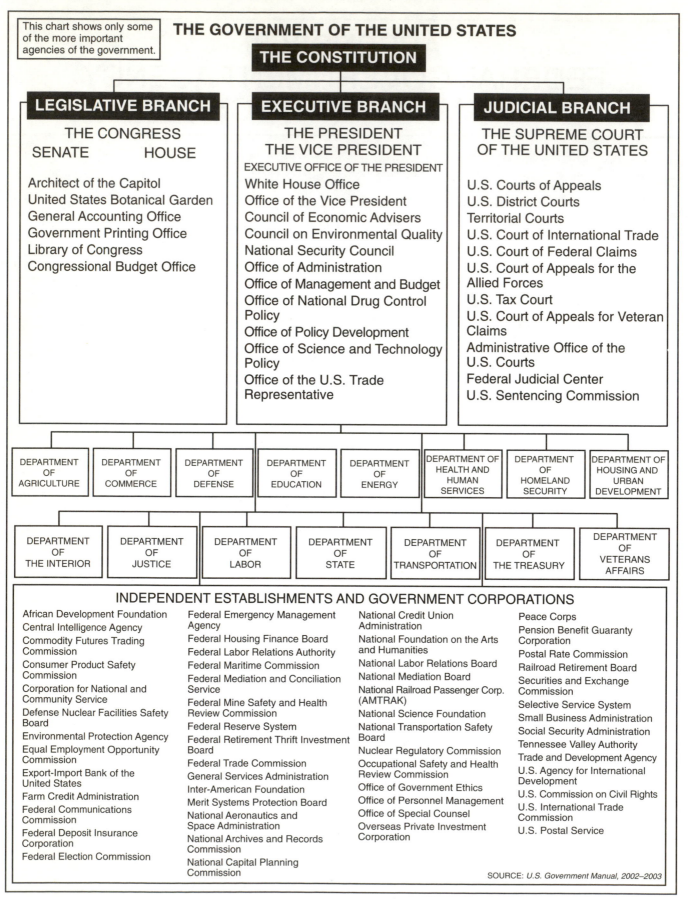

This chart shows only some of the more important agencies of the government.

THE GOVERNMENT OF THE UNITED STATES

THE CONSTITUTION

LEGISLATIVE BRANCH

THE CONGRESS
SENATE   HOUSE

Architect of the Capitol
United States Botanical Garden
General Accounting Office
Government Printing Office
Library of Congress
Congressional Budget Office

EXECUTIVE BRANCH

THE PRESIDENT
THE VICE PRESIDENT
EXECUTIVE OFFICE OF THE PRESIDENT
White House Office
Office of the Vice President
Council of Economic Advisers
Council on Environmental Quality
National Security Council
Office of Administration
Office of Management and Budget
Office of National Drug Control Policy
Office of Policy Development
Office of Science and Technology Policy
Office of the U.S. Trade Representative

JUDICIAL BRANCH

THE SUPREME COURT
OF THE UNITED STATES

U.S. Courts of Appeals
U.S. District Courts
Territorial Courts
U.S. Court of International Trade
U.S. Court of Federal Claims
U.S. Court of Appeals for the Allied Forces
U.S. Tax Court
U.S. Court of Appeals for Veteran Claims
Administrative Office of the U.S. Courts
Federal Judicial Center
U.S. Sentencing Commission

DEPARTMENT OF AGRICULTURE	DEPARTMENT OF COMMERCE	DEPARTMENT OF DEFENSE	DEPARTMENT OF EDUCATION	DEPARTMENT OF ENERGY	DEPARTMENT OF HEALTH AND HUMAN SERVICES	DEPARTMENT OF HOMELAND SECURITY	DEPARTMENT OF HOUSING AND URBAN DEVELOPMENT

DEPARTMENT OF THE INTERIOR	DEPARTMENT OF JUSTICE	DEPARTMENT OF LABOR	DEPARTMENT OF STATE	DEPARTMENT OF TRANSPORTATION	DEPARTMENT OF THE TREASURY	DEPARTMENT OF VETERANS AFFAIRS

INDEPENDENT ESTABLISHMENTS AND GOVERNMENT CORPORATIONS

African Development Foundation
Central Intelligence Agency
Commodity Futures Trading Commission
Consumer Product Safety Commission
Corporation for National and Community Service
Defense Nuclear Facilities Safety Board
Environmental Protection Agency
Equal Employment Opportunity Commission
Export-Import Bank of the United States
Farm Credit Administration
Federal Communications Commission
Federal Deposit Insurance Corporation
Federal Election Commission

Federal Emergency Management Agency
Federal Housing Finance Board
Federal Labor Relations Authority
Federal Maritime Commission
Federal Mediation and Conciliation Service
Federal Mine Safety and Health Review Commission
Federal Reserve System
Federal Retirement Thrift Investment Board
Federal Trade Commission
General Services Administration
Inter-American Foundation
Merit Systems Protection Board
National Aeronautics and Space Administration
National Archives and Records Commission
National Capital Planning Commission

National Credit Union Administration
National Foundation on the Arts and Humanities
National Labor Relations Board
National Mediation Board
National Railroad Passenger Corp. (AMTRAK)
National Science Foundation
National Transportation Safety Board
Nuclear Regulatory Commission
Occupational Safety and Health Review Commission
Office of Government Ethics
Office of Personnel Management
Office of Special Counsel
Overseas Private Investment Corporation

Peace Corps
Pension Benefit Guaranty Corporation
Postal Rate Commission
Railroad Retirement Board
Securities and Exchange Commission
Selective Service System
Small Business Administration
Social Security Administration
Tennessee Valley Authority
Trade and Development Agency
U.S. Agency for International Development
U.S. Commission on Civil Rights
U.S. International Trade Commission
U.S. Postal Service

SOURCE: *U.S. Government Manual, 2002–2003*

APPENDIX IV
FEDERAL GOVERNMENT JOBS

I. EXECUTIVE BRANCH

USAJOBS DATABASE

The U.S. Office of Personnel Management (OPM)

Search for jobs three ways by using the USAJOBS database:

- **Internet**—Job seekers can access current job vacancies as well as applications and resources such as the On-line Résumé Builder at *http://www.usajobs.opm.gov*. The USAJOBS website also provides links to federal executive agencies not covered by the database. Submit questions about the on-line application process and forms to *usajobshelp@opm.gov*. For problems associated with agency-specific application forms, links, or systems, contact the agency involved.
- **Touch Screen Computer Kiosk**—A network of self-service information kiosks in OPM offices and many federal buildings nationwide. At the touch of a finger, job seekers can access current job vacancies and other information.
- **Automated Telephone System**—An interactive voice response telephone system, which can be reached at (478) 757-3000 or TDD (478) 744-2299 or at 17 OPM service centers located nationwide. For local phone numbers, consult the blue pages of your telephone book.

EXCEPTED AGENCIES

The U.S. Office of Personnel Management does not provide application forms or information on jobs in excepted service agencies or organizations. The following list is excerpted from the *studentjobs.gov* section of the USAJOBS website.

Administrative Office of the U.S. Courts
http://www.uscourts.gov

Agency for International Development
http://www.usaid.gov

Central Intelligence Agency
http://www.cia.gov

Defense Intelligence Agency
http://www.dia.mil

Federal Bureau of Investigation
http://www.fbi.gov

Federal Reserve
http://www.federalreserve.gov

General Accounting Office
http://www.gao.gov

International Finance Corporation
http://www.ifc.org

International Monetary Fund
http://www.imf.org

Library of Congress
http://www.loc.gov

Multilateral Investment Guarantee Agency
http://www.miga.org

NASA JOBS
http://www.nasa.gov

National Security Agency
http://www.nsa.gov

Pan American Health Organization
http://www.paho.org

Postal Rates Commission
http://www.prc.gov

Postal Service
http://www.usps.gov

Tennessee Valley Authority
http://www.natasha.tva.gov/

United Nations Children's Fund
http://www.unicef.org

United Nations Development Program
http://www.undp.org

United Nations Institute for Training and Research
http://www.unitar.org

United Nations Population Fund
http://www.unfpa.org

United Nations Secretariat
http://www.un.org/documents/st.htm

U.S. Court of Federal Claims
http://www.uscfc.uscourts.gov

U.S. Department of State
http://www.state.gov

U.S. House of Representatives
http://www.house.gov

U.S. Mission to the United Nations
http://www.un.int./usa

U.S. Nuclear Regulatory Commission
http://www.nrc.gov

U.S. Senate
http://www.senate.gov

U.S. Senator Barbara Boxer
http://www.senate.gov/~boxer/

U.S. Supreme Court
http://www.supremecourtus.gov

World Bank
http://www.worldbank.org

APPENDIX V
EMPLOYMENT WEBSITES

The following are websites useful to job seekers, but keep in mind that information on the Internet is always changing. If a particular site proves unavailable at the URL listed, try a web search using keywords to find its new location or a similar resource.

I. POLITICAL

Political Resources—Political Job Board
http://www.politicalresources.com

Politix Group
http://www.politixgroup.com

II. GOVERNMENT

AllCityJobs.com
http://www.allcityjobs.com

Government Job.net
http://www.govtjob.net

Govtjobs.com
http://www.govtjobs.com

Careers in Government
http://www.careersingovernment.com

III. NONPROFIT JOBS

Community Career Center
http://www.nonprofitjobs.org

Non-Profit Career Network
http://www.nonprofitcareer.com

Opportunity NOCS
http://www.opportunitynocs.org

Idealist.org
http://www.idealist.org

IV. ENVIRONMENTAL JOBS

Environmental Jobs and Careers
http://www.ejobs.org

Environmental Career Center
http://www.environmentalcareer.com

Environmental Career Opportunities
http://www.ecojobs.com

V. HUMAN RIGHTS

Derechos Human Rights
http://www.derechos.org

OneWorld.net
http://www.oneworld.net

University of Minnesota Human Rights Center Training & Field Opportunities
http://www.hrusa.org

Human Rights Internet
http://www.hri.ca

ReliefWeb
http://www.reliefweb.int

VI. SERVICE OPPORTUNITIES

Corporation for National and Community Service
http://www.nationalservice.org

ServeNet
http://www.servenet.org

APPENDIX VI
GRADUATE SCHOOL PROGRAMS

A. PUBLIC AFFAIRS, PUBLIC ADMINISTRATION, PUBLIC POLICY

The following schools offer programs in public affairs, public administration, or public policy. For more information, check out the websites of the National Association of Schools of Public Affairs and Administration *(www.naspaa. org)* and/or the Association of Schools of Public Policy Analysis and Management *(www.appam.org)*.

ALABAMA

Auburn University at Auburn
Dept. of Political Science
8030 Haley Center
Auburn, AL 36849
http://www.auburn.edu/mpa

Birmingham-Southern College
Office of Graduate Programs
900 Arkadelphia Road
Box 549052
Birmingham, AL 35254
http://www.bsc.edu/programs/mppm/

The University of Alabama at Birmingham
Dept. of Government and Public Service
U238, 1530 3rd Avenue South
Birmingham, AL 35294-3350
http://www.uab.edu/graduate/documents/
  areas/publicad.htm

University of Alabama, Tuscaloosa
Dept. of Political Science
Box 870213
Tuscaloosa, AL 35487-0213
http://www.as.ua.edu/psc/grad.html

Auburn University at Montgomery
Dept. of Political Science and Public
  Administration
P.O. Box 244023
Montgomery, AL 36124-4023
http://sciences.aum.edu/popa/index.htm

University of South Alabama
Dept. of Political Science/Criminal
  Justice
Room 226
Mobile, AL 36688-0002
http://www.southalabama.edu/
  graduateprograms/artsandsci.html

ALASKA

University of Alaska
Dept. of Public Administration
3211 Providence Drive
Anchorage, AK 99508
http://mpa.alaska.edu

University of Alaska Southeast
Public Administration Program
11120 Glacier Highway
Juneau, AK 99801
http://www.uas.alaska.edu/uas/padmintro.
  html

ARIZONA

Arizona State University
School of Public Affairs
P.O. Box 870603
Tempe, AZ 85287-0603
http://www.asu.edu/copp/publicaffairs/

The University of Arizona
School of Public Administration and
  Policy
405 McClelland Hall
Tucson, AZ 85721
http://www.bpa.arizona.edu/programs/spa

ARKANSAS

University of Arkansas, Fayetteville
Dept. of Political Science
428 Old Main
Fayetteville, AR 72701
http://www.uark.edu/depts/plscinfo

University of Arkansas at Little Rock
Graduate Program in Public
2801 S University Avenue
Little Rock, AR 72204-1099
http://www.ualr.edu/~iog

Arkansas State University
Dept. of Political Science
P.O. Box 1750
State University, AR 72467-1750
http://graduateschool.astate.edu/

CALIFORNIA

California State University, Bakersfield
Dept. of Public Policy and Administration
9001 Stockdale Highway
Bakersfield, CA 93311-1099
http://www.csubak.edu/BPA/pagehome.ht

California State University, Chico
Dept. of Political Science
Chico, CA 95929-0455
http://www.csuchico.edu/pols/
  about-public-admin.html

California State University, Dominguez Hills
Dept. of Public Administration,
  SBS D311
School of Business and Public
  Administration
1000 E Victoria Street
Carson, CA 90747
http://som.csudh.edu/depts/pub_admin/
  Index.htm

Cal State University, Fresno
Dept. of Political Science
5340 North Campus Drive
Fresno, CA 93740-0019
http://www.csufresno.edu/PoliticalScience
  /requirements/mpa.html

California State University, Fullerton
Division of Criminal Justice and Political
  Science
P.O. Box 6848
Fullerton, CA 92834-6848
http://hss.fullerton.edu/polsci/mpa_home.
  htm

California State University, Hayward
Dept. of Public Administration
25800 Carlos Bee Boulevard
Hayward, CA 94542
http://www.csuhayward/alss/puad/

California State University, Long Beach
Graduate Center for Public Policy and
    Administration
1250 Bellflower Boulevard
Long Beach, CA 90840-4602
http://www.csulb.edu/~chhs/dptframes.ht

California State University, Los Angeles
Dept. of Political Science
5151 State University Drive
Los Angeles, CA 90032-8226
http://www.calstatela.edu/dept/pol_sci/M
    SPA1.html

California State Polytechnic University
Political Science Department
3801 West Temple Avenue
Building 94, Room 303
Pomona, CA 91768-4055
http://www.class.csupomona.edu/pls/
    pls.html

California State University, Sacramento
MPPA Program
6000 J Street
Sacramento, CA 95819-6081
http://www.csus.edu/mppa

**California State University, San
    Bernardino**
Dept. of Public Administration
Jack Bown Hall, Room 456
San Bernardino, CA 92407-2397
http://www.sbpa.csusb.edu/pa/

California State University, Stanislaus
Dept. of Political and Public
    Administration
325 North Broadway
Turlock, CA 95380
http://www.csustan.edu/ppa/index.html

California State University, Northridge
M.P.A. Program
Dept. of Political Science
18111 Nordhoff Street
Northridge, CA 91330-8362
http://www.csun.edu/~hcpol009/

Golden Gate University
Graduate School of Liberal Studies and
    Public Affairs
536 Mission Street
San Francisco, CA 94105-2968
http://www.ggu.edu/schools/ls&pa/
    public_admin/home.html

**The Monterey Institute of International
    Studies**
Graduate School of International Policy
    Studies
425 Van Buren Street
Monterey, CA 93940
http://fgsib.miis.edu/

National University
Dept. of Public Policy and Administration
11255 North Torrey Pines Road
La Jolla, CA 92037
http://www.nu.edu/academics/index.html

The Naval Postgraduate School
Department of Systems Management
555 Dyer Road
Monterey, CA 93943-5000
http://web.nps.navy.mil/~sm

Pepperdine University
School of Public Policy
24255 Pacific Coast Highway
Malibu, CA 90263
http://pepperdine.edu/PublicPolicy

The RAND Graduate School
RAND Graduate School of Policy Studies
Ph.D. in Policy Analysis
1700 Main Street
P.O. Box 2138
Santa Monica, CA 90407-2138
http://www.rgs.edu

San Diego State University
School of Public Administration and
    Urban Studies
5500 Campanile Drive
San Diego, CA 92182-4505
http://www.sdsu.edu/academicprog/
    publcadm.html

San Francisco State University
Dept. of Public Administration
1600 Holloway Avenue
San Francisco, CA 94132
http://bss.sfsu.edu/~mpa/

San Jose State University
Dept. of Political Science
One Washington Square
San Jose, CA 95112-0119
http://www.sjsu.edu/depts/PoliSci/

University of California, Berkeley
Richard and Rhoda Goldman School of
    Public Policy
2607 Hearst Avenue
Berkeley, CA 94720-7320
http://www.berkeley.edu

University of California, Los Angeles
School of Public Policy and Social
    Research
3284-D Public Policy Building
Box 951656
Los Angeles, CA 90095-1656
http://www.sppsr.ucla.edu

University of La Verne
Dept. of Public Administration
2220 3rd Street
La Verne, CA 91750
http://www.ulv.edu/acdem/dept/padm/
    padmp.html

University of San Francisco
College of Professional Studies
Dept. of Public Management
2130 Fulton Street
San Francisco, CA, 94117-1080
http://www.cps.usfca.edu/

University of Southern California
School of Policy, Planning, and
    Development
Ralph and Goldy Lewis Hall, Room 312
650 Childs Way
Los Angeles, CA 90089-0626
http://www.usc.edu/dept/sppd/index.html

COLORADO

University of Colorado at Denver
Graduate School of Public Affairs
P.O. Box 173364, Campus Box 142
Denver, CO 80217-3364
http://www.cudenver.edu/public/gspa

University of Denver
Graduate Program in Public Policy
Mary Reed Building Suite 107
2199 S University Boulevard
Denver, CO 80208
http://www.du.edu/mpp

CONNECTICUT

University of Connecticut
Master of Public Affairs Program
Box U-1106
421 Whitney Road
Storrs Mansfield, CT 06269-1106
http://www.mpa.uconn.edu/

University of New Haven
Dept. of Public Management
300 Orange Avenue
West Haven, CT 06516-1999
http://www.newhaven.edu/

DELAWARE

University of Delaware
School of Urban Affairs and Public
   Policy
182 Graham Hall
Newark, DE 19716-7301
http://www.udel.edu/suapp

DISTRICT OF COLUMBIA

American University
Dept. of Public Administration
Ward Circle Building, Room 322
Washington, DC 20016-8011
http://www.american.edu/academic.depts/
   spa/spa-home.htm

The George Washington University
Dept. of Public Administration
805 21st Street, NW
Washington, DC 20052
http://www.gwu.edu/~pad/

Georgetown University
Public Policy Institute
3600 N Street, NW
Room 200
Washington, DC 20007
http://www.georgetown.edu/grad/gppi

Howard University
Department of Political Science
112 Douglas Hall
Washington, DC 20059
http://www.howard.edu/polisci/graduate/g
   radhome

FLORIDA

Florida Atlantic University
School of Public Administration
220 SE 2nd Avenue
Fort Lauderdale, FL 33301
http://fau.edu/divdept/caupa/

Florida Gulf Coast University
Division of Public Administration
10501 FGCU Boulevard, South
Fort Myers, FL 33965-6565

Florida International University
College of Health and Urban Affairs
North Miami Campus, ACI-281
3000 NE 151st Street
North Miami, FL 33181
http://www.fiu.edu/~cupa

The Florida State University
Askew School of Public Administration
   and Policy
614 Bellamy Building
Tallahassee, FL 32306-2250
http://www.fsu.edu/~spap/

Nova Southeastern University
3100 SW Ninth Avenue
Fort Lauderdale, FL 33314
http://www.sbe.nova.edu

Troy State University
1020 N Orlando Avenue, Suite Z
Winter Park, FL 32789
http://www.troyst.edu

University of Central Florida
Dept. of Public Administration
HPA 343
Orlando, FL 32816-1395
http://www.cohpa.ucf.edu/

University of Miami
Public Administration Program
P.O. Box 248047
Coral Gables, FL 33124
http://www.miami.edu/politicalscience.htm

University of North Florida
Dept. of Political Science and Public
   Administration
4567 St. Johns Bluff Road, S
Jacksonville, FL 32250
http://www.unf.edu/coas/
   polsci-pubadmin/

University of South Florida
Dept. of Government and International
   Affairs
4202 E Fowler Avenue, SOC 107
Tampa, FL 33620-8100
http://www.cas.usf.edu/pad/index.html

The University of West Florida
Division of Administrative Studies
Building 85, Room 160
11000 University Parkway
Pensacola, FL 32514-5750
http://www.uwf.edu/~justice/

GEORGIA

Albany State University
Dept. of History and Political Science
504 College Drive
Albany, GA 31705
http://argus.asurams.edu/asu/Academics/
   pols.htm

Augusta State University
Dept. of Political Science
2500 Walton Way
Augusta, GA 30904
http://www.aug.edu/political_science

Clark Atlanta University
Dept. of Public Administration
223 James P. Brawley Drive, SW
Atlanta, GA 30314
http://www.cau.edu

Columbus State University
Dept. of Political Science
4225 University Avenue
Columbus, GA 31907-5645
http://polsci.colstate.edu/pg7.htm

Georgia College and State University
Dept. of Government and Sociology
Campus Box 18
Milledgeville, GA 31061-0490
http://www.gcsu.edu/acad_affairs/
   coll_artsci/gov_soc/

Georgia Institute of Technology
School of Public Policy
685 Cherry Street
Campus Box 0345
Atlanta, GA 30332-0345
http://www.gatech.edu/spp/

Georgia Southern University
M.P.A. Program
Dept. of Political Science
P.O. Box 8101
Statesboro, GA 30460
http://www2.gasou.edu/facstaff/mpa/

Georgia State University
Dept. of Public Administration and Urban
   Studies
University Plaza
Atlanta, GA 30303-3083
http://www.gsu.edu/~wwwsps

Kennesaw State University
M.P.A. Program
1000 Chastain Road
Kennesaw, GA 30144-5591
http://www.kennesaw.edu/pub hum.

Savannah State University
P.O. Box 20385
Savannah, GA 31404
http://www.savstate.edu/mpa

State University of West Georgia
Dept. of Political Science
1500 Maple Street
Carrollton, GA 30118
http://www.westga.edu/~polisci/

The University of Georgia
Dept. of Political Science
Baldwin Hall
Athens, GA 30602-1615
http://www.uga.edu/~pol-sci/

Valdosta State University
Dept. of Political Science
1500 N Patterson
Valdosta, GA 31698-0056
http://www.valdosta.edu/mpa/online/

GUAM

University of Guam
Dept. of Public Administration
UOG Station
Mangilao, GU 96923
http://uog2.uog.edu/cbpa/index.html

HAWAII

University of Hawaii
Public Administration Program
2424 Maile Way
Honolulu, HI 96822
http://www.puba.hawaii.edu/
   ProgramOverview.htm

IDAHO

Boise State University
Dept. of Public Policy and Administration
1910 University Drive
Boise, ID 83725
http://www.ppa.boisestate.edu

University of Idaho
Dept. of Political Science
Admin. 205
Moscow, ID 83844
http://www.uidaho.edu/bpar/mpa.html

ILLINOIS

DePaul University
Public Services Graduate Program
243 S Wabash Avenue
Room 700
Chicago, IL 60604
http://www.depaul.edu/~pubserv/

Governors State University
College of Business and Public
   Administration
Graduate Program in Public
   Administration
University Park, IL 60466
http://www.govst.edu/users/gcbpa/

Illinois Institute of Technology
M.P.A. Program
IIT Downtown Campus
Room 659
Chicago, IL 60661-3691
http://www.grad.iit.edu/graduatecollege/
   programs/pubadmin.html

Northern Illinois University
Division of Public Administration
DeKalb, IL 60115
http://www.niu.edu/pub_ad/paweb.html

Roosevelt University
School of Policy Studies
430 S Michigan Avenue
Chicago, IL 60605-1394
http://www.roosevelt.edu/mpa

Southern Illinois University, Carbondale
M.P.A. Program
Carbondale, IL 62901
http://www.siu.edu/departments/cola/
   polysci/mpa.html

**Southern Illinois University at
   Edwardsville**
Dept. of Public Administration and Policy
   Analysis
Box 1457
Edwardsville, IL 62026
http://siue.edu/papa/

University of Chicago
Harris School of Public Policy Studies
1155 East 60th Street
Suite 151A
Chicago, IL 60637
http://www.uchicago.edu/

The University of Illinois at Chicago
M.P.A. Program (M/C278)
412 South Peoria
Chicago, IL 60607-7064
http://www.uic.edu/cuppa/mpa/

University of Illinois at Springfield
School of Public Affairs and
   Administration
PAC 440, Sheppard Road
Springfield, IL 62794-9243
http://www.uis.edu/~ipa/mainhtm.htm

INDIANA

Indiana State University
Dept. of Political Science
Terre Haute, IN 47809
http://web.indstate.edu/polisci/

Indiana University, Bloomington
School of Public and Environmental
   Affairs
1315 E Tenth Street
Bloomington, IN 47405-2100
http://www.indiana.edu/~speaweb/index.
   html

Indiana University, Northwest
Division of Public and Economic Affairs
3400 Broadway
Gary, IN 46408
http://www.iun.indiana.edu/spea/
   spea.htm

**Indiana University-Purdue University,
   Fort Wayne**
Division of Public and Environmental
   Affairs
2101 Coliseum Boulevard, E
Fort Wayne, IN 46805-1499
http://www.ipfw.edu/spea/

**Indiana University-Purdue University,
   Indianapolis**
SPEA
3025B, IUPUI
801 W Michigan Street
Indianapolis, IN 46202-5152
http://www.iupui.edu/home/env.html

Indiana University South Bend Campus
SPEA
1800 Mishawaka Avenue
South Bend, IN 46615
http://www.iusb.edu/~spea/

IOWA

Drake University
Dept. of Public Administration
College of Business and Public
   Administration
Aliber Hall
Des Moines, IA 50311
http://www.drake.edu/cbpa/

Iowa State University
515 Ross Hall
Ames, IA 50011-1204
http://www.iastate.edu/~polsci/mpa.
   html

KANSAS

Kansas State University
226 Waters Hall
Manhattan, KS 66506
http://www.ksu.edu/polsci

The University of Kansas
Dept. of Public Administration
318 Blake Hall
Lawrence, KS 66045
http://www.ukans.edu/~kupa

Wichita State University
Hugo Wall School of Urban and Public
    Affairs
1845 N Fairmount Street
Wichita, KS 67260-0155
http://www.mrc.twsu.edu/kpfc/

KENTUCKY

Eastern Kentucky University
Dept. of Government
113 McCreary Hall
Richmond, KY 40475-3122
http://www.socialscience.eku.edu/
    GOV/MPA/MPAn.htm

Kentucky State University
School of Public Administration
400 E Main Street
Frankfort, KY 40601
http://www.kysu.edu/PublicAdmin/
    Default.html

Murray State University
Dept. of Political Science and Legal Studies
553 Business Building
Murray, KY 42071-3314
http://www.mursuky.edu/qacd/cbpa/
    bpa-web.htm

Northern Kentucky University
Dept. of Political Science
Landrum 217K, Nunn Drive
Highland Heights, KY 41099-2207
http://www.nku.edu/~mpa/

University of Kentucky
Martin School of Public Policy and
    Administration
415 Patterson Office Tower
Lexington, KY 40506-0027
http://www.uky.edu/rgs/martinschool/

University of Louisville
College of Business and Public
    Administration
426 W Bloom
Louisville, KY 40208
http://cbpa.louisville.edu/AcademicProgr
    ams/MPA.htm

Western Kentucky University
Public Administration Program
Dept. of Government

Bowling Green, KY 42101-3576
http://www.wku.edu/Dept/Academic/
    AHSS/Government/govt.htm

LOUISIANA

Grambling State University
Dept. of Political Science and Public
    Administration
Grambling, LA 71245
http://www.gram.edu/COLA/department_
    of_political_science.htm

Louisiana State University
Public Administration Institute
3200 CEBA
Baton Rouge, LA 70803
http://www.bus.lsu.edu/pai/

Southern University
Nelson Mandela School of Public Policy
    and Urban Affairs
Box 9656
Baton Rouge, LA 70816
http://publicpolicy.subr.edu/

University of New Orleans
College of Urban and Public Affairs
New Orleans, LA 70148
http://www.uno.edu

MAINE

The University of Maine at Augusta
Dept. of Public Administration
46 University Drive
Augusta, ME 04330
http://www.uma.maine.edu/academics/
    uacadprograms.html

University of Maine
Dept. of Public Administration
5754 N Stevens Hall
Room 239
Orono, ME 04469-5754
http://www.ume.maine.edu/pubadmin/

University of Southern Maine
Public Policy and Management Program
96 Falmouth Street
PO Box 9300
Portland, ME 04104-9300
http://www.muskie.usm.maine.edu

MARYLAND

Johns Hopkins University
Institute of Policy Studies
3400 N Charles Street
Baltimore, MD 21218
http://www.jhu.edu/~ips

University of Baltimore
Dept. of Government and Public
    Administration
School of Public Affairs
1420 N Charles Street
Baltimore, MD 21201-5779
http://www.ubalt.edu/cla_dgpa/

**University of Maryland, Baltimore
    County**
Policy Science Graduate Program
1000 Hilltop Circle
626 Administration Building
Baltimore, MD 21250
http://www.umbc.edu

University of Maryland, College Park
School of Public Affairs
2101G Van Munching Hall
College Park, MD 20742-1821
http://www.puaf.umd.edu

MASSACHUSETTS

Bridgewater State College
Dept. of Political Science
Summer Street House
Bridgewater, MA 02325
http://www.bridgew.edu/DEPTS/POLISCI
    /index.HTM

Clark University
COPACE
950 Main Street
Worcester, MA 01610-1477
http://www.copace.clarku.edu

Harvard University
The John F. Kennedy School of
    Government
79 JFK Street
Cambridge, MA 02138
http://www.ksg.harvard.edu

Northeastern University
Dept. of Political Science
303 Meserve Hall
Boston, MA 02115
http://www.casdn.neu.edu/~polisci/

Suffolk University
School of Management
8 Ashburton Place
Boston, MA 02108-2770
http://www.sawyer.suffolk.edu

University of Massachusetts, Amherst
Center for Public Policy and
    Administration
416 Thompson Hall
Amherst, MA 01003
http://pubpol1.sbs.umass.edu/

University of Massachusetts at Boston
John W. McCormack Institute of Public
    Affairs
100 Morrissey Boulevard
Boston, MA 02125-3393
http://www.mccormack.umb.edu

MICHIGAN

Central Michigan University
Dept. of Political Science
245 Anspach Hall
Mt. Pleasant, MI 48859
http://www.cmich.edu/PSC.HTML

Eastern Michigan University
Dept. of Political Science
601 Pray-Harrold
Ypsilanti, MI 48197
http://www.emich.edu/public/polisci/
    mpaprog.htm

Grand Valley State University
School of Public and Nonprofit
    Administration
401 W Fulton Street
2nd Floor
Grand Rapids, MI 49504-4100
http://www.gvsu.edu/spna

Michigan State University
Program in Public Policy and
    Administration
324 South Kedzie Hall
East Lansing, MI 48824-1032
http://www.ssc.msu.edu/~pls/mpa

Northern Michigan University
Dept. of Political Science
1401 Presque Isle Avenue
259 Magers Hall
Marquette, MI 49855-5257
http://www.nmu.edu/mpa/

Oakland University
Dept. of Political Science
418 Varner Hall
Rochester, MI 48309-4401
http://www.oakland.edu/
    political-science/mpa/index.htm

University of Michigan, Ann Arbor
The Gerald R. Ford School of Public
    Policy
440 Lorch Hall
611 Tappan Street
Ann Arbor, MI 48109-1220
http://www.Fordschool.umich.edu/

University of Michigan, Dearborn
Public Administration Program
4901 Evergreen Road
Dearborn, MI 48128-1491
http://umd.umich.edu

University of Michigan, Flint
Department of Public Administration
Flint, MI 48502
http://www.flint.umich.edu/Departments/
    graduate/MPA.htm

Wayne State University
Graduate Program in Public Administration
2049 FAB
Detroit, MI 48202
http://www.pol.sci.wayne.edu/pol.sci.2/
    grad/mpa.html

Western Michigan University
School of Public Affairs and
    Administration
Kalamazoo, MI 49008-3899
http://www.wmich.edu/spaa/

MINNESOTA

Hamline University
Graduate School of Public Administration
    and Management
1536 Hewitt Avenue, N
St. Paul, MN 55104-1284
http://web.hamline.edu/graduate/gpam/

University of Minnesota
Humphrey Institute of Public Affairs
300 Humphrey Center
301 – 19th Avenue, S
Room 163
Minneapolis, MN 55455
http://www.hhh.umn.edu

MISSISSIPPI

Jackson State University
Dept. of Public Policy and Administration
3825 Ridgewood Road
Box 18
Jackson, MS 39217
http://www.jsums.edu/liberalarts/
    pubpolicy/index.html

Mississippi State University
Dept. of Political Science
P.O. Box PC
121 Bowen Hall
Mississippi State, MS 39762
http://www.msstate.edu/Dept/
    PoliticalScience/

Mississippi Valley State University
Social Science Building, Office A
Box 7273
Itta Bena, MS 38941
http://www.msvu.edu

MISSOURI

Park College
Graduate School of Public Affairs
934 Wyandotte
Kansas City, MO 64105
http://www.park.edu/pubadm/pubadm.htm

Southwest Missouri State University
901 S National Avenue
Springfield, MO 65804-0094
http://www.smsu.edu/PolSci/MPA.htm

St. Louis University
Dept. of Public Policy Studies and
    Administration
3663 O'Donnell Hall
St. Louis, MO 63103
http://www.slu.edu/colleges/cops/

University of Missouri, Columbia
Graduate School of Public Affairs
265 McReynolds Hall
Columbia, MO 65211-2015
http://gspa.missouri.edu

University of Missouri, Kansas City
Bloch School of Business and Public
    Administration
5100 Cherry
Kansas City, MO 64110-2499
http://www.bsbpa.umkc.edu

University of Missouri, St. Louis
Public Policy Administration Program
406 Tower
8001 Natural Bridge Road
St. Louis, MO 63121-4499
http://www.umsl.edu/divisions/graduate/
    mppa

MONTANA

Montana State University
Dept. of Political Science
Bozeman, MT 59715
http://www.montana.edu/wwwpo/

NEBRASKA

University of Nebraska at Omaha
College of Public Affairs and Community
    Service
60th and Dodge Street
Omaha, NE 68182-0276
http://cid.unomaha.edu/~wwwpa/pahome.
    html

NEVADA

University of Nevada, Las Vegas
M.P.A. Program
4505 Maryland Parkway
Las Vegas, NV 89154
http://www.nscee.edu/unlv/Colleges/
  Business/PublicAdmin/pubadmn.html

NEW JERSEY

Fairleigh Dickinson University
Public Administration Institute
Mailstop H-DH2-13
1000 River Road
Teaneck, NJ 07666
http://www.fdu.edu/centers/pai.html

Kean University
Dept. of Public Administration
Morris Avenue
Union, NJ 07083
http://www.kean.edu/AcademicSchools/
  BusGovTech.htm

Princeton University
Woodrow Wilson School
Robertson Hall
Princeton, NJ 08544-1013
http://www.wws.princeton.edu/

Rutgers University, Camden
Graduate Department of Public Policy
  and Administration
401 Cooper Street
Camden, NJ 08102
http://camden-www.rutgers.edu/~publicad/

Rutgers University, Newark
Graduate Department of Public
  Administration
360 Dr. Martin L. King Boulevard
Room 701
Newark, NJ 07102
http://rutgers-newark.rutgers.edu/
  pubadmin

Seton Hall University
Center for Public Service
Kozlowski Hall
South Orange, NJ 07079
http://artsci.shu.edu/cps/

NEW MEXICO

New Mexico State University
M.P.A. Program
Dept. of Government
Las Cruces, NM 88003-0001
http://www.nmsu.edu/~mpa

The University of New Mexico
School of Public Administration
3016 Social Sciences Building
Albuquerque, NM 87131
http://www.unm.edu/~spagrad

NEW YORK

Baruch College, CUNY
School of Public Affairs
17 Lexington Avenue
Box C-0305
New York, NY 10010
http://www.baruch.cuny.edu/spa/

Binghamton University
Dept. of Political Science
P.O. Box 6000
Binghamton, NY 13902
http://www.binghamton.edu/mpa/
  index.html

Columbia University
Graduate Program in Public Policy and
  Administration
420 West 118th Street, #1417
New York, NY 10027
http://www.columbia.edu/cu/sipa

Cornell University
Institute for Public Affairs
472 Hollister Hall
Ithaca, NY 14853
http://www.cfe.cornell.edu/cipa

John Jay College, CUNY
445 West 59th Street
Room 3254, North Hall
New York, NY 10019
http://www.jjay.cuny.edu/academic/
  graduate/pub_admin/pub_admin.html

Long Island University, Brooklyn
Public Administration Program
Brooklyn Campus, University Plaza
School of Business, Public Administration
  and Information Science
Brooklyn, NY 11201
http://www.brooklyn.liunet.edu/cwis/
  bklyn/sbpais/business.html

**Long Island University, C. W. Post
  Campus**
Health Care and Public Administration
  Dept.
720 Northern Boulevard
Brookville, NY 11548
http://www.cwpost.liunet.edu/cwis/cwp/
  colofman/public/public.html

Marist College
3399 North Road
Poughkeepsie, NY 12601
http://www.marist.edu/graduate/pa.html

Medgar Evers College
Social Science Division
1650 Bedford Avenue
Office B-2015H
Brooklyn, NY 11225
http://www.mec.cuny.edu/administ.htm

New School University
R. J. Milano Graduate School of
  Management and Urban Policy
66 Fifth Avenue
7th Floor
New York, NY 10011
http://www.newschool.edu/milano/

New York University
Wagner Graduate School of Public
  Service
4 Washington Square North
New York, NY 10003
http://www.nyu.edu/wagner/

Pace University
Dept. of Public Administration
Lubin Graduate Center
1 Martine Avenue
Room 324
White Plains, NY 10606-1909
http://www.pace.edu/dyson/graduate/
  ms_public_admin.htm

The Sage Colleges
Division of Management,
  Communications, and Legal Studies
140 New Scotland Avenue
Albany, NY 12208
http://www.sage.edu/divisions/mcls/
  Welcome.html

**State University of New York (SUNY)
  at Albany**
Dept. of Public Administration and
  Policy
135 Western Avenue
Albany, NY 12222
http://www.albany.edu/gspa

**State University of New York (SUNY)
  College at Brockport**
255 Faculty Office Building
Brockport, NY 14420-2961
http://cc.brockport.edu/~pubadmin/index.
  html

Syracuse University
Dept. of Public Administration
The Maxwell School
215 Eggers Hall
Syracuse, NY 13244-1090
http://www.maxwell.syr.edu/pa/papage.ht

NORTH CAROLINA

Appalachian State University
Dept. of Political Science and Criminal
    Justice
P.O. Box 32107
Boone, NC 28608
http://www.pscj.appstate.edu/contact.html

Duke University
Terry Sanford Institute of Public Policy
Box 90239
Durham, NC 27708-0239
http://www.pubpol.duke.edu

East Carolina University
Dept. of Political Science
A-124 Brewster
Greenville, NC 27858-4353
http://www.ecu.edu/polsci/mpa_in$9elht

North Carolina Central University
Public Administration Program
P.O. Box 19552
Durham, NC 27707
http://www.nccu.edu/artsci/polysci/
    gprog_pa.htm

North Carolina State University
Dept. of Political Science and Public
    Administration
Campus Box 8102
Raleigh, NC 27695-8102
http://www.chass.ncsu.edu/pa/index.html

**University of North Carolina at Chapel
    Hill**
Institute of Government
CB#3330 Knapp Building
Chapel Hill, NC 27599-3330
http://ncinfo.iog.edu/uncmpa/

**University of North Carolina at
    Charlotte**
Dept. of Political Science
9201 University City Boulevard
Charlotte, NC 28223-0001
http://www.uncc.edu/gradmiss/

**University of North Carolina at
    Greensboro**
Dept. of Political Science
P.O. Box 26170
Greensboro, NC 27402-6170
http://www.uncg.edu/psc/mpa

**University of North Carolina at
    Pembroke**
Master of Science in Organizational
    Leadership and Management
P.O. Box 1510
Pembroke, NC 28372-1510
http://www.uncp.edu

**University of North Carolina at
    Wilmington**
Dept. of Political Science
601 S College Road
Wilmington, NC 28403-3297
http://www.uncwil.edu/mpa

Western Carolina University
Dept. of Political Science and Public
    Affairs
Cullowhee, NC 28723
http://www.wcu.edu/as/politicalscience/

NORTH DAKOTA

University of North Dakota
Dept. of Political Science and Public
    Administration
Box 8379
University Station
Grand Forks, ND 58202-8379
http://www.und.edu/dept/collegeb/

OHIO

Bowling Green State University
Master's Program in Public Administration
    and International Affairs
124 Williams Hall
Bowling Green, OH 43403
http://www.bgsu.edu/departments/pols/m
    pa/index.html

Cleveland State University
Levin College of Urban Affairs
1717 Euclid Avenue
Cleveland, OH 44115
http://urban.csuohio.edu

Kent State University
Dept. of Political Science
302 Bowman Hall
Kent, OH 44242-0001
http://www.kent.edu/mpa.htm

The Ohio State University
School of Public Policy and Management
College of Social and Behavioral
    Sciences
60 Medbrook Way
Columbus, OH 43214
http://ppm.ohio-state.edu

Ohio University
Dept. of Political Science
222 Bentley Hall
Athens, OH 45701-2979
http://www-as.phy.ohiou.edu/Departments/
    PoliSci/mpa.html

The University of Akron
Dept. of Public Administration and Urban
    Studies
265 Polsky Building
Akron, OH 44325-7904
http://www.uakron.edu/paus/

University of Cincinnati
Dept. of Political Science
1013 Crosley Tower (#375)
Cincinnati, Oh 45221
http://www.uc.edu/mpa/

University of Dayton
Dept. of Political Science
MPA Program
Dayton, OH 45469-1425
http://www.udayton.edu/~mpa

The University of Toledo
Dept. of Political Science and Public
    Administration
2801 W Bancroft Street
Toledo, OH 43606-3390
http://www.utoledo.edu/www/
    poli-sci/pshome.html

Wright State University
Dept. of Urban Affairs and Geography
166 Millett Hall
3640 Colonel Glenn Highway
Dayton, OH 45435-0001
http://www.wright.edu/cupa/
    graduate.htm

OKLAHOMA

The University of Oklahoma
Public Administration Program
455 W Lindsey Street
Room 305
Norman, OK 73019-2003
http://www.ou.edu/cas/psc/mpaprog.htm

OREGON

Portland State University
Dept. of Public Administration
730 SW Mill Street
P.O. Box 751
Portland, OR 97207
http://www.upa.pdx.edu/PA/

University of Oregon
Dept. of Planning, Public Policy and
    Management
Eugene, OR 97403-1209
http://utopia.uoregon.edu

Willamette University
Atkinson Graduate School of
    Management
900 State Street
Salem, OR 97301-3931
http://www.willamette.edu/agsm/

PENNSYLVANIA

Carnegie Mellon University
5000 Forbes Avenue
Pittsburgh, PA 15213-3890
http://www.heinz.cmu.edu

Marywood University
Dept. of Public Administration
2300 Adams Avenue
Scranton, PA 18509
http://www.marywood.edu/gas/
    departments/

**The Pennsylvania State University at
    Harrisburg**
M.P.A. Program
777 W Harrisburg Pike
Middletown, PA 17057-4898
http://www.hbg.psu.edu/spa

Shippensburg University
Dept. of Political Science
1871 Old Main Drive
Grove Hall 420
Shippensburg, PA 17257-2299
http://www.ship.edu

Slippery Rock University
Dept. of Government and Public Affairs
209 Spotts World Culture Building
Slippery Rock, PA 16057-1326
http://www.sru.edu/

University of Pennsylvania
School of Arts and Sciences
3814 Walnut Street
Philadelphia, PA 19104-6197
http://www.upenn.edu/fels/

University of Pittsburgh
GSPIA
3G07 Posvar Hall
Pittsburgh, PA 15260
http://www.gspia.pitt.edu

Villanova University
Dept. of Political Science
800 Lancaster Avenue
Villanova, PA 19085
http://www.psc.villanova.edu

PUERTO RICO

University of Puerto Rico
Graduate School of Public Administration
Box 21839
San Juan, PR 00931-1839
http://upracd.upr.clu.edu:9090/~admipubl

RHODE ISLAND

**University of Rhode Island and Rhode
    Island College**
Political Science Dept.
600 Mt. Pleasant Avenue
Providence, RI 02908
http://nick.uri.edu/prov/mpa/mpa.html
http://www.ric.edu/polisci/

SOUTH CAROLINA

Clemson University
Dept. of Political Science
Brackett Hall 230
Clemson, SC 29634-1354
http://www.business.clemson.edu/mpa

The University of Charleston
Masters of Public Administration
66 George Street
Charleston, SC 29424
http://www.cofc.edu/

The University of South Carolina
Dept. of Government and International
    Studies
349 Gambrell Hall
Columbia, SC 29208
http://www.cla.sc.edu/gint/gradmpa/
    mpa.html

SOUTH DAKOTA

The University of South Dakota
Dept. of Political Science
414 E Clark Street
Vermillion, SD 57069-2390
http://www.usd.edu/polsci/

TENNESSEE

East Tennessee State University
Master of Public Management Program
P.O. Box 70699
Johnson City, TN 37614
http://pub-mgmt.etsu.edu/

Tennessee State University
Institute of Government
330 10th Avenue, N
Nashville, TN 37203-3401
http://duke.tnstate.edu/pubadmin/

The University of Memphis
Division of Public Administration
136 McCord Hall
Memphis, TN 38152-6108
http://www.memphis.edu/~gapubaddm/
    mps.html

**The University of Tennessee at
    Chattanooga**
Dept. of Political Science
615 McCallie Avenue
Chattanooga, TN 37403
http://www.utc.edu/~mpa

The University of Tennessee at Knoxville
Dept. of Political Science
1001 McClung Tower
Knoxville, TN 37996-0410
http://www.utk.edu/~lilliard/poli-sci.html

TEXAS

Midwestern State University
Public Administration Program
College of Health and Human Services
3410 Taft Boulevard
Wichita Falls, TX 76308-2099
http://www.mwsu.edu/~hsa/hsaintro.
    html

Southwest Texas State University
Dept. of Political Science
LA 266
San Marcos, TX 78666-4616
http://www.swt.edu/acad_depts/
    public_admin.html

Stephen F. Austin State University
Dept. of Political Science
1936 North Street
Liberal Arts North Building
Room 124
Nacogdoches, TX 75962-3045
http://titan.sfasu.edu/~f_sementelAJ/
    MPASFA.html

Texas A&M University
The George Bush School of Government
    and Public Service
Bush Academic West
Suite 1098
College Station, TX 77843-4220
http://bush.tamu.edu/home/

Texas Tech University
Dept. of Political Science
Lubbock, TX 79409-1015
http://www.ttu.edu/~cps/

University of Houston
Central Campus
Public Administration Program
Dept. of Political Science
Houston, TX 77204-3474
http://www.uh.edu/

University of Houston at Clear Lake
Programs in Government and Public
    Management
2700 Bay Area Boulevard
Houston, TX 77058
http://www.cl.uh/grad/majors/pubadmin.ht

University of North Texas
Dept. of Public Administration
P.O. Box 310617
Denton, TX 76203-0617
http://www.scs.unt.edu/depts/padm

The University of Texas at Arlington
Institute of Urban Studies
P.O. Box 19588
Arlington, TX 76019
http://www.uta.edu/supa/

The University of Texas at Austin
Lyndon B. Johnson School of Public
    Affairs
2315 Red River
Austin, TX 78705
http://www.utexas.edu/lbj/

The University of Texas at Dallas
School of Social Sciences
P.O. Box 830688
Richardson, TX 75083-0688
http://www.utdallas.edu/dept/socsci

University of Texas at El Paso
Dept. of Political Science
Benedict Hall
El Paso, TX 79968-0547
http://www.utep.edu/~librats/mpa.htm

University of Texas – Pan American
Dept. of Political Science
1201 W University Drive
Edinburg, TX 78539-2999
http://www.panam.edu/dept/polsci/

University of Texas at San Antonio
Dept. of Public Administration
501 West Durango
San Antonio, TX 78207
http://csbs.utsa.edu/divisions/socrpol/
    MPA/frames.htm

UTAH

Brigham Young University
Romney Institute of Public Management
P.O. Box 23161
760A TNRB
Provo, UT 84602-3161
http://msm.byu.edu/dept/pm

The University of Utah
Public Administration Program
260 S Central Campus Drive
Room 205
Salt Lake City, UT 84112-9154
http://www.cppa.utah.edu/cppa/
    cppa-index.html

VERMONT

University of Vermont
M.P.A. Program
503 Old Mill
Burlington, VT 05405
http://www.uvm.edu/

VIRGIN ISLANDS

University of the Virgin Islands
Division of Social Sciences
St. Thomas, VI 00802
http://www.uvi.edu/
    pub-relations/divsosci.htm

VIRGINIA

The College of William and Mary
Thomas Jefferson Public Policy Program
Morton Hall
P.O. Box 8795
Williamsburg, VA 23187-8795
http://www.wm.edu/publicpolicy

George Mason University
Dept. of Public and International Affairs
4400 University Drive
MSN 3F4
Fairfax, VA 22030-4444
http://www.gmu.edu/departments/pia/

James Madison University
Public Administration Program
Dept. of Political Science
Harrisonburg, VA 22807
http://www.jmu.edu/polisci/

Old Dominion University
Dept of Economics, Public
    Administration and Urban Studies
Hughes Hall
Room 2049
Norfolk, VA 23529-0224
http://www.odu-cbpa.org/uspa/mpa.htm

Regent University
Robertson School of Government
1000 Regent University Drive
Virginia Beach, VA 23464-9800
http://www.regent.edu/acad/schgov/

Virginia Commonwealth University
Dept. of Political Science and Public
    Administration
P.O. Box 842028
Richmond, VA 23284
http://www.vcu.edu/hasweb/pos/masters.
    html

**Virginia Polytechnic Institute and State
    University**
Center for Public Administration and
    Policy
104 Draper Road
Blacksburg, VA 24061
http://civnet.com/cpap

Virginia State University
Dept. of Political Science and Public
    Administration
Box 9062
Petersburg, VA 23806
http://www.vsu.edu/politic.html

WASHINGTON

Eastern Washington University
Public Administration Program
668 N Riverport Boulevard
Suite A
Spokane, WA 99204-1660
http://www.cbpa.ewu.edu

The Evergreen State College
Graduate Program in Public
    Administration
2700 Evergreen Parkway, NW
Olympia, WA 98502
http://www.evergreen.edu/mpa/

Seattle University
Institute of Public Service
900 Broadway
Seattle, WA 98122-4460
http://www.seattleu.edu/

University of Washington
Daniel J. Evans Graduate School of
    Public Affairs
Box 353055
Seattle, WA 98195-3055
http://www.gspa.washington.edu/

Washington State University
Dept. of Public Administration
14204 NE Salmon Creek Avenue
Vancouver, WA 98686
http://baron.vancouver.wsu.edu/fac/steel/
    pgm/mpa/frame.htm

WEST VIRGINIA

West Virginia University
School of Applied Social Sciences
P.O. Box 6322
209 Knapp Hall
Morgantown, WV 26506-6322
http://www.25.wvu.edu/coll03/pubadm/
www/

WISCONSIN

University of Wisconsin, Madison
Robert M. LaFollette School of Public
Affairs
1225 Observatory Drive
Madison, WI 53706
http://www.lafollette.wisc.edu

University of Wisconsin, Milwaukee
Dept. of Political Science
Public Administration and Public Policy
P.O. Box 413
Milwaukee, WI 53201
http://www.uwm.edu/

University of Wisconsin, Oshkosh
Dept. of Political Science, MPA
Program
800 Algoma Boulevard
Oshkosh, WI 54901
http://www.uwosh.edu/grad_school/
prog-mpa.html

WYOMING

University of Wyoming
Dept. of Political Science
Box 3197
Arts and Sciences Building
Laramie, WY 82071-3197
http://www.uwyo.edu/A&S/pols/Mpa/
index.htm

B. NONPROFIT MANAGEMENT

The following schools offer graduate (degree or certificate) programs specifically in nonprofit management. Many other schools offer graduate and/or undergraduate courses related to nonprofit management through their public administration, social work, or other departments. Courses and seminars in nonprofit management also are offered through continuing-education departments and professional associations.

CALIFORNIA

Hope International University
School of Graduate Studies
Program in Business Administration
Nonprofit Management
Fullterton, CA 92831-3138
Phone: (800) 762-1294
http://www.hiu.edu

San Francisco State University
Graduate Division
College of Behavioral and Social Sciences
Public Administration Program
San Francisco, CA 94132-1722
Phone: (415) 338-2023
http://www.sfsu.edu

University of San Francisco
College of Professional Studies
Department of Public Management
Institute for Nonprofit Administration
San Francisco, CA 94117-1080
Phone: (415) 422-6000
http://www.usfca.edu

COLORADO

Regis University
School of Professional Studies
Program in Nonprofit Management
Denver, CO 80221-1099
Phone: (800) 677-9270
http://www.regis.edu

DISTRICT OF COLUMBIA

The George Washington University
School of Business and Public
Management
Department of Public Administration
Washington, DC 20052
Phone: (202) 994-6584
http://www.gwu.edu

Trinity College
School of Professional Studies
Programs in Administration
Washington, DC 20017-1094
Phone: (202) 884-9400
http://www.trinitydc.edu

FLORIDA

University of Central Florida
College of Health and Public Affairs
Program in Public Administration
Orlando, FL 32816
Phone: (407) 823-2604
http://www.ucf.edu

ILLINOIS

DePaul University
College of Liberal Arts and Sciences
Program in Public Services
Chicago, IL 60604-2287
Phone: (312) 362-5367
http://www.depaul.edu

North Central College
Graduate Programs
Department of Leadership Studies
Naperville, IL 60566-7063
Phone: (630) 637-5840
http://www.noctrl.edu

Northwestern University
The Graduate School
Kellogg Graduate School of Management
Programs in Management
Evanston, IL 60208
http://www.nwu.edu

INDIANA

Indiana University Northwest
Division of Public and Environmental
Affairs
Gary, IN 46408-1197
Phone: (219) 980-6737
http://www.iun.indiana.edu

**Indiana University-Purdue University
Indianapolis**
Center on Philanthropy
Indianapolis, IN 46202
Phone: (317) 274-4200
http://www.iupui.edu

MASSACHUSETTS

Boston University
School of Management
Program in Public and Nonprofit
Management

Boston, MA 02215
Phone: (612) 353-2312
http://www.bu.edu

Brandeis University
Heller Graduate School
Program in Management
Waltham, MA 02454-9110
Phone: (800) 279-4105
http://www.brandeis.edu

Lesley University
School of Management
Cambridge, MA 02138-2790
Phone: (617) 349-8690
http://www.lesley.edu

Suffolk University
Frank Sawyer School of Management
Department of Public Management
Boston, MA 02108-2770
Phone: (617) 573-8302
http://www.suffolk.edu

Tufts University
Division of Graduate and Continuing
    Studies and Research
Professional and Continuing Studies
Management of Community
    Organizations Program
Medford, MA 02155
Phone: (617) 627-3700
http://www.tufts.edu

Worcester State College
Graduate Studies
Program in Non-Profit Management
Worcester, MA 01602-2597
Phone: (508) 929-8120
http://www.worcester.edu

MINNESOTA

Hamline University
Graduate School of Public Administration
    and Management
St. Paul, MN 55104-1284
Phone: (651) 523-2284
http://www.hamline.edu

Metropolitan State University
College of Management
St. Paul, MN 55106-5000
Phone: (612) 373-2724
http://www.metrostate.edu

St. Cloud State University
School of Graduate Studies
College of Social Studies
Program in Public and Nonprofit
    Institutions

St. Cloud, MN 56301-4498
Phone: (320) 255-2113
http://www.stcloudstate.edu

University of St. Thomas
Graduate Studies
Graduate School of Business
St. Paul, MN 55105-1096
Phone: (651) 962-4226
http://www.stthomas.edu

NEW JERSEY

Seton Hall University
College of Arts and Sciences
Center for Public Service
Program in Management of Nonpofit
    Organizations
South Orange, NJ 07079-2697
Phone: (973) 761-9510
http://www.shu.edu

NEW YORK

The College of Saint Rose
Graduate Studies
School of Business
Not for Profit Management Department
Albany, NY 12203-1419
Phone: (518) 454-5137
http://www.strose.edu

New School University
Robert J. Milano Graduate School of
    Management and Urban Policy
Program in Nonprofit Management
New York, NY 10011-8603
Phone: (212) 229-5462
http://www.newschool.edu

New York University
Robert F. Wagner Graduate School of
    Public Service
Program in Public Administration
New York, NY 10012-1019
Phone: (212) 998-7414
http://www.nyu.edu

Pace University
White Plains Campus
Dyson College of Arts and Sciences
Department of Public Administration
White Plains, NY 10603
Phone: (914)-422-4283
http://www.pace.edu

OHIO

Case Western Reserve University
Weatherhead School of Management
Mandel Center for Nonprofit Organizations

Cleveland, OH 44106
Phone: (216) 368-58566
http://www.cwru.edu

OKLAHOMA

Oral Roberts University
School of Business
Tulsa, OK 74171-0001
Phone: (918) 495-6236
http://www.oru.edu

OREGON

Willamette University
George H. Atkinson Graduate School of
    Management
Salem, OR 97301-3931
Phone: (503) 370-6167
http://www.willamette.edu

PENNSYLVANIA

Carlow College
Division of Professional Leadership
Pittsburgh, PA 15213-3165
Phone: (412) 578-8764
http://www.carlow.edu

Eastern College
Graduate Business Programs
Program in Nonprofit Management
St. Davids, PA 19087-3696
Phone: (610) 341-5972
http://www.eastern.edu

TEXAS

St. Edward's University
College of Professional and Graduate
    Studies
Program in Business Administration
Austin, TX 78704-6489
Phone: (512) 448-8600
http://www.stedwards.edu

WASHINGTON

Seattle University
College of Arts and Sciences
Institute of Public Service
Program in Not-for-Profit Leadership
Seattle, WA 98122
Phone: (206) 296-5900
http://www.seattleu.edu

C. URBAN AND REGIONAL PLANNING

The following is a list of universities in North America offering programs in planning accredited by the Planning Accreditation Board (PAB). Most are master's degree programs, but the list also includes undergraduate programs in planning. The list is revised annually. Changes are updated on the PAB's website, which can be accessed through the American Planning Association's education section (www.planning.org).

ALABAMA

Alabama A&M University
Department of Community Planning and Urban Studies
School of Agricultural and Environmental Sciences
308 Dawson Building
Normal, Alabama 35762
Phone: (256) 858-4990
http://www.aamu.edu/saes/HTDOCS/Departments.htm
Bachelor of Science in Urban Planning, Master of Urban and Regional Planning

ARIZONA

Arizona State University
School of Planning and Landscape Architecture
College of Architecture and Environmental Design
Architecture Building North, Room 158
Tempe, Arizona 85287-2005
Phone: (480) 965-7167
Master of Environmental Planning

The University of Arizona
School of Planning
College of Architecture, Planning, and Landscape Architecture
Architecture Building, Room 214
Tucson, Arizona 85721-0075
Phone: (520) 621-9597
http://capla.arizona.edu/planning
Master of Science in Planning

CALIFORNIA

California Polytechnic State University, San Luis Obispo
City and Regional Planning Department
College of Architecture and Environmental Design
San Luis Obispo, California 93407
Phone: (805) 756-1315
http://www.calpoly.edu/~crp/
Bachelor of Science in City and Regional Planning
Master of City and Regional Planning

California State Polytechnic University, Pomona
Department of Urban and Regional Planning
College of Environmental Design
3801 W Temple Avenue
Pomona, California 91768-4048
Phone: (909) 869-2688
http://www.csupomona.edu/~urp
Bachelor of Science in Urban and Regional Planning
Master of Urban and Regional Planning

San Jose State University
Urban and Regional Planning Department
College of Social Work
One Washington Square
San Jose, California 95192-0185
Phone: (408) 924-5882
Master of Urban Planning

University of California at Berkeley
Department of City and Regional Planning
College of Environmental Design
228 Wurster Hall
Berkeley, California 94720-1850
Phone: (510) 642-3256
http://www.ced.berkeley.edu/city_planning
Master of City Planning

University of California, Irvine
Department of Urban and Regional Planning
School of Social Ecology
Social Ecology I, Room 202
Irvine, California 92697-7075
Phone: (949) 824-3480
http://www.seweb.uci.edu/dept/urp_home.html
Master of Urban and Regional Planning

University of California, Los Angeles
Department of Urban Planning
School of Public Policy and Social Research
3250 Public Policy Building
Los Angeles, California 90095-1656
Phone: (310) 825-4025
http://www.sppsr.ucla.edu
Master of Arts in Urban Planning

University of Southern California
School of Policy, Planning and Development
Ralph and Goldy Lewis Hall, Room 108
University Park Campus
Los Angeles, California 90089-0626
Phone: (213) 740-6842
http://www.use.edu\sppd\
Master of Planning

COLORADO

University of Colorado at Denver
Department of Planning and Design
College of Architecture and Planning
Campus Box 126, P.O. Box 173364
Denver, Colorado 80217-3364
Phone: (303) 556-4866
http://www.cudenver.edu/public/AandP
Master of Urban and Regional Planning

FLORIDA

Florida Atlantic University
Department of Urban and Regional Planning
College of Architecture, Urban and Public Affairs
220 SE 2nd Avenue
Fort Lauderdale, Florida 33301
Phone: (954) 762-5652
www.fau.edu/divdept/cupa/depts/urp.htm
Master of Urban and Regional Planning

Florida State University
Department of Urban and Regional Planning
College of Social Sciences
311 Bellamy Building
Tallahassee, Florida 32306-2280
Phone: (850) 644-4510
http://www.fsu.edu/~durp
Master of Science in Planning

University of Florida
Urban and Regional Planning Department
College of Architecture
P.O. Box 115706
Gainesville, Florida 32611-5706

Phone: (352) 392-0997, x423
http://www.arch.ufl.edu/arc/urp
Master of Arts in Urban and Regional
   Planning

GEORGIA

Georgia Institute of Technology
Graduate Program in City Planning
College of Architecture
245 Fourth Street, NW, Room 204
Atlanta, Georgia 30332-0155
Phone: (404) 894-2350
http://www.arch.gatech/cp/
Master of City Planning

HAWAII

University of Hawaii at Manoa
Department of Urban and Regional
   Planning
College of Social Sciences
2424 Maile Way, Room 107
Honolulu, Hawaii 96822
Phone: (808) 956-7381
http://www.durp.hawaii.edu
Master of Urban and Regional Planning

ILLINOIS

University of Illinois at Chicago
Urban Planning and Policy Program
College of Urban Planning and Public
   Affairs
412 S Peoria Street, Suite 215
Chicago, Illinois 60607-7065
Phone: (312) 996-5240
http://www.uic.edu/cuppa/upp
Master of Urban Planning and Policy

**University of Illinois at Urbana-
   Champaign**
Department of Urban and Regional
   Planning
College of Fine and Applied Arts
111 Temple Buell Hall, 611 Taft Drive
Champaign, Illinois 61820
Phone: (217) 333-3890
http://www.urban.uiuc.edu
Bachelor of Arts in Urban Planning
Master of Urban Planning

INDIANA

Ball State University
Department of Urban Planning
College of Architecture and Planning
Architecture Building 327

Muncie, Indiana 47306-0315
Phone: (765) 285-1963
Bachelor of Urban Planning and
   Development
Master of Urban and Regional Planning

IOWA

Iowa State University
Department of Community and Regional
   Planning
College of Design
126 College of Design
Ames, Iowa 50011
Phone: (515) 294-8958
http://www.public.iastate.edu/~design/
   crp/crp.html
Bachelor of Science in Community and
   Regional Planning
Master of Community and Regional
   Planning

University of Iowa
Graduate Program in Urban and Regional
   Planning
347 Jessup Hall
Iowa City, Iowa 52242
Phone: (319) 335-0032
http://www.uiowa.edu/~urp/
Master of Arts or Master of Science in
   Urban and Regional Planning

KANSAS

Kansas State University
Department of Landscape Architecture/
   Regional and Community Planning
College of Architecture, Planning and
   Design
302 Seaton Hall
Manhattan, Kansas 66506
Phone: (785) 532-2440
Master of Regional and Community
   Planning

University of Kansas
Graduate Program in Urban Planning
School of Architecture and Urban Design
317 Marvin Hall
Lawrence, Kansas 66045
Phone: (785) 864-4184
http://www.arch.ukans.edu/urban/new/
   index.htm
Master of Urban Planning

LOUISIANA

University of New Orleans
Urban and Regional Planning Program

College of Urban and Public Affairs
New Orleans, Louisiana 70148
Phone: (504) 280-6277
   or (504) 280-5473
http://www.uno.edu/~cupa
Master of Urban and Regional Planning

MARYLAND

Morgan State University
Graduate Program in City and Regional
   Planning
Institute of Architecture and Planning
1700 E Cold Spring Lane and Hillen Road
Montebello, Room B107
Baltimore, Maryland 21251
Phone: (443) 885-3225
http://jewel.morgan.edu/~iap/programs/
   programs_CRP
Master of City and Regional Planning

University of Maryland at College Park
Program of Urban Studies and Planning
Caroline Hall 0129
College Park, Maryland 20742-9150
Phone: (301) 405-6791
Fax: (301) 314-9897
http://www.arch.umd.edu/URSP/
   Academics
Master of Community Planning

MASSACHUSETTS

Harvard University
Department of Urban Planning and Design
Graduate School of Design
48 Quincy Street, Room 312
Cambridge, Massachusetts 02138
Phone: (617) 495-2521
http://www.gsd.harvard.edu
Master in Urban Planning

Massachusetts Institute of Technology
Department of Urban Studies and
   Planning
77 Massachusetts Avenue, Bldg. 7, No. 337
Cambridge, Massachusetts 02139
Phone: (617) 253-1907
http://www.web.mit.edu/dusp/www/
Master in City Planning

University of Massachusetts-Amherst
Department of Landscape Architecture
   and Regional Planning
College of Food and Natural Resources
109 Hills North
Amherst, Massachusetts 01003-4010
Phone: (413) 545-2255
http://www.umass.edu/larp.
Master of Regional Planning

MICHIGAN

Eastern Michigan University
Urban and Regional Planning Program
Department of Geography and Geology
College of Arts and Sciences
Ypsilanti, Michigan 48197-2219
Phone: (734) 487-8656
http://planning.emich.edu
Bachelor of Science/Major in Urban and
    Regional Planning

Michigan State University
Urban and Regional Planning Program
Department of Geography
College of Social Science
201 UPLA Building
East Lansing, Michigan 48824-1221
Phone: (517) 353-9054
http://www.ssc.msu.edu/~urp/
Bachelor of Science in Urban and
    Regional Planning
Master in Urban and Regional Planning

University of Michigan
Urban and Regional Planning Program
A. Alfred Taubman College of
    Architecture and Urban Planning
2000 Bonisteel Boulevard
Ann Arbor, Michigan 48109-2069
Phone: (734) 764-1300
http://www.caup.umich.edu/
Master of Urban Planning

Wayne State University
Department of Geography and Urban
    Planning
College of Urban, Labor and
    Metropolitan Affairs
225 State Hall
Detroit, Michigan 48202
Phone: (313) 577-2701
http://www.culma.wayne.edu
Master of Urban Planning

MINNESOTA

University of Minnesota
Master of Urban and Regional Planning
    Program
Hubert H. Humphrey Institute of Public
    Affairs
301 Nineteenth Avenue, S
Minneapolis, Minnesota 55455
Phone: (612) 625-8092
http://www.hhh.umn.edu/gpo/degrees/
    murp/
Master of Urban and Regional Planning

NEBRASKA

University of Nebraska-Lincoln
Department of Community and Regional
    Planning
College of Architecture
302 Architecture Hall
Lincoln, Nebraska 68588-0105
Phone: (402) 472-9280
http://www.unl.edu/archcoll/crp/index.html
Master of Community and Regional
    Planning

NEW JERSEY

**Rutgers, The State University of New
Jersey**
Department of Urban Planning and Policy
    Development
Edward J. Bloustein School of Planning
    and Public Policy
33 Livingston Avenue, Suite 302
New Brunswick, New Jersey 08901-1987
Phone: (732) 932-3822 x741
http://www.policy.rutgers.edu
Master of City and Regional Planning

NEW MEXICO

University of New Mexico
Community and Regional Planning
    Program
School of Architecture and Planning
2414 Central, SE
Albuquerque, New Mexico 87131
Phone: (505) 277-5068
http://www.unm.edu/~saap/crp
Master of Community and Regional
    Planning

NEW YORK

Columbia University
Urban Planning Program
Graduate School of Architecture,
    Planning and Preservation
1172 Amsterdam Avenue, Avery Hall 413
New York, New York 10027
Phone: (212) 854-3513
http://www.arch.columbia.edu/UP
Master of Science in Urban Planning

Cornell University
Department of City and Regional Planning
College of Architecture, Art, and Planning
105 West Sibley Hall
Ithaca, New York 14853
Phone: (607) 255-4331
http://www.crp.cornell.edu/
Master of Regional Planning

Hunter College, CUNY
Graduate Program in Urban Planning
Department of Urban Affairs and
    Planning
695 Park Avenue
New York, New York 10021
Phone: (212) 772-5518
http://maxweber.hunter.cuny.edu/urban/
Master of Urban Planning

New York University
Program in Urban Planning
Robert F. Wagner Graduate School of
    Public Service
4 Washington Square, N
New York, New York 10003
Phone: (212) 998-7400
http://www.nyu.edu/wagner/
Master of Urban Planning

Pratt Institute
Graduate Center for Planning and the
    Environment
School of Architecture
200 Willoughby Avenue
Brooklyn, New York 11205
Phone: (718) 399-4314
http://www.pratt.edu/arch/gcpe
Master of Science in City and Regional
    Planning

State University of New York at Albany
Department of Geography and Planning
College of Arts and Sciences
Earth Science 218
Albany, New York 12222
Phone: (518) 442-4770
http://www.albany.edu/gp/
Master of Regional Planning

State University of New York at Buffalo
Department of Planning
School of Architecture and Planning
3435 Main Street, 116 Hayes Hall
Buffalo, New York 14214-3087
Phone: (716) 829-2133, x109
http://www.ap.buffalo.edu/planning
Master of Urban Planning

NORTH CAROLINA

**The University of North Carolina at
Chapel Hill**
Department of City and Regional Planning
College of Arts and Sciences
New East Building, Campus Box 3140
Chapel Hill, North Carolina 27599-3140
Phone: (919) 962-3983
http://www.unc.edu/depts/dcrpweb
Master of Regional Planning

OHIO

University of Cincinnati
School of Planning
College of Design, Architecture, Art, and
Planning
6210 DAAP Building
Cincinnati, Ohio 45221-0016
Phone: (513) 556-4943
http://ucplanning.uc.edu
Bachelor of Urban Planning
Master of Community Planning

Cleveland State University
Maxine Goodman Levin College of
Urban Affairs
Department of Urban Studies
1717 Euclid Avenue, UB112E
Cleveland, Ohio 44115
Phone: (216) 687-2136
http://www.urban.csuohio.edu
Master of Urban Planning, Design, and
Development

The Ohio State University
City and Regional Planning Program
Knowlton School of Architecture
109 Brown Hall, 190 W 17th Avenue
Columbus, Ohio 43210
Phone: (614) 292-1012
http://www.crp.ohio-state.edu
Master of City and Regional Planning

OKLAHOMA

University of Oklahoma
Regional and City Planning Division
College of Architecture
162 Gould Hall
Norman, Oklahoma 73019-0263
Phone: (405) 325-2444
http://www.ou.edu/Architecture/RCPL
Master of Regional and City Planning

OREGON

Portland State University
School of Urban Studies and Planning
College of Urban and Public Affairs
P.O. Box 751-USP
Portland, Oregon 97207-0751
Phone: (503) 725-4045
http://www.upa.pdx.edu/USP/murp.htm/
Master of Urban and Regional Planning

University of Oregon
Graduate Program in Community and
Regional Planning
Department of Planning, Public Policy
and Management

School of Architecture and Allied Arts
Hendricks Hall
Eugene, Oregon 97403-1209
Phone: (541) 346-3635
http://utopia.uoregon.edu
Master of Community and Regional
Planning

PENNSYLVANIA

University of Pennsylvania
Department of City and Regional Planning
Graduate School of Fine Arts
127 Meyerson Hall
Philadelphia, Pennsylvania 19104-6311
Phone: (215) 898-8329
http://www.upenn.edu/gsfa/cpln
Master of City Planning

PUERTO RICO

University of Puerto Rico
Graduate School of Planning
P.O. Box 23354
San Juan, Puerto Rico 00931
Phone: (787) 764-0000 x5010
Master in Planning

RHODE ISLAND

University of Rhode Island
Department of Community Planning and
Landscape Architecture
College of the Environment and Life
Sciences
Rodman Hall, 94 West Alumni Avenue,
Suite 1
Kingston, Rhode Island 02881-0815
Phone: (401) 874-2248
http://www.uri.edu/cels/cpla
Master of Community Planning

SOUTH CAROLINA

Clemson University
Department of Planning and Landscape
Architecture
College of Architecture, Arts and
Humanities
121 Lee Hall, Box 340511
Clemson, South Carolina 29634-0511
Phone: (864) 656-3926
http://www.clemson.edu/aah/pla/
Master of City and Regional Planning

TENNESSEE

University of Memphis
Graduate Program in City and Regional
Planning

226 Johnson Hall
Memphis, Tennessee 38152
Phone: (901) 678-2161
http://planning.memphis.edu
Master of City and Regional Planning

University of Tennessee, Knoxville
School of Planning
College of Arts and Sciences
1401 Cumberland Avenue, 108 Hoskins
Library
Knoxville, Tennessee 37996-4015
Phone: 423/974-5227
http://www.planning.cap.utk.edu
Master of Science in Planning

TEXAS

Texas A & M University
Department of Landscape Architecture
and Urban Planning
College of Architecture
MS 3137
College Station, Texas 77843-3137
Phone: (409) 845-1019
http://taz.tamu.edu/LAUP
Master in Urban Planning

University of Texas at Arlington
City and Regional Planning Program
School of Urban and Public Affairs
P.O. Box 19588
Arlington, Texas 76019-0588
Phone: (817) 272-3340
http://www.uta.edu/supa/03
academics/cirp.htm
Master of City and Regional Planning

The University of Texas at Austin
Graduate Program in Community and
Regional Planning
School of Architecture and Planning
Goldsmith Hall 2.308 B7500
Austin, Texas 78712-1160
Phone: (512) 471-1922
http://www.ar.utexas.edu/Planning/index.
html
Master of Science in Community and
Regional Planning

VIRGINIA

University of Virginia
Department of Urban and Environmental
Planning
Campbell Hall, P.O. Box 400122
Charlottesville, Virginia 22904-4122
Phone: (804) 924-1339

http://minerva.acc.Virginia.EDU/~arch/
dept/urban.html
Bachelor of Urban and Environmental
Planning
Master of Urban and Environmental
Planning

Virginia Commonwealth University
Department of Urban Studies and Planning
812 W Franklin Street
VCU Box 842008
Richmond, Virginia 23284-2008
Phone: (804) 828-2489
http://www.has.vcu.edu/usp/
Master of Urban and Regional Planning

**Virginia Polytechnic Institute and State
University**
Department of Urban Affairs and
Planning
College of Architecture and Urban Studies
201 Architecture Annex
Blacksburg, Virginia 24061
Phone: (540) 231-5485
http://www.uap.vt.edu
Master of Urban and Regional Planning

WASHINGTON

Eastern Washington University
Department of Urban Planning, Public
and Health Administration

College of Business and Public
Administration
668 N Riverpoint Boulevard., Suite A
Spokane, Washington 99202-1660
Phone: (509) 358-2230
http://www.ebpa.ewu.edu/~planning/
Bachelor of Arts in Urban and Regional
Planning
Master of Urban and Regional Planning

University of Washington
Department of Urban Design and
Planning
College of Architecture and Urban
Planning
410 Gould Hall, Box 355740
Seattle, Washington 98195-5740
Phone: (206) 543-4190
http://www.caup.washington.edu/html/
urbdp/
Master of Urban Planning 1999; 1941

WISCONSIN

University of Wisconsin-Madison
Department of Urban and Regional
Planning
College of Letters and Science and
College of Agriculture and Life
Sciences
925 Bascom Mall/Old Music Hall
Madison, Wisconsin 53706

Phone: (608) 262-1005
http://www.wisc.edu/urpl/
Master of Science in Urban and Regional
Planning

University of Wisconsin-Milwaukee
Department of Urban Planning
School of Architecture and Urban
Planning
P.O. Box 413
Milwaukee, Wisconsin 53201-0413
Phone: (414) 229-5563
http://www.uwm.edu/SARUP//planning/
index.html
Master of Urban Planning

CANADA

BRITISH COLUMBIA

The University of British Columbia
School of Community and Regional
Planning
433-6333 Memorial Road
Vancouver, British Columbia
Canada V6T 1Z2
Phone: (604) 822-3276
http://www.scarp.ubc.ca
Master of Arts or Master of Science
(Planning)

D. POLITICAL/CAMPAIGN MANAGEMENT

New programs and seminars in political/campaign management have sprung up in response to the growing complexity
of political campaigns. Programs fall into two basic types:
degree-granting and shorter intensive courses. Political science and related departments also offer useful courses, as
do professional associations.

CALIFORNIA

University of California/Davis
Political Campaign Management Institute
University Extension, UC Davis
Davis, CA 95616-4852
Phone: (530) 757-8878
http://universityextension.ucdavis.edu/pcm

CONNECTICUT

Yale University
Women's Campaign School
P.O. Box 3307
New Haven, CT 06515
Phone: (203) 734-7385 or 1-800-353-2878

Fax: (203) 734-7547
E-mail: wcsyale@aol.com
http://www.yale.edu/wcsyale.org.
One-day and five-day sessions
(cosponsored by Yale Law School and
the Yale Women and Gender Studies
Program) for women who wish to enter
politics or move up the political ladder.

DISTRICT OF COLUMBIA

American University
Campaign Management Institute
4400 Massachusetts Avenue, NW
Washington, DC 20016

Phone: (202) 885-6251
Fax: (202) 885-1038
E-mail: ccps@american.edu
http://www.american.edu/ccps
The Campaign Management Institute
(CMI) offers intensive two-week
campaign management certification
programs in January and May, which
are taught by campaign
professionals. Participants prepare
campaign plans for actual
candidates.

American University
Center for Congressional and Presidential
Studies

4400 Massachusetts Avenue, NW
Washington, DC 20016
Phone: (202) 885-3491
Fax: (202) 885-1038
E-mail: ccps@american edu
http://www.american.edu/ccps
The Center for Congressional and
Presidential Studies offers courses in
campaign management and lobbying
and forums throughout the year. The
center was awarded a grant from the
Pew Charitable Trusts to study
campaign conduct.

American University
Lobbying Institute
4400 Massachusetts Avenue, NW
Washington, DC 20016
Phone: (202) 885-6296
Fax: (202) 885-1038
E-mail: ccps@american.edu
http://www.american.edu/ccps
Twice a year Lobbying Institute offers
students and professionals a two-week
intensive course on the tactics and
daily strategies of lobbying within the
democratic political process.

**Campaigns and Elections Magazine—
Seminar and Political Training
Division**
1414 22nd Street, NW
Washington, DC 20037
Phone: (202) 887-8590
Fax: (202) 463-7085
http://www.campaignline.com
A nonpartisan political training program
with the Annual Political Campaign
Training Seminar and Trade Show as
well as private, customized training
programs, seminars, conferences, and
briefings are offered.

George Washington University
The Graduate School of Political
Management
2147 F Street, NW
Washington, DC 20052
Phone: (202) 994-8782
Fax: (202) 994-6000
E-mail: law@gwu.edu
http://www.gwu.edu/~gspm/

FLORIDA

**University of Florida—Political
Campaign Program**
3324 Turlington Hall
Gainesville, FL 32611
Phone: (904) 392-0262
Fax: (904) 392-8127

MASSACHUSETTS

**Suffolk University Graduate Program
in Political Science**
41 Temple Street
Boston, MA 02114
Phone: (617) 573-8126
Fax: (617) 367-4623
E-mail: jberg@acad.suffolk.edu
The program offers a one-year master's
degree in either professional politics
(campaigning, advocacy/lobbying) or
international relations (human rights,
trade, nongovernmental organizations);
study includes internship.

NEW YORK

New York University
Political Campaign Management
Department of Politics
715 Broadway, 4th Floor
New York, NY 10003

Phone: (212) 998-8530
Fax: (212) 995-4184
http://www.nyu.edu/gsas/dept/politics

NORTH CAROLINA

**University of North Carolina,
Wilmington**
Institute of Political Leadership
601 S College Road, Westside Hall
Wilmington, NC 28403
Phone: 910-962-7585
E-mail: iopl@uncwil.edu
http://www.uncwil.edu/iopl

OHIO

The University of Akron
Bliss Institute of Applied Politics
Akron, OH 44325-1914
Phone: (330) 972-5182
Fax: (330) 972-5479
E-mail: bliss@uakron.edu
The Bliss Institute of Applied Politics at
the University of Akron offers a
master's degree in applied politics and
certification in applied politics to
graduate and undergraduate students
interested in careers in campaign
management, political parties,
lobbying, and election of government
officials.

VIRGINIA

**Regent University School of
Government**
1000 Regent University Drive
Virginia Beach, VA 23464
Phone: (888) 800-7735
Fax: (757) 226-4536
E-mail: govschool@regent.edu

E. POLITICAL SCIENCE

Because of the multitude of undergraduate programs in political science, students can find political science as a major at most colleges or universities. Publications available through the American Political Science Association's website (*http://www.apsanet.org/pubs*) include *Political Science: An Ideal Liberal Arts Major, Careers and the Study of Political Science: A Guide for Undergraduates,* and *Studying in Washington: A Guide to Academic Internships in the Nation's Capital.*

The following is a list of master's degree programs (all also offer undergraduate majors) in political science provided by the American Political Science Association. Schools not on this list may offer master's degrees in public affairs, public administration, or public policy and/or doctoral programs in political science. For updated information, check *Peterson's Guide to Graduate Programs in the Humanity and Social Sciences* in libraries and on-line (*http://www.petersons.com*)

ALABAMA

Birmingham-Southern College
Behavioral and Social Sciences
900 Arkadelphia Road
Birmingham, AL 35254
Phone: (205) 226-4847
http://www.bsc.edu

Jacksonville State University
Political Science and Public Administration
221 Curtiss Hall
Jacksonville, AL 36265
Phone: (256) 782-5669
http://www.jsu.edu/depart/polsci/polsci.
    html

University of Alabama-Birmingham
Government and Public Service
U 238
1530 3rd Avenue, S
Birmingham, AL 35294-3350
Phone: (205) 934-9896
http://www.uab.edu/gps

University of Alabama-Huntsville
Political Science
Morton Hall 250
Huntsville, AL 35899
Phone: (256) 824-6949
http://www.uah.edu

University of South Alabama
Political Science and Criminal Justice
Humanities Building 226
Mobile, AL 36688
Phone: (334) 460-6567
http://www.southalabama.edu/polscie/

ARKANSAS

Arkansas State University
Political Science
P.O. Box 1750
State University, AR 72467-1750
Phone: (870) 972-2720
http://www.cas.astate.edu/posc

University of Arkansas-Fayetteville
Political Science
428 Old Main
Fayetteville, AR 72701
Phone: (501) 575-6432
http://www.uark.edu/depts/plasinfo

CALIFORNIA

California State University-Chico
Political Science
1st and Normal Street
Chico, CA 95929-0455
Phone: (530) 898-6910
http://www.csuchico.edu/pols

California State University-Fullerton
Political Science
P.O. Box 6848
Fullerton, CA 92834-6848
Phone: (714) 278-3524
http://www.fullerton.edu

California State University-Long Beach
Political Science
1250 Bellflower Boulevard
Long Beach, CA 90840-4605
Phone: (562) 985-4979
http://www.csulb.edu/~posc

California State University-Los Angeles
Political Science
5151 State University Drive
Los Angeles, CA 90032-8226
Phone: (213) 343-6452
http://www.calstatela.edu/dept/polsci/
    index.html

California State University-Northridge
Political Science
18111 Nordhoff Avenue
Northridge, CA 91330-8254
Phone: (818) 677-4502
http://www.csun.edu

California State University-Sacramento
Government Department
6000 J Street
Sacramento, CA 95819-6089
Phone: (916) 278-6488
http://www.csus.edu/govt/index.html

**Monterey Institute of International
    Studies**
Graduate School of International Policy
    Studies
425 Van Buren Street
Monterey, CA 93940
Phone: (831) 647-4199
http://www.miis.edu

San Diego State University
Political Science
5500 Campanile Drive
San Diego, CA 92182-4427
Phone: (619) 594-7302
http://www.sdsu.edu/dept/polsciwb/
    polsci.html

San Francisco State University
Political Science
1600 Holloway Avenue
San Francisco, CA 94132-4155
Phone: (415) 338-2391
http://www.sfsu.edu/~polisci

Sonoma State University
Political Science
1801 East Cotati Avenue
Rohnert Park, CA 94928
Phone: (707) 664-3920
http://www.sonoma.edu

University of San Diego
Political Science and International
    Relations
5998 Alcala Park
San Diego, CA 92110
Phone: (619) 260-6840
http://www.acusd.edu

COLORADO

University of Colorado-Denver
Political Science
1200 Larimer Street
CB 190
Denver, CO 80217
Phone: (303) 556-6041
http://www.cudenver.edu/public/polisci/
    pols.html

CONNECTICUT

Southern Connecticut State University
Political Science
501 Crescent Street
New Haven, CT 06515
Phone: (203) 392-5670
http://www.scsu.ctstateu.edu

FLORIDA

Florida Atlantic University
Political Science
777 Glades Road
P.O. Box 3081
Boca Raton, FL 33431-0991
Phone: (561) 367-2997
http://www.fau.edu/polsci/index.html

Florida Atlantic University
Social Sciences
2912 College Avenue
Davie, FL 33314
Phone: (954) 236-1150
http://www.fau.edu

University of Central Florida
Political Science
P.O. Box 161356
Orlando, FL 32816-1356

Phone: (407) 823-0051
pegasus.cc.ucf.edu/~politics/

University of Miami
Political Science
P.O. Box 248047
314 Jenkins Building
5250 University Drive
Miami, FL 33124-6534
Phone: (305) 284-3636
http://www.bus.miami.edu/~pol

University of South Florida
Government and International Affairs
4202 East Fowler Avenue, SOC 107
Tampa, FL 33620-8100
Phone: (813) 974-0832
http://www.usf.edu

University of West Florida
Government
11000 University Parkway
Pensacola, FL 32514
Phone: (850) 473-7001
http://www.uwf.edu/~govt/

GEORGIA

Augusta State University
Political Science, Public Administration,
    International Studies, and Philosophy
2500 Walton Way
Augusta, GA 30904-2200
Phone: (706) 667-4116
http://www.aug.edu/political_science

Georgia College and State University
Government and Sociology
Milledgeville, GA 31061
http://www.gcsu.edu/acad_affairs/
    coll_artsci/gov_

Georgia Institute of Technology
Sam Nunn School of International Affairs
781 Marietta Street, NW
Atlanta, GA 30332-0610
Phone: (404) 894-1900
http://www.inta.gatech.edu

Georgia Southern University
Political Science
P.O. Box 8101
Statesboro, GA 30460
Phone: (912) 681-5348
http://www.gasou.edu/psc

**North Georgia College and State
    University**
Political Science and Criminal Justice
Young Social Science Center
Dahlonega, GA 30597

Phone: (706) 864-1874
http://www.ngcsu.edu

State University of West Georgia
Political Science
1601 Maple Street
Carrollton, GA 30118
Phone: (770) 836-4665
http://www.westga.edu/~polisci

ILLINOIS

Eastern Illinois University
Political Science
600 Lincoln Avenue
Charleston, IL 61920
Phone: (217) 581-2926
http://www.eiu.edu/~polisci

Illinois State University
Politics and Government
306 Schroeder Hall
Campus Box 4600
Normal, IL 61790-4600
Phone: (309) 438-7638
http://www.ilstu.edu/depts/polisci/
    pos.htm

Northeastern Illinois University
Political Science
5500 N St. Louis Avenue
Chicago, IL 60625
Phone: (773) 442-4900
http://www.neiu.edu/~psci/

Roosevelt University
Political Science
430 S Michigan Avenue
Chicago, IL 60605-1394
Phone: (312) 341-3762
http://www.roosevelt.edu/academics/
    caas/sps

University of Illinois-Springfield
Political Studies
Public Affairs Center
P.O. Box 19243
Springfield, IL 62794-9243
Phone: (217) 206-7807
http://www.uis.edu/politicalstudies/

Western Illinois University
Political Science
Morgan Hall #422
Macomb, IL 61455-1390
Phone: (309) 298-1857
http://www.wiu.edu

INDIANA

Ball State University
Political Science
Muncie, IN 47306-0515
Phone: (765) 285-5345
http://www.bsu.edu/poli-sci

Indiana State University
Political Science
Holmstedt Hall 301
Terre Haute, IN 47809
Phone: (812) 237-3445
http://web.indstate.edu/polisci

University of Indianapolis
History and Political Science
1400 E Hanna Avenue
Indianapolis, IN 46227-3264
Phone: (317) 788-3480
http://www.uindy.edu

IOWA

Iowa State University
Political Science
503 Ross Hall
Ames, IA 50011
http://www.iastate.edu/~polisci

University of Northern Iowa
Political Science
321 Sabin Hall
Cedar Falls, IA 50614-0404
Phone: (319) 273-7108
http://www.uni.edu/polisci/

KANSAS

Kansas State University
Political Science
226 Waters Hall
Manhattan, KS 66506-4030
Phone: (785) 532-2339
http://www.ksu.edu/polsci

Pittsburg State University
Social Science
235 Whitesit Hall
Pittsburg, KS 66762
Phone: (316) 235-8020
http://www.pittstate.edu/sosci

Wichita State University
Political Science
1845 Fairmount
Box 17
Wichita, KS 67260
Phone: (316) 978-7132
http://www.wichita.edu

KENTUCKY

Eastern Kentucky University
Government Department
113 McCreary Hall
521 Lancaster Avenue
Richmond, KY 40475-3102
Phone: (859) 622-8019
http://www.government.eku.edu

Murray State University
Political Science and Legal Studies
553 Business Building
Murray, KY 42071-3314
Phone: (270) 762-3482
http://www.murraystate.edu/

Northern Kentucky University
Political Science
Landrum Building 217
Highland Heights, KY 41099-2207
Phone: (606) 572-6184
http://www.nku.edu/~psc

University of Louisville
Political Science
Ford Hall
Louisville, KY 40292
Phone: (502) 852-7923
http://www.louisville.edu/www/a-s/polisci

Western Kentucky University
Government Department
1 Big Red Way
Bowling Green, KY 42101-3576
Phone: (270) 745-2945
http://www.wku.edu/dept/academic/ahss/
    government/govt.htm

LOUISIANA

Grambling State University
Political Science and Public
    Administration
GSU Box 4266
Grambling, LA 71245
Phone: (318) 274-3427
http://www.gram.edu

Southern University
Political Science
P.O. Box 9656
Baton Rouge, LA 70813
Phone: (225) 771-3105
http://www.subr.edu

MARYLAND

University of Baltimore
Government and Public Administration
1304 St. Paul Street
Baltimore, MD 21201
Phone: (410) 837-6094
    or (410) 837-6175
http://www.ubalt.edu/cla_spa

MASSACHUSETTS

Bridgewater State College
Political Science
Summer Street House
180 Summer Street
Bridgewater, MA 02325
Phone: (508) 279-6106
http://www.bridgew.edu

Suffolk University
Government Department
8 Ashburton Place
Boston, MA 02108-2770
http://www.suffolk.edu

MICHIGAN

Central Michigan University
Political Science
247 Anspach Hall
Mount Pleasant, MI 4885
Phone: (989) 774-1136
http://www.chsbs.cmich.edu/
    Political_Science

Eastern Michigan University
Political Science
601 Pray-Harrold
Ypsilanti, MI 48197
Phone: (734) 487-3340
http://www.emich.edu/public/polisci/
    polisci.htm

Northern Michigan University
Political Science
1401 Presque Isle Avenue
Marquette, MI 49855
Phone: (906) 227-1819
http://www.nmu.edu/politicalscience

Oakland University
Political Science
Rochester, MI 48309-4488
Phone: (248) 370-4299
http://www.oakland.edu/polisci/

University of Detroit Mercy
Political Science
4001 W McNichols Road
Detroit, MI 48221-9987
Phone: (313) 993-1166
http://www.udmercy.edu

MINNESOTA

Minnesota State University-Mankato
Political Science and Law Enforcement
109 Morris Hall
Mankato, MN 56001
Phone: (507) 389-6377
http://www.mankato.msus.edu/dept/psle

Minnesota State University-Moorhead
Political Science
1104 7th Avenue, S
Moorhead, MN 56563
Phone: (218) 236-2845
http://www.mnstate.edu/polsci

MISSISSIPPI

Delta State University
Social Sciences
Cleveland, MS 38733
Phone: (662) 846-4016
http://www.deltast.edu/index-acad.html

Jackson State University
Political Science
1400 J. R. Lynch Street
P.O. Box 18420
Jackson, MS 39217
Phone: (601) 968-2904
http://www.jsums.edu

Mississippi College
History and Political Science
Box 4006
Clinton, MS 39058
Phone: (601) 925-3932
http://www.mc.edu/organizations/acad/his/

University of Southern Mississippi
Political Science
Box 5108
Hattiesburg, MS 39406-5108
Phone: (601) 266-4172
http://www.dept.usm.edu/~psc

MISSOURI

Southeast Missouri State University
Political Science
One University Plaza, MS 2920
Cape Girardeau, MO 63701
Phone: (573) 651-2695
http://www.semo.edu

Southwest Missouri State University
Political Science
Public Affairs Classroom Building 307
Springfield, MO 65804
Phone: (417) 836-6655
http://www.smsu.edu/polsci/

Webster University
History, Politics and Law
470 East Lockwood
Saint Louis, MO 63119-3194
Phone: (314) 968-7403
http://www.webster.edu/depts/artsci/
    hpl/hpl.html

MONTANA

Montana State University-Bozeman
Political Science
2-143 Wilson Hall
Bozeman, MT 59717
Phone: (406) 994-6692
http://www.montana.edu/wwwpo

University of Montana
Political Science
Missoula, MT 59812
Phone: (406) 243-4076
http://www.umt.edu/polsci

NEBRASKA

University of Nebraska-Omaha
Political Science
6001 Dodge Street
Arts and Sciences 275
Omaha, NE 68182-0271
Phone: (402) 554-4860
http://www.unomaha.edu/~psci

NEW HAMPSHIRE

University of New Hampshire
Political Science
321 Horton Social Science Center
20 College Road
Durham, NH 03824
Phone: (603) 862-0178
http://www.unh.edu/political-science

NEW JERSEY

Fairleigh Dickinson University
Political and International Studies
1000 River Road
Teaneck, NJ 07666
Phone: (201) 692-9096
http://www.fdu.edu

New Jersey Institute of Technology
Humanities and Social Sciences
University Heights
Newark, NJ 07102-1982
http://www.nit.edu

Rutgers University
Eagleton Institute and Public Policy
New Brunswick, NJ 08901
http://www.rci.rutgers.edu/~eagleton

Rutgers University-Newark
Political Science
Hill Hall
360 M. L. King Boulevard
Newark, NJ 07102
Phone: (973) 353-5103
http://www.tech.rutgers.edu/
    politicalscience

NEW MEXICO

New Mexico Highlands University
History and Political Science
Las Vegas, NM 87701
Phone: (505) 454-0026
http://www.nmhu.edu

New Mexico State University
Government Department
P.O. Box 30001
Las Cruces, NM 88003-8001
Phone: (505) 646-2052
http://www.nmsu.edu/~govdept

NEW YORK

College of Saint Rose
History and Political Science
432 Western Avenue
Albany, NY 12203
Phone: (518) 458-5446
http://www.strose.edu

CUNY-Brooklyn College
Political Science
James Hall
2900 Bedford Street
Brooklyn, NY 11210
Phone: (718) 951-4833
http://www.brooklyn.edu

CUNY-City College of New York
Political Science
138th and Convent Avenue
New York, NY 10031
Phone: (212) 271-7915
http://www.ccny.cuny.edu

Long Island University
Political Science
University Plaza-Humanities Building
Brooklyn, NY 11201
Phone: (718) 488-1086
http://www.liunet.edu

Long Island University
Political Science and International Studies
C. W. Post Campus
Brookville, NY 11548
http://www.liunet.edu.cwis/cwp/post.html

NEVADA

University of Nevada-Las Vegas
Political Science
4505 Maryland Parkway
Box 455029
Las Vegas, NV 89154-5029
Phone: (702) 895-1065
http://www.unlv.edu

NORTH CAROLINA

Appalachian State University
Political Science and Criminal Justice
College Street, Whitener Hall
Boone, NC 28608
Phone: (828) 262-2947
http://www.acs.appstate.edu/dept/ps-cj

East Carolina University
Political Science
125-A Brewster Building
Greenville, NC 27858-4353
Phone: (252) 328-4134
http://www.ecu.edu/polsci

Fayetteville State University
Government and History
1200 Murchison Road
Fayetteville, NC 28301
Phone: (910) 672-1090
http://www.uncfsu.edu/w4/ghp/index.htm

University of North Carolina-Charlotte
Political Science
9201 University City Boulevard
Charlotte, NC 28223-0001
Phone: (704) 687-3497
http://www.uncc.edu/polisci

**University of North Carolina-
    Greensboro**
Political Science
P.O. Box 26170
Greensboro, NC 27402-6170
Phone: (336) 334-4315
http://www.uncg.edu/psc

Western Carolina University
Political Science and Public Affairs
Stillwell 101
Cullowhee, NC 28723
Phone: (828) 227-7647
http://www.wcu.edu/as/politicalscience

NORTH DAKOTA

North Dakota State University
Political Science
P.O. Box 5075
Fargo, ND 58105
Phone: (701) 231-6545
http://www.ndsu.nodak.edu/
    Political_Science

OHIO

Bowling Green State University
Political Science
122 William Hall
Bowling Green, OH 43403
Phone: (419) 372-8494
http://www.bgsu.edu/departments/pols/
    index.html

Wright State University
Political Science
124 Allyn Hall
Dayton, OH 45435-0001
Phone: (937) 775-3301
http://www.wright.edu

Ohio University
Political Science
222 Bentley Hall
Athens, OH 45701
Phone: (740) 593-0394
http://www.ohio.edu/pols

University of Akron
Political Science
Olin Hall, Room 237
Akron, OH 44325-1904
Phone: (330) 972-8841
http://www.uakron.edu/polisci

University of Dayton
Political Science
227 St. Joseph Hall
300 College Park
Dayton, OH 45469
Phone: (937) 229-3900
http://www.as.udayton.edu/~polsci

University of Toledo
Political Science and Public
    Administration
2801 W Bancroft Street
1032 Scott Hall
Toledo, OH 43606-3390
Phone: (419) 530-4199
http://www.utoledo.edu/poli-sci/
    pshome.html

OKLAHOMA

Oklahoma State University
Political Science
519 Math Sciences
Stillwater, OK 74078-1060
Phone: (405) 744-6534
http://www.okstate.edu

University of Central Oklahoma
Political Science
100 N University Drive
Edmond, OK 73034-5209
Phone: (405) 974-3832
http://www.libarts.ucok.edu/political

OREGON

Portland State University
Political Science
P.O. Box 751
Portland, OR 97207-0751
Phone: (503) 725-8444
http://www.pdx.edu/POLISCI/

PENNSYLVANIA

East Stroudsburg University
Political Science
200 Prospect Street
East Stroudsburg, PA 18301
Phone: (570) 422-3198
http://www.esu.edu

Indiana University of Pennsylvania
Political Science
390 Pratt Drive
103 E Annex
Indiana, PA 15705-1069
Phone: (724) 357-3810
http://www.chss.iup.edu/ps

Kutztown University
Political Science
P.O. Box 730
Kutztown, PA 19530
Phone: (610) 683-4603
http://www.kutztown.edu/academics/
    liberal_arts

Lehigh University
Political Science
9 W Packer Avenue
Bethlehem, PA 18015
Phone: (610) 758-6554
http://www.lehigh.edu/~ingov/
    homepage.html

Shippensburg University
Political Science
1871 Old Main Drive
Grove Hall 424
Shippensburg, PA 17257
Phone: (717) 477-4030
http://www.ship.edu

Slippery Rock University
Government and Public Affairs
Slippery Rock, PA 16057
Phone: (724) 738-2314
http://www.sru.edu/depts/artsci/gov/
    gov.htm

Villanova University
Political Science
800 Lancaster Avenue
Villanova, PA 19085
Phone: (610) 519-7487
http://www.villanova.edu

RHODE ISLAND

University of Rhode Island
Political Science
Washburn Hall
80 Upper College Road
Kingston, RI 02881-0817
Phone: (401) 874-4072
http://www.uri.edu/artsci/psc/

SOUTH CAROLINA

Clemson University
Political Science
232 Brackett Hall
Clemson, SC 29634-1354
Phone: (864) 656-0690
http://www.business.clemson.edu/business/
    polisci.html

SOUTH DAKOTA

University of South Dakota
Political Science
414 E Clark Street
Vermillion, SD 57069-2390 USA
Phone: (605) 677-6302
http://www.usd.edu/polsci/

TENNESSEE

University of Memphis
Political Science
Clement Hall, Room 437
Memphis, TN 38152-3539
Phone: (901) 678-2983
http://www.memphis.edu/

TEXAS

Angelo State University
Government
Box 10896 ASU Station
2601 W Avenue, N
San Angelo, TX 76909
Phone: (915) 942-2307
http://www.angelo.edu/dept/gov

Baylor University
Political Science
P.O. Box 97276
500 Speight
Waco, TX 76798-7264
Phone: (976) 798-7276 or (254) 710-
3122
http://www.baylor.edu/~Political_Science
/welcome.html

Lamar University
Political Science
P.O. Box 10030
211 Red Bird Lane
Beaumont, TX 77710
Phone: (409) 880-8710
http://www.lamar.edu

Midwestern State University
Political Science
3410 Taft Boulevard
Wichita Falls, TX 76308-2099
Phone: (940) 397-4865
http://www.mwsu.edu

Sam Houston State University
Political Science
P.O. Box 2149
Huntsville, TX 77341-2149
Phone: (936) 294-4172
http://www.shsu.edu/~pol

Southwest Texas State University
Political Science
601 University Drive
San Marcos, TX 78666
Phone: (512) 245-7815
http://www.polisci.swt.edu/

St. Mary's University
Political Science
One Camino Santa Maria
San Antonio, TX 78228-8571
Phone: (210) 431-4336
http://www.stmarytx.edu

Stephen F. Austin State University
Political Science
Box 13045 SFA Station
Nacogdoches, TX 75962

Phone: (936)-468-2732
http://www.sfasu.edu

Sul Ross State University
Behavioral and Social Sciences
208B Lawrence Hall
Hwy 90 E
Alpine, TX 79832
Phone: (915) 837-8146
http://www.sulross.edu

Tarleton State University
Social Sciences
Box T-0660
Stephenville, TX 76402
Phone: (254) 968-9798
http://www.tarleton.edu/~socsci

Texas A&M International University
Social Sciences
5201 University Boulevard
Laredo, TX 78041-1999
Phone: (956) 326-2464
http://www.tamiu.edu

Texas A&M University-Kingsville
Political Science
MSC 165
700 University Boulevard
Kingsville, TX 78363
Phone: (361) 593-3502
http://www.tamuk.edu

Texas Woman's University
History and Government
P.O. Box 425889
Denton, TX 76204
Phone: (940) 898-2130
http://www.twu.edu/as/histgov/

University of Houston
African American Studies Program
4800 Calhoun Street
Houston, TX 77004-3474
Phone: (713) 743-3927
http://www.uh.edu

University of Texas-Arlington
Political Science
P.O. Box 19539
Arlington, TX 76019
Phone: (817) 272-2525
http://www.uta.edu/pols/pols.htm

University of Texas-El Paso
Political Science
Benedict Hall
El Paso, TX 79968-0547
Phone: (915) 747-5400
http://www.utep.edu/pols/

University of Texas-Pan American
Political Science
1201 W University Drive
Edinburg, TX 78539
Phone: (956) 381-2805
http://www.panam.edu/dept/polsci.html

University of Texas-San Antonio
Political Science and Geography
6900 N Loop 1604 W
San Antonio, TX 78249-0655
Phone: (210) 458-5430
http://www.utsa.edu

University of Texas-Tyler
Social Sciences
3900 University Boulevard
Tyler, TX 75799
Phone: (903) 566-7377
http://www.uttyler.edu

West Texas A&M University
History and Political Science
WTAMU Box 60807
Canyon, TX 79016
Phone: (806) 651-2601
http://www.wtamu.edu

UTAH

Utah State University
Political Science
0725 Old Main Hill
Logan, UT 84322-0725
Phone: (435) 797-3751
http://www.usu.edu/~polisci

VERMONT

Goddard College
Social Inquiry
Plainfield, VT 05667
Phone: (802) 454-8017
http://www.goddard.edu

University of Vermont
Political Science
94 University Place
532 Old Mill
Burlington, VT 05405-0114
Phone: (802) 656-0758
http://www.uvm.edu/~polisci/

VIRGINIA

College of William and Mary
Government
P.O. Box 8795
Williamsburg, VA 23187-8795
Phone: (757) 221-1868
http://www.wm.edu

George Mason University
Public and International Affairs Bldg.
Robinson, Room A201
4400 University Dr.
MSN 3F4
Fairfax, VA 22030-4444
Phone: (703) 993-1399
http://www.gmu.edu/departments/pia

James Madison University
Political Science
MSC 1101
Harrisonburg, VA 22807
Phone: (540) 568-8021
http://www.jmu.edu/polisci/outline.html

Regent University
Robertson School of Government
1000 Regent University Drive
Virginia Beach, VA 23464-9800
Phone: (757) 226-4643
http://www.regent.edu

Virginia Commonwealth University
Political Science and Public
   Administration
923 West Franklin Street
Richmond, Va 23284-2028

Phone: (804) 828-7463
http://www.vcu.edu

Virginia Tech
Political Science
531 Major Williams Hall (mail code 130)
Blacksburg, VA 24061
Phone: (540) 231-6078
http://www.vt.edu

WASHINGTON

Western Washington University
Political Science
Arntzen Hall 415
516 High Street
Bellingham, WA 98225-9082
Phone: (360) 650-2800
http://www.wwu.edu/~polsci

WASHINGTON, D.C.

George Washington University
Graduate School of Political Management
805 21st Street, NW, Suite 401
Washington, DC 20052
Phone: (202) 994-6006
http://www.gwu.edu/~gspm

WEST VIRGINIA

Marshall University
Political Science
One John Marshall Drive
Huntington, WV 25755-2668
Phone: (304) 696-3245
http://www.marshall.edu/polsci

WISCONSIN

Marquette University
Political Science
Wehr Physics 428
P.O. Box 1881
Milwaukee, WI 53201-1881
Phone: (414) 288-3360
http://www.marquette.edu/dept/polisci

WYOMING

University of Wyoming
Political Science
P.O. Box 3197
16th and Gibbon
Laramie, WY 82071
Phone: (307) 766-6771
http://www.uwyo.edu/pols

F. INTERNATIONAL AFFAIRS

Graduate programs in international affairs might also be called by similar titles such as international studies or international relations. Joint degrees with other academic programs, including business, law, and public affairs, are common. For more information, see *Peterson's Graduate Programs in the Humanities, Arts & Social Sciences* (*http://www.petersons.com*).

Alliant International University
College of Arts and Sciences
Department of Global Liberal Studies
San Diego, CA 92131-1799
Phone: (858) 635-4772
http://www.alliant.edu

American University
School of International Service
Washington, DC 20016-8001
Phone: (202) 885-1599
http://www.american.edu

Angelo State University
Graduate School
College of Liberal and Fine Arts
Department of Government
San Angelo, TX 76909
Phone: (915) 942-2262
http://www.angelo.edu

Antioch University McGregor
Graduate Programs
Individualized Master of Arts Programs
Department of Intercultural Relations
Yellow Springs, OH 45387-1609
Phone: (937) 769-1825
http://www.mcgregor.edu

Baylor University
Graduate School
Hankamer School of Business
Department of Economics
Waco, TX 76798
Phone: (254) 710-3588
http://www.baylor.edu

Boston University
Graduate School of Arts and Sciences
Department of International Relations
Boston, MA 02215

Phone: (617) 353-9349
http://www.bu.edu

Brandeis University
Graduate School of International
   Economics and Finance
Waltham, MA 02454-9110
Phone: (781) 736-4829
http://www.brandeis.edu

Brigham Young University
The David M. Kennedy Center for
   International and Area Studies
Provo, UT 84602-1001
Phone: (801) 378-7402
http://www.byu.edu

Brock University
Graduate Studies and Research
Division of Social Sciences

Department of Political Science
St. Catharines, ON L2S 3A1
Canada
Phone: (905) 688-5488
http://www.brocku.ca

California State University, Fresno
Division of Graduate Studies
College of Social Sciences
Department of Political Science
Program in International Relations
Fresno, CA 93740-8027
Phone: (559) 278-3005
http://www.scufresno.edu

California State University, Sacramento
Graduate Studies
College of Social Sciences and
    Interdisciplinary Studies
Program in International Affairs
Sacramento, CA 95819-6048
Phone: (916) 278-6557
http://www.csus.edu

California State University, Stanislaus
Graduate Programs
College of Arts, Letters, and Sciences
Department of History
Turlock, CA 95382
Phone: (209) 667-3238
http://www.csustan.edu

Carleton University
Faculty of Graduate Studies
Faculty of Public Affairs and Management
Norman Paterson School of International
    Affairs
Ottawa, ON K1S 5B6
Canada
Phone: (613) 520-2600 ext. 6660
http://www.carleton.ca/npsia/

The Catholic University of America
School of Arts and Sciences
Department of Politics
Program in International Affairs
Washington DC 20064
Phone: (202) 319-5057
http://www.cua.edu

Central Connecticut State University
School of Graduate Studies
Program in Interdisciplinary Area Studies
New Britain, CT 06050-4010
Phone: (860) 832-2921
http://www.ccsu.edu

Central Michigan University
College of Extended Learning
Program in Administration
Mount Pleasant, MI 48859

Phone: (800) 950-1144, x3865
http://www.cmich.edu

**City College of the City University of
    New York**
Graduate School
College of Liberal Arts and Science
Division of Social Science
Program in International Relations
New York, NY 10031-9198
Phone: (212) 650-5846
http://www.ccny.cuny.edu

Claremont Graduate University
Graduate Programs
School of Politics and Economics
Department of Politics and Policy
Claremont, CA 91711-6160
Phone: (909) 621-8699
http://www.cgu.edu

Clark Atlanta University
School of International Affairs and
    Development
Atlanta, GA 30314
Phone: (800) 688-3228
http://www.cau.edu

Columbia University
School of International and Public Affairs
Program in International Affairs
New York, NY 10027
Phone: (212) 854-6216
http://www.columbia.edu

Cornell University
Graduate School
Graduate Fields of Arts and Sciences
Field of Government
Ithaca, NY 14853-0001
Phone: (607) 255-3567
http://www.cornell.edu

Creighton University
Graduate School
College of Arts and Sciences
Program in International Relations
Omaha, NE 68178-0001
Phone: (402) 280-2870
http://www.creighton.edu

DePaul University
College of Liberal Arts and Sciences
Program in International Studies
Chicago, IL 60604-2287
Phone: (773) 325-4548
http://www.depaul.edu

Dominican University of California
Graduate Programs
School of Business and International
    Studies

Program in International Economic and
    Political Assessment
Bertrand Hall, Room 26B
50 Acacia Ave
San Rafael, CA 94901-2298
Phone: (415) 485-3238
http://www.dominican.edu

East Carolina University
Graduate School
College of Arts and Sciences
Program in International Studies
Greenville, NC 27858-4353
Phone: (252) 328-6012
http://www.ecu.edu

Fairleigh Dickinson University
Teaneck-Hackensack Campus
University College
Arts, Sciences, and Professional Studies
School of Political and International
    Studies
Program in International Studies
Teaneck, NJ 07666-1914
Phone: (201) 692-2272
http://www.fdu.edu

Florida International University
College of Arts and Sciences
Department of International Relations
Miami, FL 33199
Phone: (305) 348-2556
http://www.fiu.edu

Florida State University
Graduate Studies
College of Social Sciences
Program in International Affairs
Tallahassee, FL 32306
Phone: (850) 644-4418
http://www.fsu.edu

George Mason University
School of Public Policy
Program in International Commerce and
    Policy
Fairfax, VA 22030-4444
Phone: (703) 993-8099
http://www.gmu.edu

Georgetown University
Graduate School of Arts and Sciences
Edmund A. Walsh School of Foreign
    Service
Washington, DC 20057
Phone: (202) 687-5696
http://www.georgetown.edu

The George Washington University
Elliott School of International Affairs
Program in International Affairs
Washington, DC 20052

Phone: (202) 994-7050
http://www.gwu.edu

Georgia Institute of Technology
Graduate Studies and Research
Ivan Allen College of Policy and
    International Affairs
Sam Nunn School of International Affairs
Atlanta, GA 30332-0001
Phone: (404) 894-3195
http://www.gatech.edu

Harvard University
Graduate School of Arts and Sciences
Department of Government
Cambridge, MA 02138
Phone: (617) 496-6100
http://www.harvard.edu\

Johns Hopkins University
Paul H. Nitze School of Advanced
    International Studies
Baltimore, MD 21218-2699
Phone: (202) 663-5700
http://www.jhu.edu

Kansas State University
Graduate School
College of Arts and Sciences
Department of Political Science
Program in Political Science
Manhattan, KS 66506
Phone: (785) 532-6842
http://www.ksu.edu

Kent State University
College of Arts and Sciences
Department of Political Science
Kent, OH 44242-0001
Phone: (330) 672-2060
http://www.kent.edu

Lesley University
Graduate School of Arts and Social
    Sciences
Program in Intercultural Relations
Cambridge, MA 02138-2790
Phone: (800) 999-1959
http://www.lesley.edu

Long Island University
C. W. Post Campus
College of Liberal Arts and Sciences
Department of Political
    Science/International Studies
Brookville, NY 11548-1300
Phone: (516) 299-3025
http://www.cwpost.liu.edu

Loyola University Chicago
Graduate School
Department of Political Science
Chicago, IL 60611-2196

Phone: (773) 508-3068
http://www.luc.edu

Marquette University
Graduate School
College of Arts and Sciences
Department of Political Science
Milwaukee, WI 53201-1881
Phone: (414) 288-3360
http://www.mu.edu

Michigan State University
Graduate School
College of Social Science
Interdisciplinary Program
East Lansing, MI 48824
Phone: (517) 355-0301
http://www.msu.edu

**Monterey Institute of International
    Studies**
Graduate School of International Policy
    Studies
Monterey, CA 93940-2691
Phone: (831) 647-4123
http://www.miis.edu

Morgan State University
School of Graduate Studies
College of Liberal Arts
Department of Political Science and
    International Studies
Baltimore, MD 21251
http://www.morgan.edu

New School University
New School Program in International
    Affairs
New York, NY 10011-8603
Phone: (212) 229-5630
http://www.newschool.edu

New York University
Graduate School of Arts and Science
Department of Politics
New York, NY 10012-1019
Phone: (212) 998-8500
http://www.nyu.edu

North Carolina State University
Graduate School
College of Humanities and Social Sciences
Department of Political Science and
    Public Administration
Program in International Studies
Raleigh, NC 27695
Phone: (919) 515-3755
http://www.ncsu.edu

Northeastern University
College of Arts and Sciences
Department of Political Science
Boston, MA 02115-5096

Phone: (617) 373-4404
http://www.neu.edu

Ohio University
Graduate Studies
Center for International Studies
Program in Communications and
    Development Studies
Athens, OH 45701-2979
Phone: (740) 593-1840
http://www.ohio.edu

Oklahoma City University
Petree College of Arts and Sciences
Program in Liberal Arts
Oklahoma City, OK 73106-1402
Phone: (800) 633-7242 ext. 4
http://www.okcu.edu

Oklahoma State University
Graduate College
Program in International Studies
Stillwater, OK 74078
Phone: (405) 744-6606
http://www.okstate.edu

Old Dominion University
College of Arts and Letters
Programs in International Studies
Norfolk, VA 23529
Phone: (757) 683-5700
http://www.odu.edu

Princeton University
Graduate School
Woodrow Wilson School of Public
    and International Affairs
Princeton, NJ 08544-1019
Phone: (609) 258-4836
http://www.princeton.edu

**Rutgers, The State University
    of New Jersey, Newark**
Graduate School
Center for Global Change and Governance
Newark, NJ 07102
Phone: (973) 353-5585
http://www.rutgers.edu

St. John Fisher College
School of Adult and Graduate Education
International Studies Program
Rochester, NY 14618-3597
Phone: (716) 385-8344
http://www.sjfc.edu

St. Mary's University of San Antonio
Graduate School
Interdisciplinary Program in International
    Relations
San Antonio, TX 78228-8507

Phone: (210) 436-3101
http://www.stmarytx.edu

Salve Regina University
Graduate School
Program in International Relations
Newport, RI 02840-4192
Phone: (401) 847-6650
http://www.salve.edu

San Francisco State University
Graduate Division
College of Behavioral and Social Sciences
Department of International Relations
San Francisco, CA 94132-1722
Phone: (415) 338-2234
http://www.sfsu.edu

School for International Training
Graduate Programs
Master's Programs in Intercultural
    Management, Leadership, and Service
Brattleboro, VT 05302-0676
Phone: (802) 258-3265
http://www.sit.edu

Seton Hall University
School of Diplomacy and International
    Relations
South Orange, NJ 07079-2697
Phone: (973) 275-2515
http://www.shu.edu

Southwest Missouri State University
Graduate College
College of Humanities and Public Affairs
Department of Political Science
Program in International Affairs and
    Administration
Springfield, MO 65804-0094
Phone: (417) 836-8472
http://www.smsu.edu

Southwest Texas State University
Graduate School
Interdisciplinary Studies
Program in International Studies
San Marcos, TX 78666
Phone: (512) 245-2107
http://www.swt.edu

Stanford University
School of Humanities and Sciences
Program in International Policy Studies
Stanford, CA 94305-9991
Phone: (650) 723-4547
http://www.stanford.edu

Syracuse University
Graduate School
Maxwell School of Citizenship and
    Public Affairs

Program in International Relations
Syracuse, NY 13244-0003
Phone: (315) 443-9346
http://www.syr.edu

Texas A&M University
College of Liberal Arts
George Bush School of Government and
    Public Service
Program in International Affairs
College Station, TX 77843
Phone: (979) 458-2276
http://www.tamu.edu

Tufts University
Fletcher School of Law and Diplomacy
Medford, MA 02155
Phone: (617) 627-3040
http://www.tufts.edu

The University of British Columbia
Faculty of Graduate Studies
Institute of Asian Research
Vancouver, BC V6T 1Z1
Canada
Phone: (604) 822-2746
http://www.ubc.ca

University of California, Berkeley
Graduate Division
Haas School of Business and
Group in International and Area Studies
Berkeley, CA 94720-1500
Phone: (510) 642-1405
http://www.berkeley.edu

University of California, San Diego
Graduate Studies and Research
School of International Relations
    and Pacific Studies
La Jolla, CA 92093-0520
Phone: (858) 534-5914
http://www.ucsd.edu

University of California, Santa Cruz
Graduate Division
Division of Social Sciences
Program in International Economics
Santa Cruz, CA 95064
Phone: (831) 459-2301
http://www.ucsc.edu

University of Central Oklahoma
College of Graduate Studies and Research
College of Liberal Arts
Department of Political Science
Program in International Affairs
Edmond, OK 73034-5209
http://www.ucok.edu

University of Chicago
Division of Social Sciences

Committee on International Relations
Chicago, IL 60637-1513
Phone: (773) 702-8415
http://www.uchicago.edu

University of Colorado at Boulder
Graduate School
College of Arts and Sciences
Department of Political Sciences
Boulder, CO 80309
Phone: (303) 492-7872
http://www.colorado.edu

University of Connecticut
Graduate School
College of Liberal Arts and Sciences
Department of International Studies
Storrs, CT 06269
Phone: (860) 486-3617
http://www.uconn.edu

University of Delaware
College of Arts and Sciences
Department of Political Science and
    International Relations
Newark, DE 19716
Phone: (302) 831-2355
http://www.udel.edu

University of Denver
Graduate School of International
    Studies
Denver, CO 80208
Phone: (303) 871-2544
http://www.du.edu

University of Detroit Mercy
College of Liberal Arts
Department of Political Science
Program in International Politics and
    Economics
Detroit, MI 48219-0900
Phone: (313) 993-1245
    or (800) 635-5020
http://www.udmercy.edu

University of Florida
Graduate School
College of Liberal Arts and Sciences
Department of Political Science
Program in International Relations
Gainesville, FL 32611
Phone: (352) 392-0262 ext. 282
http://www.ufl.edu

University of Kentucky
Patterson School of Diplomacy
    and International Commerce
Lexington, KY 40506-0032
Phone: (859) 257-4613
http://www.uky.edu

University of Miami
Graduate School
School of International Studies
Coral Gables, FL 33124
Phone: (305) 284-3117
http://www.miami.edu

University of Missouri-St. Louis
Graduate School
College of Arts and Sciences
Center for International Studies
St. Louis, MO 63121-4499
Phone: (314) 516-6928
http://www.umsl.edu

University of New Orleans
Graduate School
College of Liberal Arts
Department of Political Science
New Orleans, LA 70148
Phone: (504) 280-6671
http://www.uno.edu

**University of Northern British
    Columbia**
Office of Graduate Studies
Prince George, BC Y2N 4Z9
Canada
Phone: (250) 960-6336
http://www.unbc.ca

University of Notre Dame
Graduate School
College of Arts and Letters
Division of Social Science
Department of Government and
    International Studies
Notre Dame, IN 46556
Phone: (219)-631-7706
http://www.nd.edu

University of Oklahoma
Graduate College
International Academic Programs
Norman, OK 73019-0390
Phone: (405) 325-1396
http://www.ou.edu

University of Oregon
Graduate School
College of Arts and Sciences
Program in International Studies
Eugene, OR 97403
Phone: (541) 346-3201
http://www.uoregon.edu

University of Pennsylvania
Feis Center of Government
Philadelphia, PA 19104
Phone: (215) 898-6520
http://www.upenn.edu

University of Pittsburgh
Graduate School of Public and
    International Affairs
International Affairs Division
Pittsburgh, PA 15260
Phone: (412) 648-7643
http://www.pitt.edu

University of Rhode Island
Graduate School
College of Arts and Sciences
Department of Political Science
Kingston, RI 02881
Phone: (401) 874-2183
http://www.uri.edu

University of San Diego
College of Arts and Sciences
Department of Political Science
San Diego, CA 92110-2492
Phone: (619) 260-4524
http://www.sandiego.edu

University of South Carolina
Graduate School
College of Liberal Arts
Department of Government and
    International Studies
Program in International Studies
Columbia, SC 29208
Phone: (803) 777-6801
http://www.sc.edu

University of Southern California
Graduate School
College of Letters, Arts and Sciences
School of International Relations
Los Angeles, CA 90089
Phone: (213) 740-8629
http://www.usc.edu

University of the Pacific
McGeorge School of Law
Sacramento, CA 95817
Phone: (916) 739-7105
http://www.uop.edu

University of Toronto
School of Graduate Studies
Social Sciences Division
Collaborative Program in International
    Relations
Toronto, ON M5S 1A1
Canada
Phone: (401) 926-2301
http://www.utoronto.ca

University of Virginia
College and Graduate School of Arts
    and Sciences

Department of Government and Foreign
    Affairs
Program in Foreign Affairs
Charlottesville, VA 22903
Phone: (804) 924-7184
http://www.virginia.edu

University of Washington
Graduate School
College of Arts and Sciences
Henry M. Jackson School of International
    Studies
Seattle, WA 98195
Phone: (206) 543-6001
http://www.u.washington.edu

University of Wyoming
Graduate School
College of Arts and Sciences
Program in International Studies
Laramie, WY 82071
Phone: (307) 766-3423
http://www.uwyo.edu

**Virginia Polytechnic Institute
    and State University**
Graduate School
College of Architecture and Urban
    Studies
Department of Urban Affairs and
    Planning
Program in Public and International
    Affairs
Blacksburg, VA 24061
Phone: (540) 231-8306 or (540) 231-6691
http://www.vt.edu

Webster University
College of Arts and Sciences
Department of History, Politics and Law
Program in International Relations
St. Louis, MO 63119-3194
Phone: (314) 968-7100
http://www.webster.edu

West Virginia University
Eberly College of Arts and Sciences
Department of Political Science
Morgantown, WV 26506
Phone: (304) 293-3811 ext. 5271
http://www.wvu.edu

Yale University
Graduate School of Arts and Sciences
Graduate Program in International
    Relations
New Haven, CT 06520
Phone: (203) 432-3418
http://www.yale.edu

APPENDIX VII
ADVOCACY GROUPS

What follows is a sampling of advocacy groups chosen because they have state/regional chapters, affiliates, or other indications of local activity. All have websites to help you get involved. Many organizations list employment opportunities on their websites. Use this list only as a starting point. Follow the news to familiarize yourself with the activities of other groups, particularly at the local level.

A. POLITICAL PARTIES AND GOVERNMENT REFORM

The Association of State Green Parties
P.O. Box 18452
Washington, DC 20036
Phone: (202) 232-0335
http://www.greenparties.org/
The Green platform supports social justice and equal opportunity, nonviolence, and community-based economics.

Common Cause
1250 Connecticut Avenue, NW, Suite 600
Washington, DC 20036
Phone: (202) 833-1200
Fax: (202) 659-3716
E-mail: commoncause@aol.com
http://www.commoncause.org
Common Cause works to promote open, honest, and accountable government.

Democratic National Committee
430 S Capitol Street, SE
Washington, DC 20003
Phone: (202) 863-8000
http://www.democrats.org/
Founded in 1792 by Thomas Jefferson, the Democratic Party, in its current platform, calls for prosperity, progress, and peace.

League of Women Voters
1730 M Street, NW
Washington, DC 20036
Phone: (202) 429-1965, (800) 249-VOTE
Fax: (202) 429-0854

E-mail: 1wv@1wv.org
http://www.1wv.org
The League of Women Voters is a multiissue organization dedicated to encouraging the informed and active participation of citizens in government.

National Libertarian Party
2600 Virginia Avenue, NW, Suite 100
Washington, DC 20037
Phone: (202) 333-0008
    or (800) ELECT-US
http://www.1p.org
Libertarians advocate a system that encourages all people to choose what they want from life.

National Women's Political Caucus
1630 Connecticut Avenue, NW
Suite 201
Washington, DC 20009
Phone: (202) 785-1100
Fax: (202) 785-3605
E-mail: info@nwpc.org
http://www.nwpc.org
The National Women's Political Caucus's (NWPC's) mission is to identify, recruit, train, and support women seeking elected and appointed office, with the help of hundreds of state and local chapters.

Reform Party
3281 N Meadow Mine Place
Tucson, AZ 85745

Phone: (877) GO-REFORM
http://www.reformparty.org
The Reform Party works to reestablish trust in government by supporting political candidates dedicated to fiscal responsibility and political accountability.

Republican National Committee
310 First Street, SE
Washington, DC 20003
Phone: (202) 863-8500
Fax: (202) 863-8820
E-mail: info@rnc.org
http://www.rnc.org
The Republican Party, over its 150-year history, has called for government based on the principles of freedom and personal liberty.

Rock the Vote
10635 Santa Monica Boulevard
Box 22
Los Angeles, CA 90015
Phone: (310) 234-0665
Fax: (310) 234-0666
E-mail: nmail@rockthevote.org
http://www.rockthevote.org
Rock the Vote is dedicated to protecting freedom of expression and to helping young people realize and utilize their power to affect change in the civic and political lives of their communities.

B. ENVIRONMENT AND CONSUMER ADVOCACY

Clean Water Action
4455 Connecticut Avenue, NW
Suite A300
Washington, DC 20008-2328
Phone: (202) 895-0420

Fax: (202) 895-0438
E-mail: cwa@cleanwater.org
http://www.cleanwateraction.org
Clean Water Action is a national citizens' organization working for clean, safe, and

affordable water; prevention of health-threatening pollution; creation of environmentally safe jobs and businesses; and empowerment of people to make democracy work.

Greenpeace USA
1436 U Street, NW
Washington, DC 20009
Phone: (202) 462-1177
Fax: (202) 462-4507
E-mail: greenpeace.usa@
    wdc.greenpeace.org
http://www.greenpeace.org/index.shtml
Greenpeace, which works to expose and
solve global environmental problems, has
offices in Washington, D.C., New York,
San Francisco, Seattle, and Chicago, and
throughout the world.

National Audubon Society
700 Broadway
New York, NY 10003
Phone: (212) 979-3000
Fax: (212) 979-3188
http://www.audubon.org
The National Audubon Society works to
conserve and restore natural ecosystems,
focusing on birds and other wildlife.

The Nature Conservancy
1815 N Lynn Street
Arlington, VA 22209
Phone: (703) 841-5300 or (800) 628-6860
Fax: (703) 841-1283
http://www.tnc.org

The Nature Conservancy works to pre-
serve habitats and species by buying the
lands and waters they need to survive.

Public Citizen, Inc.
1600 20th Street, NW
Washington, DC 20009
Phone: (202) 588-1000
    or (800) 239-3787
E-mail: public_citizen@citizen.org
http://www.citizen.org
Founded in 1971 by Ralph Nader, Public
Citizen, Inc., works for safer drugs and
medical devices, cleaner and safer energy
sources, a cleaner environment, fair
trade, and a more open and democratic
government.

Sierra Club
85 2nd Street, Second Floor
San Francisco, CA 94105-3441
Phone: (415) 977-5500
Fax: (415) 977-5799
E-mail: information@sierraclub.org
http://www.sierraclub.org
The Sierra Club is a nonprofit, member-
supported public interest organization that
promotes conservation of the natural environment.

**Student Environmental Action
    Coalition**
P.O. Box 31909
Philadelphia, PA 19104-0609
Phone: (215) 222-4711
Fax: (215) 222-2896
http://www.seac.org
The Student Environmental Action Coalition (SEAC) (pronounced "seek") is a stu-
dent- and youth-run national network of
organizations and individuals working on
environmental issues.

**United States Public Interest Research
    Group**
218 D Street, SE
Washington, DC 20003-1900
Phone: (202) 546-9707
Fax: (202) 546-2461
E-mail: uspirg@pirg.org
http://www.uspirg.org/
The United States Public Interest Research
Group uses investigative research, media
exposés, grass roots organizing, advocacy,
and litigation to fight dangers to public
health and well-being.

C. COMMUNITY AND SOCIAL ISSUES

AIDS Action Council
1906 Sunderland Place, NW
Washington, DC 20036
Phone: (202) 530-8030
Fax: (202) 530-8031
E-mail: aidsaction@aidsaction.org
http://www.aidsaction.org
Founded in 1984, AIDS Action is dedicated to
improved care and services for acquired
immunodeficiency syndrome (AIDS) patients
as well as medical research and prevention of
the disease.

**Association of Community
    Organizations for Reform Now**
739 8th Street, SE
Washington, DC 20002
Phone: (202) 547-2500
Fax: (202) 546-2483
http://www.acorn.org
The Association of Community Organiza-
tions for Reform Now (ACORN) works to
organize and win power for low- and mod-
erate-income people, with offices in New
York, Little Rock, New Orleans, and
Washington, D.C.

Children's Defense Fund
25 E Street, NW
Washington, DC 20001
Phone: (202) 628-8787
Fax: (202) 662-3510
E-mail: cdfinfo@childrensdefense.org
http://www.childrensdefense.org
The Children's Defense Fund (CDF)
works to provide a strong and effective
voice for the children of America.

Habitat for Humanity
121 Habitat Street
Americus, GA 31709
Phone: (229) 924-6935
http://www.habitat.org
Habitat for Humanity members build
houses in communities around the world.

Mothers against Drunk Driving
P.O. Box 541688
Dallas, TX 75354-1688
Phone: (800) GET-MADD
E-mail: info@madd.org
http://www.madd.org

Mothers against Drunk Driving (MADD)
works to stop drunk driving and to support
victims of the crime.

National Coalition for the Homeless
1012 14th Street, NW, #600
Washington, DC 20005-3410
Phone: (202) 737-6444
Fax: (202) 737-6445
E-mail: info@nationalhomeless.org
http://nationalhomeless.org
The National Coalition for the Homeless is
committed to ending homelessness through
public education, policy advocacy, grassroots organizing, and technical assistance.

USAction
1341 G Street, NW
10th Floor
Washington, DC 20005
Phone: (202) 661-0216
Fax: (202) 737-9197
http://www.usaction.org
USAction is a national coalition of social
action organizations.

D. CIVIL RIGHTS AND LIBERTIES

American Association for Retired Persons
601 E Street, NW
Washington, DC 20049
Phone: (800) 424-3410
Fax: (202) 434-6484
E-mail: member@aarp.org
http://www.aarp.org
The American Association for Retired Persons (AARP) is dedicated to helping older Americans achieve lives of independence, dignity, and purpose.

American Civil Liberties Union
125 Broad Street
New York, NY 10004-2400
Phone: (212) 944-9800
Fax: (212) 869-9065
E-mail: info@aclu.org
http://www.aclu.org
The American Civil Liberties Union (ACLU) is involved in litigating, legislating, and educating the public on a broad array of issues affecting individual freedom in the United States.

National Association for the Advancement of Colored People
4805 Mt. Hope Drive
Baltimore, MD 21215
Phone: (410) 521-4939
Fax: (410) 486-9257
http://www.naacp.org

The National Association for the Advancement of Colored People (NAACP) works to ensure the political, educational, social, and economic equality of minority group citizens of the United States.

National Council of La Raza
1111 19th Street, NW, Suite 1000
Washington, DC 20036
Phone: (202) 785-1670
Fax: (202) 776-1792
http://www.nclr.org
The National Council of La Raza, which has affiliates throughout the nation, was established in 1968 to reduce poverty and discrimination and improve life opportunities for Hispanic Americans.

National Gay and Lesbian Task Force
1700 Kalorama Road, NW
Washington, DC 20009-2624
Phone: (202) 332-6483
Fax: (202) 332-0207
E-mail: ngltf@ngltf.org
http://www.ngltf.org
The National Gay and Lesbian Task Force (NGLTF) serves as a national lobbying, organizing, and resource center for gay and lesbian civil rights.

National Organization on Disability
910 16th Street, NW
Washington, DC 20006

Phone: (202) 293-5960
Fax: (202) 293-7999
E-mail: ability@nod.org
http://www.nod.org
The National Organization on Disability promotes full and equal participation of America's millions of men, women, and children with disabilities in all aspects of life.

National Organization for Women
1000 16th Street, NW, Suite 700
Washington, DC 20036
Phone: (202) 331-0066
Fax: (202) 785-8576
E-mail: now@now.org
http://www.now.org
The National Organization for Women (NOW) is dedicated to legal, political, social, and economic equality for women.

National Urban League
120 Wall Street
New York, NY 10005
Phone: (212) 558-5300
E-mail: info@nul.org
http://www.nul.org
The mission of the National Urban League is to assist African Americans in the achievement of social and economic equality.

E. PEACE AND INTERNATIONAL AFFAIRS

American Friends Service Committee
1501 Cherry Street
Philadelphia, PA 19102
Phone: 215-241-7000
Fax: 215-241-7275
E-mail: afscinfo@afsc.org
http://www.afsc.org
The American Friends Service Committee is an independent Quaker organization, supported by people of different persuasions, that carries out programs of service, development, justice, and peace, with several regional offices around the nation.

Amnesty International, USA
322 Eighth Avenue
New York, NY 10001
(212) 807-8400
Fax: (212) 627-1451
E-mail: amnestyis@amnesty.org or
    admin-us@aiusa.org
http://www.amnesty.org or
    http://www.aiusa.org

Amnesty International opposes institutional abuses of human rights such as torture and imprisonment without trial.

Bread for the World
50 F Street, NW
Suite 500
Washington, DC 20001
Phone: (202) 639-9400 or (800) 82-Bread
Fax: 301-608-2401
http://www.bread.org
Bread for the World advocates for the hungry people of the world.

Human Rights Watch
1630 Connecticut Avenue, NW
Suite 500
Washington, DC 20009
Phone: (202) 612-4321
Fax: (202) 612-4333
http://www.hrw.org
Human Rights Watch is dedicated to protecting the human rights of people around the world.

Peace Action (formerly SANE/FREEZE)
1819 H Street, NW, #420
Washington, DC 20006
Phone: (202) 862-9740
Fax: (202) 862-9762
http://www.peace-action.org.
Peace Action, with over 100 local chapters, works to promote global nuclear disarmament, cut military spending, and end the international arms trade.

United Nations Association of the United States of America
1779 Massachusetts Avenue, NW
Suite 610
Washington, DC 20036
Phone: (202) 462-3446
Fax: (202) 462-3448
E-mail: unadc@unausa.org
http://www.unausa.org
The United Nations Association of the United States of America (UNA-USA) is a nonprofit, nonpartisan national organiza-

tion, with chapters throughout the nation, dedicated to enhancing U.S. participation in the United Nation and strengthening of the United Nations.

World Federalist Associations
420 7th Street, SE

Washington, DC 20003
Phone: (202) 546-3950
    or (800) WFA-0123
http://wfa.org/
The World Federalist Association works toward the abolition of war, the preservation of a sustainable global environment, and a just world community through the development of enforceable world law (other offices are in New York, Boston, San Francisco, Los Angeles, Pittsburgh, and Chicago).

APPENDIX VIII
HOW TO RUN FOR POLITICAL OFFICE—
THE BASICS

Before deciding to run for office, you should know what is involved in getting your name on the ballot and your campaign off to a running start. For more information, read How to Run for Local Office *by Robert J. Thomas and* How to Win Your First Election *by Susan Guber, which were both valuable sources for this Appendix. Also search the Internet for information from local and state election departments. This guide is not intended to be a substitute for seeking the services of political parties and/or campaign professionals.*

STEP ONE: ASK YOURSELF THE HARD QUESTIONS

Insiders recommend that you ask yourself the following questions before deciding to run for office. If you answer no to any of them, you might want to think again:

- Do I have a background of community and/or political party involvement?
- Am I interested in issues of concern to most voters?
- Am I willing to ask people for money?
- Am I prepared for the rough-and-tumble world of politics?

STEP TWO: FILE THE NECESSARY PAPERWORK

Your local Clerk's Office and/or Election Department can provide valuable assistance to candidates running for public office. People in these offices can inform you of elected positions you might not have previously considered; point out the differences between competing for the party's nomination and running as an independent; provide lists of items for sale; and refer you elsewhere if necessary for what you need to get started, including

- Election schedule
- Declaration of candidacy
- Election cycle financial reports
- Nomination petitions
  - Collect more than the number of signatures required for the position
  - Inform anyone collecting signatures for you of the necessary requirements

STEP THREE: ORGANIZE YOUR CAMPAIGN

Although a campaign committee may not be absolutely necessary, it will help you receive and disburse funds and handle record keeping:

- Choose a name for your committee (e.g., Citizens for Smith)
- Appoint your campaign manager and treasurer: organize other helpers
- Set up a bank account
- Ask the Clerk's Office or Election Department about purchasing voter registration lists, maps, and so on, to help target likely voters
- Set up campaign headquarters in a home or rented office
- Write a campaign plan with your campaign manager

STEP FOUR: CONDUCT A VIGOROUS CAMPAIGN

Typical activities for this phase of the campaign include

- Designing campaign literature, ads, and signs
- Knocking on doors and talking to people
- Raising campaign funds
- Seeking endorsements
- Appearing at events
- Preparing for debates

STEP FIVE: GEAR UP FOR ELECTION DAY

As Election Day approaches, you will need to

- Line up poll workers
- Activate phone banks
- Set up a committee for an election returns party
- Write two speeches—one for victory, the other for defeat

STEP SIX: DEAL WITH THE ELECTION'S AFTERMATH

Your job is not quite done after the polls close because you will still need to

- Make a victory or concession speech
- Thank staff and volunteers
- Remove campaign signs
- Rest: You deserve it!

APPENDIX IX
TRADE PUBLICATIONS

The following publications are of interest to individuals in the public sector. They commonly include career information and/or job ads.

Campaigns & Elections Magazine
1414 22nd Street, NW
Washington, DC 20037
Phone: (202) 887-8530
http://www.campaignline.com

The Chronicle of Philanthropy
1255 Twenty-third Street, NW
Washington, DC 20037
Phone: (800) 842-7817
http://www.philanthropy.com

Governing
1100 Connecticut Avenue, NW
#1300
Washington, DC 20036

Phone: (202) 862-8802
http://www.governing.com

The Hill
733 15th Street, NW
Suite 1140
Washington, DC 20005
Phone: (202) 628-8500
http://www.hillnews.com

Nonprofit Times
120 Littleton Road
Suite 120
Parsippany, NJ 07054-1803
Phone: (973) 394-1800
http://www.nptimes.com

Public Administration Times
American Society for Public
   Administration
1120 G Street, NW
Suite 700
Washington, DC 20005
Phone: (202) 393-7878
http://www.aspanet.org

Roll Call
50 S Frank, NW
Washington, DC 20001
Phone: (202) 824-6800
http://www.rollcall.com

APPENDIX X
ASSOCIATIONS

I. POLITICS, GOVERNMENT, ACTIVISM—GENERAL

American Political Science Association
1527 New Hampshire Avenue, NW
Washington, DC 20036-1208
Phone: (202) 483-2512
http://www.apsanet.org

American Society for Public Administration
1120 G Street, NW
Suite 700
Washington, DC 20005
Phone: (202) 393-7878
http://www.aspanet.org

Association for Public Policy Analysis and Management
P.O. Box 18766
Washington, DC 20036-8766
Phone: (202) 261-5788
http://www.appam.org

The National Association of Schools of Public Affairs and Administration
1120 G Street, NW
Suite 730
Washington, DC 20005
Phone: (202) 628-8965
http://www.naspaa.org

POLITICAL CAMPAIGNS

American Association for Public Opinion Research
426 Thompson Street
P.O. Box 1248
Ann Arbor, M1 48106-1248
Phone: (734) 764-3341
http://www.aapor.org

American Association of Political Consultants
600 Pennsylvania Avenue, SE
Suite 330
Washington, DC 20003

Phone: (202) 544-9815
http://www.theaapc.org

College Democrats of America
430 S Capitol Street, SE
Washington, DC 20003
Phone: (202) 863-8151
http://www.collegedems.com

College Republican National Committee
600 Pennsylvania Avenue, SE
Suite 207
Washington, DC 20003
Phone: (888) 765-3564
http://www.crnc.org

International Association of Political Consultants
927 15th Street, SW
Suite 1000
Washington, DC 20005
Phone: (202) 659-4300
http://www.iapc.org

Young Democrats of America
430 S Capitol Street, SE
Washington, DC 20003
Phone: (202) 863-8150
http://www.yda.org

Young Republicans
Young Republican National Federation, Inc.
620 Pennsylvania Avenue, SE
Suite 302
Washington, DC 20003
Phone: (202) 608-1417
http://www.yrock.com

POLITICAL OFFICE

The Council of State Governments
2760 Research Park Drive
P.O. Box 11910
Lexington, KY 40578¹910

Phone: (859) 244-8001
http://www.csg.org

National Conference of State Legislatures
Denver Office
7700 East First Place
Denver CO 80230
Phone: (303) 364-7700
Washington Office
444 N. Capitol Street, NW
Washington DC 20001
Phone: (202) 624-5400
http://www.ncsl.org

National District Attorneys Association
99 Canal Center Plaza
Suite 510
Alexandria, VA 22314
Phone: (703) 519-1689
http://www.ndaa-apri.org

National Governors' Association
Hall of States
444 N Capitol Street
Washington, DC 20001-1512
Phone: (202) 624-5300
http://www.nga.org

The National League of Cities
1301 Pennsylvania Avenue, NW
Washington, DC 20004-1763
Phone: (202) 626-3000
http://www.nlc.org

The U.S. Conference of Mayors
1620 Eye Street, NW
Washington, DC 20006
Phone: (202)-293-7330
http://www.usmayors.org

II. GOVERNMENT

GENERAL POSITIONS

American Federation of State, County, and Municipal Employees
1625 L Street, NW
Washington, DC 20036-5687
Phone: (202) 429-1000
http://www.afscme.org

The City-County Communications and Marketing Association
P.O. Box 20278
Washington-Dulles International
  Airport
Washington, D.C. 20041
Phone: (202) 488-7100
http://www.3cma.org

National Association of Government Employees
159 Burgin Park
Quincy, MA 02169
Phone: (617) 376-0285
http://www.nage.org

LOCAL GOVERNMENT

Council for Urban Economic Development
1730 K Street, NW
Suite 700
Washington, DC 20006
Phone: (202) 223-4735
http://www.cued.org

Economic Development
American Economic Development
  Council
1030 Higgins Road, Suite 301
Park Ridge, IL 60068
Phone: (847) 692-9944
http://www.aedc@aedc.org

The Election Center
12543 Westella
Suite 100
Houston, TX 77077-3929
Phone: (281) 293-0101
http://www.electioncenter.org

International City/County Management Association
777 North Capitol Street, NE
Suite 500
Washington, DC 20002-4201
Phone: (202) 962-3680
http://www.icma.org

International Institute of Municipal Clerks
1212 N San Dimas Canyon Road
San Dimas, CA 91773
Phone: (909) 592-4462
http://www.iimc.com

National Association of Housing and Redevelopment Officials
630 Eye Street, NW
Washington, DC 20001-3736
Phone: (203) 289-3500
http://www.nahro.org

Public Housing Authorities Directors Association
511 Capitol Court, NE
Washington, DC 20002-4937
Phone: (202) 546-5445
http://www.phada.org

Recreation Supervisor
National Recreation and Park
  Association
22377 Belmont Ridge Road
Ashburn, VA 20148
Phone: (703) 858-0784
http://www.nrpa.org

Urban and Regional Planner
American Planning Association
1313 E 60th Street
Chicago, IL 60637
Phone: (312) 955-9100
http://www.planning.org

LOCAL/STATE SPECIALISTS

American Public Human Services Association
810 First Street, NE
Suite 500
Washington, D.C. 20002-4267
(202) 682-0100
http://www.aphsa.org

Association of State and Territorial Health Officials
1275 K Street, NW
Suite 800
Washington, DC 20005-4006
Phone: (202) 371-9090
http://www.astho.org

Council on Government Ethics Laws
910 Charles Street
Fredericksburg, VA 22401
Phone: (540) 370-0106
http://www.cogel.org

The Environmental Careers Organization
179 South Street
Boston, MA 02111
Phone: (617) 426-4375
http://www.eco.org

Environmental Council of the States
444 N Capitol Street, NW
Suite 445
Washington, DC 20001
Phone: (202) 624-3660
http://www.ecos.org

International Association of Emergency Managers
111 Park Place
Falls Church, VA 22046-4123
Phone: (703) 538-1795
http://www.iaem.com

International Personnel Management Association
1617 Duke Street
Alexandria, VA 22314
Phone: (703) 549-7100
http://www.ipma-hr.org

National Association of County and City Health Officials
1100 17th Street, NW
Second Floor
Washington, D.C. 20036
Phone: (202) 783-5550
http://www.naccho.org

National Association of Environmental Professionals
Three Adams Street
South Portland, ME 04106-1606
Phone: (888) 251-9902
http://www.naep.org

National Association of Local Government Auditors
2401 Regency Road
Suite 302
Lexington, KY 40503
Phone: (859) 276-0686
http://www.nalga.org

National Association of Local Government Environmental Professionals
1350 New York Avenue, NW
Suite 2200
Washington, DC 20005
Phone: (202) 393-2866
http://www.nalgep.org

National Association of Social Workers
750 First Street, NE
Suite 700
Washington, DC 20002-4241
(202) 408-8600 or (800) 638-8799
http://www.naswdc.org

National Association of State Auditors,
  Comptrollers, and Treasurers
2401 Regency Road
Suite 302
Lexington, KY 40503
Phone: (859) 276-1147
http://www.nasact.org

National Emergency Management
  Association
c/o Council of State Governments
P.O. Box 11910
Lexington, KY 40578
Phone: (859) 244-8000
http://www.nemaweb.org

National Public Employer Labor
  Relations Association
1620 I Street, NW
3rd Floor
Washington, DC 20006
Phone: (202) 296-2230
http://www.npelra.org

Public Health
Association of Schools of Public Health
1101 15th Street, NW
Suite 910
Washington, DC 10005
Phone: (202) 296-1099
http://www.asph.org

Student Conservation Association
P.O. Box 550
Charlestown, NH 03603
Phone: (603) 543-1700
http://www.sca-inc.org

LEGISLATIVE

Congressional Legislative Staff
  Association
(leadership changes annually)
P.O. Box 1991
Long Wharf Office Building
Washington D.C. 20515
Phone: (202) 226-7709

Congressional Research Employees
  Association
Library of Congress
101 Independence Avenue, SE
LM-412
Washington, DC 20540-7999
Phone: (202) 707-7636
http://www.crealocal75.org

House Administrative Assistants
  (Chiefs of Staff) Association
U.S. House of Representatives
1974 Longworth House Office
  Buildings
Washington, D.C. 20515

National Conference of State
  Legislatures
1560 Broadway
Suite 700
Denver, Colorado 80202
Phone: (303) 830-2200
http://www.ncsl.org

STATE/FEDERAL

American Association for Paralegal
  Education
2965 Flowers Road, S
Suite 105
Atlanta, GA 30341
Phone: (770) 452-9877
http://www.aafpe.org

American Bar Association
750 N Lake Shore Drive
Chicago, IL 60611
Phone: (800) 285-2221
http://www.abanet.org

National Association for Law
  Placement
1666 Connecticut Avenue, NW
Washington, DC 20009
Phone: (202) 667-1666
http://www.nalp.org

National Association of Government
  Communicators
10301 Democracy Lane
Suite 203
Fairfax, VA 22030
Phone: (703) 691-0377
http://www.nagc.com

National Association of Legal
  Assistants
1516 S Boston
#200
Tulsa, OK 74119
Phone: (918) 587-6828
http://www.nala.org

National Federation of Paralegal
  Associations
P.O. Box 33108
Kansas City, MO 64114-0108
Phone: (816) 941-2725
http://www.paralegals.org

Public Relations Society of America
23 Irving Place
New York, NY 10003-2376
Phone: (212) 995-2230
http://www.prsa.org

INTERNATIONAL

American Foreign Service Association
2101 E. Street, NW
Washington, DC 20037
Phone: (202) 338-4045
http://www.afsa.org

Association of Former Intelligence
  Officers
6723 Whittier Avenue
Suite 303A
McLean, VA 22101-4533
Phone: (703) 790-0320
http://www.afio.com

III. ACTIVISM

GENERAL NONPROFIT

Alliance for Nonprofit Management
1899 L. Street, NW, 6th Floor
Washington, DC 20036
Phone: (202) 955-8406
http://www.allianceonline.org

American Society of Association Executives
1575 I Street, NW
Washington, DC 20005-1103
Phone: (202) 626-2723
http://www.asaenet.org

Association of Fundraising Professionals
1101 King Street
Suite 700
Alexandria, VA 22314
Phone: (703) 684-0410
http://www.afpnet.org

Council on Foundations
1828 L Street, NW
Washington, DC 20036
Phone: (202) 466-6512
http://www.cof.org

The Independent Sector
1200 18th Street, SW
Suite 200
Washington, DC 20036
Phone: (202) 467-6100
http://www.IndependentSector.org

The National Council of Nonprofit Associations
1001 Connecticut Avenue, NW
Suite 900
Washington, DC 20036
Phone: (202) 833-5740
http://www.ncna.org

Public Relations Society of America
23 Irving Place
New York, NY 10003-2376
Phone: (212) 995-2230
http://www.prsa.org

The Society for Nonprofit Organizations
6314 Odana Road
Suite 1
Madison, WI 53719-1141
Phone: (608) 274-9777
http://www.dancenet.org/snpo

ENVIRONMENTAL/ CONSUMER

Consumer Federation of America
1424 16th Street, NW
Suite 604
Washington, DC 20036
Phone: (202) 387-6121
http://www.consumerfed.org

The Environmental Careers Organization
179 South Street
Boston, MA 02111
Phone: (617) 426-4375
http://www.eco.org

Equal Justice Works
(Formerly National Association for Public Interest Law)
212 L Street, NW
Suite 450
Washington, DC 20037
Phone: (202) 466-3686
http://www.equaljusticeworks.org

National Association of Environmental Professionals
Three Adams Street
South Portland, ME 04106-1606
Phone: (888) 251-9902
http://www.naep.org

Student Conservation Association
P.O. Box 550
Charlestown, NH 03603
Phone: (603) 543-1700
http://www.sca-inc.org

COMMUNITY, SOCIAL, AND INTERNATIONAL

Association for Conflict Resolution
1527 New Hampshire Avenue, NW
Washington, DC 20036-1206
Phone: (202) 667-9700
http://www.acresolution.org

Consortium on Peace, Research, Education, and Development
c/o The Evergreen State University
Mailstop: Seminar 3127
Olympia, WA 98505
Phone: (360) 867-6196
http://www.evergreen.edu

National Association for Community Mediation
1527 New Hampshire Avenue, NW
Washington, DC 20036-1206
Phone: (202) 667-9700
http://www.nafcm.org

National Congress for Community Economic Development
1030 15th Street, NW
Suite 325
Washington, DC 20005
Phone: (202) 289-9020
http://www.ncced.org

National Council of Women's Organizations
733 15th Street, NW
Suite 1011
Washington, DC 20005
Phone: (202) 393-7122
http://www.womensorganizations.org

National Organizers Alliance
715 G Street, SE
Washington, DC 20003
Phone: (202) 543-6603
http://www.noacentral.org

The National Women's Studies Association
University of Maryland
7100 Baltimore Boulevard
Ste. 500
College Park, MD 20740
Phone: (301) 403-4137
http://www.nwsa.org

Peace Studies Association
Drawer 105
Earlham College
Richmond, IN 47374
Phone: (317) 983-1305
http://www.earlham.edu

LOBBIES, UNIONS/ ASSOCIATIONS, AND RESEARCH CENTERS

AFL-CIO Organizing Institute
815 16th Street, NW
Washington, DC 20006
Phone: (800) 848-3021
http://www.aflcio.org/orginst

American League of Lobbyists
P.O. Box 30005
Alexandria, VA 22310
Phone: (703) 960-4070
http://www.alldc.org

American Society of Association Executives
The ASAE Building
15756 I Street, NW
Washington, DC 20005-1103
Phone: (202) 626-2803
http://www.asaenet.org

National Association of Business Political Action Committees
2300 Clarendon Boulevard
Suite 401
Arlington, VA 22201
Phone: (713) 516-4708
http://www.nabpac.org

SERVICE

AmeriCorps
Corporation for National Service
1201 New York Avenue, NW
Washington, DC 20525
Phone: (800) 942-2677
http://www.americorps.org

AmeriCorps Alums, Inc.
1400 I Street, NW
Suite 800
Washington, DC 20005
Phone: (202) 729-8102
http://www.americorpsalums.org

Peace Corps
National Peace Corps Association
1900 L Street, NW
Suite 205
Washington, DC 20036
Phone: (800) 424-8580
http://www.peacecorps.gov

BIBLIOGRAPHY

Public Sector Careers

Dumbaugh, Kerry, and Gary Serota. *Capitol Jobs: An Insider's Guide to Finding a Job in Congress.* Washington, D.C.: Tilden Press, 1984.

Jebens, Harley. *100 Jobs in Social Change.* New York: Macmillan, 1996.

Krannich, Ronald L., and Caryl Rae Krannich. *The Complete Guide to Public Employment.* Manassas Park, Va.: Impact Publications, 1995.

Lauber, Daniel. *Government Job Finder.* River Forest, Ill.: Planning/Communications, 1997.

Males, Anne Marie, contributing authors Julie Czernada and Victoria Vincent. *Great Careers for People Fascinated by Government and the Law.* Detroit: UXL.

Maxwell, Bruce. *Finding a Job in Washington.* Washington, D.C.: Congressional Quarterly Press, 2000.

Porter, Christopher. *How to Get a Job in Congress (Without Winning an Election).* Arlington, Va.: Blutarsky Media, 2000.

U.S. Department of Labor, Bureau of Labor Statistics. *Occupational Outlook Handbook. 2000–2001.* Washington, D.C.: U.S. Government Printing Office, 2000.

Environmental Careers

Doyle, Kevin, and Tanya Stubby, eds. Environmental Careers Organization. *The Complete Guide to Environmental Careers in the 21st Century.* Washington, D.C.: Island Press, 1998.

Green, Kathleen. "We've Got the Whole World in Our Hands: Environmental Careers," *Occupational Outlook Quarterly* (winter 1994–1995). Copies available from Bureau of Labor Statistics at *blsdata_staff@bls.gov* or at 202-691-5200.

Quintana, Debra. *100 Jobs in the Environment.* New York: Macmillan, 1996.

Student Conservation Association Staff (Compiler) and Scott D. Izzo. *Guide to Graduate Environmental Programs.* Washington D.C.: Island Press, 1997.

International Careers

Carland, Maria Pinto, and Michael Trucano, eds. *Careers in International Affairs.* Washington, D.C.: Georgetown University Press, 1997.

Kocher, Eric, and Nina Segal. *International Jobs: Where They Are, How to Get Them,* 5th ed. Reading, Mass.: Perseus Books, 1999.

Nonprofit Careers

Colvin, Donna, eds. *Good Works: A Guide to Careers in Social Change.* Preface by Ralph Nader. New York: Barricade Books, 1994.

Crosby, Olivia. "Paid Jobs in Charitable Nonprofits," *Occupational Outlook Quarterly* (summer 2001): 11–23.

Krannich, Ron, and Caryl Krannich. *Jobs and Careers with Non-Profit Organizations.* Manassas Park, Va.: Impact Publications, 1999.

Political Science/Public Policy

Bardach, Eugene. *The Eight-Step Path of Policy Analysis: A Handbook for Practice.* Berkeley, Calif.: Berkeley Academic Press, 1996.

Beck, Paul Allen. *Party Politics in America,* 8th ed. New York: Addison Wesley Longman, 1997.

Bibby, John E. *Politics, Parties, and Elections in America.* Chicago: Nelson-Hall Publishers, 1992.

Johnson, Dennis W. *No Place for Amateurs: How Political Consultants Are Reshaping American Democracy.* New York: Routledge, 2001.

Light, Paul. *The New Public Service.* Washington, D.C.: Brookings Institution Press, 1999.

O'Connor, Karen, and Larry J. Sabato. *American Government: Roots and Reform.* Boston: Allyn & Bacon, 1993.

——— *The Essentials of American Government: Continuity and Change.* New York: Addison Wesley Longman, 2000.

Radin, Beryl A. *Beyond Machiavelli: Policy Analysis Comes of Age.* Washington, D.C.: Georgetown University Press, 2000.

Sabato, Larry. *The Rise of Political Consultants.* New York: Basic Books, 1981.

———. *PAC Power: Inside the World of Political Action Committees.* New York: W. W. Norton, 1984.

Sandak, Cass R. *Lobbying.* New York: Twenty-First Century Books, 1995.

Smith, James A. *The Idea Brokers: Think Tanks and the Rise of the New Policy Elite.* New York: The Free Press, 1999.

Thurber, James A., and Candice J. Nelson (Editors). *Campaign Warriors: Political Consultants in Elections.* Washington, D.C.: Brookings Institution Press, 2000.

Zeigler, Harmon, and Michael A. Baer. *Lobbying: Interaction and Influence in American State Legislatures.* Belmont, Calif.: Wadsworth Publishing Company, 1969.

Elected Office

Barber, James David. *The Presidential Character: Predicting Performance in the White House.* Englewood Cliffs, N.J.: Prentice-Hall, 1985.

Cuomo, Mario M. *Diaries of Mario M. Cuomo: The Campaign for Governor.* New York: Random House, 1984.

Guber, Susan. *How to Win Your First Election.* Boca Raton, Fla.: St. Lucie Press, 1997.

Herrnson, Paul S. *Congressional Elections: Campaigning at Home and in Washington.* Washington, D.C.: CQ Press, 1998.

Hughes, Emmet John. *The Living Presidency.* New York: Coward, McCann & Geoghegan, 1972.

Rosenthal, Alan. *Legislative Life: People, Process and Performance in the States.* New York: Harper & Row, 1981.

Rossiter, Clinton. *The American Presidency.* New York: Harcourt, Brace & World, 1960.

Sabato, Larry. *Goodbye to Good-Time Charlie: The American Governorship Transformed,* 2d ed. Washington, D.C.: Congressional Quarterly, 1983.

Thomas, Robert J. *How to Run for Local Office: A Complete Guide for Winning a Local Election.* Westland, Mich.: R & T Enterprises, 1999.

Intelligence/International Affairs

Agee, Philip. *CIA Diary: Inside the Company.* New York: Penguin Books, 1975.

American Foreign Service Association. *Inside a U.S. Embassy: How the Foreign Service Works for America.* Washington, D.C.: American Foreign Service Association, 1996.

The New York Times. "Dining with the Devil: The Future of the C.I.A." Available online. URL: *www.nytimes.com.*

The New York Times. "Interrogation, CIA-Style: Many Mean Ways to Loosen Cold-War Tongues." *The New York Times,* February 9, 1997. Available online. URL: *www.nytimes.com.*

Shirley, Edward G. "Can't Anybody Here Play This Game?" *The Atlantic,* February 1998. Available online. URL: *www.theatlantic.com.*

Weiner, Tim. "Spies Wanted." *The New York Times,* Jan. 24, 1999. Available online. URL: *www.nytimes.com.*

Law

Abrams, Lisa L. *The Official Guide to Legal Specialties: An Insider's Guide to Every Major Practice Area.* Chicago: Harcourt Legal & Professional Publications, 2000.

Bernardo, Barbara. *Paralegal,* 3d ed. Princeton, N.J.: Peterson's, 1997.

DeBroff, Stacy M., Jill P. Martyn, and Alexa Shabecoff. *Public Interest Job Search Guide 2001–2002: Harvard Law School's Handbook & Directory for Law Students and Lawyers Seeking Public Service Work,* 12th ed. Cambridge, Mass.: Harvard Law School, 2001.

Snyder, A. Kurt, ed. *American Bar Association Guide to Approved Law Schools.* Hoboken, NY: Hungry Minds, 2000.

Nonprofit/Activism

Brophy, Paul C., and Alice Shabecoff. A *Guide to Careers in Community Development.* Washington, D.C.: Island Press, 2001.

Campbell, Katherine Noyes, and Susan J. Ellis. *The (Help!) I-Don't Have-Enough-Time Guide to Volunteer Management.* Philadelphia: Energize, 1995.

Crosby, Olivia. "Paid Jobs in Charitable Nonprofits." *Occupational Outlook Quarterly* (summer 2001): 11–23.

"A Crucial Test for Feminism: Some Scholars Think the Field of Women's Studies Is Having a Midlife Crisis." November 17, 2000, *Newsweek,* 70.

Edles, L. Peter. *Fundraising: Hands-on Tactics for Nonprofit Groups.* New York: McGraw-Hill, 1993.

Felder, David W. *How to Work for Peace.* Tallahassee: Florida A&M University Press, 1991.

Hummel, Joan M. *Starting and Running a Nonprofit Organization,* 2nd ed. Minneapolis: University of Minnesota Press, 1996.

Klein, Kim. *Fundraising for Social Change,* 4th ed. Oakland, Calif.: Chardon Press, 2000.

Mancuso, Anthony. *How to Form a Nonprofit Corporation in all 50 States,* 3d ed. Occidental, Calif.: Nolo.com, 1998.

Mort, Jo-Ann, ed. *Not Your Father's Union Movement: Inside the AFL-CIO.* New York: Verso, 1998.

Steinem, Gloria. "Advice to Old Fems." *Ms.,* February/March 2000, 93–95.

Speechwriting

Brake, Mike. "Nine Steps to Effective Speech-Writing." *Writer's Digest,* July 1999, 40–43.

Hertzberg, Hendrik. "Behind the Lines with Peggy Noonan." *The New Yorker,* February 2, 1998, 72–76.

Noonan, Peggy. *Simply Speaking: How to Communicate Your Ideas with Style, Substance, and Clarity.* New York: HarperCollins, 1998.

Safire, William. *Lend Me Your Ears: Great Speeches in History.* New York: Norton, 1997.

DIRECTORIES

Directories are particularly helpful when looking for prospective employers in various fields. Use this list only as a starting point. Browse libraries and career centers for additional resources.

Colvin, Donna, ed. *Good Works: A Guide to Careers in Social Change.* Preface by Ralph Nader. New York: Barricade Books, 1994.

Congressional Quarterly, *Politics in America* (published every two years).

Eldridge, Grant, ed. *Government Research Center Directory 2001,* 14th ed. Detroit: Gale Group, 2000.

Encyclopedia of Associations. Farmington Hills, Mich.: Gale Group, 1999.

National Journal Group. *The Almanac of American Politics* (published every two years). Washington, D.C.: National Journal Group, 2001.

INDEX